REX MUNDI
Book Three

LES ARMES DES SALAM

Et in Arcadia ego...

ER NOSTER QVI EST IN COEL

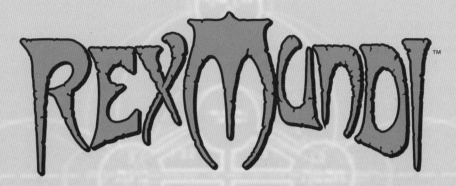

REX MUNDI

• BOOK THREE •

The Lost Kings

writer ARVID NELSON

artist, chapters one and two ERICJ

color artist, chapters one and two JEROMY COX

artist, chapters three and four JIM DI BARTOLO

artist, chapters five and six JUAN FERREYRA

cover artist JUAN FERREYRA

Rex Mundi created by ARVID NELSON and ERICJ

DARK HORSE BOOKS™

publisher
MIKE RICHARDSON

editor
SCOTT ALLIE

assistant editors
MATT DRYER and DAVE MARSHALL

letterer and newspaper designer
ARVID NELSON

book designer
AMY ARENDTS

art director
LIA RIBACCHI

Special thanks to Jason Rickerd.
Archival photographs: Eugène Atget.

REX MUNDI BOOK THREE: THE LOST KINGS

This volume collects issues twelve through seventeen of the comic-book
series *Rex Mundi* originally published by Image Comics.

Published by
Dark Horse Books
A division of Dark Horse Comics, Inc.
10956 SE Main Street
Milwaukie, OR 97222

darkhorse.com

To find a comics shop in your area, call the Comic Shop Locator
Service toll-free at 1-888-266-4226

First edition: September 2006
ISBN-10: 1-59307-651-7
ISBN-13: 978-1-59307-651-1

10 9 8 7 6 5 4 3 2 1

Printed in China

LOVELY, PROVOCATIVE REX

REX MUNDI IS BY FAR, in my humble opinion, one of the finest comics being produced today. Arvid and his associates have truly made something remarkable. This series is full of intrigue, dispelled lies, mystery, politics, religious notions and (depending on your point of view) heresy.

Within its pages you will discover theories that lead to some very "truthful" insights into what we believe to be Christianity and its history. This series is willing to provoke thought and discussion on the religious politics of the West and East that are so prevalent in today's news headlines. This is what makes *Rex Mundi* extremely relevant, and a must-read for anyone who is interested in anything beyond what the nightly newscasts want us to know.

As the series unfolds its mysteries of the world before us, you can't help but feel that you are reading something truly important. Not just from or about comics, but about the world we live in. This is one of those very rare instances where a comic reaches beyond its colorful panels to say something that will give pause, food for our propaganda-addled brains. It causes us to consider the possibilities of lies being told. I'm not one to go in for conspiracy. However, when presented with the ideas being shown by Arvid, I must stop and think about our reality for a time.

Rex Mundi, with all of its delicious secrets to be divulged, is something I truly look forward to every single issue, and I relish it even more in collected form. I guess another bit I should touch on is the fact that this series addresses the use of magic in the context of Christian religious beliefs. This is something that is very bold to consider: the idea that certain aspects of Christianity have been stolen, for lack of a better term, from pagan influences. Just one more layer to be pondered: the origins of modern religions of all types.

I feel when all is said and done this series will be looked upon by future readers as one of the more truly important pieces of comics work to make it to the published arena. My hope is that it will find its way to every bookshelf, beyond those of comics readers, and that all will give it a chance, and read this material with an intelligent, open mind. It deserves at least that.

J. H. Williams III

Artist and writer, whose work includes *Promethea,*
Desolation Jones, Chase and more

Appropriately written on Easter weekend, 2006

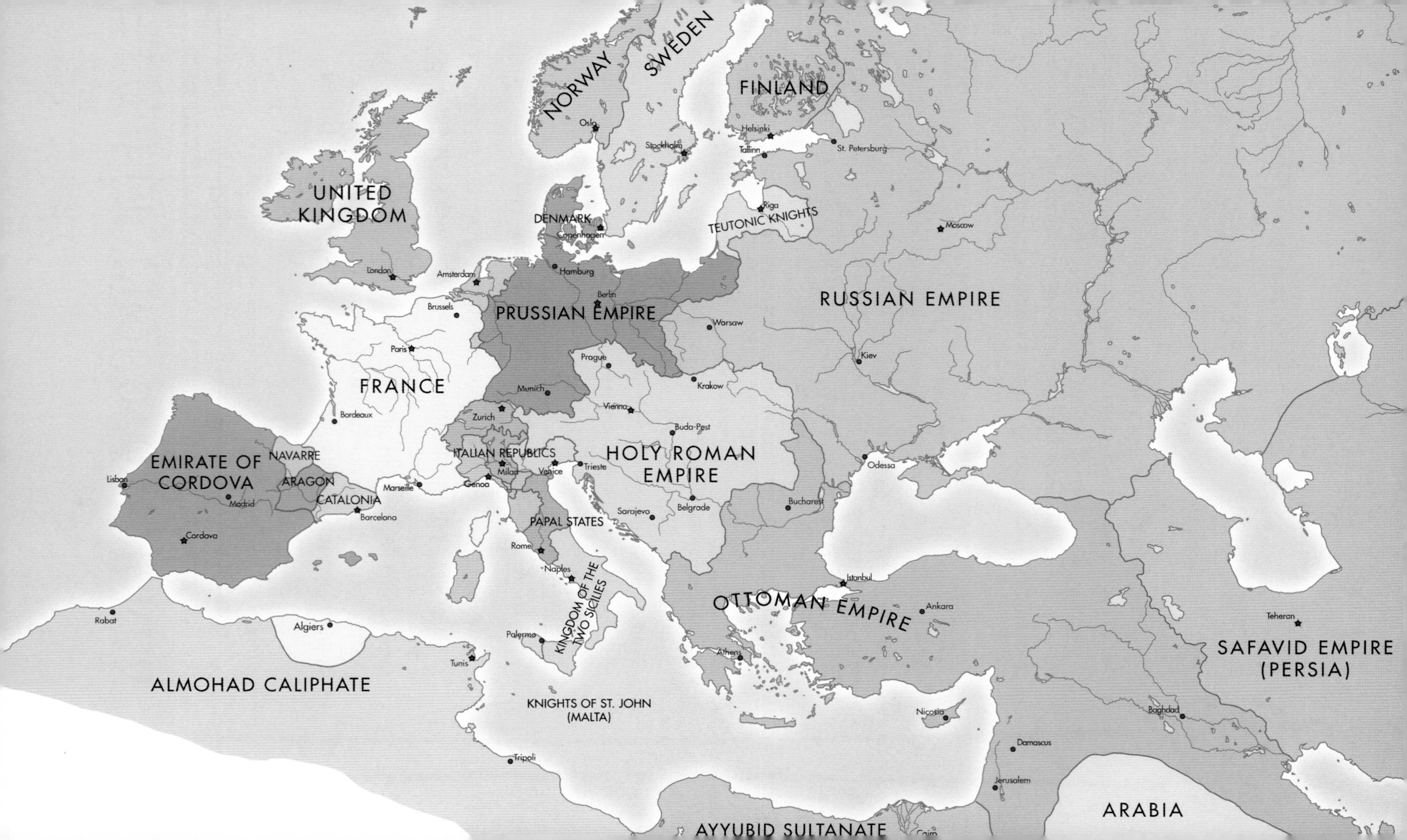
NORWAY
SWEDEN
FINLAND
Oslo
Stockholm
Helsinki
Tallinn
St. Petersburg
UNITED KINGDOM
DENMARK
Copenhagen
Riga
TEUTONIC KNIGHTS
Moscow
London
Amsterdam
Hamburg
Berlin
Brussels
RUSSIAN EMPIRE
PRUSSIAN EMPIRE
Warsaw
Paris
Prague
Kiev
Krakow
FRANCE
Munich
Vienna
Zurich
Bordeaux
Buda-Pest
HOLY ROMAN EMPIRE
ITALIAN REPUBLICS
EMIRATE OF CORDOVA
NAVARRE
Milan
Venice
Trieste
Odessa
Lisbon
ARAGON
Marseille
Genoa
Madrid
CATALONIA
Bucharest
Barcelona
Sarajevo
Belgrade
PAPAL STATES
Cordova
Rome
Naples
Istanbul
KINGDOM OF THE TWO SICILIES
OTTOMAN EMPIRE
Ankara
Rabat
Algiers
Teheran
Palermo
Tunis
Athens
SAFAVID EMPIRE (PERSIA)
ALMOHAD CALIPHATE
KNIGHTS OF ST. JOHN (MALTA)
Nicosia
Baghdad
Damascus
Tripoli
Jerusalem
ARABIA
AYYUBID SULTANATE

PARIS, 1933. THE PROTESTANT REFORMATION failed. Europe is in the grip of feudalism, and sorcerers stalk the streets at night. This is the world of *Rex Mundi*.

Master Physician Julien Saunière is on the trail of a secret society with origins in the murky history of the First Crusade. The order has infiltrated the highest ranks of government, and is manipulating rising political tensions to bring about a devastating world war.

The conspirators are devoted to a common cause: the Holy Grail itself. The Grail, it seems, is not a cup, but a secret with explosive spiritual and political implications. A secret that threatens to drown the world in blood.

Saunière stumbled onto the mystery when an encrypted medieval scroll was stolen from longtime friend Father Gérard Marin. Marin had been having an affair with a prostitute, and told her about the scroll and its terrible importance. A mysterious assassin in a white suit murdered Marin and the prostitute, setting Saunière on a path that has now taken over his life.

A trail of corpses has led him to the powerful Duke of Lorraine, apparent mastermind of the mysterious secret society and the coming war. Lorraine may be a long-lost descendant of the Merovingian Dynasty, the first Christian kings of France, who fell from power after betrayal by the Holy Church.

Genevieve Tournon, Saunière's old flame and fellow doctor, has been appointed Lorraine's personal physician. She is having an affair with the powerful Duke while trying to protect Saunière at the same time.

Now Saunière has run afoul of the Holy Inquisition. He must say goodbye to confidant Rabbi Albert Maiselles, who is being forced to flee Europe in a rising wave of anti-Semitism. Meanwhile, Lorraine is meeting with his supporters from across the English Channel . . .

"Then Judas, which betrayed him, answered and said, Master, is it I?
He said unto him, Thou hast said."

—Matthew 26:25

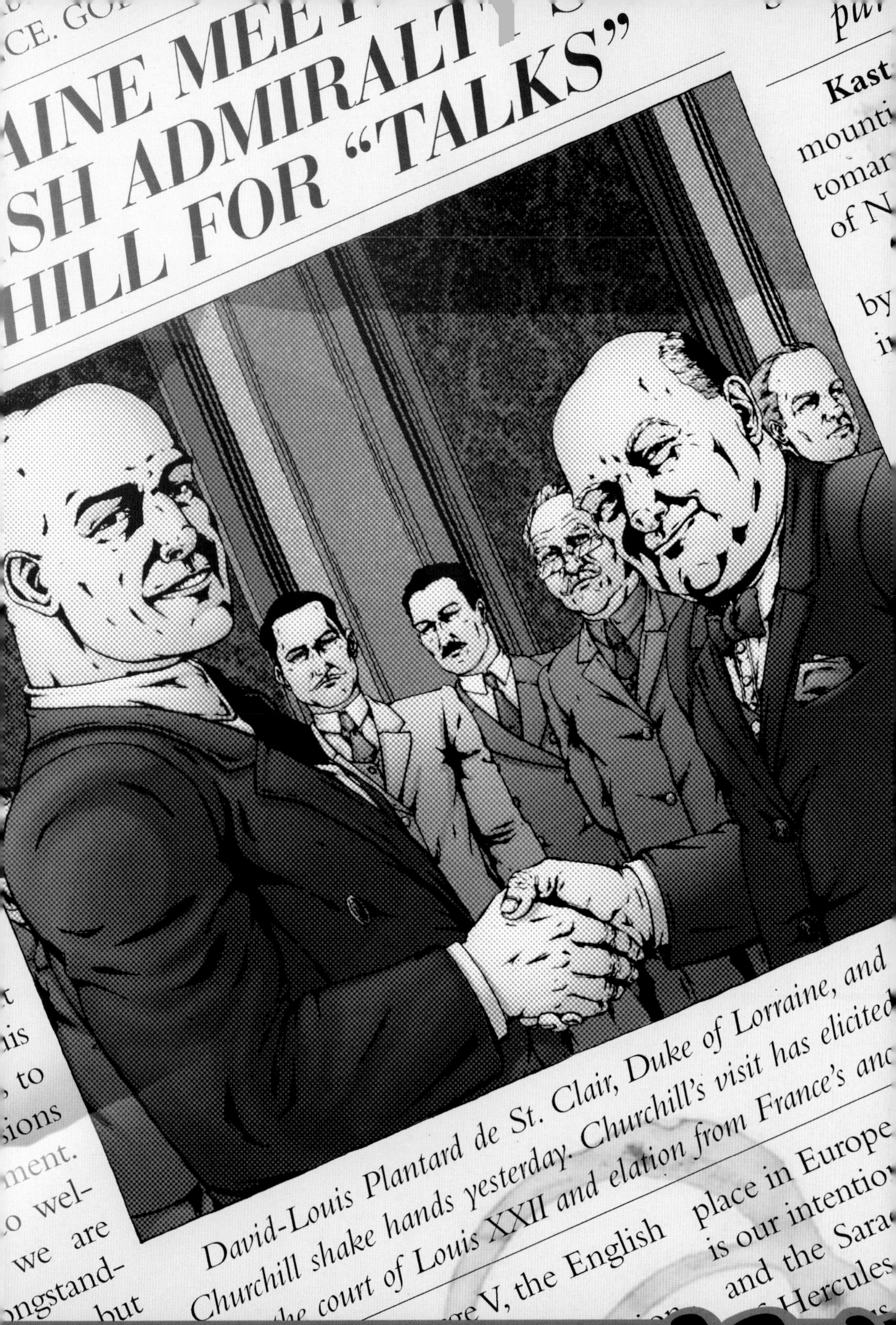

AINE MEET
SH ADMIRALT
HILL FOR "TALKS"
Kast
mounti
tomar
of N
David-Louis Plantard de St. Clair, Duke of Lorraine, and
Churchill shake hands yesterday. Churchill's visit has elicited
the court of Louis XXII and elation from France's anc
V, the English
place in Europe
is our intentio
and the Sara
Hercules
ment.
o wel-
we are
ngstand-
but

CHAPTER ONE

THE SWAN KNIGHT

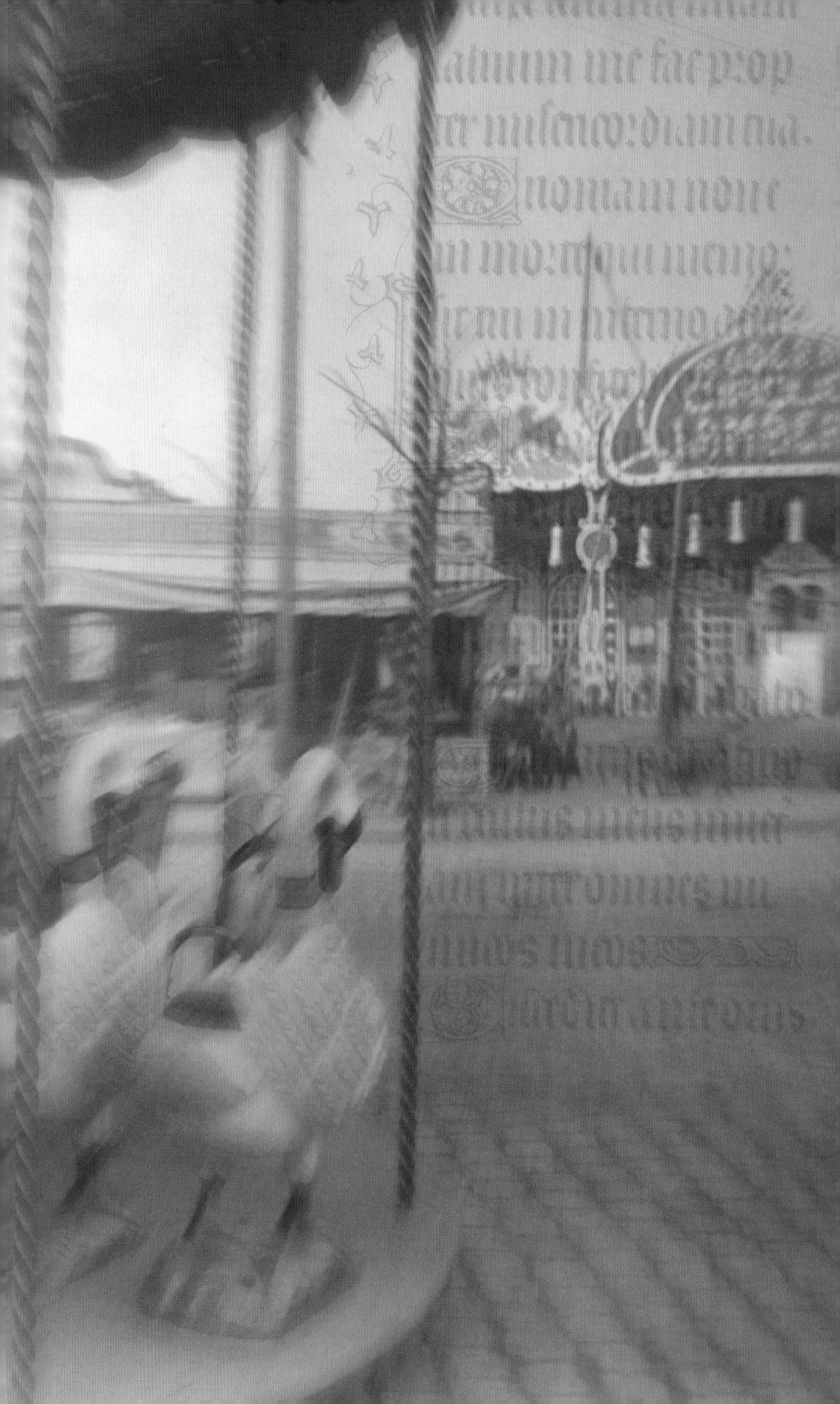

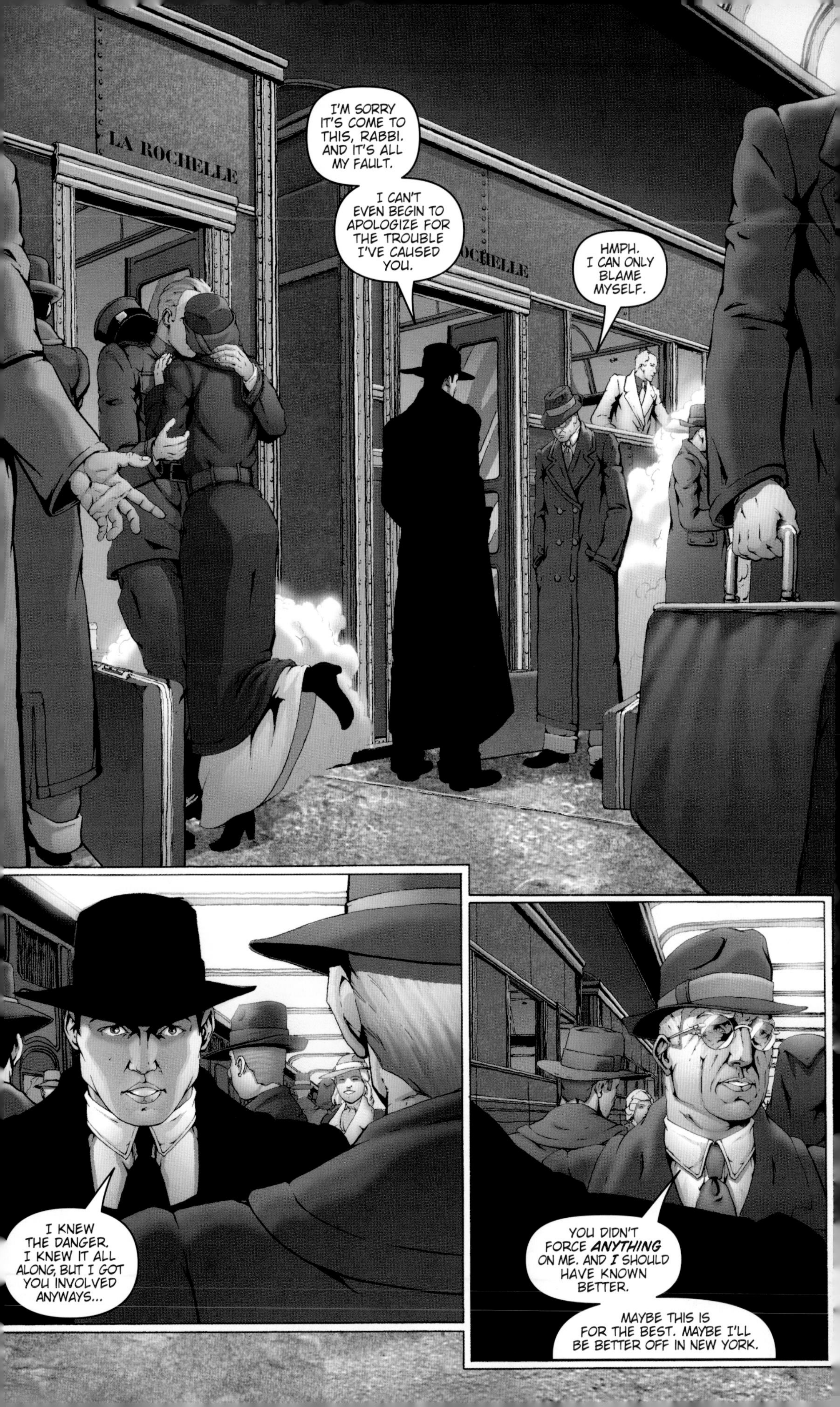
LA ROCHELLE
I'M SORRY IT'S COME TO THIS, RABBI. AND IT'S ALL MY FAULT.
I CAN'T EVEN BEGIN TO APOLOGIZE FOR THE TROUBLE I'VE CAUSED YOU.
HMPH. I CAN ONLY BLAME MYSELF.
I KNEW THE DANGER. I KNEW IT ALL ALONG, BUT I GOT YOU INVOLVED ANYWAYS...
YOU DIDN'T FORCE ***ANYTHING*** ON ME. AND ***I*** SHOULD HAVE KNOWN BETTER.
MAYBE THIS IS FOR THE BEST. MAYBE I'LL BE BETTER OFF IN NEW YORK.

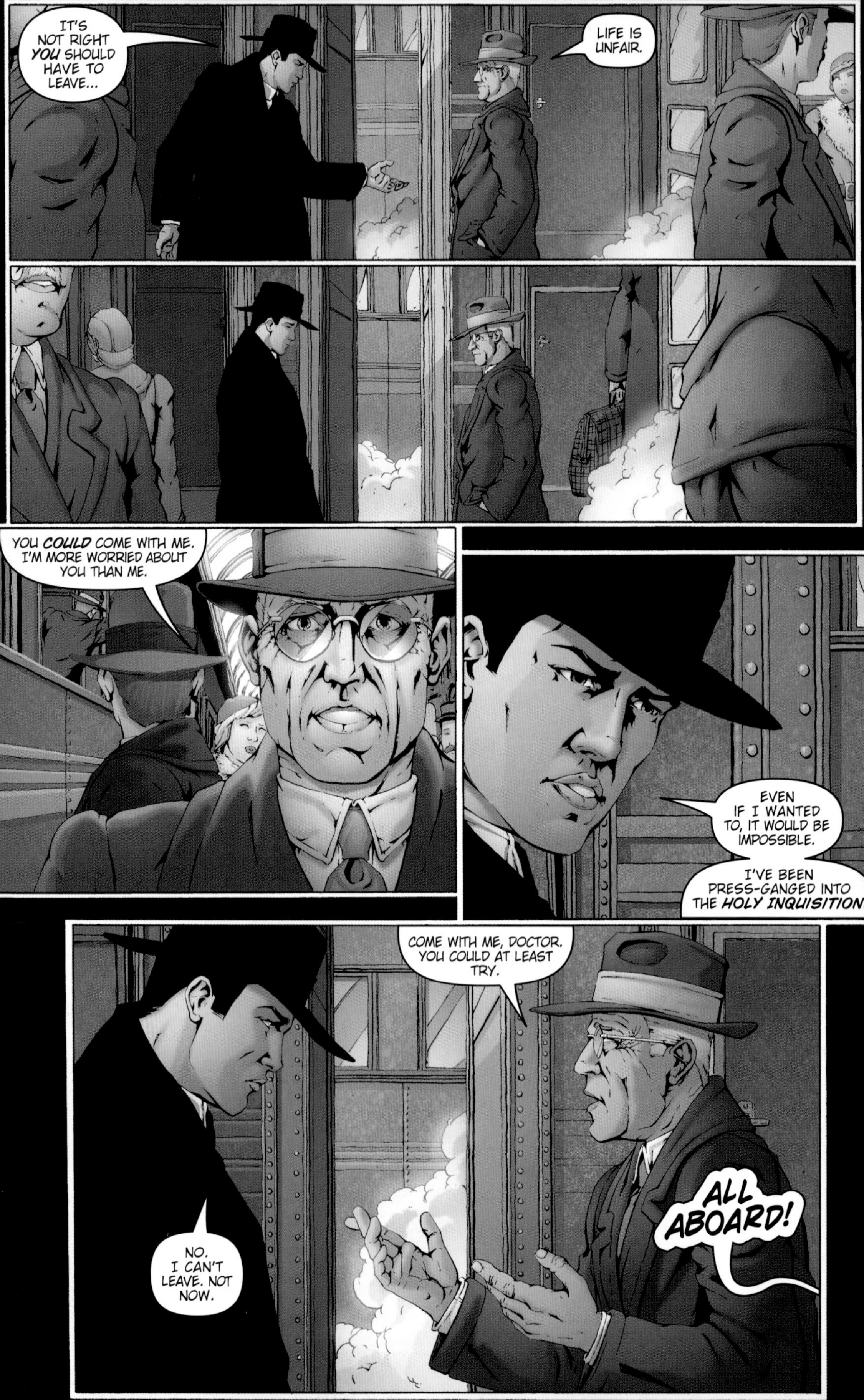
IT'S NOT RIGHT *YOU* SHOULD HAVE TO LEAVE...
LIFE IS UNFAIR.
YOU *COULD* COME WITH ME. I'M MORE WORRIED ABOUT YOU THAN ME.
EVEN IF I WANTED TO, IT WOULD BE IMPOSSIBLE.
I'VE BEEN PRESS-GANGED INTO THE *HOLY INQUISITION*.
COME WITH ME, DOCTOR. YOU COULD AT LEAST TRY.
NO. I CAN'T LEAVE. NOT NOW.
ALL ABOARD!

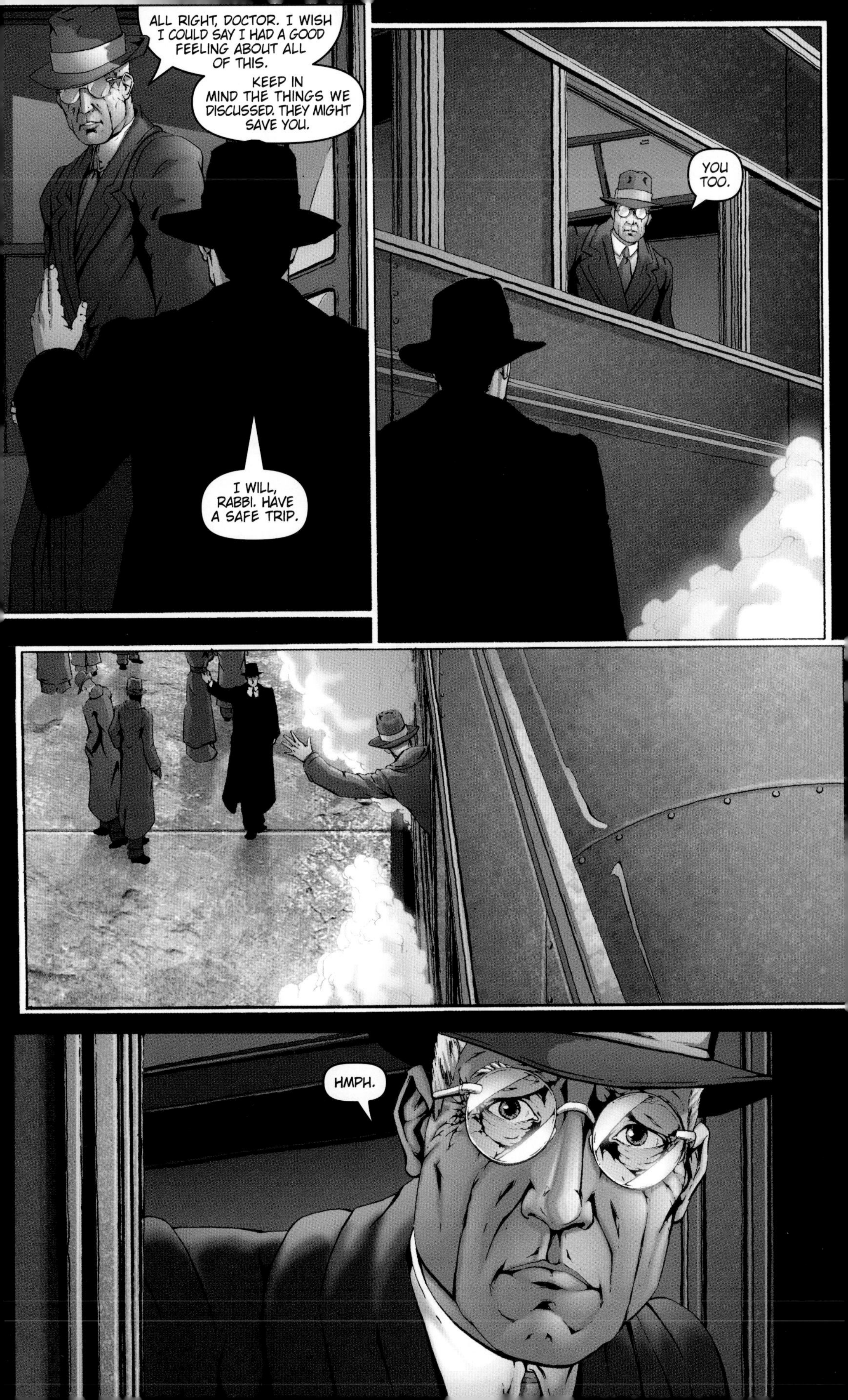
ALL RIGHT, DOCTOR. I WISH I COULD SAY I HAD A GOOD FEELING ABOUT ALL OF THIS.
KEEP IN MIND THE THINGS WE DISCUSSED. THEY MIGHT SAVE YOU.
I WILL, RABBI. HAVE A SAFE TRIP.
YOU TOO.
HMPH.

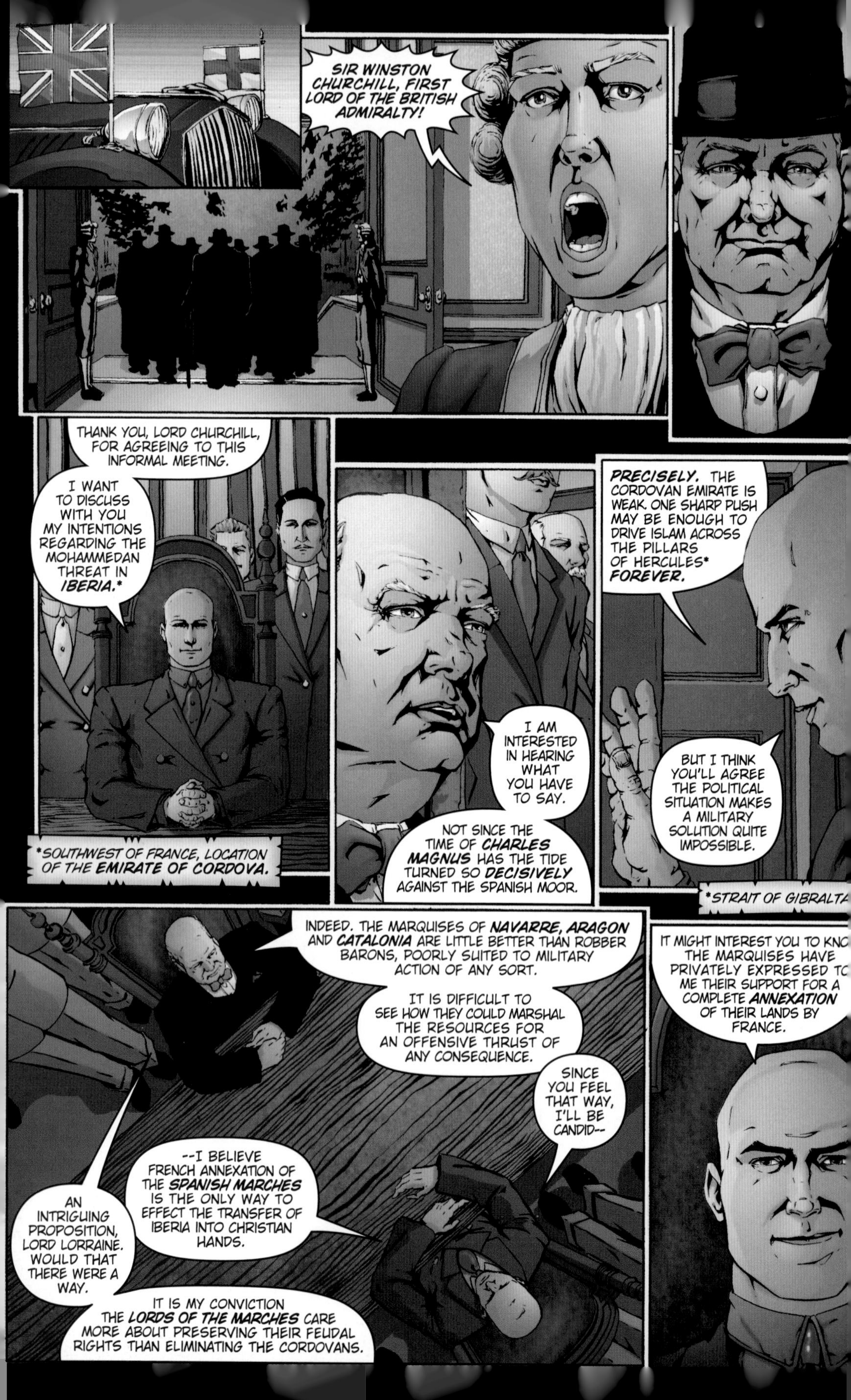
SIR WINSTON CHURCHILL, FIRST LORD OF THE BRITISH ADMIRALTY!
THANK YOU, LORD CHURCHILL, FOR AGREEING TO THIS INFORMAL MEETING.
I WANT TO DISCUSS WITH YOU MY INTENTIONS REGARDING THE MOHAMMEDAN THREAT IN IBERIA.*
*SOUTHWEST OF FRANCE, LOCATION OF THE EMIRATE OF CORDOVA.
I AM INTERESTED IN HEARING WHAT YOU HAVE TO SAY.
NOT SINCE THE TIME OF CHARLES MAGNUS HAS THE TIDE TURNED SO DECISIVELY AGAINST THE SPANISH MOOR.
PRECISELY. THE CORDOVAN EMIRATE IS WEAK. ONE SHARP PUSH MAY BE ENOUGH TO DRIVE ISLAM ACROSS THE PILLARS OF HERCULES* FOREVER.
BUT I THINK YOU'LL AGREE THE POLITICAL SITUATION MAKES A MILITARY SOLUTION QUITE IMPOSSIBLE.
*STRAIT OF GIBRALTA
INDEED. THE MARQUISES OF NAVARRE, ARAGON AND CATALONIA ARE LITTLE BETTER THAN ROBBER BARONS, POORLY SUITED TO MILITARY ACTION OF ANY SORT.
IT IS DIFFICULT TO SEE HOW THEY COULD MARSHAL THE RESOURCES FOR AN OFFENSIVE THRUST OF ANY CONSEQUENCE.
IT MIGHT INTEREST YOU TO KNO THE MARQUISES HAVE PRIVATELY EXPRESSED TO ME THEIR SUPPORT FOR A COMPLETE ANNEXATION OF THEIR LANDS BY FRANCE.
SINCE YOU FEEL THAT WAY, I'LL BE CANDID--
--I BELIEVE FRENCH ANNEXATION OF THE SPANISH MARCHES IS THE ONLY WAY TO EFFECT THE TRANSFER OF IBERIA INTO CHRISTIAN HANDS.
AN INTRIGUING PROPOSITION, LORD LORRAINE. WOULD THAT THERE WERE A WAY.
IT IS MY CONVICTION THE LORDS OF THE MARCHES CARE MORE ABOUT PRESERVING THEIR FEUDAL RIGHTS THAN ELIMINATING THE CORDOVANS.

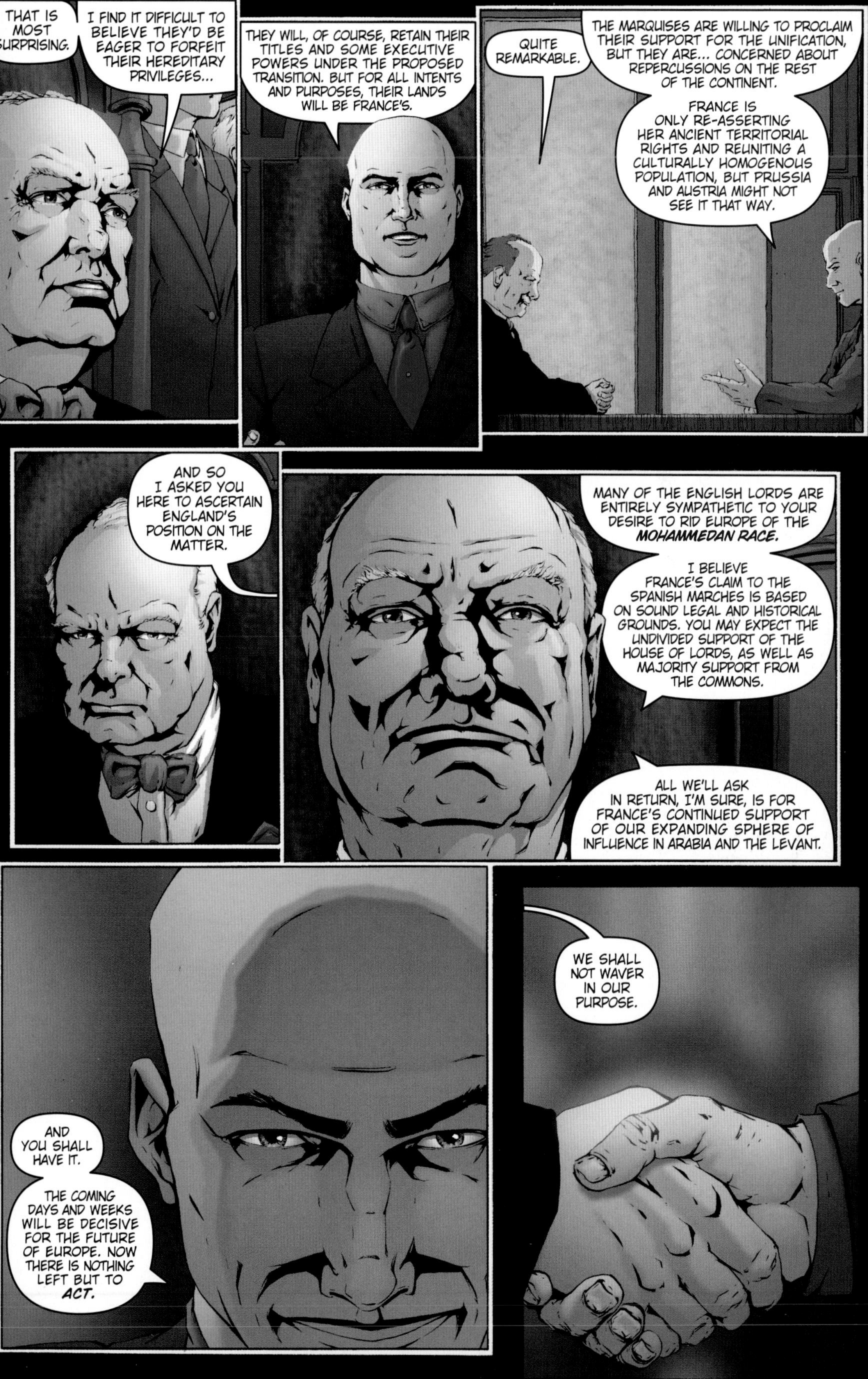
THAT IS MOST SURPRISING.
I FIND IT DIFFICULT TO BELIEVE THEY'D BE EAGER TO FORFEIT THEIR HEREDITARY PRIVILEGES...
THEY WILL, OF COURSE, RETAIN THEIR TITLES AND SOME EXECUTIVE POWERS UNDER THE PROPOSED TRANSITION. BUT FOR ALL INTENTS AND PURPOSES, THEIR LANDS WILL BE FRANCE'S.
QUITE REMARKABLE.
THE MARQUISES ARE WILLING TO PROCLAIM THEIR SUPPORT FOR THE UNIFICATION, BUT THEY ARE... CONCERNED ABOUT REPERCUSSIONS ON THE REST OF THE CONTINENT.
FRANCE IS ONLY RE-ASSERTING HER ANCIENT TERRITORIAL RIGHTS AND REUNITING A CULTURALLY HOMOGENOUS POPULATION, BUT PRUSSIA AND AUSTRIA MIGHT NOT SEE IT THAT WAY.
AND SO I ASKED YOU HERE TO ASCERTAIN ENGLAND'S POSITION ON THE MATTER.
MANY OF THE ENGLISH LORDS ARE ENTIRELY SYMPATHETIC TO YOUR DESIRE TO RID EUROPE OF THE ***MOHAMMEDAN RACE.***
I BELIEVE FRANCE'S CLAIM TO THE SPANISH MARCHES IS BASED ON SOUND LEGAL AND HISTORICAL GROUNDS. YOU MAY EXPECT THE UNDIVIDED SUPPORT OF THE HOUSE OF LORDS, AS WELL AS MAJORITY SUPPORT FROM THE COMMONS.
ALL WE'LL ASK IN RETURN, I'M SURE, IS FOR FRANCE'S CONTINUED SUPPORT OF OUR EXPANDING SPHERE OF INFLUENCE IN ARABIA AND THE LEVANT.
AND YOU SHALL HAVE IT.
THE COMING DAYS AND WEEKS WILL BE DECISIVE FOR THE FUTURE OF EUROPE. NOW THERE IS NOTHING LEFT BUT TO ***ACT.***
WE SHALL NOT WAVER IN OUR PURPOSE.

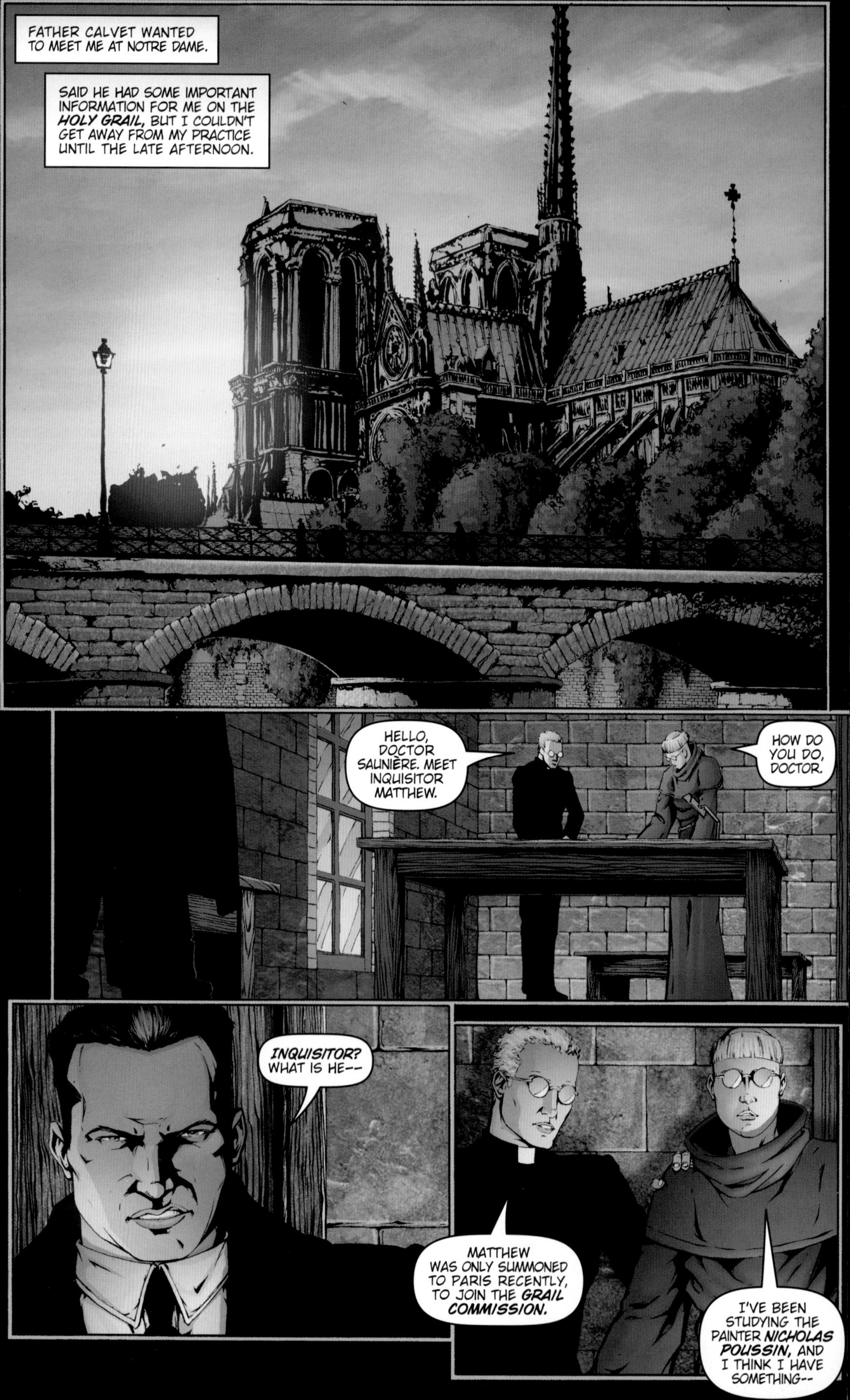
FATHER CALVET WANTED TO MEET ME AT NOTRE DAME.
SAID HE HAD SOME IMPORTANT INFORMATION FOR ME ON THE HOLY GRAIL, BUT I COULDN'T GET AWAY FROM MY PRACTICE UNTIL THE LATE AFTERNOON.
HELLO, DOCTOR SAUNIÈRE. MEET INQUISITOR MATTHEW.
HOW DO YOU DO, DOCTOR.
INQUISITOR? WHAT IS HE--
MATTHEW WAS ONLY SUMMONED TO PARIS RECENTLY, TO JOIN THE GRAIL COMMISSION.
I'VE BEEN STUDYING THE PAINTER NICHOLAS POUSSIN, AND I THINK I HAVE SOMETHING--

HOW DID YOU TWO MEET, EXACTLY?

I HAD ACCESS TO THE REPORTS MONITORING YOUR PROGRESS, SO I KNEW YOU WERE INVESTIGATING FATHER MARIN'S MURDER.

DILIGENTLY, IF NOT DISCREETLY.

WHEN I SAW FATHER CALVET ATTENDING THE ARCHBISHOP DURING YOUR INTERROGATION THE OTHER DAY,* IT WAS OBVIOUS HE WAS INVOLVED SOMEHOW.

*BOOK TWO, CHAPTER SIX.

WELL... WHY DID YOU RISK SO MUCH OVER THE PAST FEW WEEKS?

I'M SURE YOU HAVE YOUR REASONS, AND SO DO I. MAYBE I JUST LIKE A GOOD MYSTERY.

...ND ...Y ARE ...EING SO ...OUS WITH ...VER YOU ...VE?

...GHT.

...S ...UT ...N?

BEFORE THAT, I THINK THERE'S SOMETHING YOU SHOULD KNOW ABOUT THE CATHARS.*

YES, THE ARCHBISHOP MENTIONED THEM...

THERE'S MUCH MORE THAN HE TOLD YOU.

*A HERESY EXTERMINATED BY THE CHURCH IN THE EARLY THIRTEENTH CENTURY. FOR MORE INFORMATION

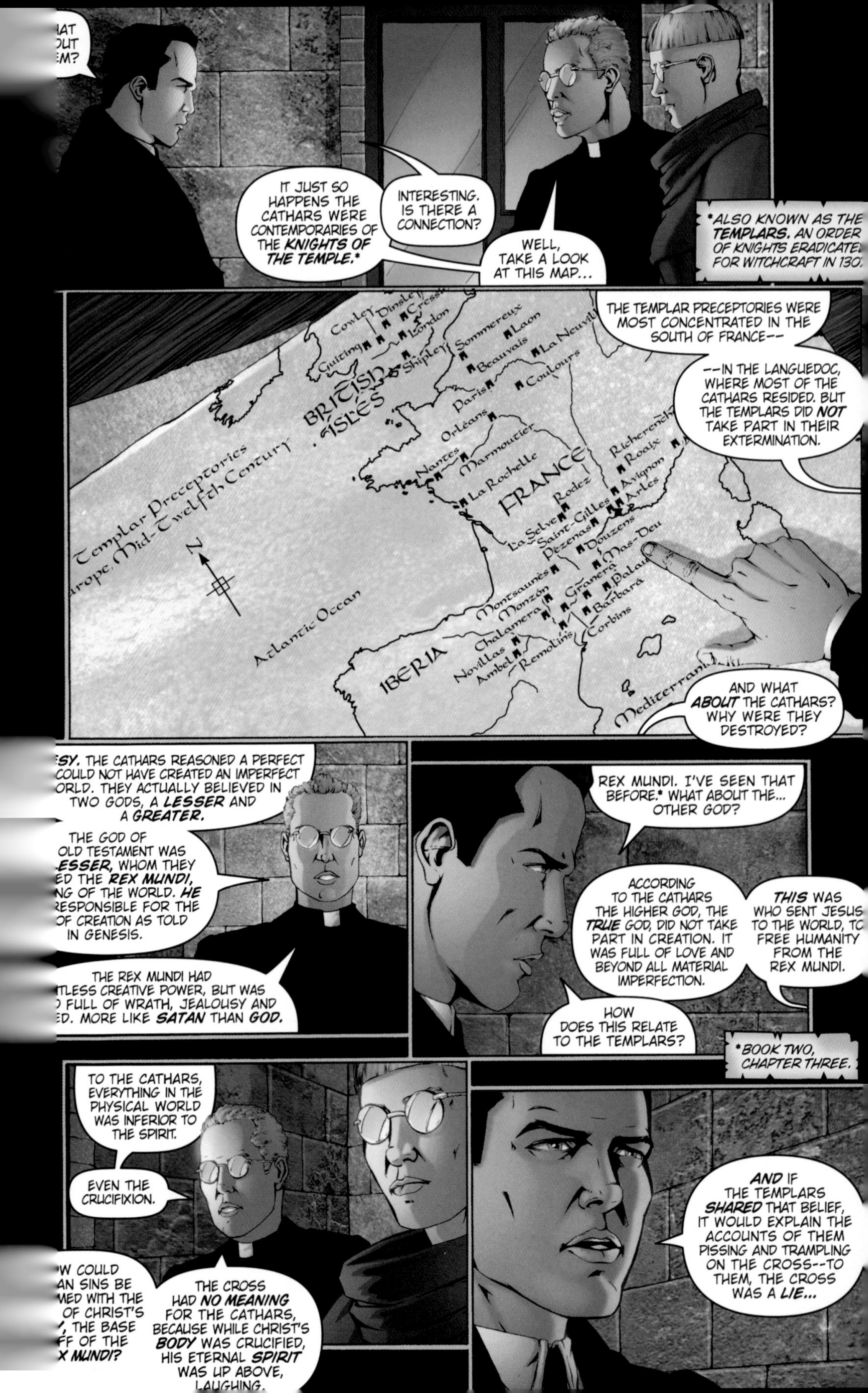

...HAT ...OUT ...EM?
IT JUST SO HAPPENS THE CATHARS WERE CONTEMPORARIES OF THE KNIGHTS OF THE TEMPLE.*
INTERESTING. IS THERE A CONNECTION?
WELL, TAKE A LOOK AT THIS MAP...
*ALSO KNOWN AS THE TEMPLARS. AN ORDER OF KNIGHTS ERADICATE... FOR WITCHCRAFT IN 130...
Templar Preceptories ...rope, Mid-Twelfth Century
N
Atlantic Ocean
BRITISH ISLES
Cowley
Dinsley
Cressing
London
Guiting
Shipley
Sommereux
Laon
La Neuville
Beauvais
Coulours
Paris
Orléans
Marmoutier
Nantes
La Rochelle
FRANCE
Richerenche
Roaix
Avignon
Arles
Rodez
Saint-Gilles
La Selve
Pezenas
Douzens
Mas-Deu
Montsaunès
Monzón
Granera
Palau
Chalamera
Barbara
Corbins
Novillas
Ambel
Remolins
IBERIA
Mediterran...
THE TEMPLAR PRECEPTORIES WERE MOST CONCENTRATED IN THE SOUTH OF FRANCE--
--IN THE LANGUEDOC, WHERE MOST OF THE CATHARS RESIDED. BUT THE TEMPLARS DID NOT TAKE PART IN THEIR EXTERMINATION.
AND WHAT ABOUT THE CATHARS? WHY WERE THEY DESTROYED?
...SY. THE CATHARS REASONED A PERFECT ... COULD NOT HAVE CREATED AN IMPERFECT ...ORLD. THEY ACTUALLY BELIEVED IN TWO GODS, A LESSER AND A GREATER.
THE GOD OF ... OLD TESTAMENT WAS ...LESSER, WHOM THEY ...ED THE REX MUNDI, ...NG OF THE WORLD. HE ... RESPONSIBLE FOR THE ... OF CREATION AS TOLD IN GENESIS.
THE REX MUNDI HAD ...TLESS CREATIVE POWER, BUT WAS ... FULL OF WRATH, JEALOUSY AND ...ED. MORE LIKE SATAN THAN GOD.
REX MUNDI. I'VE SEEN THAT BEFORE.* WHAT ABOUT THE... OTHER GOD?
ACCORDING TO THE CATHARS THE HIGHER GOD, THE TRUE GOD, DID NOT TAKE PART IN CREATION. IT WAS FULL OF LOVE AND BEYOND ALL MATERIAL IMPERFECTION.
THIS WAS WHO SENT JESUS TO THE WORLD, TO FREE HUMANITY FROM THE REX MUNDI.
HOW DOES THIS RELATE TO THE TEMPLARS?
*BOOK TWO, CHAPTER THREE.
TO THE CATHARS, EVERYTHING IN THE PHYSICAL WORLD WAS INFERIOR TO THE SPIRIT.
EVEN THE CRUCIFIXION.
...W COULD ...AN SINS BE ...MED WITH THE ... OF CHRIST'S ..., THE BASE ...FF OF THE ...X MUNDI?
THE CROSS HAD NO MEANING FOR THE CATHARS, BECAUSE WHILE CHRIST'S BODY WAS CRUCIFIED, HIS ETERNAL SPIRIT WAS UP ABOVE, LAUGHING.
AND IF THE TEMPLARS SHARED THAT BELIEF, IT WOULD EXPLAIN THE ACCOUNTS OF THEM PISSING AND TRAMPLING ON THE CROSS--TO THEM, THE CROSS WAS A LIE...

HOLD ON. WE'RE ASSUMING THE CATHARS SOMEHOW TRANSMITTED THEIR BELIEFS TO THE TEMPLARS.

BUT IS IT POSSIBLE THE *TEMPLARS* SOMEHOW CAME TO THE SAME CONCLUSIONS AS THE CATHARS WHILE IN THE HOLY LAND?

WHAT DO YOU MEAN?

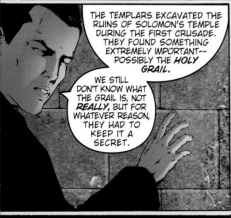

THE TEMPLARS EXCAVATED THE RUINS OF SOLOMON'S TEMPLE DURING THE FIRST CRUSADE. THEY FOUND SOMETHING EXTREMELY IMPORTANT-- POSSIBLY THE *HOLY GRAIL.*

WE STILL DON'T KNOW WHAT THE GRAIL IS, NOT *REALLY,* BUT FOR WHATEVER REASON, THEY HAD TO KEEP IT A SECRET.

MAYBE WHATEVER IT WAS SOMEHOW *CONFIRMED* WHAT THE CATHARS BELIEVED.

WHEN THE TEMPLARS RETURN FROM THE HOLY LAND WITH THEIR NEW-FOUND KNOWLEDGE, THEY FIND WILLING CO-CONSPIRATORS IN THE CATHARS, WHOM THEY ENTRUST WITH THE GRAIL.

AND THE SECRET OF THE GRAIL WAS LOST TO THE CHURCH WITH THE SMALL BAND OF CATHARS WHO ESCAPED DESTRUCTION.

BUT *WHAT* COULD HAVE CAUSED THE TEMPLARS TO DIVERGE SO VIOLENTLY FROM THE CHURCH THEY FOUGHT AND DIED FOR?

THAT JUST MIGHT BE THE KEY TO UNDERSTANDING THE *TRUE* NATURE OF THE HOLY GRAIL.

AND THE GRAIL IS ONLY HALF THE STORY.

EXPLAIN.

THE MEDIEVAL EPICS ALSO TELL OF A GRAIL *FAMILY.* THE ORIGINS OF THIS FAMILY ARE VAGUE, BUT THEY HAVE A HEREDITARY DUTY TO PROTECT THE GRAIL.

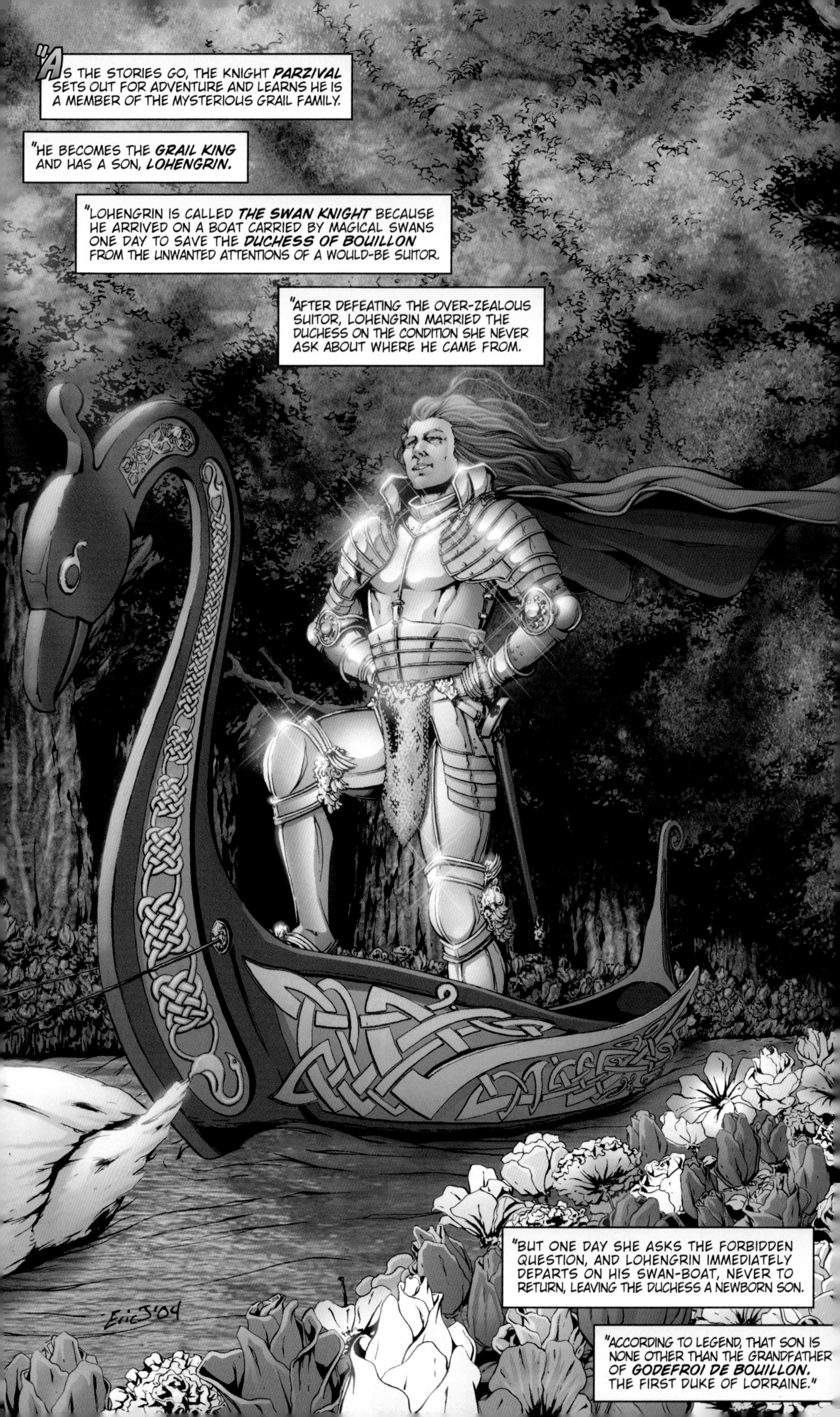
"AS THE STORIES GO, THE KNIGHT PARZIVAL SETS OUT FOR ADVENTURE AND LEARNS HE IS A MEMBER OF THE MYSTERIOUS GRAIL FAMILY.
"HE BECOMES THE GRAIL KING AND HAS A SON, LOHENGRIN.
"LOHENGRIN IS CALLED THE SWAN KNIGHT BECAUSE HE ARRIVED ON A BOAT CARRIED BY MAGICAL SWANS ONE DAY TO SAVE THE DUCHESS OF BOUILLON FROM THE UNWANTED ATTENTIONS OF A WOULD-BE SUITOR.
"AFTER DEFEATING THE OVER-ZEALOUS SUITOR, LOHENGRIN MARRIED THE DUCHESS ON THE CONDITION SHE NEVER ASK ABOUT WHERE HE CAME FROM.
Eric J'04
"BUT ONE DAY SHE ASKS THE FORBIDDEN QUESTION, AND LOHENGRIN IMMEDIATELY DEPARTS ON HIS SWAN-BOAT, NEVER TO RETURN, LEAVING THE DUCHESS A NEWBORN SON.
"ACCORDING TO LEGEND, THAT SON IS NONE OTHER THAN THE GRANDFATHER OF GODEFROI DE BOUILLON, THE FIRST DUKE OF LORRAINE."

WHAT?

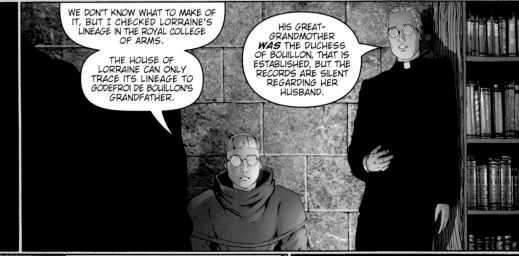

WE DON'T KNOW WHAT TO MAKE OF IT, BUT I CHECKED LORRAINE'S LINEAGE IN THE ROYAL COLLEGE OF ARMS.

THE HOUSE OF LORRAINE CAN ONLY TRACE ITS LINEAGE TO GODEFROI DE BOUILLON'S GRANDFATHER.

HIS GREAT-GRANDMOTHER *WAS* THE DUCHESS OF BOUILLON, THAT IS ESTABLISHED, BUT THE RECORDS ARE SILENT REGARDING HER HUSBAND.

OKAY. IF THIS IS BASED IN FACT... AND THAT'S A *BIG* IF... THEN THE CURRENT DUKE OF LORRAINE IS IN FACT A DESCENDANT OF *PARZIVAL*, THE HERO OF GRAIL EPICS--WHO IS NOT A LEGEND, BUT A REAL PERSON.

THAT WOULD MAKE THE *CURRENT* DUKE OF LORRAINE...

...A MEMBER OF THE *GRAIL FAMILY* ITSELF.

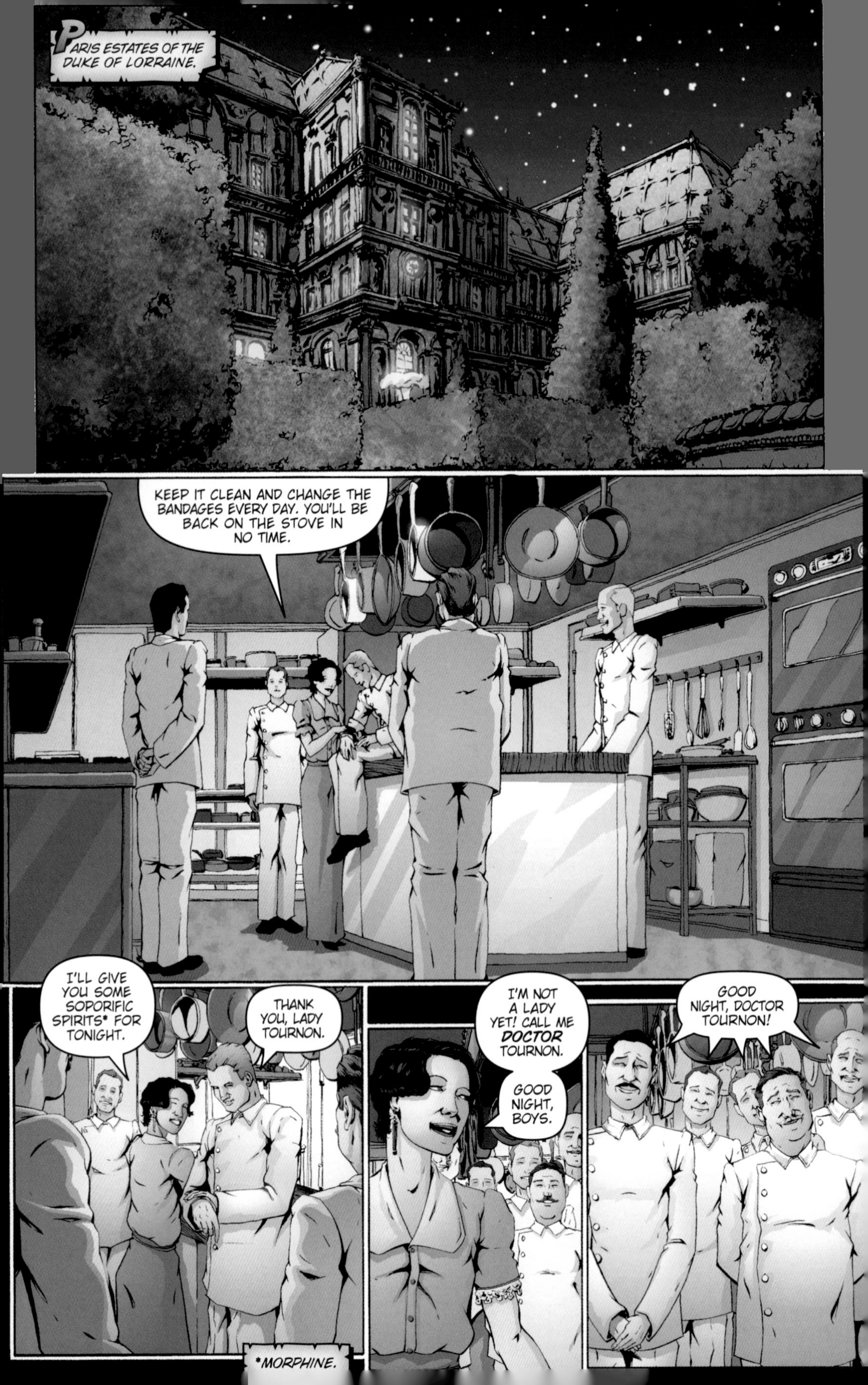
PARIS ESTATES OF THE DUKE OF LORRAINE.
KEEP IT CLEAN AND CHANGE THE BANDAGES EVERY DAY. YOU'LL BE BACK ON THE STOVE IN NO TIME.
I'LL GIVE YOU SOME SOPORIFIC SPIRITS* FOR TONIGHT.
THANK YOU, LADY TOURNON.
*MORPHINE.
I'M NOT A LADY YET! CALL ME DOCTOR TOURNON.
GOOD NIGHT, BOYS.
GOOD NIGHT, DOCTOR TOURNON!

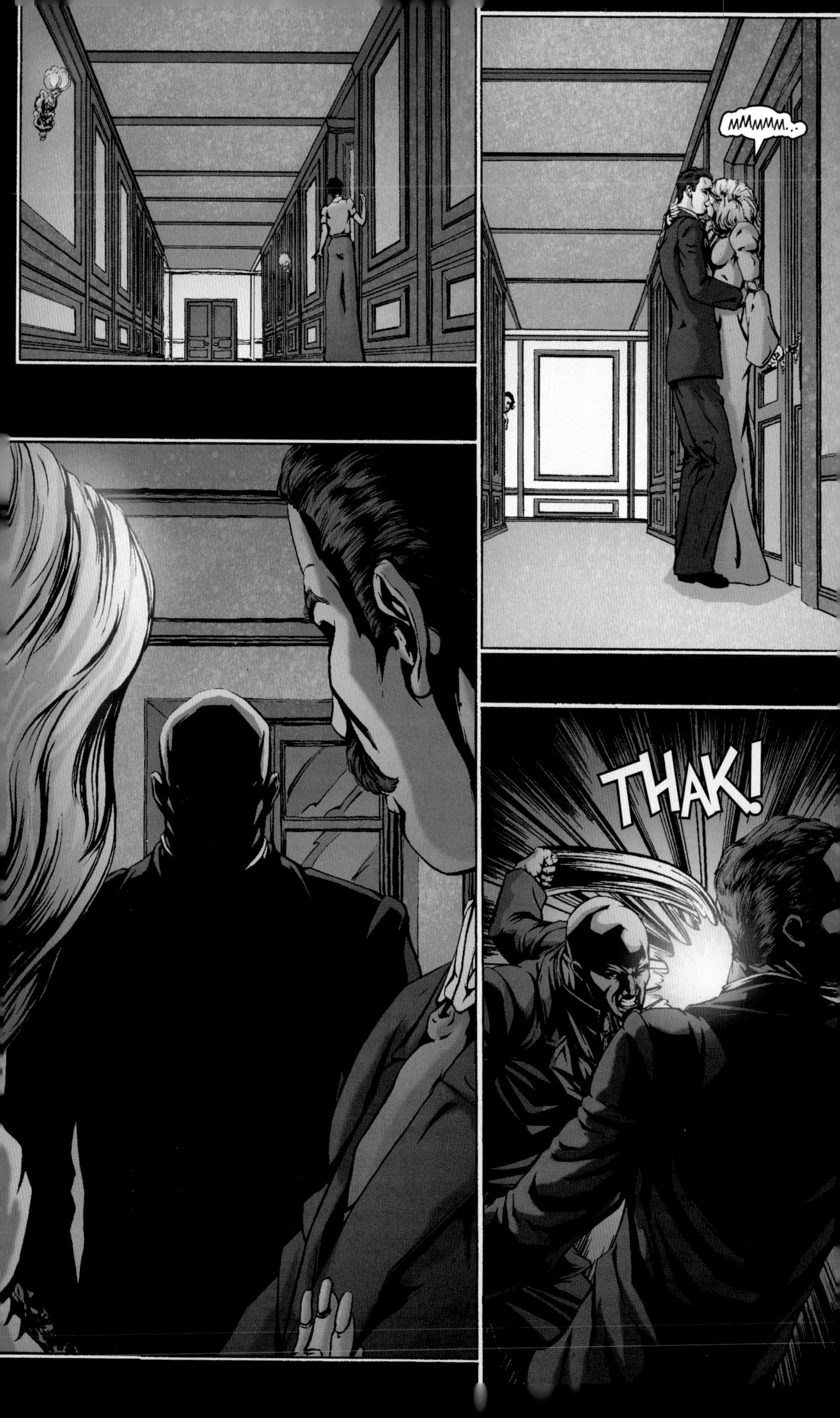
MMMMM...
THAK!

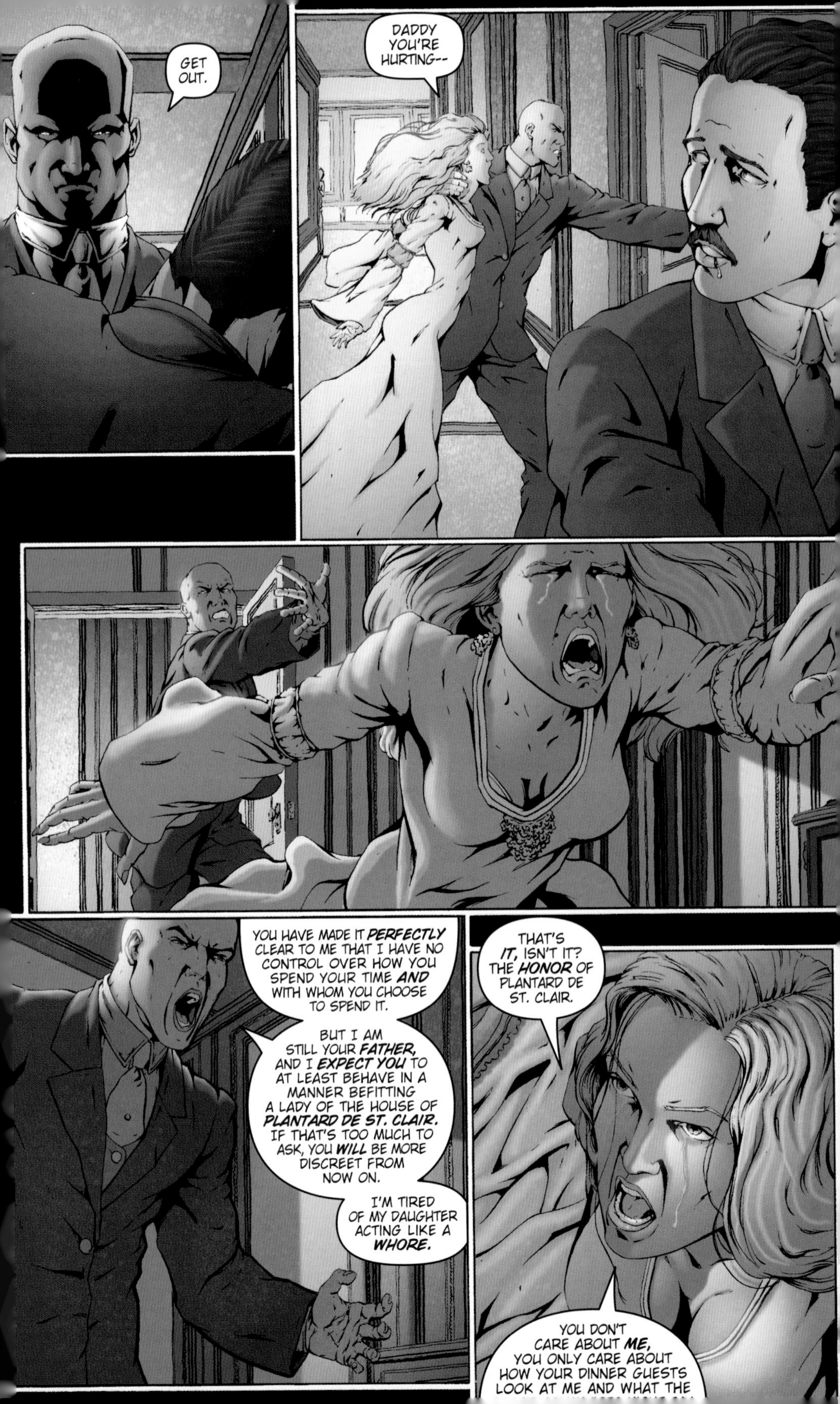
GET OUT.
DADDY YOU'RE HURTING--
YOU HAVE MADE IT PERFECTLY CLEAR TO ME THAT I HAVE NO CONTROL OVER HOW YOU SPEND YOUR TIME AND WITH WHOM YOU CHOOSE TO SPEND IT.
BUT I AM STILL YOUR FATHER, AND I EXPECT YOU TO AT LEAST BEHAVE IN A MANNER BEFITTING A LADY OF THE HOUSE OF PLANTARD DE ST. CLAIR. IF THAT'S TOO MUCH TO ASK, YOU WILL BE MORE DISCREET FROM NOW ON.
I'M TIRED OF MY DAUGHTER ACTING LIKE A WHORE.
THAT'S IT, ISN'T IT? THE HONOR OF PLANTARD DE ST. CLAIR.
YOU DON'T CARE ABOUT ME, YOU ONLY CARE ABOUT HOW YOUR DINNER GUESTS LOOK AT ME AND WHAT THE

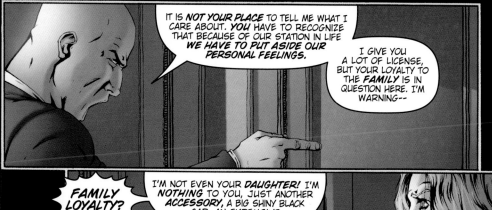

IT IS **NOT YOUR PLACE** TO TELL ME WHAT I CARE ABOUT. **YOU** HAVE TO RECOGNIZE THAT BECAUSE OF OUR STATION IN LIFE **WE HAVE TO PUT ASIDE OUR PERSONAL FEELINGS.**

I GIVE YOU A LOT OF LICENSE, BUT YOUR LOYALTY TO THE **FAMILY** IS IN QUESTION HERE. I'M WARNING--

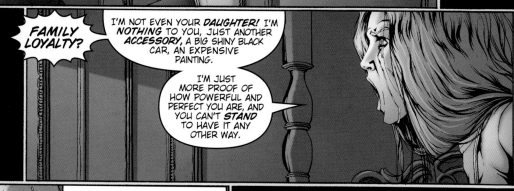

FAMILY LOYALTY?

I'M NOT EVEN YOUR **DAUGHTER!** I'M **NOTHING** TO YOU, JUST ANOTHER **ACCESSORY**, A BIG SHINY BLACK CAR, AN EXPENSIVE PAINTING.

I'M JUST MORE PROOF OF HOW POWERFUL AND PERFECT YOU ARE, AND YOU CAN'T **STAND** TO HAVE IT ANY OTHER WAY.

OUR **FAMILY HISTORY** GOES BACK A LOT FURTHER THAN YOU REALIZE, AND I WILL **NOT** TOLERATE ANY MORE DISSENT FROM YOU.

DON'T TEST MY **PATIENCE, ISABELLE!** I **WILL** CUT YOU OFF IF I HAVE TOO.

THAT'S YOUR SOLUTION FOR EVERYTHING, **ISN'T** IT?

CUT ME OFF.

BELITTLE ME.

MAKE ME **INSIGNIFICANT.**

JUST LIKE ALL YOUR ENEMIES. BUT ONCE THAT'S DONE, WHAT'S LEFT FOR YOU? **NOTHING.**

NONE OF IT IS GOING TO BRING MY MOTHER BACK.

DON'T YOU **DARE** SPEAK OF YOUR MOTHER--

YOU'RE **PATHETIC!** YOU'RE NOT EVEN A REAL **PERSON**, YOU'RE JUST A BAG OF SKIN PUFFED UP WITH A LOT OF EMPTY IDEAS ABOUT **HONOR** AND **HISTORY** AND **SOCIAL GRACE.**

I DON'T **CARE** HOW MANY SPEECHES YOU GIVE OR HOW MANY WARS YOU FIGHT, YOU'RE **NOTHING** BUT...

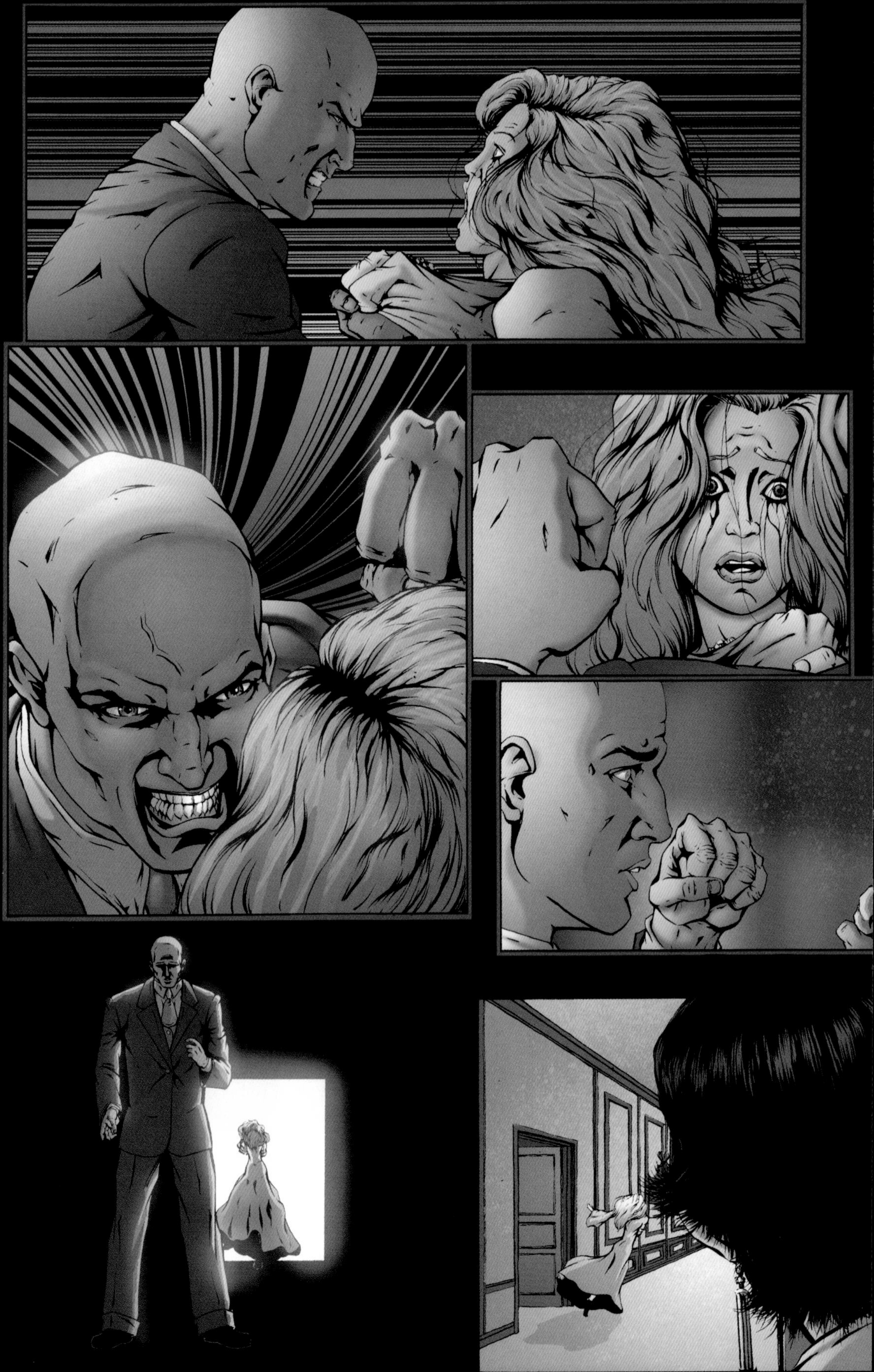

The Descent of the True Kings of France

Dagobert II
Sigisbert IV – Comte de Razes (681)
Guillaume de Gellone (Guillaume I)
Sigisbert V
Sigisbert VI
Guillaume II
Guillaume III
Arnaud
Bera VI
Sigisbert VII
Hugues I
Jean I
Hugues III (Lohengrin)
Mahaut de Louvain

WHAT?

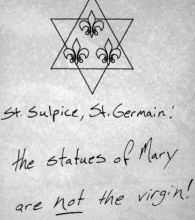

St. Sulpice, St. Germain!

the statues of Mary
are *not* the virgin!

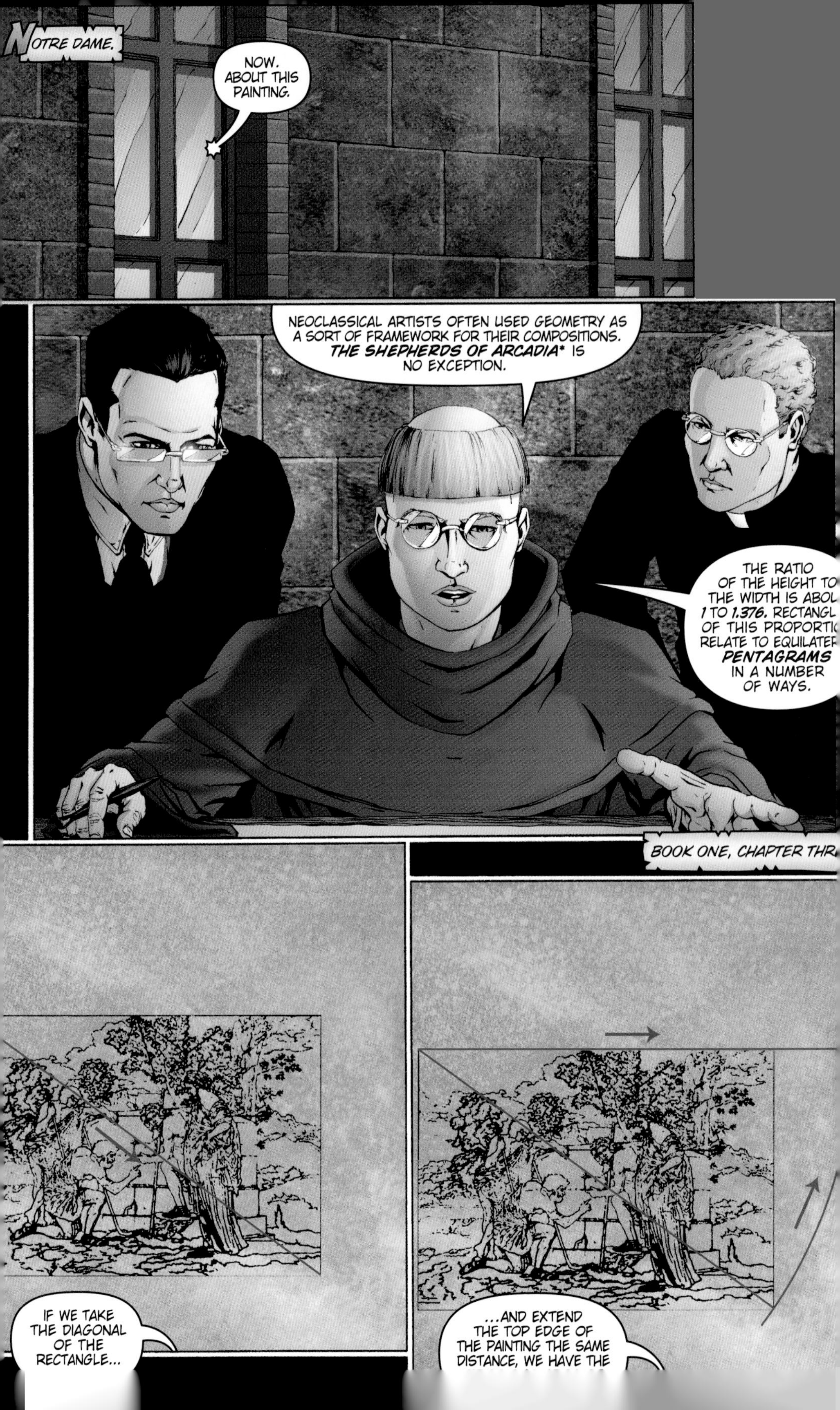
NOTRE DAME.
NOW. ABOUT THIS PAINTING.
NEOCLASSICAL ARTISTS OFTEN USED GEOMETRY AS A SORT OF FRAMEWORK FOR THEIR COMPOSITIONS. THE SHEPHERDS OF ARCADIA* IS NO EXCEPTION.
THE RATIO OF THE HEIGHT TO THE WIDTH IS ABOU 1 TO 1.376. RECTANGL OF THIS PROPORTI RELATE TO EQUILATER PENTAGRAMS IN A NUMBER OF WAYS.
BOOK ONE, CHAPTER THR
IF WE TAKE THE DIAGONAL OF THE RECTANGLE...
...AND EXTEND THE TOP EDGE OF THE PAINTING THE SAME DISTANCE, WE HAVE THE

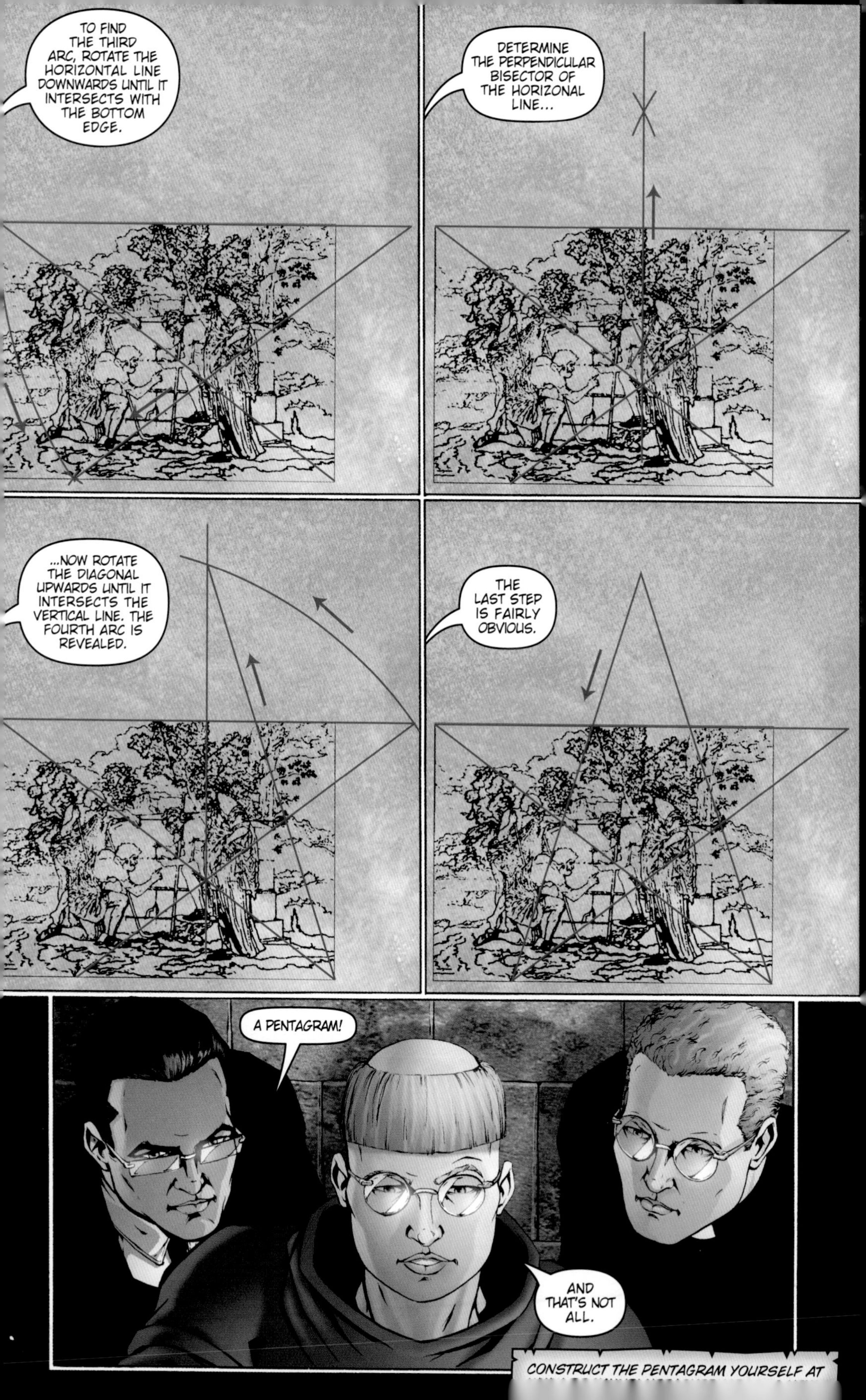
TO FIND THE THIRD ARC, ROTATE THE HORIZONTAL LINE DOWNWARDS UNTIL IT INTERSECTS WITH THE BOTTOM EDGE.
DETERMINE THE PERPENDICULAR BISECTOR OF THE HORIZONAL LINE...
...NOW ROTATE THE DIAGONAL UPWARDS UNTIL IT INTERSECTS THE VERTICAL LINE. THE FOURTH ARC IS REVEALED.
THE LAST STEP IS FAIRLY OBVIOUS.
A PENTAGRAM!
AND THAT'S NOT ALL.
CONSTRUCT THE PENTAGRAM YOURSELF AT

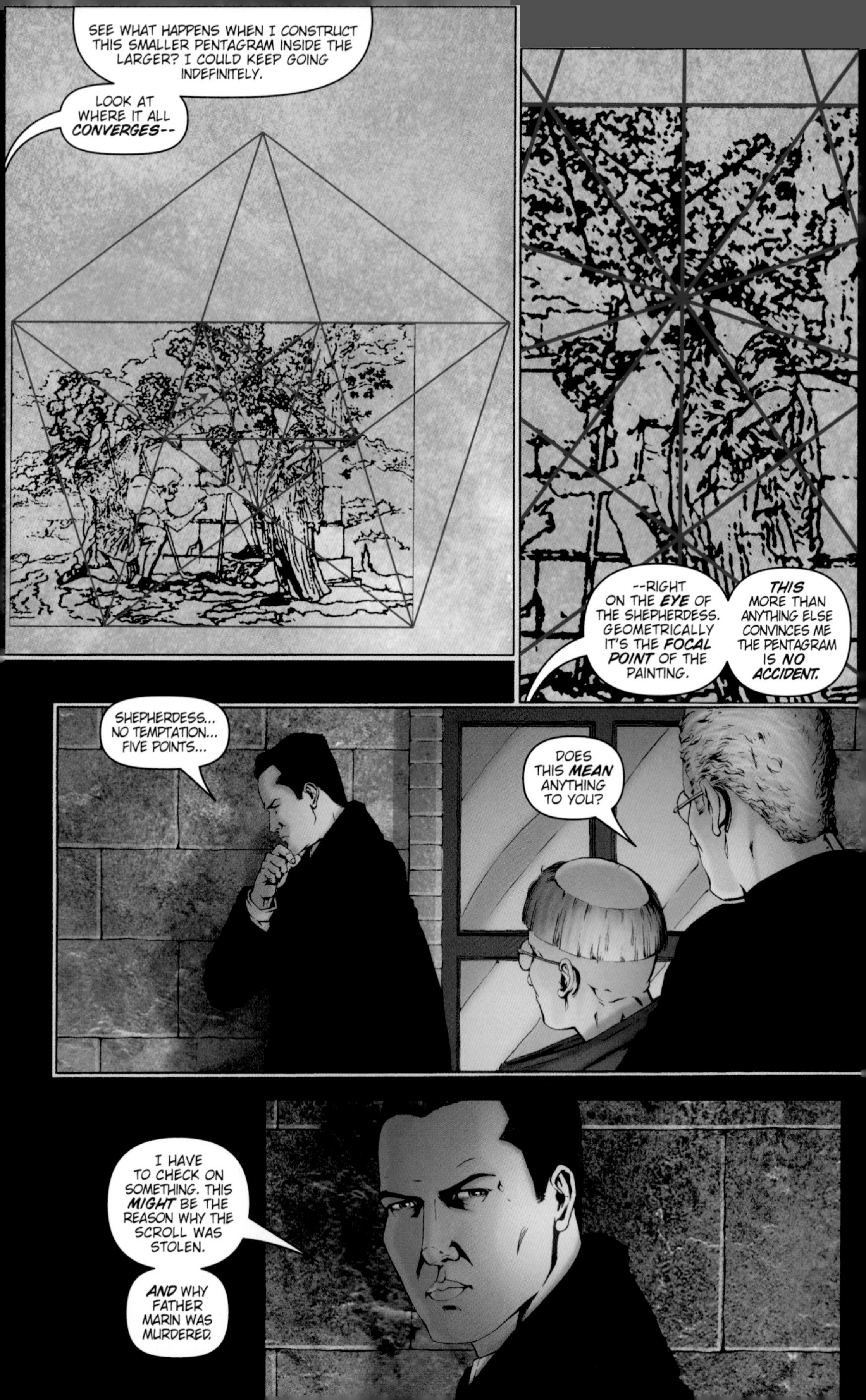
SEE WHAT HAPPENS WHEN I CONSTRUCT THIS SMALLER PENTAGRAM INSIDE THE LARGER? I COULD KEEP GOING INDEFINITELY.
LOOK AT WHERE IT ALL **CONVERGES**--
--RIGHT ON THE **EYE** OF THE SHEPHERDESS. GEOMETRICALLY IT'S THE **FOCAL POINT** OF THE PAINTING.
THIS MORE THAN ANYTHING ELSE CONVINCES ME THE PENTAGRAM IS **NO ACCIDENT.**
SHEPHERDESS... NO TEMPTATION... FIVE POINTS...
DOES THIS **MEAN** ANYTHING TO YOU?
I HAVE TO CHECK ON SOMETHING. THIS **MIGHT** BE THE REASON WHY THE SCROLL WAS STOLEN.
AND WHY FATHER MARIN WAS MURDERED.

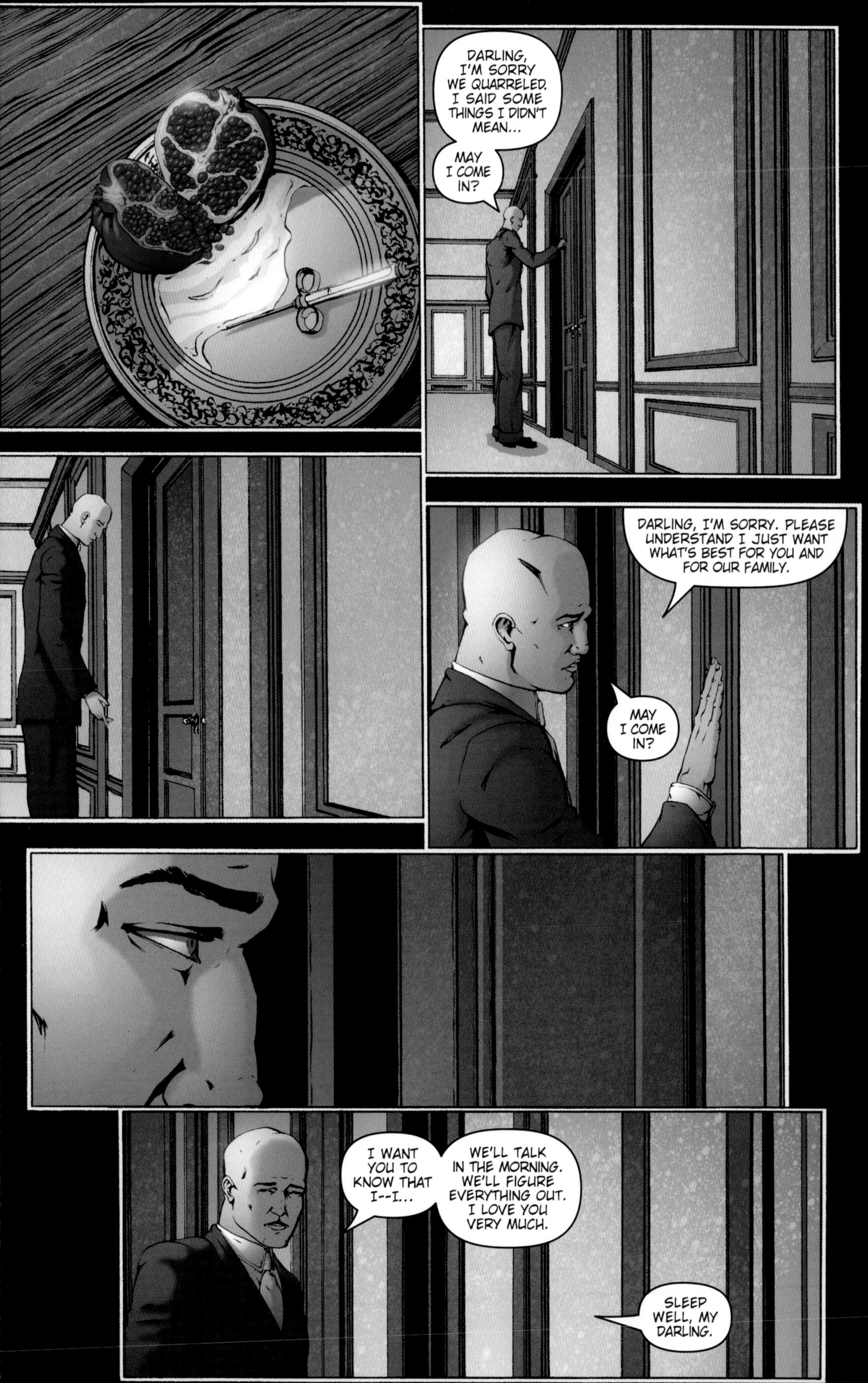
DARLING, I'M SORRY WE QUARRELED. I SAID SOME THINGS I DIDN'T MEAN...
MAY I COME IN?
DARLING, I'M SORRY. PLEASE UNDERSTAND I JUST WANT WHAT'S BEST FOR YOU AND FOR OUR FAMILY.
MAY I COME IN?
I WANT YOU TO KNOW THAT I--I...
WE'LL TALK IN THE MORNING. WE'LL FIGURE EVERYTHING OUT. I LOVE YOU VERY MUCH.
SLEEP WELL, MY DARLING.

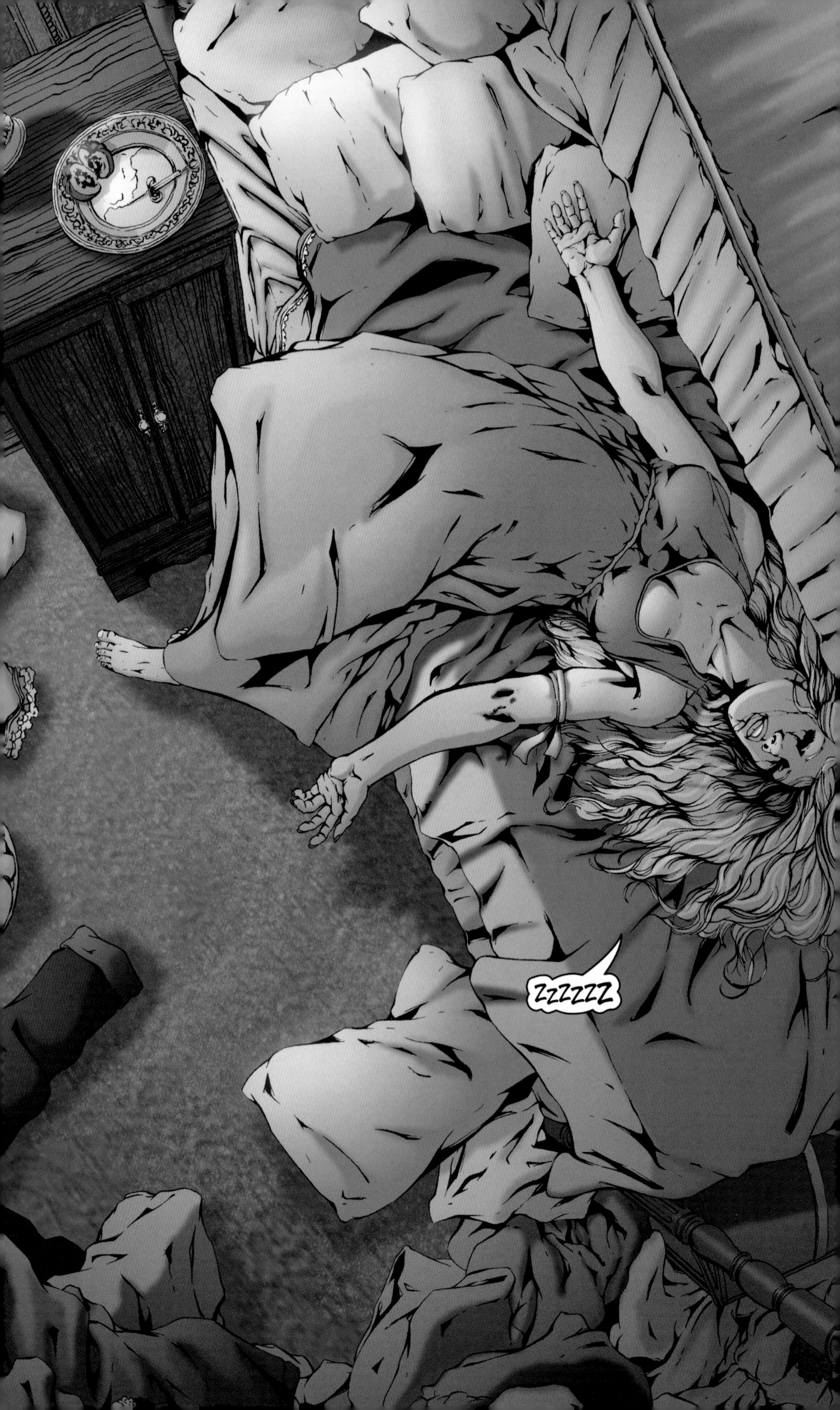
ZZZZZZ

Le Journal de la Liberté

Paris' leading anglophone newspaper • vol. 205, no. 103 • Oct. 29, MCMXXXIII

Editors in Chief: M. Tait Bergstrom, M. Matthew Pasteris. **Story Editor:** M. Arvid Nelson. **Art Editors:** M. EricJ, M. Jeromy Cox. **Photography Editor:** M. Alexander Waldman. **Layout Supervisor:** M. William Kartalopoulos. **Editors Emeritus:** M. Clark A. Smith, M. Howard P. Lovecraft, M. Robert E. Howard. Redacted by the Holy Parisian Inquisition under the direction of His Excellency Archbishop Emile-Jean Ireneaux. Le Journal de la Liberté is printed under the benign auspices of his most puissant majesty KING LOUIS XXII of FRANCE. GOD SAVE THE KING.

Papal seal

of Approval

DUKE OF LORRAINE MEETS SENIOR BRITISH DIPLOMAT SIR WINSTON CHURCHILL FOR "TALKS"

Duke and Influential British Politician Hint at Announcement of a "Major Initiative."

Paris – Eminent British politician and diplomat Winston Churchill met King Louis XXII of France at Versailles yesterday, confirming the close ties across the English Channel.

But Churchill's visit comes at an awkward time for King Louis, as he attempts to defuse pan-continental tensions and reign in an unruly parliament.

"We welcome Sir Winston and are happy to reiterate our longstanding friendship with Britain," Charles Martel, Louis XXII's mayor of the court, said. "However, his warlike attitude gives us some concern."

Martel referred specifically to Churchill's aggressive stance on Islam. In many ways Churchill's policies mirror those of the Duke of Lorraine in France.

As is the case for Lord Lorraine, Churchill's hawkish position has won him great favor in parliament but also the displeasure of his king, George V of England. Lorraine finds his policies similarly blocked by Louis XXII.

The two eminent politicians are scheduled an "informal" meeting today to discuss "matters of mutual concern." Aides of Louis XXII said the French king is "troubled" by the idea.

David-Louis Plantard de St. Clair, Duke of Lorraine, and Sir Winston Churchill shake hands yesterday. Churchill's visit has elicited mixed reactions from the court of Louis XXII and elation from France's ancient noble houses.

"By publicly proclaiming support for one another they are undermining their respective sovereigns. It is flagrantly disrespectful, if not downright treasonous," a source close to King Louis said.

Churchill and Lorraine dismiss this notion.

"Lord Lorraine and Sir Winston want the same things: to strengthen the positions of their respective nations," Baron Robert Teniers, a spokesman for Lorraine, said. "They share their respective monarchs' commitments to strength and stability."

This oft-repeated claim draws sharp criticism from the court of Louis XXII.

"It is a king's G-d-given right to decide foreign policy. It is not a matter on which he must consult a national diet," Martel said. "Expansionism will almost certainly lead to war with our eastern neighbors, and that is something no nation can afford at the present time."

Lorraine and Churchill refused to give details about what they would discuss in their meeting, save that it would be "to determine the viability of a major initiative."

Islam is almost certain to be on their agenda.

"Mohammedism has no place in Europe," Lorraine said. "That is the simple truth. It is our intention to drive the Moor and the Saracen across the pillars of Hercules in the West and the Bosporous in the East."

"The time is at hand for the Christian nations to rise up and turn the tide of Islam from the shores of Europe forever," Churchill said in a speech to the House of Lords earlier this year.

"We shall each establish our spheres of influence across the globe, and we shall support France in her quest to civilize the peripheral peoples of the world."

Representatives of the Cordovan Emirate and the Ottoman Empire, the two Islamic states with holdings in Europe, vigorously condemn the "incendiary rhetoric" of Lorraine and Churchill.

"We are a peace-loving people, but we are more than capable of defending ourselves against warmongering crusaders like Lorraine and Churchill," Ali Al-Faddiq, Ottoman ambassador to France, said.

Lorraine's statements have also angered France's Christian neighbors. The Prussians and Austrians are pursuing colonial policies of their own and see direct competitors in France and England.

"Prussia reserves the right to pursue her interests at home and abroad," Kaiser Wilhelm III asserted in a radio address the other day. "No nation can stand in her way. The German race is made of iron."

Prussia boasts the largest and the most technologically advanced army in the world. The kaiser has invested a considerable amount in "panzer" machines, fast-moving tracked vehicles with "impregnable" armor plating and massive firepower.

Lorraine and Churchill disputed the idea that a war with Prussia would doom England and France.

"Wars are fought on sea as well
continued on page A2

GREEK NATIONALISTS INCREASE RAIDS IN OTTOMAN TERRITORIES

Sultan vows to "crush" partisan activity

Kastoria, Greece – There's mounting trouble for the Ottoman Sultan in the rugged hills of Northern Greece.

Greek nationals, emboldened by a perceived weakening of the Turkish presence in Europe, have stepped up raids on military outposts in recent weeks.

Although the raids are individually small, "no more than a few dozen partisans partaking in any one attack," according to Fariz Kuyvvet, the Emir of Greece, the increased frequency of the raids is "a nuisance."

The Ottomans have held Greece for over 500 years and are reluctant to give it up.

"The Greek people already enjoy a large degree of autonomy
continued on page A9

⊹ INSIDE ⊹

Our new food columnist, the sultry Baroness Bareback Contessa, shows you how to cook heart-stoppingly delicious meals. She'll even help you throw a *"fabulous"* dinner party. Her secret: paper plates and lots of butter and alcohol! **C1**

Special: The Spanish Marches

Plus opinion pieces by eds. A. Nelson and EricJ

LE JOURNAL SPECIAL: THE SPANISH MARCHES

Bordeaux
Pamplona
FRANCE
NAVARRE
ARAGON
CATALONIA
Marseille
Lisbon
Madrid
Zaragoza
Barcelona
Cordova
EMIRATE OF CORDOVA
Balearic Islands (Cordovan)
ALMOHAD CALIPHATE
ALGERIA (FRANCE)
Rabat
Algiers

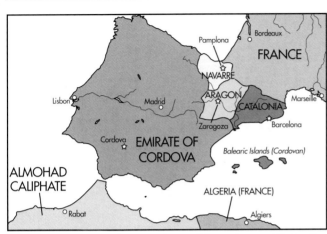

This map clearly demonstrates the precarious location of Navarre, Aragon and Castile, collectively known as the Spanish Marches. For hundreds of years the Lords of the Marches have kept the Cordovan moors away from France's borders.

The words "march" and "marquis" are derived from the Latin word for border, *margo*. A marquis, therefore, is a person of noble birth with lands on the edges of his monarch's domains.

Since frontiers are susceptible to attack and invasion, marquises are often a king's first line of defense. Nowhere is this more true than in Navarre, Aragon and Catalonia, known collectively as the "Spanish Marches."

The lords of the Spanish Marches have kept France safe from the incursions of the Cordovan Emirate for many generations.

And yet, times have changed– No emir has threatened France in living memory. Have the Lords of the Marches lost their mandate, or are the Cordovans still a threat? In this *Le Journal* Special we examine the glorious past and complicated present-day politics of Navarre, Aragon and Catalonia.

Charlemagne and the Reconquista

Early in the eighth century, the moors of Northern Africa invaded and conquered the Iberian Peninsula. The campaign lasted just five years, and the muslims never left.

Charlemagne took part in the quest to expel the moors, called the *Reconquista*, the reconquering. No subsequent king would match even his limited success. In many ways the Reconquista never ended.

Charlemagne pried the rugged, mountainous lands to the southwest of France from the moors, but Islamist forces repulsed further advance.

As a defense against moorish invasions, Charlemagne created the territories of Navarre, Aragon and Catalonia. He made his three best commanders marquises and placed them in charge of the lands.

The descendants of these Carolingian warlords, known as the Lords of the Marches, rule Navarre, Aragon and Catalonia to this day. Though technically subjects of the French kings, the Lords enjoy virtual autonomy in return for defending France from moorish aggression.

The arrangement has proven useful to France. Over the centuries, the Marquises have played a decisive role in defeating Cordovan military expeditions.

"Who knows? France might have fallen to Islam if not for the Spanish Lords," Baron Jean-Pierre Doinel, an aide to King Louis and a historian of the Spanish Marches, said. "France owes the Lords of the Marches a great debt."

The Cordovan Emirate

Charles the Hammer, Charlemagne's grandfather, turned the tide of Islam away from France at the Battle of Tours in 732 AD. Islam would never again reach far past the Pyrenees mountains.

But for centuries after Tours, Christendom was still on the defensive. The Cordovan emirs, descendants of the Umayyad Dynasty, launched numerous expeditions with the aim of conquering France, the most recent of which took place in 1844.

"Every time, the French Kings relied upon the Spanish Marquises, and every time, the Marquises were decisive in defeating the Mohammedans," Baron Doinel said. No emir ever succeeded in conquering France.

"The invasion of 1844 was rather laughable. The moors were defeated in a few weeks. I doubt they'll ever have the resources or will to invade again." Doinel said.

Relations between the Cordovans and the French have improved considerably since then. Still, the two powers are cautious of each other.

"It has been said we lack the will to fight. But make no mistake; Cordova is a den of lions," Mohammed al-Mundhir, viceroy to the Emir of Cordova, said. Some take these threats seriously.

"We must always be vigilant when it comes to the forces of Islam. The world is not so different today from the days of Charlemagne," the Duke of Lorraine said.

Others disagree.

"All this rabble-rousing about the 'moorish threat' is pure nonsense," Charles Martel, mayor of the Court to Louis XXII, said. "It's dishonest rhetoric used by people with ulterior motives. The Cordovans are long past their prime."

Faded Glory?

The same debate is being raised about the Lords themselves.

"There's something to be said for having a strong foe nearb compels one to stay fit," M said. "The absence of pressure f Cordova has made the Lords of Marches soft. They have very l military value to France."

A growing movement in Hall of the Sword also believes Spanish Lords are ineffectual w riors, but they see it as a weak in France's defences.

"The Cordovans may lau an assault at a moment's no Can we really expect the Lord the Marches to repulse a mod invasion force?" the Duke of L raine said in a speech to the Ha the Sword. He even hinted at possibility of a French takeove the Marches.

"Unity is strength. Together can better defend ourselves aga the Mohammedans," he said.

"The people of the Nava Aragon and Castile share our guage, culture and history," on Robert Teniers, a spokes for the Duke of Lorraine, s "Reunification makes a cer amount of sense."

But the notion of "reunif tion" is denounced as "anne tion" by critics. The idea aro suspicion amongst the Europ monarchs—Including King L himself.

"His Majesty King Louis no desire to expand into Ibe Martel said. "He respects the lo standing feudal privileges of Lords of the Marches."

Even Lorraine acknowle that expansion into Iberia is " ficult to conceive of given pre circumstances."

And the Lords of the Marc will ultimately decide their fate. They fiercely deny the ch they have grown soft.

"The blood of Charlema flows in our veins," Diego Inc Ramírez de Gonzaga, Marqui Aragon, said. "Such blood not run thin."

Still, he did not rule out possibility of annexation. Nor his peers, the Marquises of Nav and Catalonia.

"Times have changed, and must look to France for streng Arturo Mendoza de León, the M quis of Catalonia, said.

It is not clear the Lords the Spanish Marches fully end Lorraine's overtures.

"We have always prided selves in our independence self-reliance," Juan Carlos Men Diaz, Marquis of Navarre, said. " understand the need for unity, we will think very carefully be forfeiting our feudal rights."

Navarre

Aragon

Catalonia

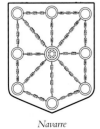

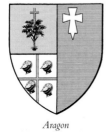

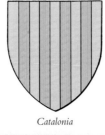

The crests of the Lords of the Marches. Are the ancient privileges of the Spanish Lords a relic of the past or a vital defense against Islam? Debate rages in the Robe and the Sword.

CHAPTER TWO

THE LOST KINGS

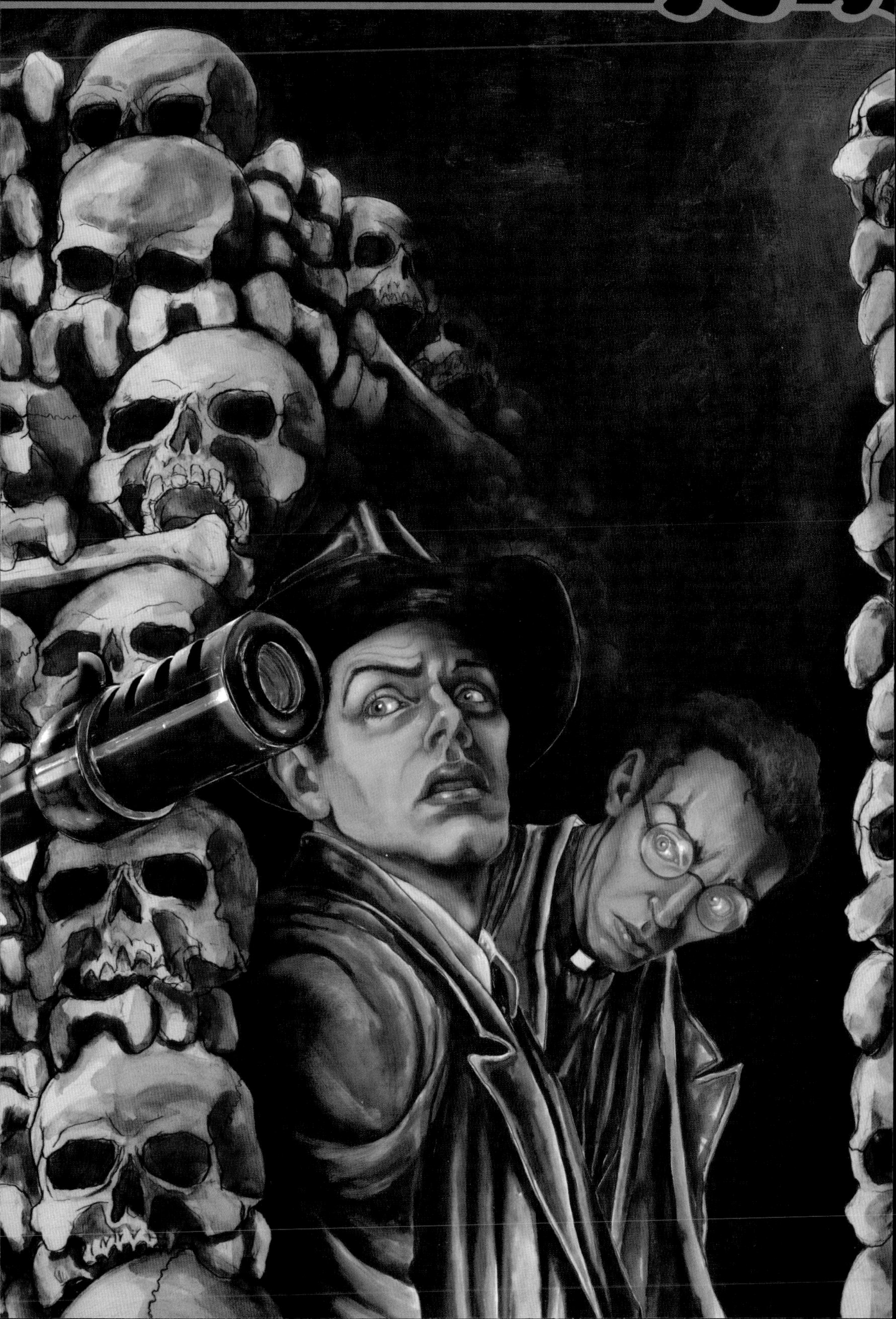

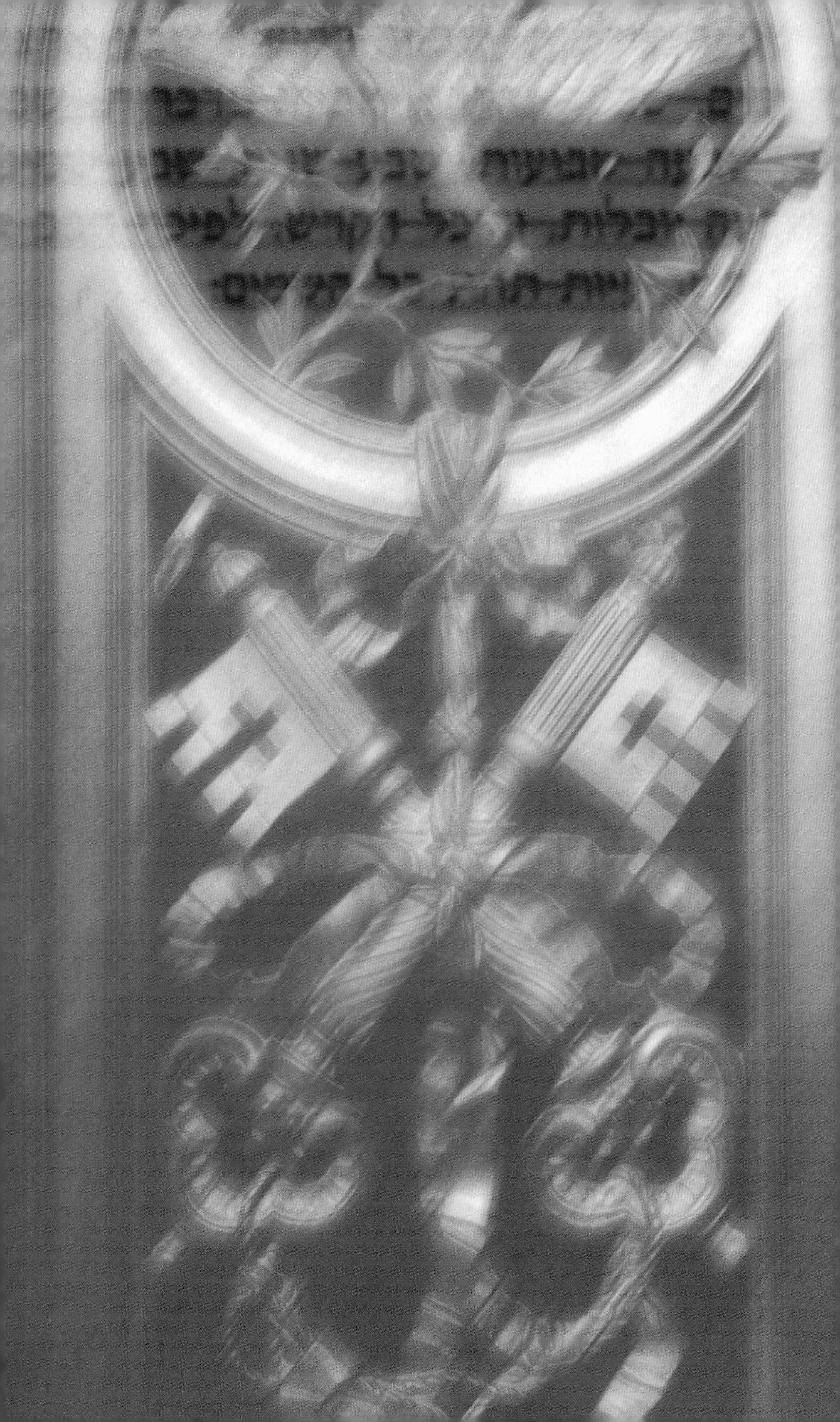

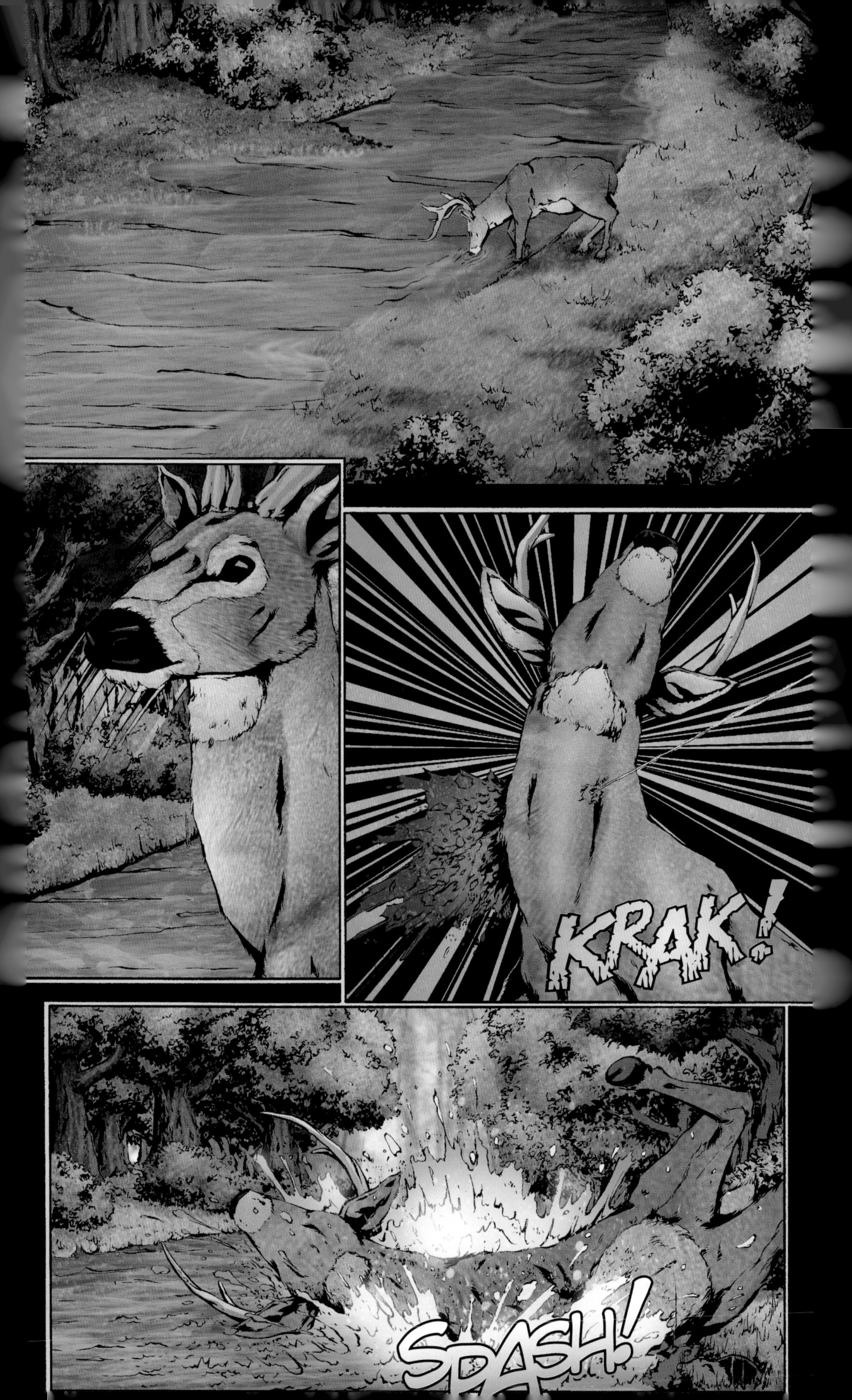
KRAK!
SPASH!

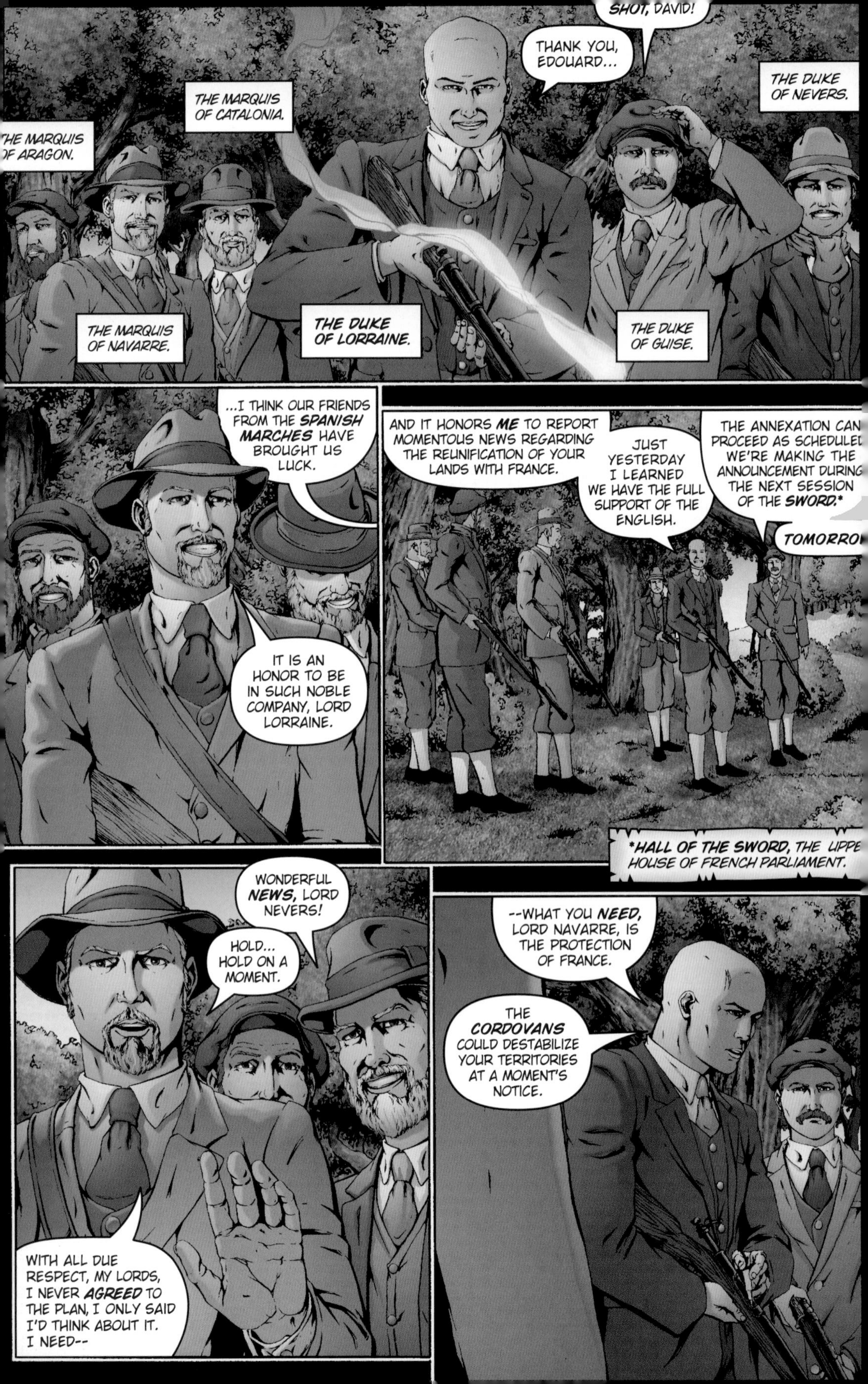

SHOT, DAVID!
THANK YOU, EDOUARD...
THE MARQUIS OF CATALONIA.
THE DUKE OF NEVERS.
THE MARQUIS OF ARAGON.
THE MARQUIS OF NAVARRE.
THE DUKE OF LORRAINE.
THE DUKE OF GUISE.
...I THINK OUR FRIENDS FROM THE SPANISH MARCHES HAVE BROUGHT US LUCK.
IT IS AN HONOR TO BE IN SUCH NOBLE COMPANY, LORD LORRAINE.
AND IT HONORS ME TO REPORT MOMENTOUS NEWS REGARDING THE REUNIFICATION OF YOUR LANDS WITH FRANCE.
JUST YESTERDAY I LEARNED WE HAVE THE FULL SUPPORT OF THE ENGLISH.
THE ANNEXATION CAN PROCEED AS SCHEDULED. WE'RE MAKING THE ANNOUNCEMENT DURING THE NEXT SESSION OF THE SWORD.*
TOMORRO
*HALL OF THE SWORD, THE UPPE HOUSE OF FRENCH PARLIAMENT.
WONDERFUL NEWS, LORD NEVERS!
HOLD... HOLD ON A MOMENT.
WITH ALL DUE RESPECT, MY LORDS, I NEVER AGREED TO THE PLAN, I ONLY SAID I'D THINK ABOUT IT. I NEED--
--WHAT YOU NEED, LORD NAVARRE, IS THE PROTECTION OF FRANCE.
THE CORDOVANS COULD DESTABILIZE YOUR TERRITORIES AT A MOMENT'S NOTICE.

THE CORDOVANS, MY DUKE, HAVE NOT ORGANIZED A RAID OF ANY CONSEQUENCE IN LIVING MEMORY. THEY ARE WEAK, AND I AM PERFECTLY CAPABLE OF DEALING WITH BANDITRY AND SPORADIC LAWLESSNESS ON MY OWN.

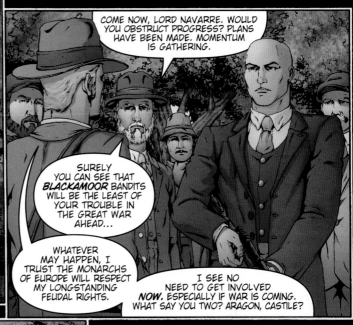

COME NOW, LORD NAVARRE. WOULD YOU OBSTRUCT PROGRESS? PLANS HAVE BEEN MADE. MOMENTUM IS GATHERING.

SURELY YOU CAN SEE THAT *BLACKAMOOR* BANDITS WILL BE THE LEAST OF YOUR TROUBLE IN THE GREAT WAR AHEAD...

WHATEVER MAY HAPPEN, I TRUST THE MONARCHS OF EUROPE WILL RESPECT MY LONGSTANDING FEUDAL RIGHTS.

I SEE NO NEED TO GET INVOLVED *NOW*. ESPECIALLY IF WAR IS COMING. WHAT SAY YOU TWO? ARAGON, CASTILE?

FRANKLY, WE'RE IN COMPLETE AGREEMENT WITH LORRAINE. SINCE MEROVINGIAN TIMES WE HAVE HAD A SPECIAL RELATIONSHIP WITH FRANCE. A CLOSE, CULTURAL CONNECTION.

IN REALITY, AREN'T WE TALKING ABOUT *REUNION?* ONE LAND AND ONE RACE?

OUR PEOPLE *ARE* ONE, NAVARRE.

TOGETHER, WE COULD ACCOMPLISH WHAT CHARLEMAGNE COULD NOT-- *DRIVE THE MOORS INTO THE SEA.*

I AM *EXTREMELY* UNEASY ABOUT...

THEREAFTER WE STRIKE *PALESTINE*, RESTORE THE HOLY CITY TO CHRISTENDOM.

THIS *COULD* BE THE CRUCIBLE OF A NEW EUROPE, THE *PURE* EUROPE OF OUR ANCESTORS!

I...

I CAN'T DECIDE *HERE*, I SIMPLY MUST HAVE SOME TIME...

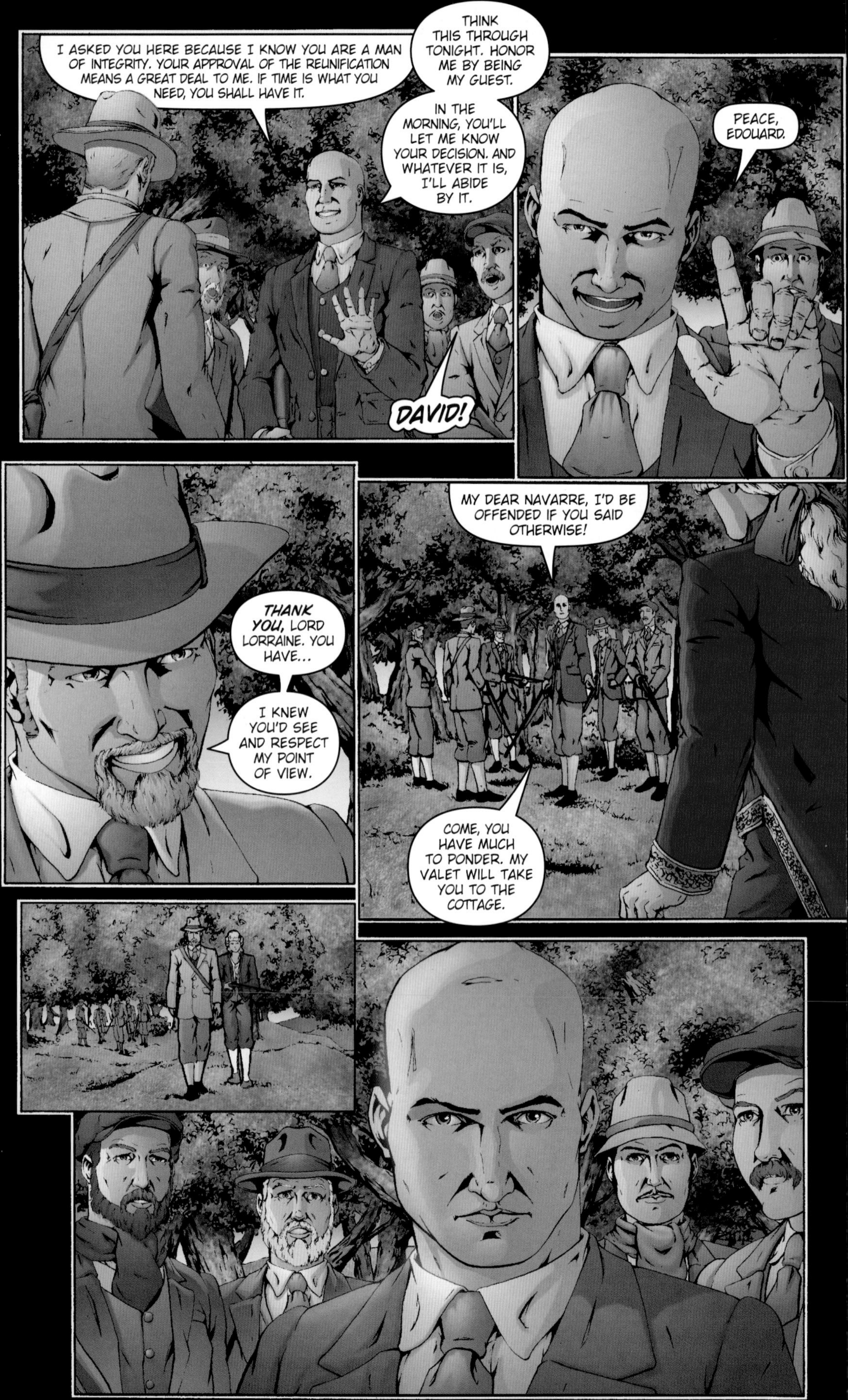
I ASKED YOU HERE BECAUSE I KNOW YOU ARE A MAN OF INTEGRITY. YOUR APPROVAL OF THE REUNIFICATION MEANS A GREAT DEAL TO ME. IF TIME IS WHAT YOU NEED, YOU SHALL HAVE IT.
THINK THIS THROUGH TONIGHT. HONOR ME BY BEING MY GUEST.
IN THE MORNING, YOU'LL LET ME KNOW YOUR DECISION. AND WHATEVER IT IS, I'LL ABIDE BY IT.
DAVID!
PEACE, EDOUARD.
THANK YOU, LORD LORRAINE. YOU HAVE...
I KNEW YOU'D SEE AND RESPECT MY POINT OF VIEW.
MY DEAR NAVARRE, I'D BE OFFENDED IF YOU SAID OTHERWISE!
COME, YOU HAVE MUCH TO PONDER. MY VALET WILL TAKE YOU TO THE COTTAGE.

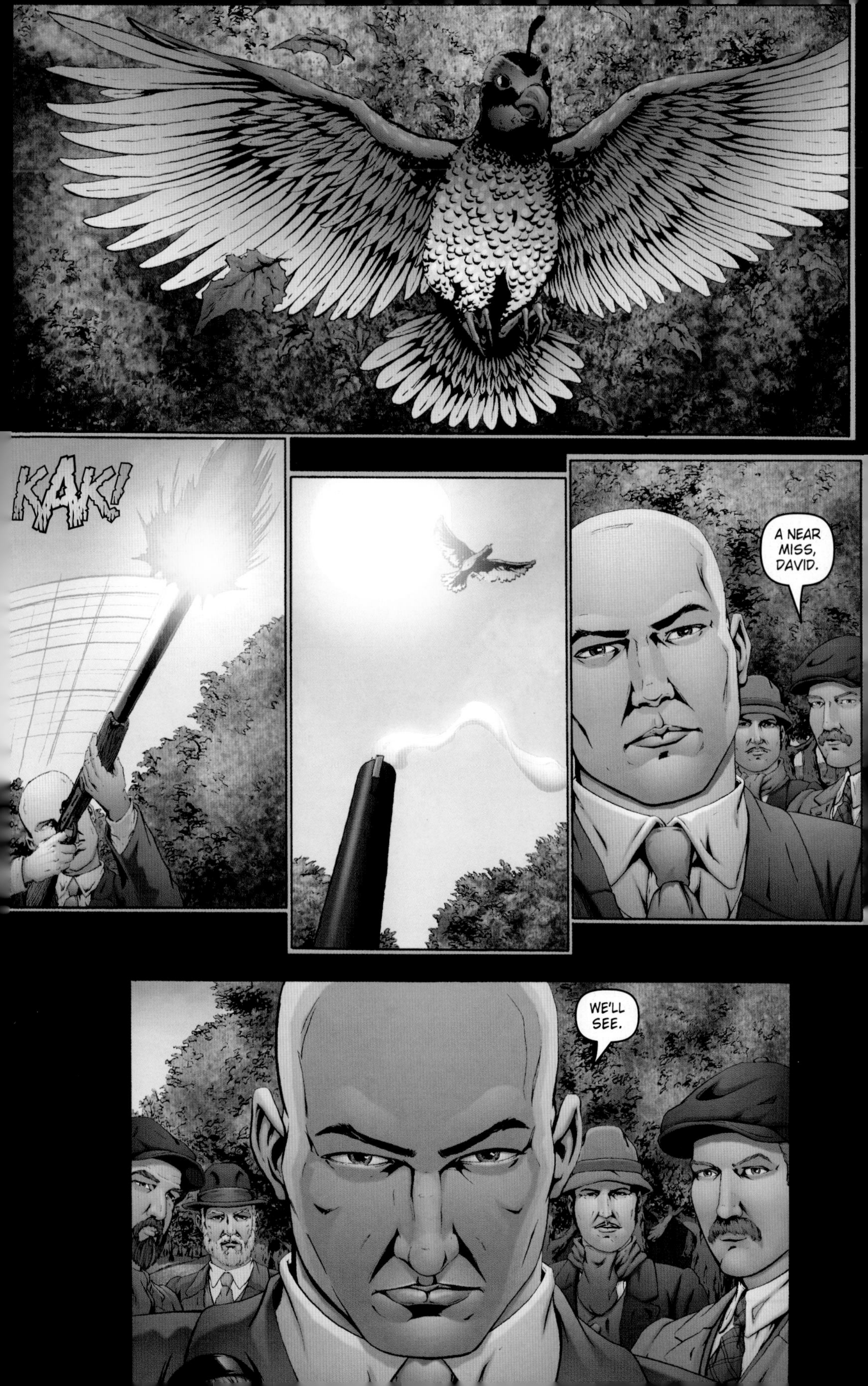
KAK!
A NEAR MISS, DAVID.
WE'LL SEE.

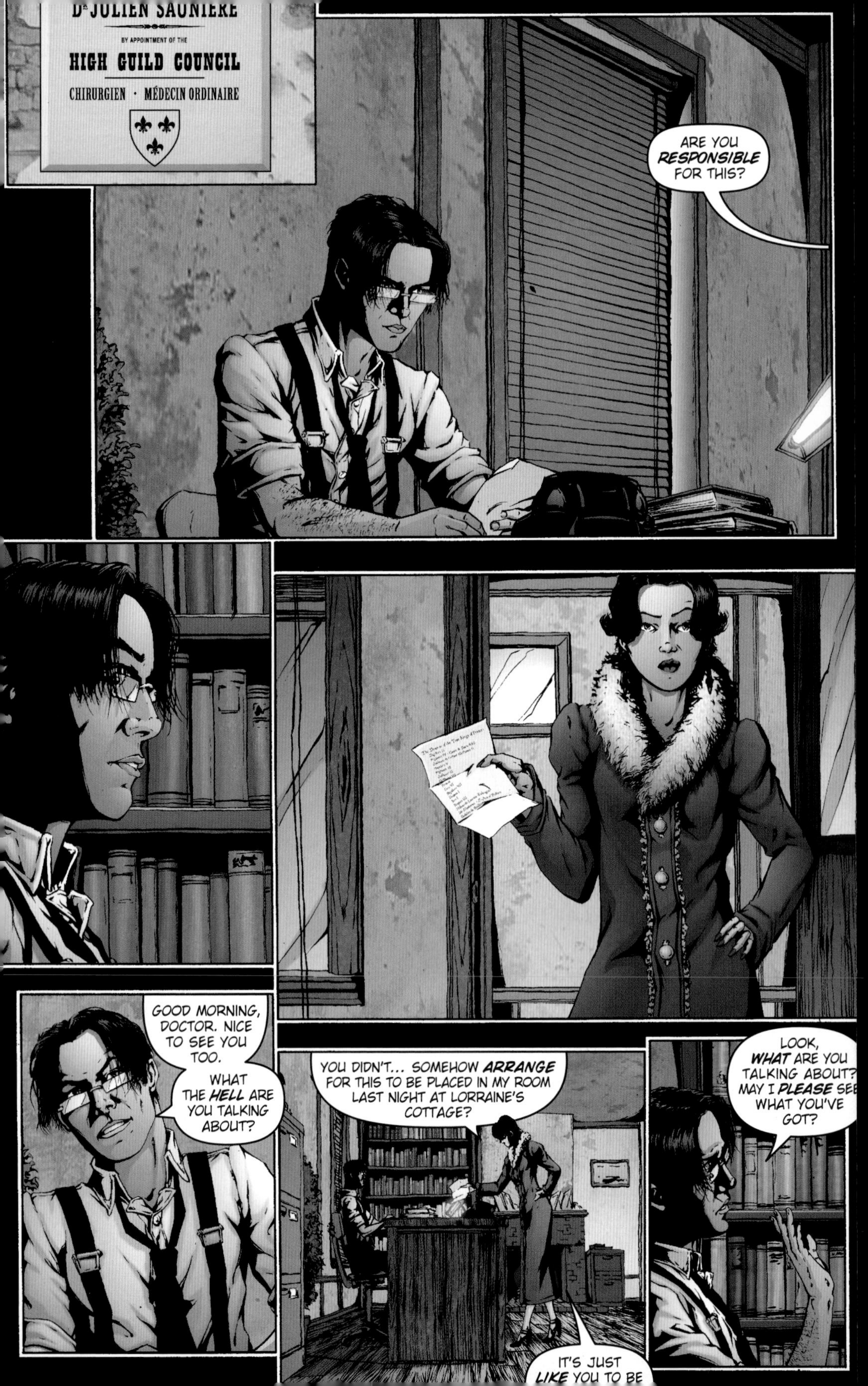
Dr JULIEN SAUNIERE
BY APPOINTMENT OF THE
HIGH GUILD COUNCIL
CHIRURGIEN · MÉDECIN ORDINAIRE
ARE YOU RESPONSIBLE FOR THIS?
GOOD MORNING, DOCTOR. NICE TO SEE YOU TOO.
WHAT THE HELL ARE YOU TALKING ABOUT?
YOU DIDN'T... SOMEHOW ARRANGE FOR THIS TO BE PLACED IN MY ROOM LAST NIGHT AT LORRAINE'S COTTAGE?
IT'S JUST LIKE YOU TO BE
LOOK, WHAT ARE YOU TALKING ABOUT? MAY I PLEASE SEE WHAT YOU'VE GOT?

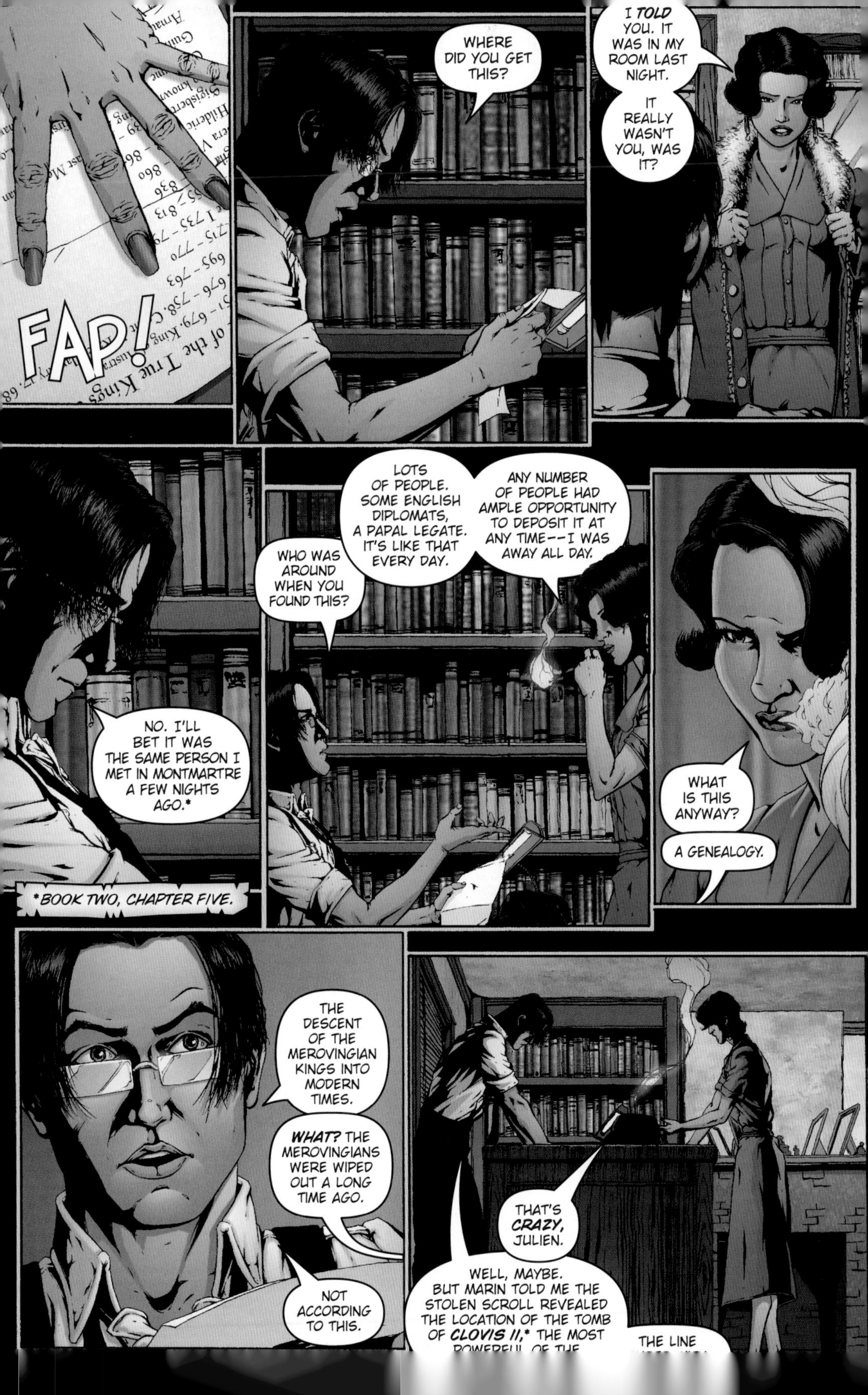
FAP!
WHERE DID YOU GET THIS?
I *TOLD* YOU. IT WAS IN MY ROOM LAST NIGHT.
IT REALLY WASN'T YOU, WAS IT?
NO. I'LL BET IT WAS THE SAME PERSON I MET IN MONTMARTRE A FEW NIGHTS AGO.*
*BOOK TWO, CHAPTER FIVE.
WHO WAS AROUND WHEN YOU FOUND THIS?
LOTS OF PEOPLE. SOME ENGLISH DIPLOMATS, A PAPAL LEGATE. IT'S LIKE THAT EVERY DAY.
ANY NUMBER OF PEOPLE HAD AMPLE OPPORTUNITY TO DEPOSIT IT AT ANY TIME--I WAS AWAY ALL DAY.
WHAT IS THIS ANYWAY?
A GENEALOGY.
THE DESCENT OF THE MEROVINGIAN KINGS INTO MODERN TIMES.
WHAT? THE MEROVINGIANS WERE WIPED OUT A LONG TIME AGO.
NOT ACCORDING TO THIS.
THAT'S *CRAZY,* JULIEN.
WELL, MAYBE. BUT MARIN TOLD ME THE STOLEN SCROLL REVEALED THE LOCATION OF THE TOMB OF *CLOVIS II,** THE MOST
THE LINE

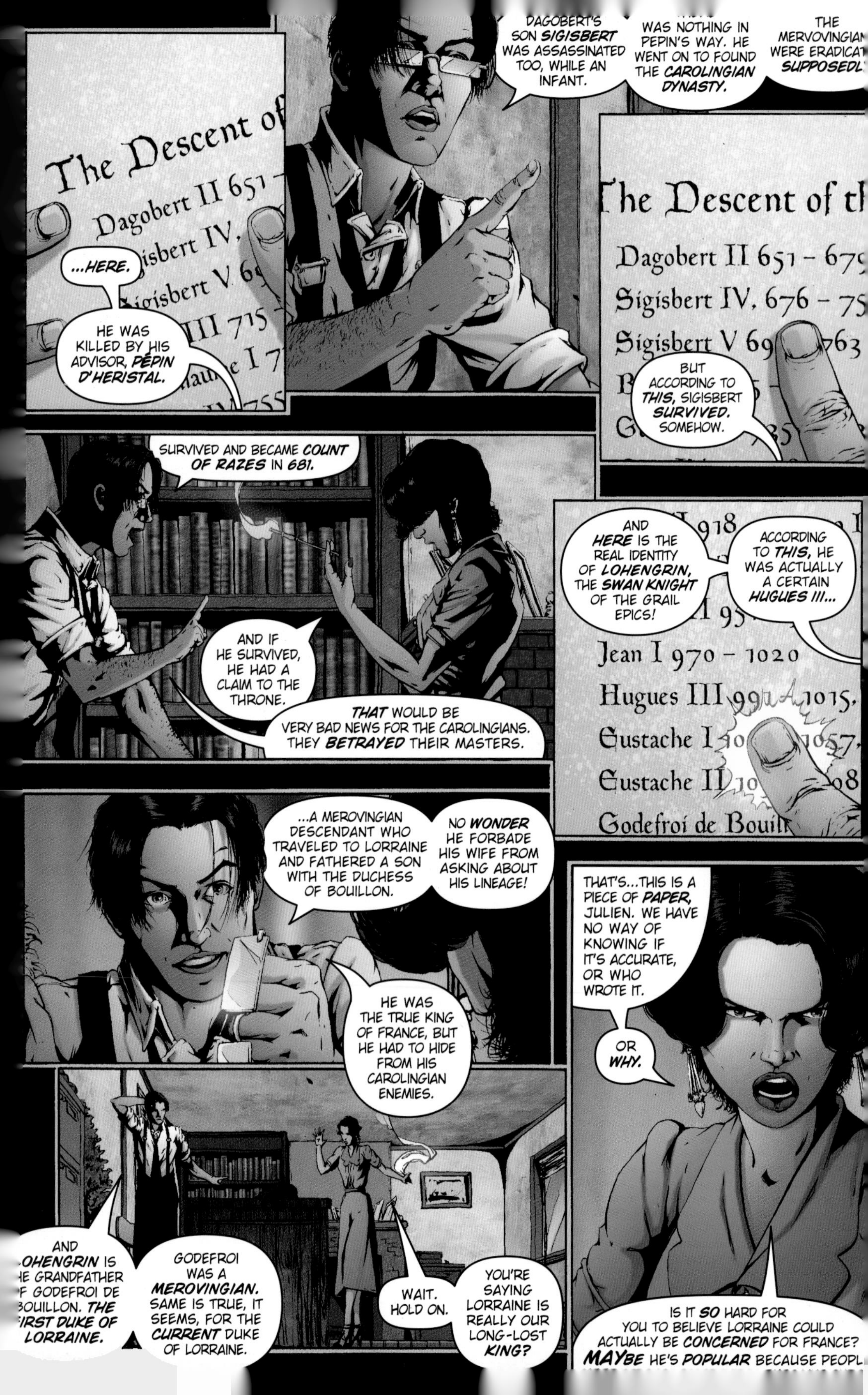

The Descent of
Dagobert II 651 –
...HERE.
HE WAS KILLED BY HIS ADVISOR, PÉPIN D'HERISTAL.
DAGOBERT'S SON SIGISBERT WAS ASSASSINATED TOO, WHILE AN INFANT.
WAS NOTHING IN PEPIN'S WAY. HE WENT ON TO FOUND THE CAROLINGIAN DYNASTY.
THE MERVOVINGIAN WERE ERADICAT SUPPOSEDL
The Descent of
Dagobert II 651 – 679
Sigisbert IV, 676 – 75
Sigisbert V 69 763
BUT ACCORDING TO THIS, SIGISBERT SURVIVED. SOMEHOW.
SURVIVED AND BECAME COUNT OF RAZES IN 681.
AND IF HE SURVIVED, HE HAD A CLAIM TO THE THRONE.
THAT WOULD BE VERY BAD NEWS FOR THE CAROLINGIANS. THEY BETRAYED THEIR MASTERS.
AND HERE IS THE REAL IDENTITY OF LOHENGRIN, THE SWAN KNIGHT OF THE GRAIL EPICS!
ACCORDING TO THIS, HE WAS ACTUALLY A CERTAIN HUGUES III...
Jean I 970 – 1020
Hugues III 99 1015
Eustache I 1057
Eustache II
Godefroi de Bouil
...A MEROVINGIAN DESCENDANT WHO TRAVELED TO LORRAINE AND FATHERED A SON WITH THE DUCHESS OF BOUILLON.
NO WONDER HE FORBADE HIS WIFE FROM ASKING ABOUT HIS LINEAGE!
HE WAS THE TRUE KING OF FRANCE, BUT HE HAD TO HIDE FROM HIS CAROLINGIAN ENEMIES.
AND OHENGRIN IS HE GRANDFATHER F GODEFROI DE OUILLON. THE IRST DUKE OF LORRAINE.
GODEFROI WAS A MEROVINGIAN. SAME IS TRUE, IT SEEMS, FOR THE CURRENT DUKE OF LORRAINE.
WAIT. HOLD ON.
YOU'RE SAYING LORRAINE IS REALLY OUR LONG-LOST KING?
THAT'S...THIS IS A PIECE OF PAPER, JULIEN. WE HAVE NO WAY OF KNOWING IF IT'S ACCURATE, OR WHO WROTE IT.
OR WHY.
IS IT SO HARD FOR YOU TO BELIEVE LORRAINE COULD ACTUALLY BE CONCERNED FOR FRANCE? MAYBE HE'S POPULAR BECAUSE PEOPL

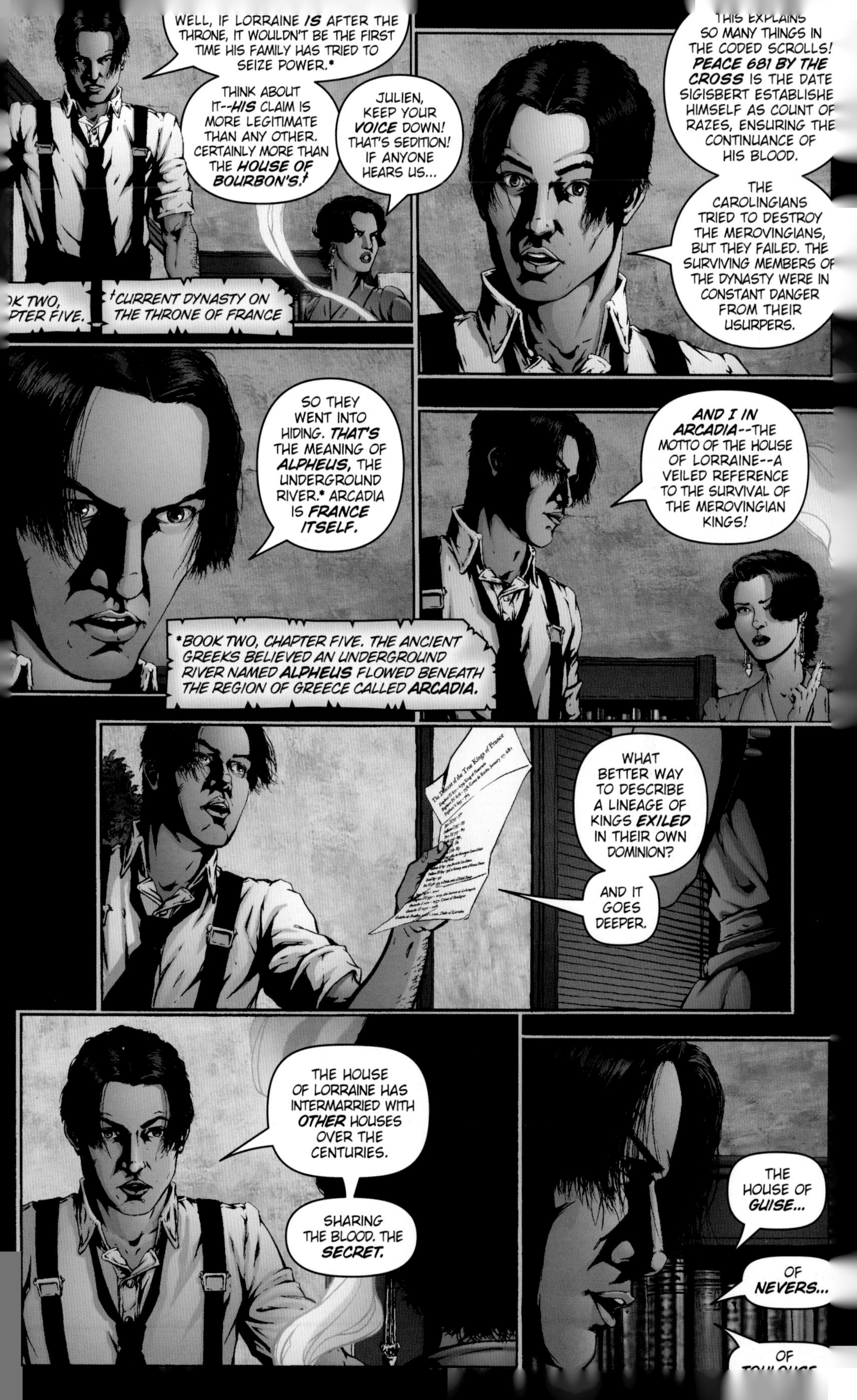

WELL, IF LORRAINE *IS* AFTER THE THRONE, IT WOULDN'T BE THE FIRST TIME HIS FAMILY HAS TRIED TO SEIZE POWER.*
THINK ABOUT IT--*HIS* CLAIM IS MORE LEGITIMATE THAN ANY OTHER. CERTAINLY MORE THAN THE *HOUSE OF BOURBON'S.*†
JULIEN, KEEP YOUR *VOICE* DOWN! THAT'S SEDITION! IF ANYONE HEARS US...
OK TWO, PTER FIVE.
†CURRENT DYNASTY ON THE THRONE OF FRANCE
THIS EXPLAINS SO MANY THINGS IN THE CODED SCROLLS! *PEACE 681 BY THE CROSS* IS THE DATE SIGISBERT ESTABLISHE HIMSELF AS COUNT OF RAZES, ENSURING THE CONTINUANCE OF HIS BLOOD.
THE CAROLINGIANS TRIED TO DESTROY THE MEROVINGIANS, BUT THEY FAILED. THE SURVIVING MEMBERS OF THE DYNASTY WERE IN CONSTANT DANGER FROM THEIR USURPERS.
SO THEY WENT INTO HIDING. *THAT'S* THE MEANING OF *ALPHEUS,* THE UNDERGROUND RIVER.* ARCADIA IS *FRANCE ITSELF.*
*BOOK TWO, CHAPTER FIVE. THE ANCIENT GREEKS BELIEVED AN UNDERGROUND RIVER NAMED *ALPHEUS* FLOWED BENEATH THE REGION OF GREECE CALLED *ARCADIA.*
AND I IN ARCADIA--THE MOTTO OF THE HOUSE OF LORRAINE--A VEILED REFERENCE TO THE SURVIVAL OF THE MEROVINGIAN KINGS!
WHAT BETTER WAY TO DESCRIBE A LINEAGE OF KINGS *EXILED* IN THEIR OWN DOMINION?
AND IT GOES DEEPER.
THE HOUSE OF LORRAINE HAS INTERMARRIED WITH *OTHER* HOUSES OVER THE CENTURIES.
SHARING THE BLOOD. THE *SECRET.*
THE HOUSE OF *GUISE...*
OF *NEVERS...*
OF

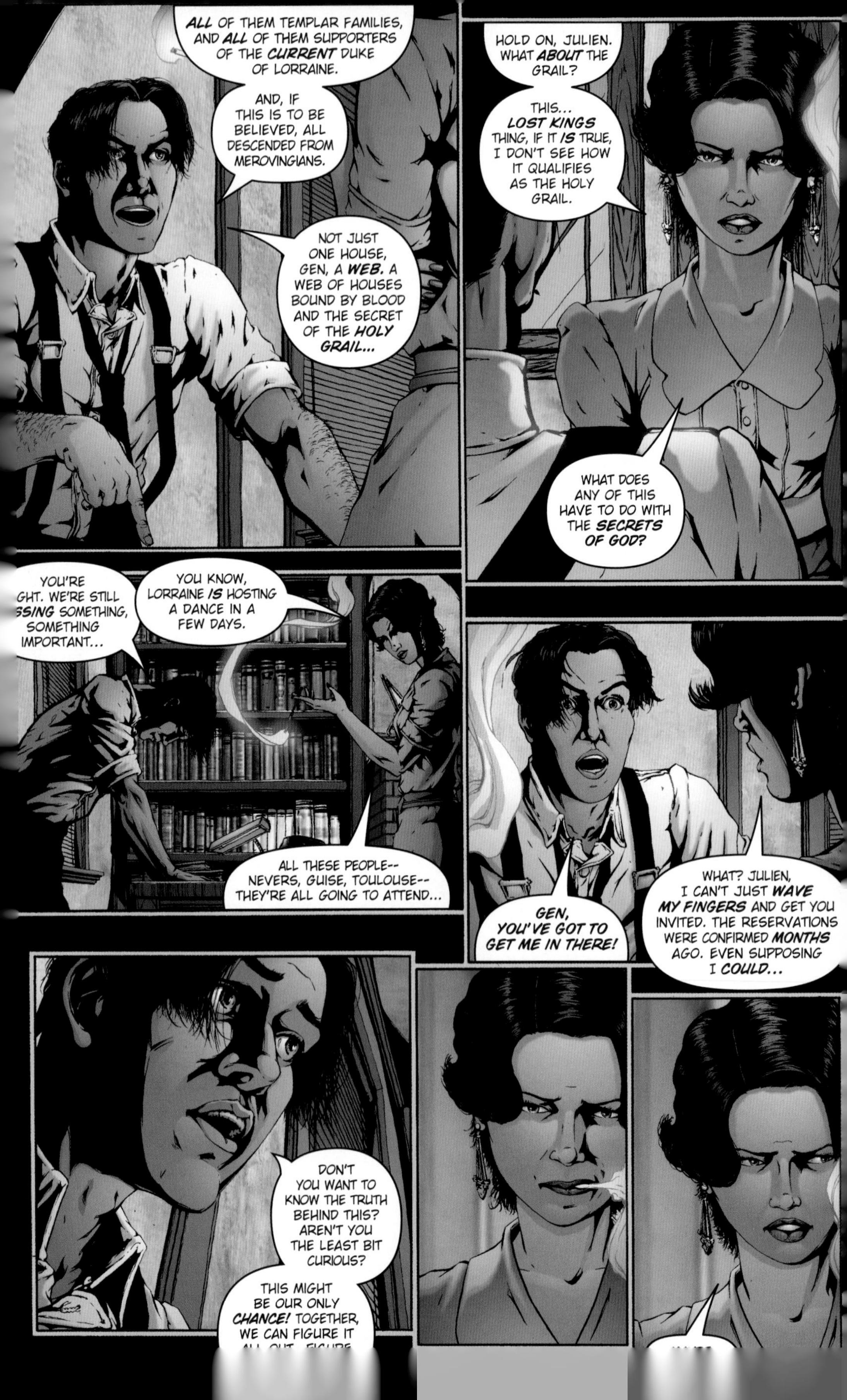
ALL OF THEM TEMPLAR FAMILIES, AND ALL OF THEM SUPPORTERS OF THE CURRENT DUKE OF LORRAINE.
AND, IF THIS IS TO BE BELIEVED, ALL DESCENDED FROM MEROVINGIANS.
NOT JUST ONE HOUSE, GEN, A WEB. A WEB OF HOUSES BOUND BY BLOOD AND THE SECRET OF THE HOLY GRAIL...
HOLD ON, JULIEN. WHAT ABOUT THE GRAIL?
THIS... LOST KINGS THING, IF IT IS TRUE, I DON'T SEE HOW IT QUALIFIES AS THE HOLY GRAIL.
WHAT DOES ANY OF THIS HAVE TO DO WITH THE SECRETS OF GOD?
YOU'RE
GHT. WE'RE STILL
SSING SOMETHING,
SOMETHING
IMPORTANT...
YOU KNOW, LORRAINE IS HOSTING A DANCE IN A FEW DAYS.
ALL THESE PEOPLE-- NEVERS, GUISE, TOULOUSE-- THEY'RE ALL GOING TO ATTEND...
GEN, YOU'VE GOT TO GET ME IN THERE!
WHAT? JULIEN, I CAN'T JUST WAVE MY FINGERS AND GET YOU INVITED. THE RESERVATIONS WERE CONFIRMED MONTHS AGO. EVEN SUPPOSING I COULD...
DON'T YOU WANT TO KNOW THE TRUTH BEHIND THIS? AREN'T YOU THE LEAST BIT CURIOUS?
THIS MIGHT BE OUR ONLY CHANCE! TOGETHER, WE CAN FIGURE IT

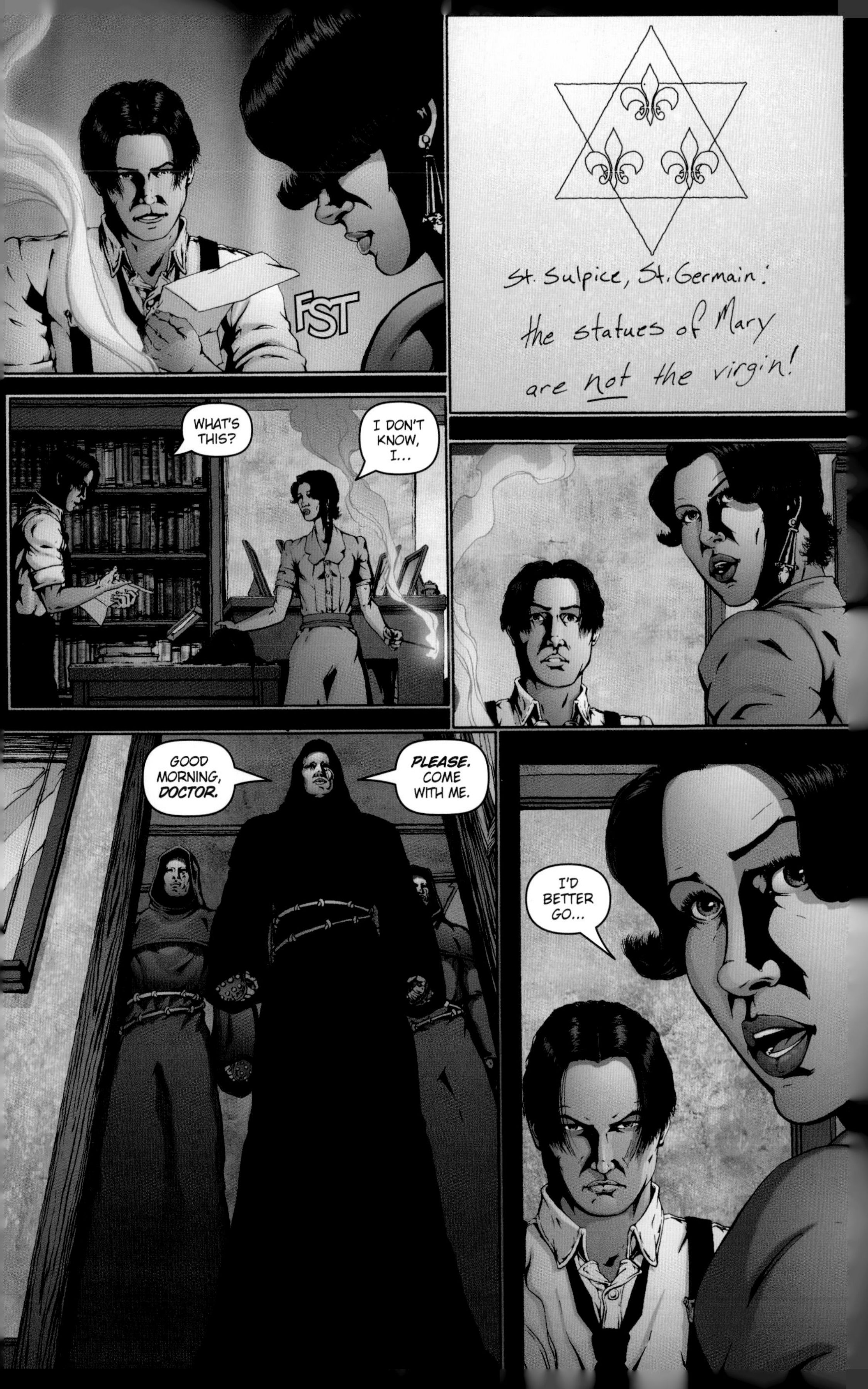
FST
St. Sulpice, St. Germain:
the statues of Mary
are not the virgin!
WHAT'S THIS?
I DON'T KNOW, I...
GOOD MORNING, DOCTOR.
PLEASE. COME WITH ME.
I'D BETTER GO...

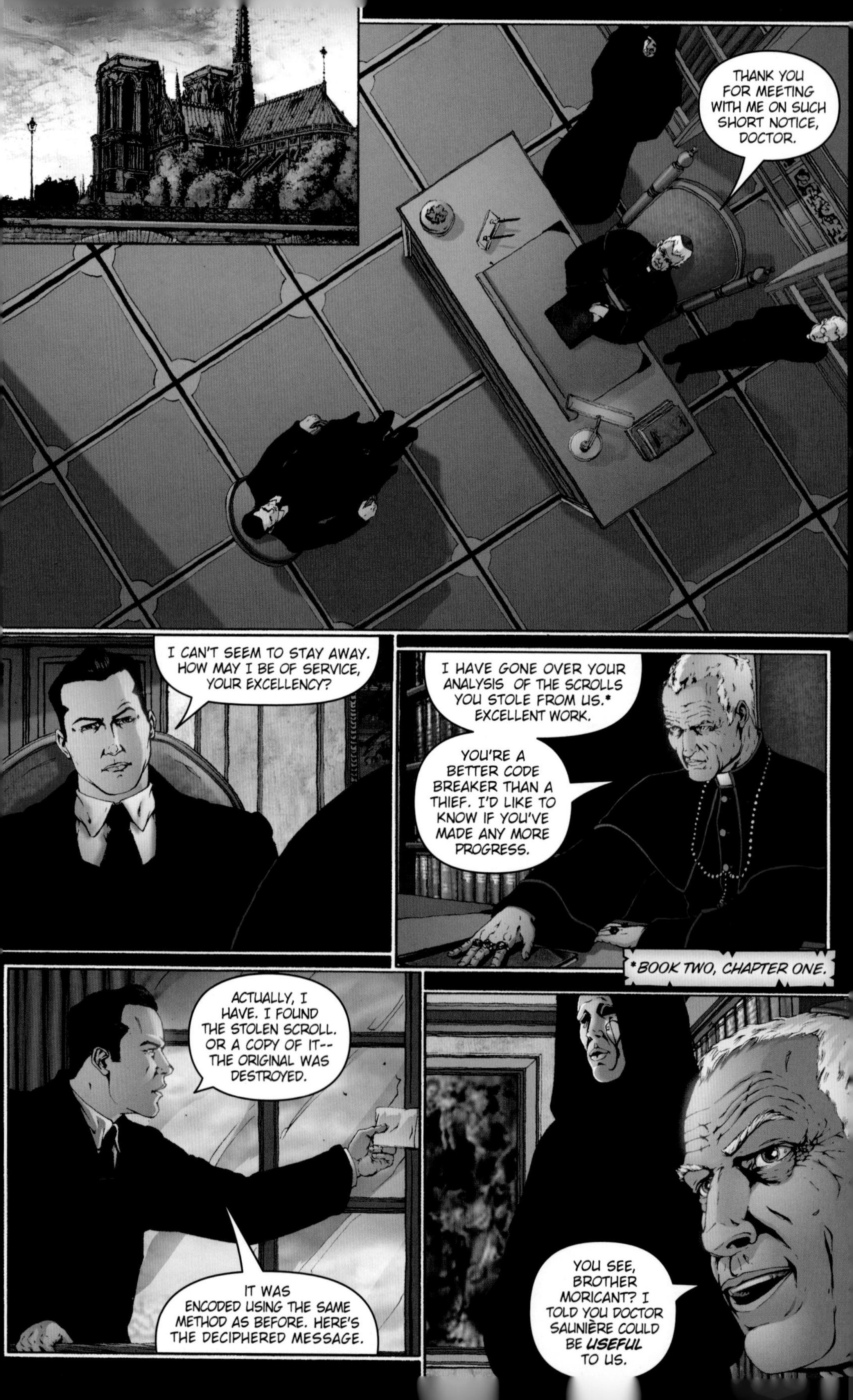
THANK YOU FOR MEETING WITH ME ON SUCH SHORT NOTICE, DOCTOR.
I CAN'T SEEM TO STAY AWAY. HOW MAY I BE OF SERVICE, YOUR EXCELLENCY?
I HAVE GONE OVER YOUR ANALYSIS OF THE SCROLLS YOU STOLE FROM US.* EXCELLENT WORK.
YOU'RE A BETTER CODE BREAKER THAN A THIEF. I'D LIKE TO KNOW IF YOU'VE MADE ANY MORE PROGRESS.
*BOOK TWO, CHAPTER ONE.
ACTUALLY, I HAVE. I FOUND THE STOLEN SCROLL. OR A COPY OF IT-- THE ORIGINAL WAS DESTROYED.
IT WAS ENCODED USING THE SAME METHOD AS BEFORE. HERE'S THE DECIPHERED MESSAGE.
YOU SEE, BROTHER MORICANT? I TOLD YOU DOCTOR SAUNIÈRE COULD BE ***USEFUL*** TO US.

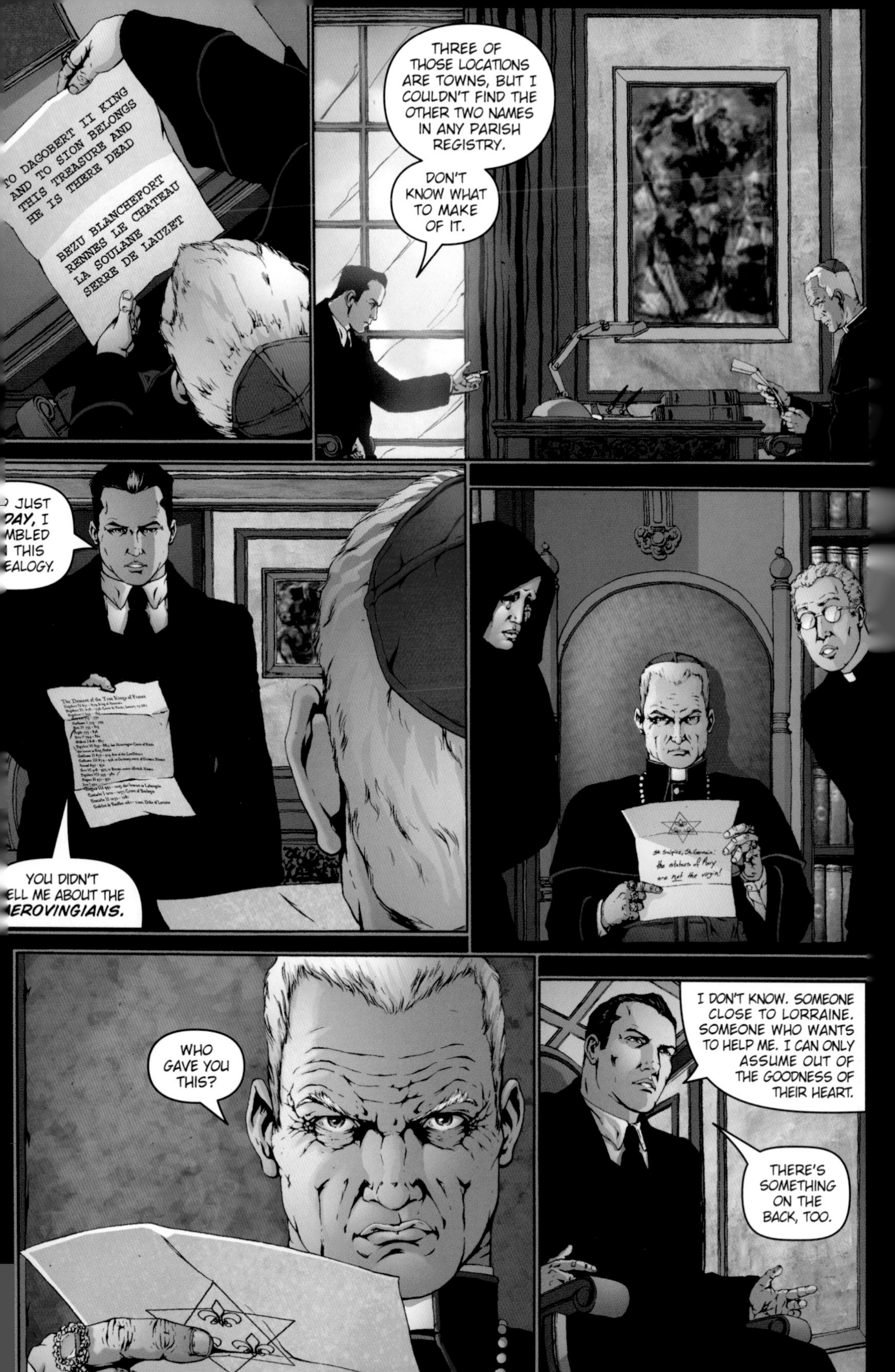
TO DAGOBERT II KING
AND TO SION BELONGS
THIS TREASURE AND
HE IS THERE DEAD
BEZU BLANCHEFORT
RENNES LE CHATEAU
LA SOULANE
SERRE DE LAUZET
THREE OF THOSE LOCATIONS ARE TOWNS, BUT I COULDN'T FIND THE OTHER TWO NAMES IN ANY PARISH REGISTRY.
DON'T KNOW WHAT TO MAKE OF IT.
JUST
DAY, I
MBLED
THIS
EALOGY.
The Descent of the True Kings of France
YOU DIDN'T
ELL ME ABOUT THE
EROVINGIANS.
St. Sulpice, St. Germain:
the statues of Mary
are not the virgin!
WHO GAVE YOU THIS?
I DON'T KNOW. SOMEONE CLOSE TO LORRAINE. SOMEONE WHO WANTS TO HELP ME. I CAN ONLY ASSUME OUT OF THE GOODNESS OF THEIR HEART.
THERE'S SOMETHING ON THE BACK, TOO.

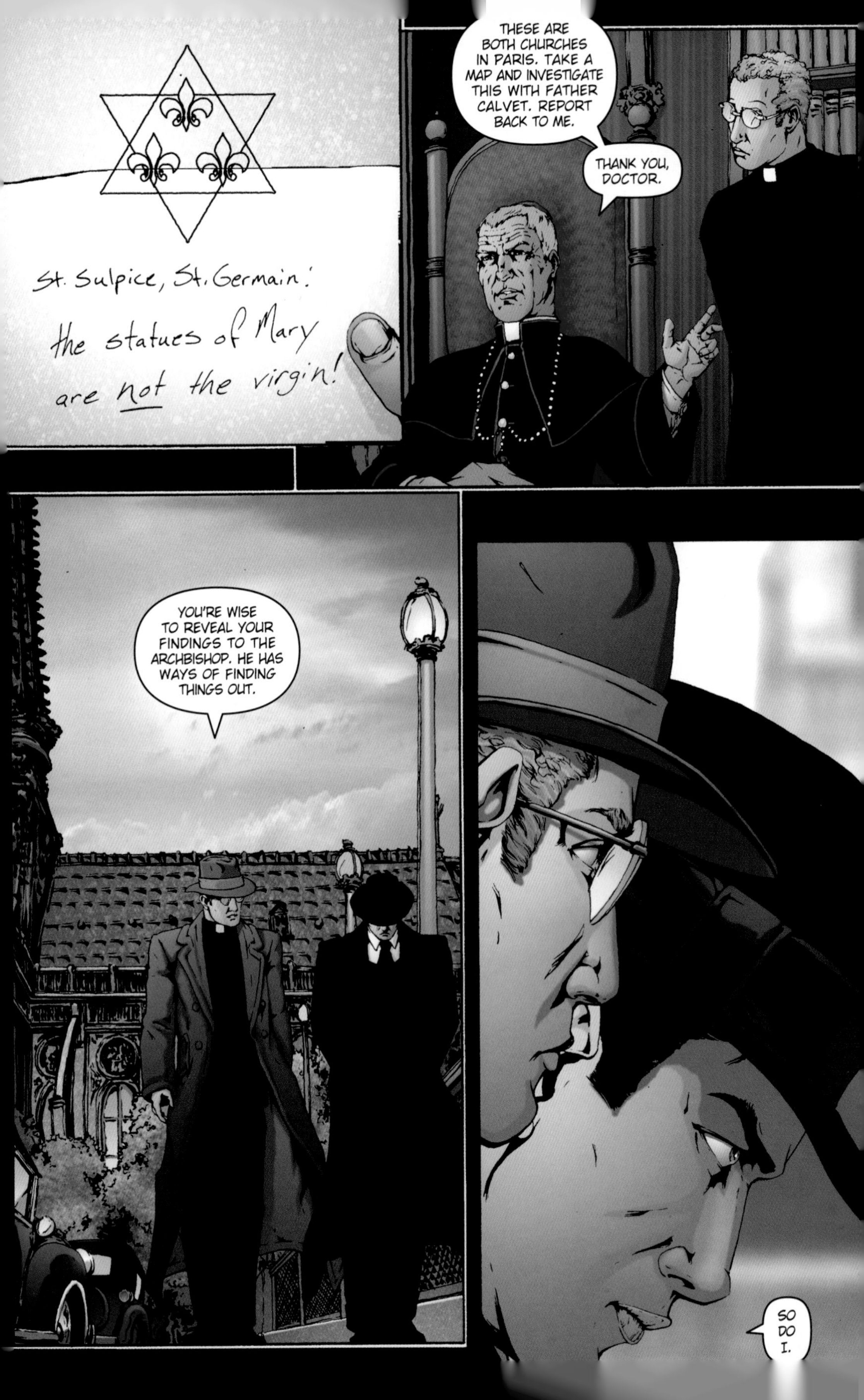
St. Sulpice, St. Germain:
the statues of Mary are not the virgin!
THESE ARE BOTH CHURCHES IN PARIS. TAKE A MAP AND INVESTIGATE THIS WITH FATHER CALVET. REPORT BACK TO ME.
THANK YOU, DOCTOR.
YOU'RE WISE TO REVEAL YOUR FINDINGS TO THE ARCHBISHOP. HE HAS WAYS OF FINDING THINGS OUT.
SO DO I.

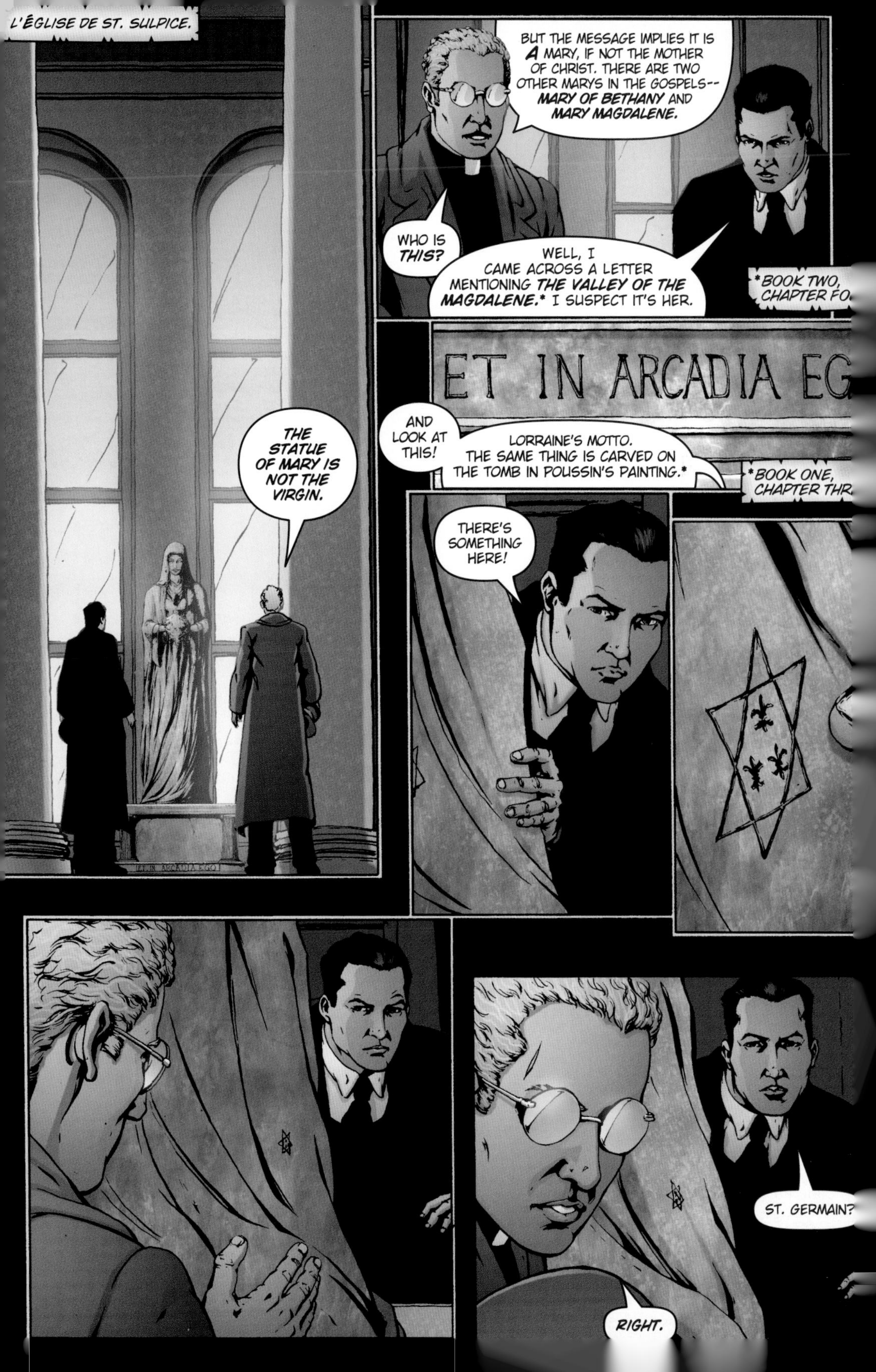
L'ÉGLISE DE ST. SULPICE.
BUT THE MESSAGE IMPLIES IT IS A MARY, IF NOT THE MOTHER OF CHRIST. THERE ARE TWO OTHER MARYS IN THE GOSPELS-- MARY OF BETHANY AND MARY MAGDALENE.
WHO IS THIS?
WELL, I CAME ACROSS A LETTER MENTIONING THE VALLEY OF THE MAGDALENE.* I SUSPECT IT'S HER.
*BOOK TWO, CHAPTER FO
THE STATUE OF MARY IS NOT THE VIRGIN.
ET IN ARCADIA EG
AND LOOK AT THIS!
LORRAINE'S MOTTO. THE SAME THING IS CARVED ON THE TOMB IN POUSSIN'S PAINTING.*
*BOOK ONE, CHAPTER THR
THERE'S SOMETHING HERE!
ST. GERMAIN?
RIGHT.

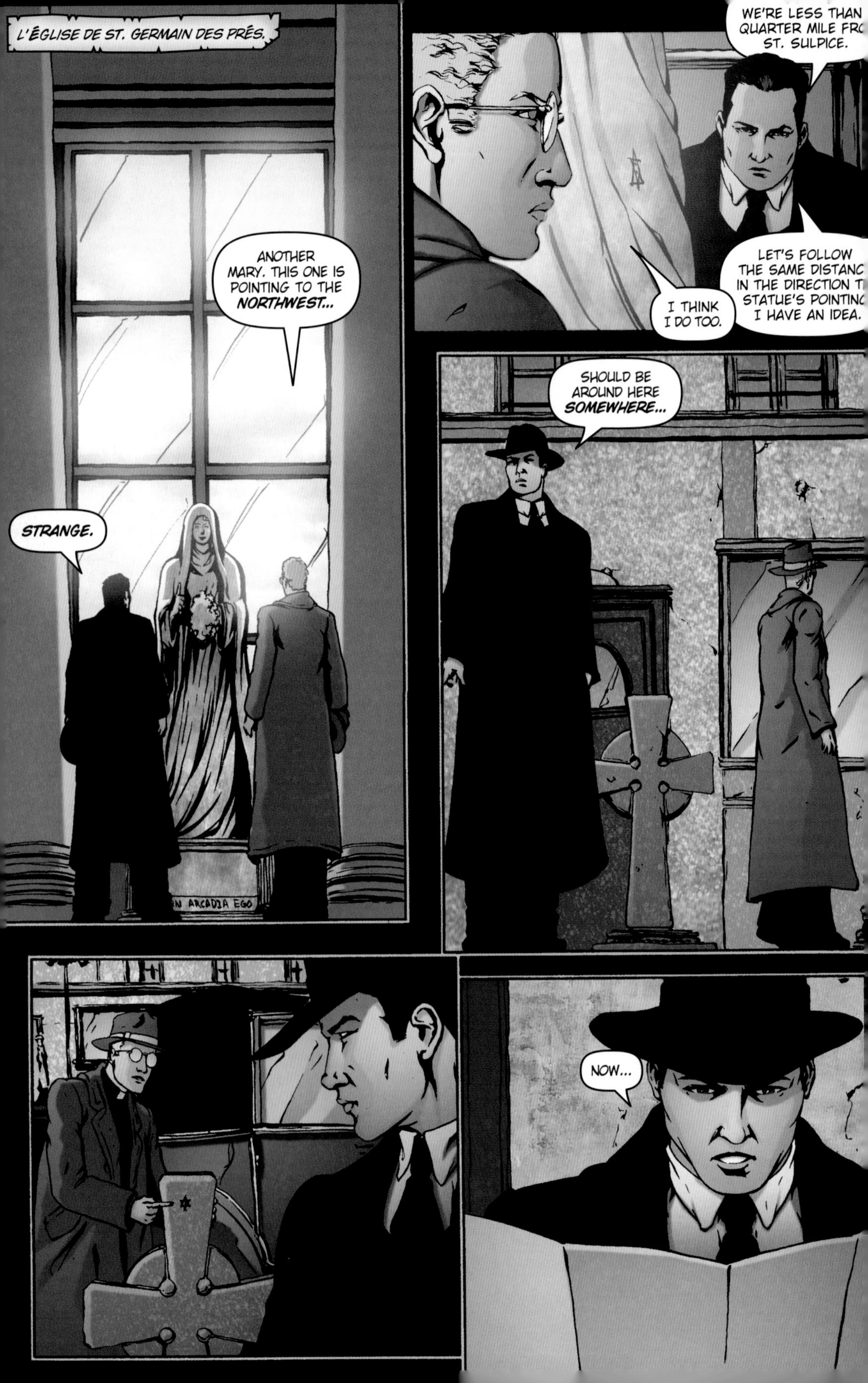

L'ÉGLISE DE ST. GERMAIN DES PRÉS.
ANOTHER MARY. THIS ONE IS POINTING TO THE *NORTHWEST...*
STRANGE.
N ARCADIA EGO
WE'RE LESS THAN QUARTER MILE FR ST. SULPICE.
LET'S FOLLOW THE SAME DISTAN IN THE DIRECTION T STATUE'S POINTIN I HAVE AN IDEA.
I THINK I DO TOO.
SHOULD BE AROUND HERE *SOMEWHERE...*
NOW...

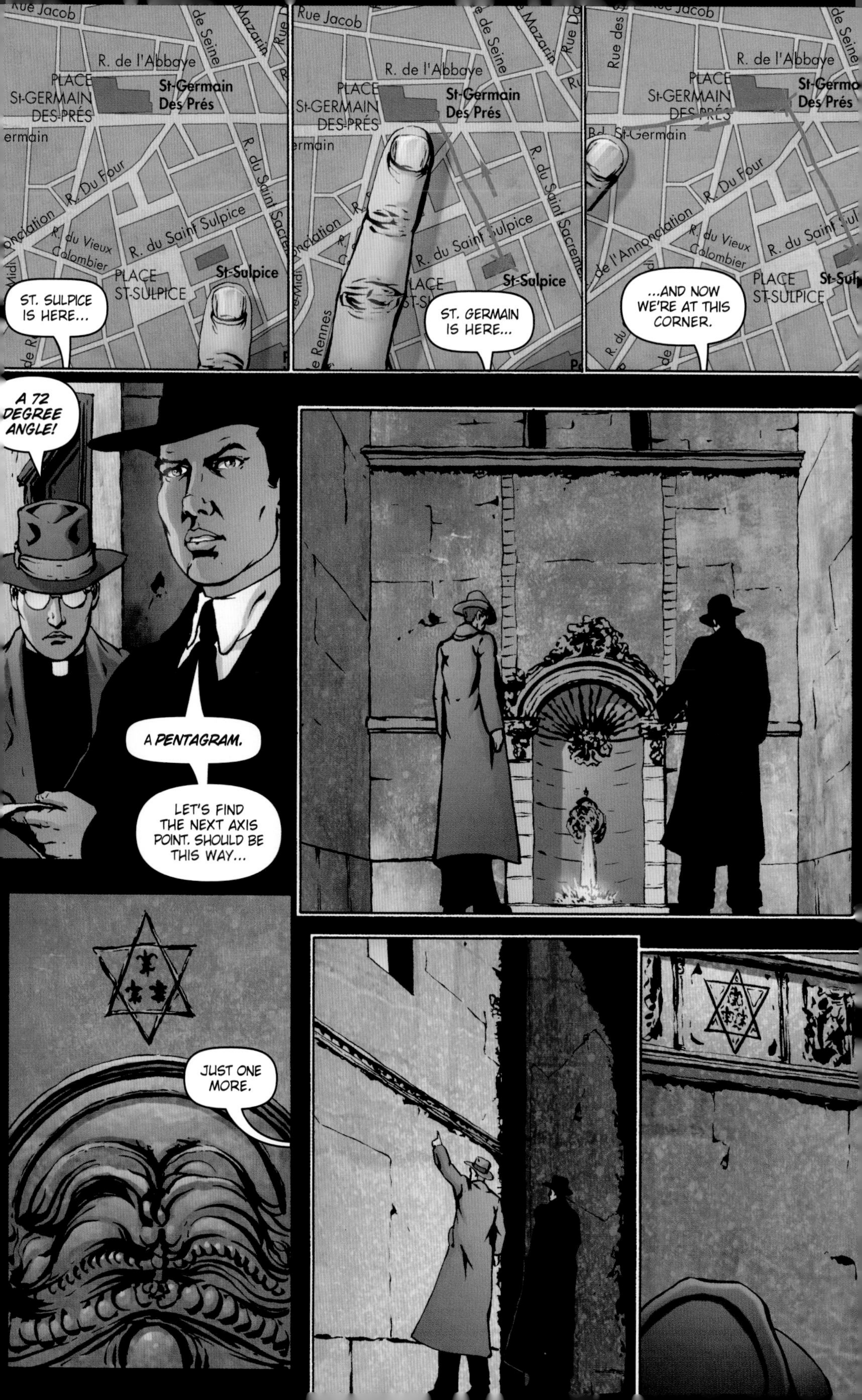
Rue Jacob
R. de l'Abbaye
PLACE
St-GERMAIN
DES-PRÉS
St-Germain
Des Prés
R. Du Four
R. du Vieux
Colombier
R. du Saint Sulpice
PLACE
ST-SULPICE
St-Sulpice
ST. SULPICE IS HERE...
ST. GERMAIN IS HERE...
...AND NOW WE'RE AT THIS CORNER.
A 72 DEGREE ANGLE!
A PENTAGRAM.
LET'S FIND THE NEXT AXIS POINT. SHOULD BE THIS WAY...
JUST ONE MORE.

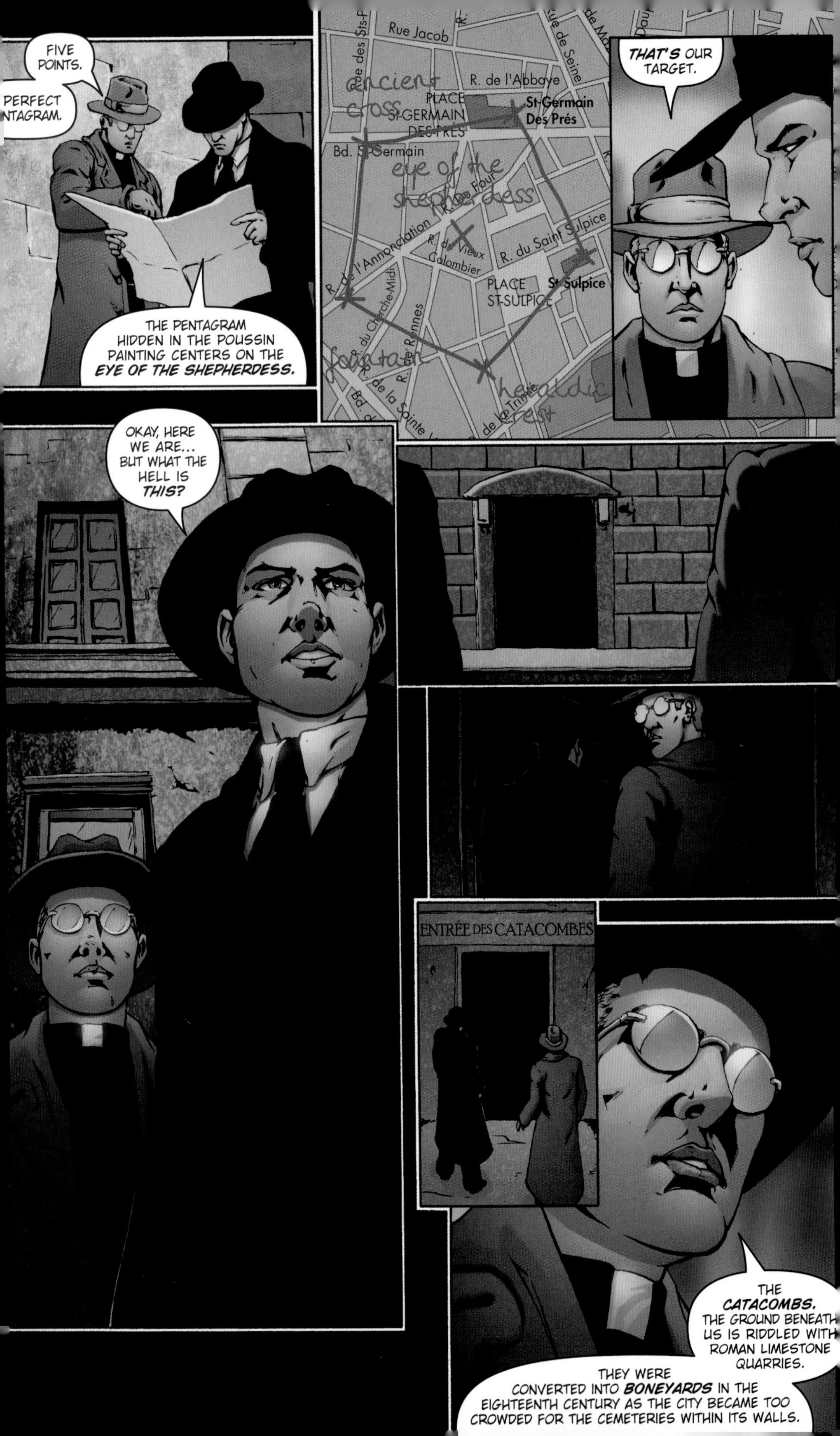
FIVE POINTS.
PERFECT
NTAGRAM.
THE PENTAGRAM HIDDEN IN THE POUSSIN PAINTING CENTERS ON THE EYE OF THE SHEPHERDESS.
Rue Jacob
R. de l'Abbaye
PLACE ST-GERMAIN DES PRÉS
St-Germain Des Prés
Bd. St-Germain
ancient cross
eye of the shepherdess
R. du Four
R. de l'Annonciation
R. du Vieux Colombier
R. du Saint Sulpice
PLACE ST-SULPICE
St Sulpice
R. du Cherche-Midi
R. de Rennes
fountain
heraldic crest
THAT'S OUR TARGET.
OKAY, HERE WE ARE... BUT WHAT THE HELL IS THIS?
ENTRÉE DES CATACOMBES
THE CATACOMBS. THE GROUND BENEATH US IS RIDDLED WITH ROMAN LIMESTONE QUARRIES.
THEY WERE CONVERTED INTO BONEYARDS IN THE EIGHTEENTH CENTURY AS THE CITY BECAME TOO CROWDED FOR THE CEMETERIES WITHIN ITS WALLS.

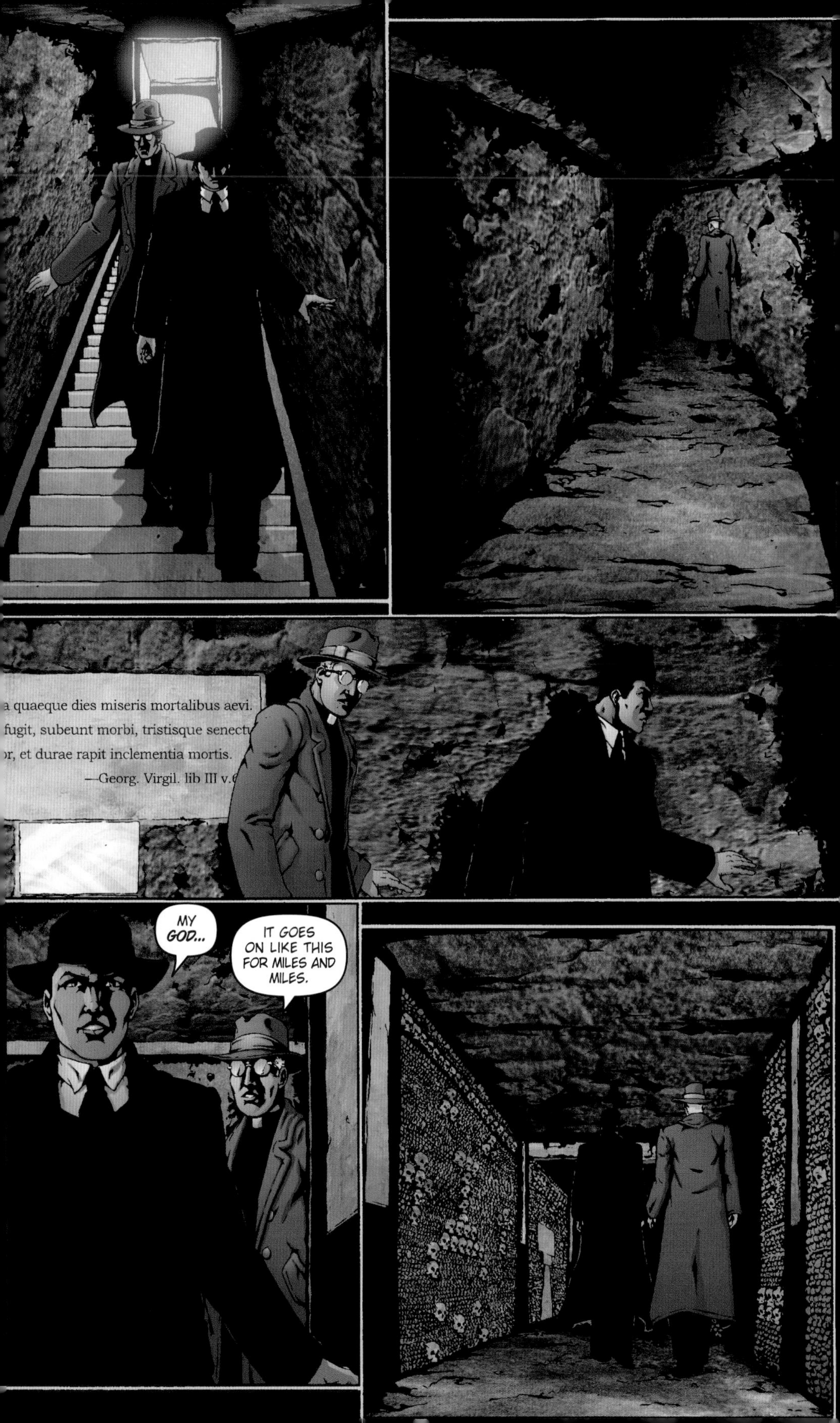
a quaeque dies miseris mortalibus aevi.
fugit, subeunt morbi, tristisque senect
or, et durae rapit inclementia mortis.
—Georg. Virgil. lib III v.6
MY GOD...
IT GOES ON LIKE THIS FOR MILES AND MILES.

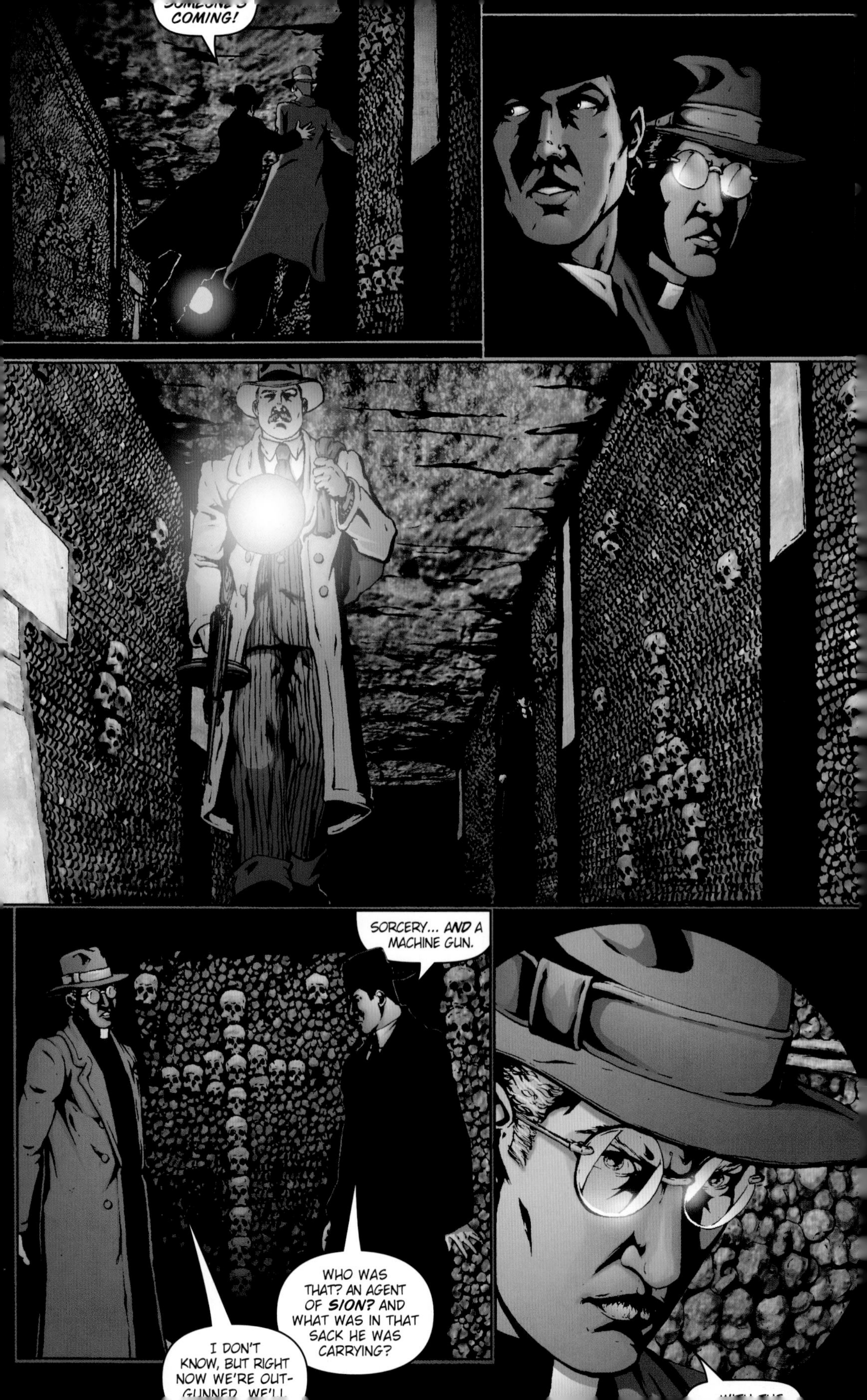
COMING!
SORCERY... AND A MACHINE GUN.
WHO WAS THAT? AN AGENT OF SION? AND WHAT WAS IN THAT SACK HE WAS CARRYING?
I DON'T KNOW, BUT RIGHT NOW WE'RE OUT-

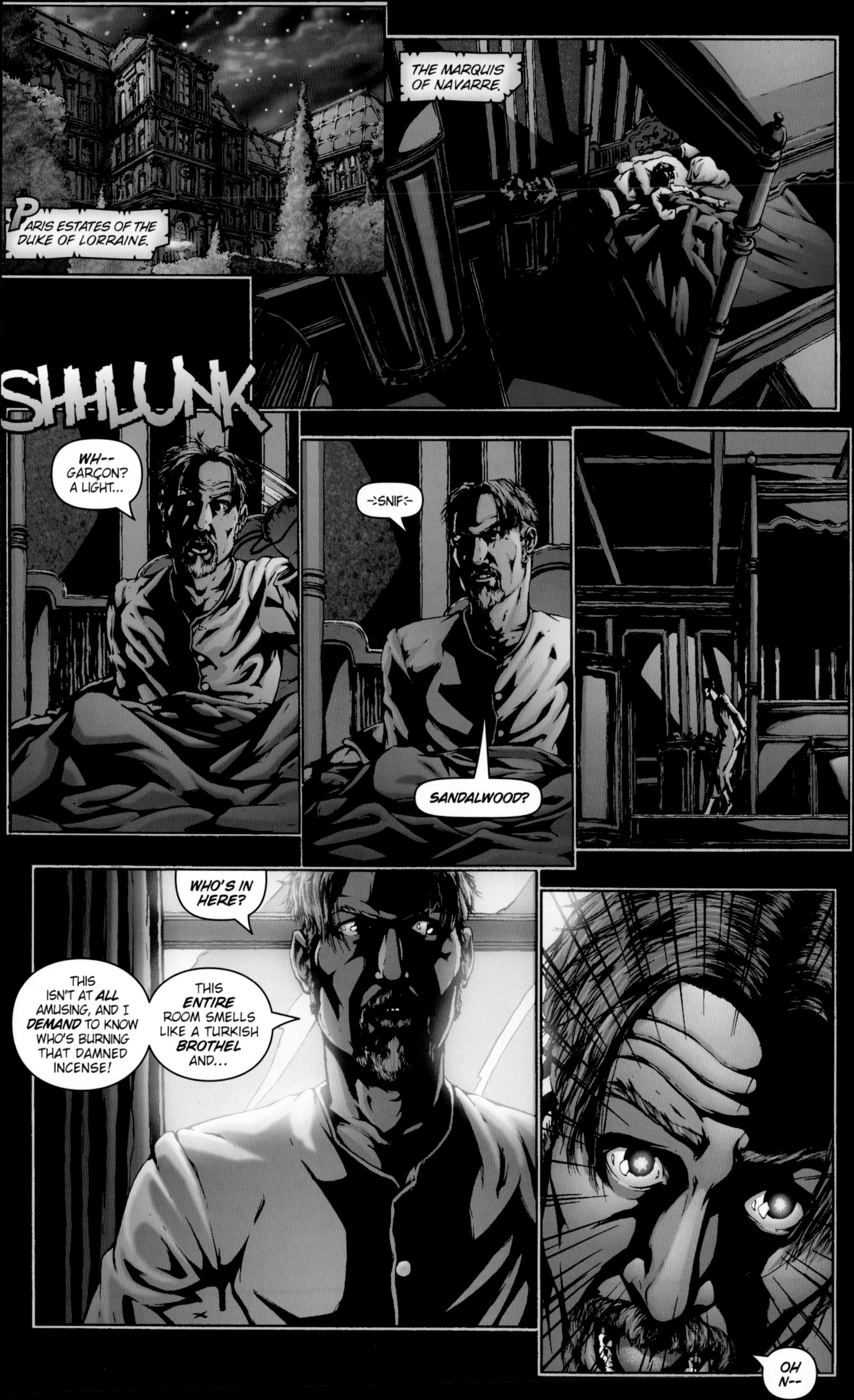
PARIS ESTATES OF THE DUKE OF LORRAINE.
THE MARQUIS OF NAVARRE.
SHHLUNK
WH-- GARÇON? A LIGHT...
-SNIF-
SANDALWOOD?
WHO'S IN HERE?
THIS ISN'T AT ALL AMUSING, AND I DEMAND TO KNOW WHO'S BURNING THAT DAMNED INCENSE!
THIS ENTIRE ROOM SMELLS LIKE A TURKISH BROTHEL AND...
OH N--

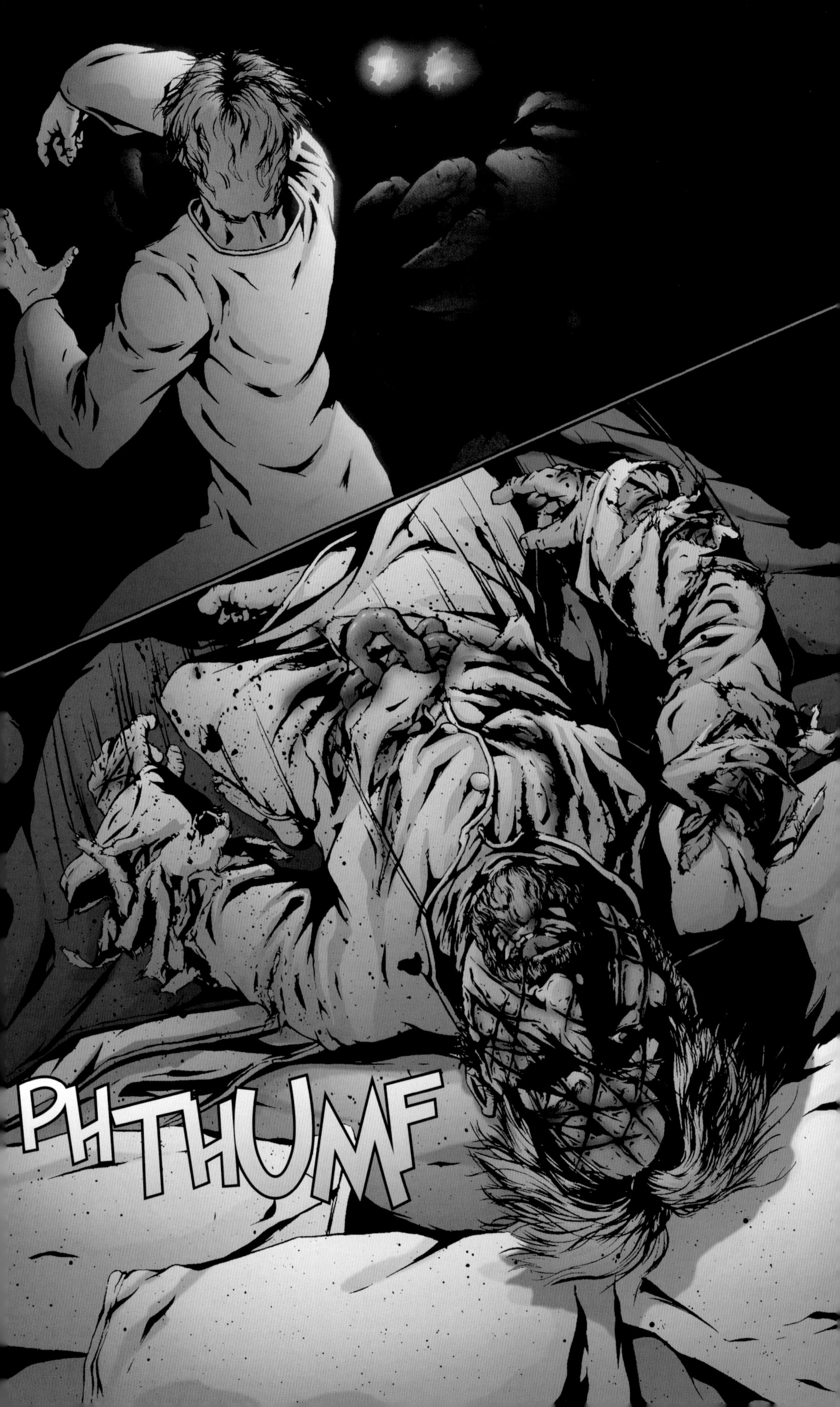
PHTHUMF

Le Journal de la Liberté

Paris' leading anglophone newspaper • vol. 205, no. 97 • Oct. 30, MCMXXXIII

Editors in Chief: M. Tait Bergstrom, M. Matthew Pasteris. **Story Editor:** M. Arvid Nelson.
Art Editor: M. Eric J. **Photography Editor:** M. Alexander Waldman.
Layout Supervisor: M. William Kartalopoulos. **Editors Emeritus:** M. Clark A. Smith,
M. Howard P. Lovecraft, M. Robert E. Howard. Redacted by the Holy Inquisition under the direction of
His Excellency Archbishop Emile-Jean Ireneaux. *Le Journal de la Liberté* is printed under the benign auspices of
His Most Puissant Majesty KING LOUIS XXII of FRANCE. GOD SAVE THE KING.

Papal seal

of Approval

SIGHTINGS OF CATACOMB "DARKLINGS" ON THE RISE

Strange, Bestial Homunculi Terrify Municipal Workers, Subterranean Pedestrians; Officials Deny Existence of Strange Creatures.

Goblins, trolls and elves are the uff of fairy tails. Or are they?

Legends of so-called "darklings," malicious demi-humans that stalk he sunless catacombs beneath Paris, xtend back farther than anyone an remember.

Real or imagined, sightings of he creatures have not diminished ver the centuries. In fact, over the ast year alone, alleged encounters ave gone up ten percent.

The reports have a core constency: underground wayfarers umble on a small, human-like reature which attacks without rovocation or warning.

"I mistook it for a child at first," woman who claims to have enountered a darkling on an underround shortcut to her workplace aid. She asked not to be named.

"When I got closer, I could see ts skin was gray and all scaly," she aid. "It didn't have no whites in its yes, and its teeth were real sharp. So were its ears." The woman said he diminutive terror chased her until she reached the surface.

"It was fast, too. Ran on all fours and started hissing like a viper. Don't know what I would've one if it caught me."

Some who encounter the trange creatures are not so lucky. M. Berenger Poulain, a city employee, said he was severely bitten nd slashed by a group of darklings vhile conducting maintenance of sewer line.

"There were about a half-dozen of them. It was a struggle for

my life. Knocked one of the vicious little brutes into the effluent channel. Hope I did it in," he said.

Poulain says he won't be returning to the sewers again without a comrade. "I don't mind admitting I'm a bit shaken," he said.

As to the origin and nature of the darklings, opinions differ.

"I believe they come from Hell itself," Father Eustache of the St. Sulpice Seminary said. "There was an explosion in the darkling population when the remains from the graveyards inside Paris were moved to the catacombs in the 1700s. They feed on the flesh of corpses." But most ecclesiastical authorities deny the existence of darklings.

"I don't think there's any validity to the claims," Monsignor Eric Grimaldi, a Vatican expert on the occult, said. "Where in scripture is there any evidence for the existence of goblins or elves?"

Academics and government officials also dismiss the reports.

"This is most likely a case of mass delusion or hysteria," Dr. Sigmund Freud, a renowned Viennese alienist, said.

Dr. Urbain Bénichou, curator of biology at the Royal Institute of Natural Sciences, is a rare voice of dissent in academia.

"I believe it is possible for a race of demi-human creatures to have developed naturally and to have coexisted with humans in complete secrecy for many centuries, even millennia. How much do we really
continued on page B3

Quel merveilleux exploit d'athlète! Busy Parisians take time out of their day to enjoy a display of acrobatics and pugilism in the Jardin du Luxembourg.

UNREST IN HOLY ROMAN EMPIRE; RUDOLF III TO VISIT SARAJEVO

Mass demonstrations broke out in Ljubjana, Belgrade and Sarajevo yesterday. The protesters were largely slavic nationalists who resent Austrian rule, according to officials. Civil authorities in those cities reported widespread violence and civil disorder.

Ferdinand Beust, Chancellor of the Holy Roman Empire, was uncharacteristically blunt. "We are one step away from open rebellion," he said.

Some sources within the Foreign Ministry of the Holy Roman Empire claim Habsburg diplomats are meeting with the highest levels of the Prussian military to discuss the possibility of a "temporary occupation" of the Sudetenland and Hungary in the event of a pan-Slavic uprising.

Such an occupation, they say, would allow the Austrian military to focus its might on rebellious Serbia and Herzegovina. Officials publicly denounced these claims.

"We categorically deny these

harmful rumors and condemn those who spread them in the strongest terms possible," Viscount Felix Von Schwartzenberg, a spokesperson for the Holy Roman Emperor, said.

Prussian Chancellor Karl von Haugwitz also denied the claims.

Nonetheless, rumors of Prussian military intervention have added fuel to the cause of minority separatists within the HRE.

"Is this any surprise? The Prussians are German. The Austrians are German. The Germans have tried to keep the Slavic race down for many centuries," Enis Jevric, a Serbian nationalist who took part in yesterday's demonstrations, said.

In an apparent attempt to ease tensions, the Austrian Emperor Rudolph III announced late yesterday his intention to visit the restive city of Sarajevo. It will be the first time he has visited his Serbian subjects.

"Emperor Rudolf is looking forward to this visit. He is not concerned for his safety at all. His Maj-
continued on page A7

Special Joint Session of Parliament Convenes Today; Duke of Lorraine to Propose New Policy Initiative

Lord Lorraine's call for the first-ever joint session of Parliament, which convenes today, demonstrates just how effectively he has rallied France's ancient noble houses and common people alike under the cause of global French imperialism, dubbed the "Greater France" movement by Lorraine's supporters.

Lorraine's policies have not gained universal acceptance, but support grows virtually day by day.

He has won over several vocal opponents in recent weeks, most notably Baronet Aristide deMandeville, speaker for the House of the Robe and formerly one of King Louis' staunchest advocates.

Baronet deMandeville dramatically declared his support for Lorraine in a speech delivered to the Hall of the Robe several days ago.

Although Lorraine's ancestral holdings are in the north of France, the core of his political lies

further south, in the region of the Languedoc.

"It's only natural. The southern houses are geographically much closer to the Muslim threat," Baron Robert Teniers, a spokesperson for Lord Lorraine, said. "They are forced to appreciate the precarious situation France finds herself in. It takes a man of great perspicacity, a man like Lord Lorraine, to comprehend the gravity of the moment
continued on page B2

THE DESCENT OF THE TRUE KINGS OF FRANCE

Dagobert II 651 – 679, King of Austrasia

The Counts of Razès

Sigisbert IV, 676 – 758, first Count of Razès, Jan. 17, 681
Sigisbert V 695 – 763
Bera III 715 – 770
Guillaume I 735 – 793
Bera IV 755 – 813
Argila 775 – 836
Bera V 794 – 860
Hilderic I 818 – 867
Sigisbert VI 839 – 884, Prince Ursus

The Lost Kings

Guillaume II 857 – 914, first of the Lost Princes
Guillaume III 874 – 936, source of German Houses
Arnaud 897 – 952
Bera VI 918 – 975, source of English Houses
Sigisbert VII 939 – 982
Hugues II 951 – 971
Jean I 970 – 1020
Hugues III 991 – 1015, also known as Lohengrin

Eustache I 1010 – 1057, Count of Boulogne
Eustache II 1032 – 1081
Godefroi de Bouillon 1061 – 1100, first Duke of Lorraine

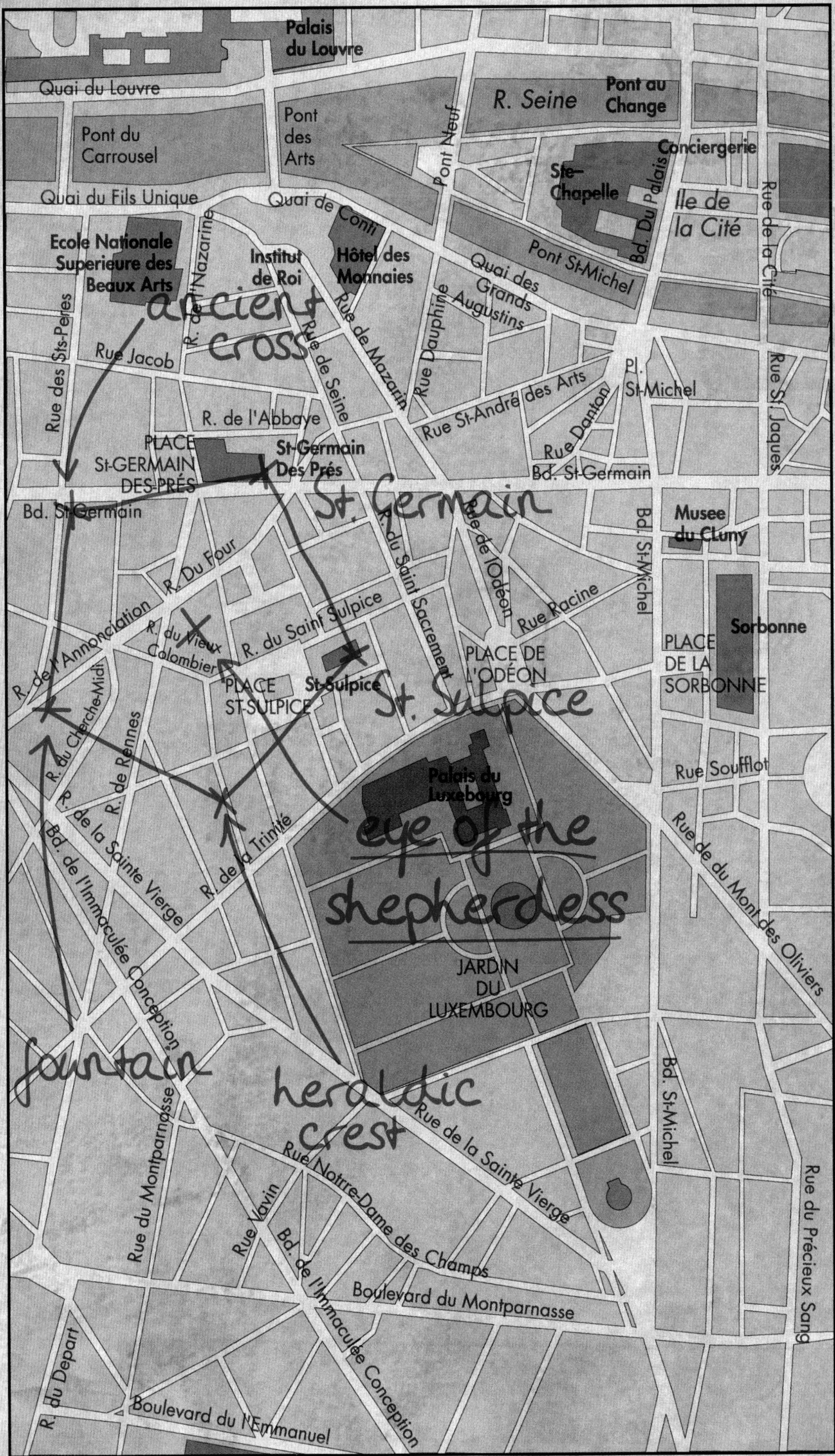

Palais du Louvre
Quai du Louvre
R. Seine
Pont au Change
Pont du Carrousel
Pont des Arts
Pont Neuf
Conciergerie
Ste-Chapelle
Quai du Fils Unique
Quai de Conti
Bd. Du Palais
Ile de la Cité
Rue de la Cité
Ecole Nationale Superieure des Beaux Arts
Institut de Roi
Hôtel des Monnaies
Pont St-Michel
Quai des Grands Augustins
R. de l'Nazarine
ancient cross
Rue des Sts-Peres
Rue Jacob
Rue de Seine
Rue de Mazarin
Rue Dauphine
Pl. St-Michel
Rue St-André des Arts
Rue St Jaques
R. de l'Abbaye
Rue Danton
PLACE ST-GERMAIN DES-PRÉS
St-Germain Des Prés
Bd. St-Germain
St. Germain
Bd. St-Germain
R. du Saint Sacrement
Rue de l'Odéon
Bd. St-Michel
Musee du CLuny
R. Du Four
R. de l'Annonciation
R. du Vieux Colombier
R. du Saint Sulpice
Rue Racine
Sorbonne
PLACE DE L'ODÉON
PLACE DE LA SORBONNE
PLACE ST-SULPICE
St-Sulpice
St. Sulpice
R. du Cherche-Midi
R. de Rennes
Palais du Luxebourg
Rue Soufflot
R. de la Sainte Vierge
Bd. de l'Immaculée Conception
R. de la Trinité
eye of the shepherdess
Rue de du Mont des Oliviers
JARDIN DU LUXEMBOURG
fountain
heraldic crest
Rue de la Sainte Vierge
Bd. St-Michel
Rue du Montparnasse
Rue Notrre-Dame des Champs
Rue Vavin
Bd. de l'Immaculée Conception
Rue du Précieux Sang
Boulevard du Montparnasse
R. du Depart
Boulevard du l'Emmanuel

LES ARMES DES

Et in Arcadia ego...

TER NOSTER QVI EST IN COEL

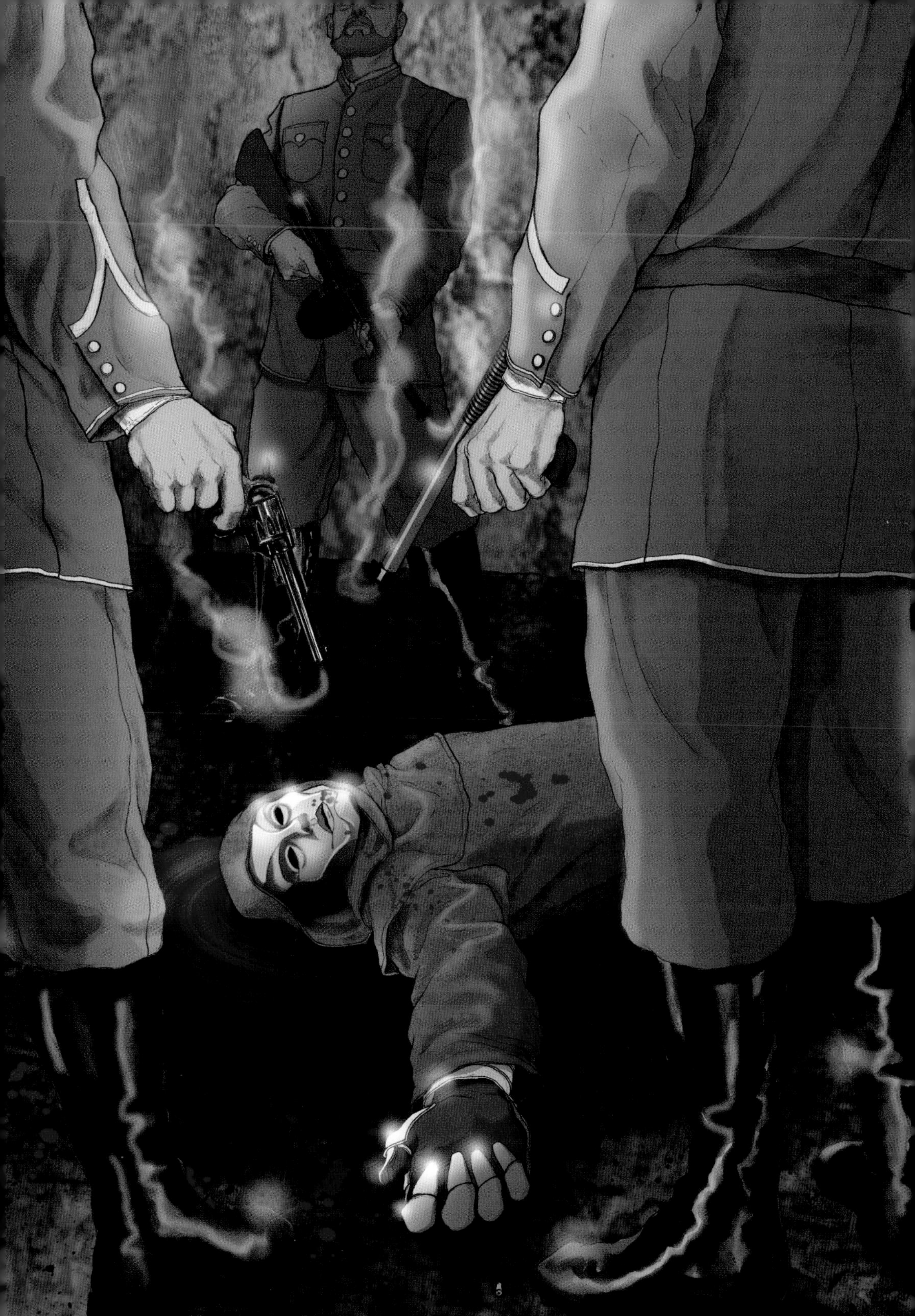

CHAPTER THREE
CITY OF THE DEAD

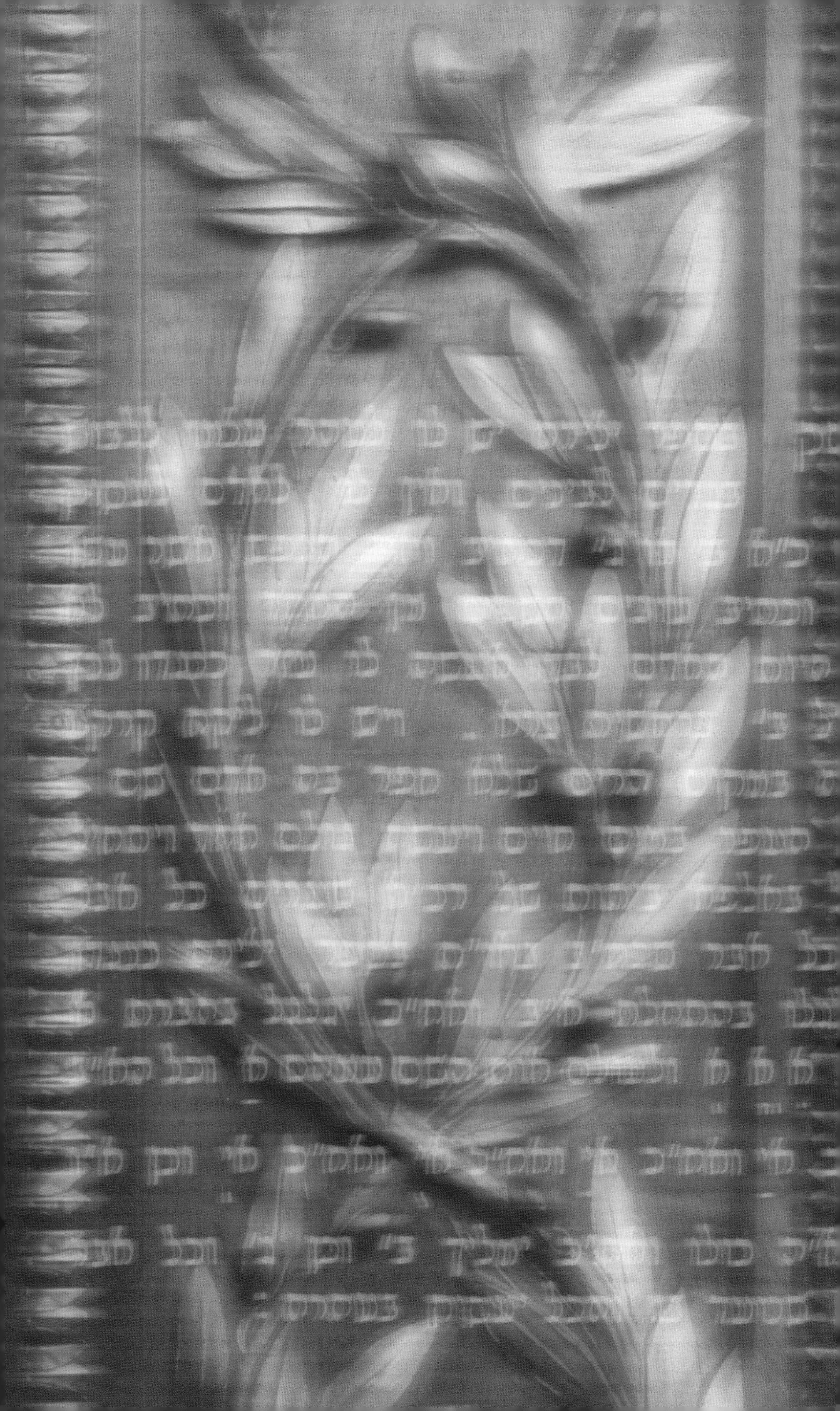

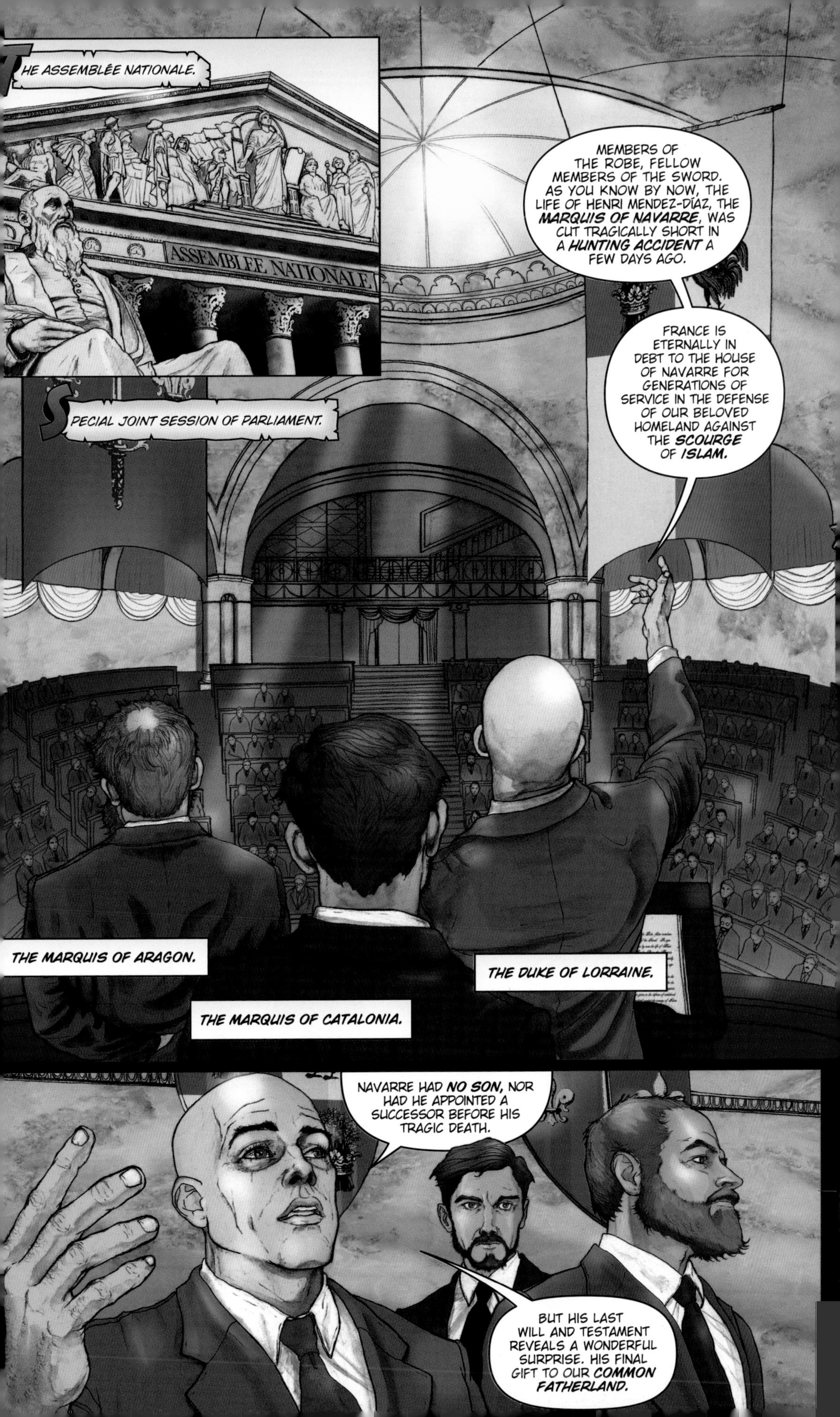
THE ASSEMBLÉE NATIONALE.
ASSEMBLEE NATIONALE
SPECIAL JOINT SESSION OF PARLIAMENT.
MEMBERS OF THE ROBE, FELLOW MEMBERS OF THE SWORD. AS YOU KNOW BY NOW, THE LIFE OF HENRI MENDEZ-DÍAZ, THE MARQUIS OF NAVARRE, WAS CUT TRAGICALLY SHORT IN A HUNTING ACCIDENT A FEW DAYS AGO.
FRANCE IS ETERNALLY IN DEBT TO THE HOUSE OF NAVARRE FOR GENERATIONS OF SERVICE IN THE DEFENSE OF OUR BELOVED HOMELAND AGAINST THE SCOURGE OF ISLAM.
THE MARQUIS OF ARAGON.
THE DUKE OF LORRAINE.
THE MARQUIS OF CATALONIA.
NAVARRE HAD NO SON, NOR HAD HE APPOINTED A SUCCESSOR BEFORE HIS TRAGIC DEATH.
BUT HIS LAST WILL AND TESTAMENT REVEALS A WONDERFUL SURPRISE. HIS FINAL GIFT TO OUR COMMON FATHERLAND.

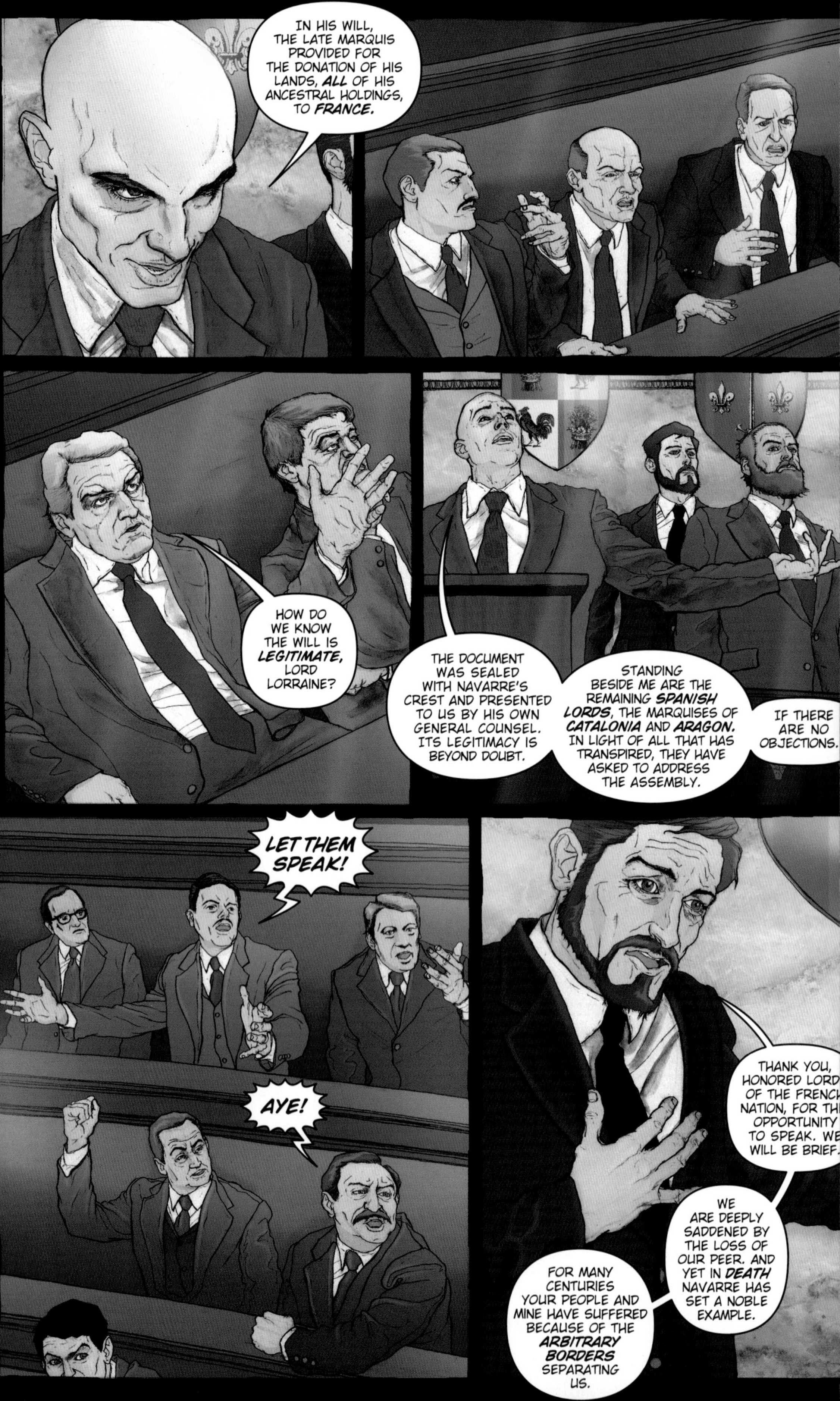
IN HIS WILL, THE LATE MARQUIS PROVIDED FOR THE DONATION OF HIS LANDS, ALL OF HIS ANCESTRAL HOLDINGS, TO FRANCE.
HOW DO WE KNOW THE WILL IS LEGITIMATE, LORD LORRAINE?
THE DOCUMENT WAS SEALED WITH NAVARRE'S CREST AND PRESENTED TO US BY HIS OWN GENERAL COUNSEL. ITS LEGITIMACY IS BEYOND DOUBT.
STANDING BESIDE ME ARE THE REMAINING SPANISH LORDS, THE MARQUISES OF CATALONIA AND ARAGON. IN LIGHT OF ALL THAT HAS TRANSPIRED, THEY HAVE ASKED TO ADDRESS THE ASSEMBLY.
IF THERE ARE NO OBJECTIONS.
LET THEM SPEAK!
AYE!
THANK YOU, HONORED LORD OF THE FRENCH NATION, FOR THE OPPORTUNITY TO SPEAK. WE WILL BE BRIEF.
WE ARE DEEPLY SADDENED BY THE LOSS OF OUR PEER. AND YET IN DEATH NAVARRE HAS SET A NOBLE EXAMPLE.
FOR MANY CENTURIES YOUR PEOPLE AND MINE HAVE SUFFERED BECAUSE OF THE ARBITRARY BORDERS SEPARATING US.

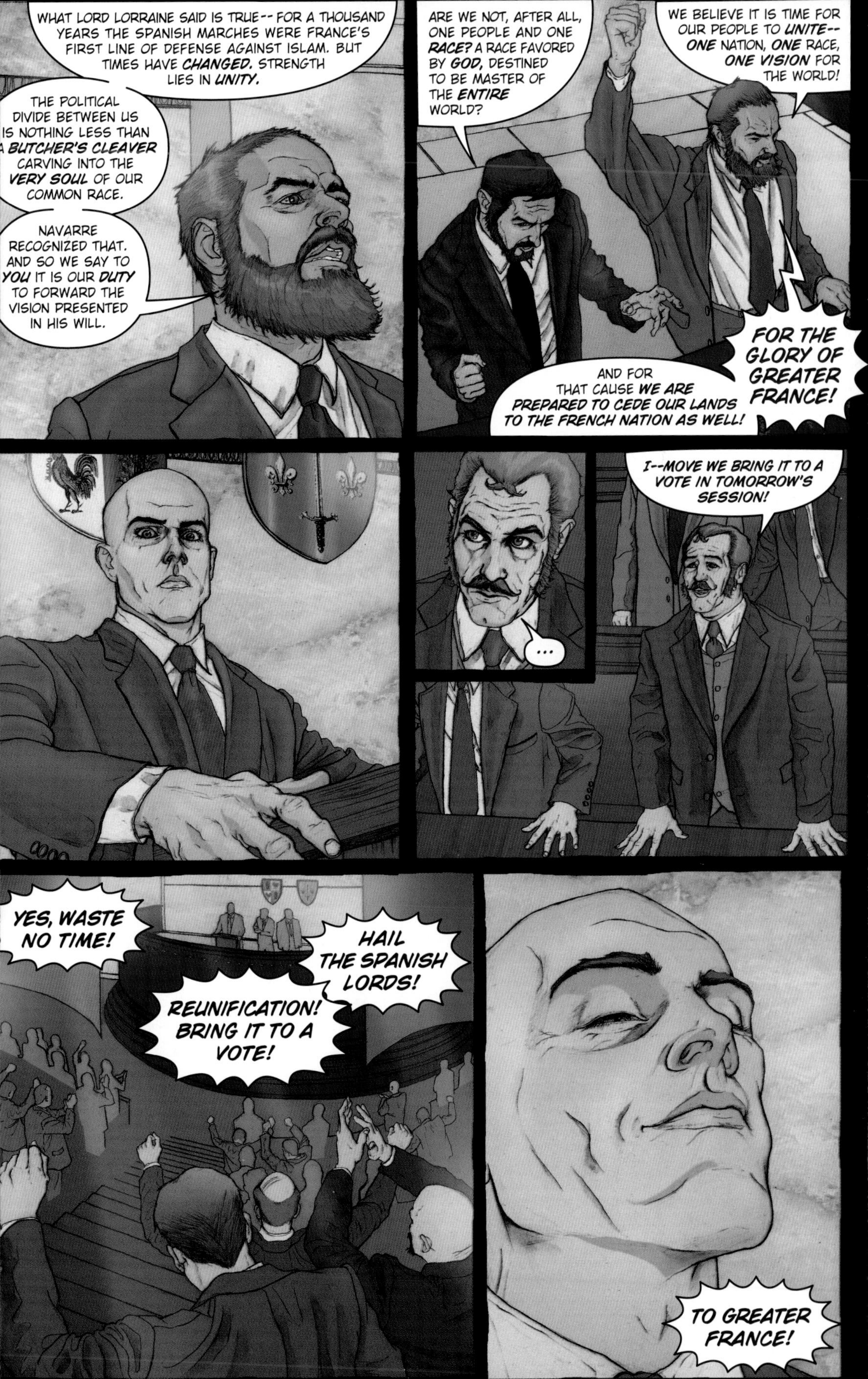
WHAT LORD LORRAINE SAID IS TRUE-- FOR A THOUSAND YEARS THE SPANISH MARCHES WERE FRANCE'S FIRST LINE OF DEFENSE AGAINST ISLAM. BUT TIMES HAVE CHANGED. STRENGTH LIES IN UNITY.
THE POLITICAL DIVIDE BETWEEN US IS NOTHING LESS THAN A BUTCHER'S CLEAVER CARVING INTO THE VERY SOUL OF OUR COMMON RACE.
NAVARRE RECOGNIZED THAT. AND SO WE SAY TO YOU IT IS OUR DUTY TO FORWARD THE VISION PRESENTED IN HIS WILL.
ARE WE NOT, AFTER ALL, ONE PEOPLE AND ONE RACE? A RACE FAVORED BY GOD, DESTINED TO BE MASTER OF THE ENTIRE WORLD?
WE BELIEVE IT IS TIME FOR OUR PEOPLE TO UNITE-- ONE NATION, ONE RACE, ONE VISION FOR THE WORLD!
AND FOR THAT CAUSE WE ARE PREPARED TO CEDE OUR LANDS TO THE FRENCH NATION AS WELL!
FOR THE GLORY OF GREATER FRANCE!
...
I--MOVE WE BRING IT TO A VOTE IN TOMORROW'S SESSION!
YES, WASTE NO TIME!
HAIL THE SPANISH LORDS!
REUNIFICATION! BRING IT TO A VOTE!
TO GREATER FRANCE!

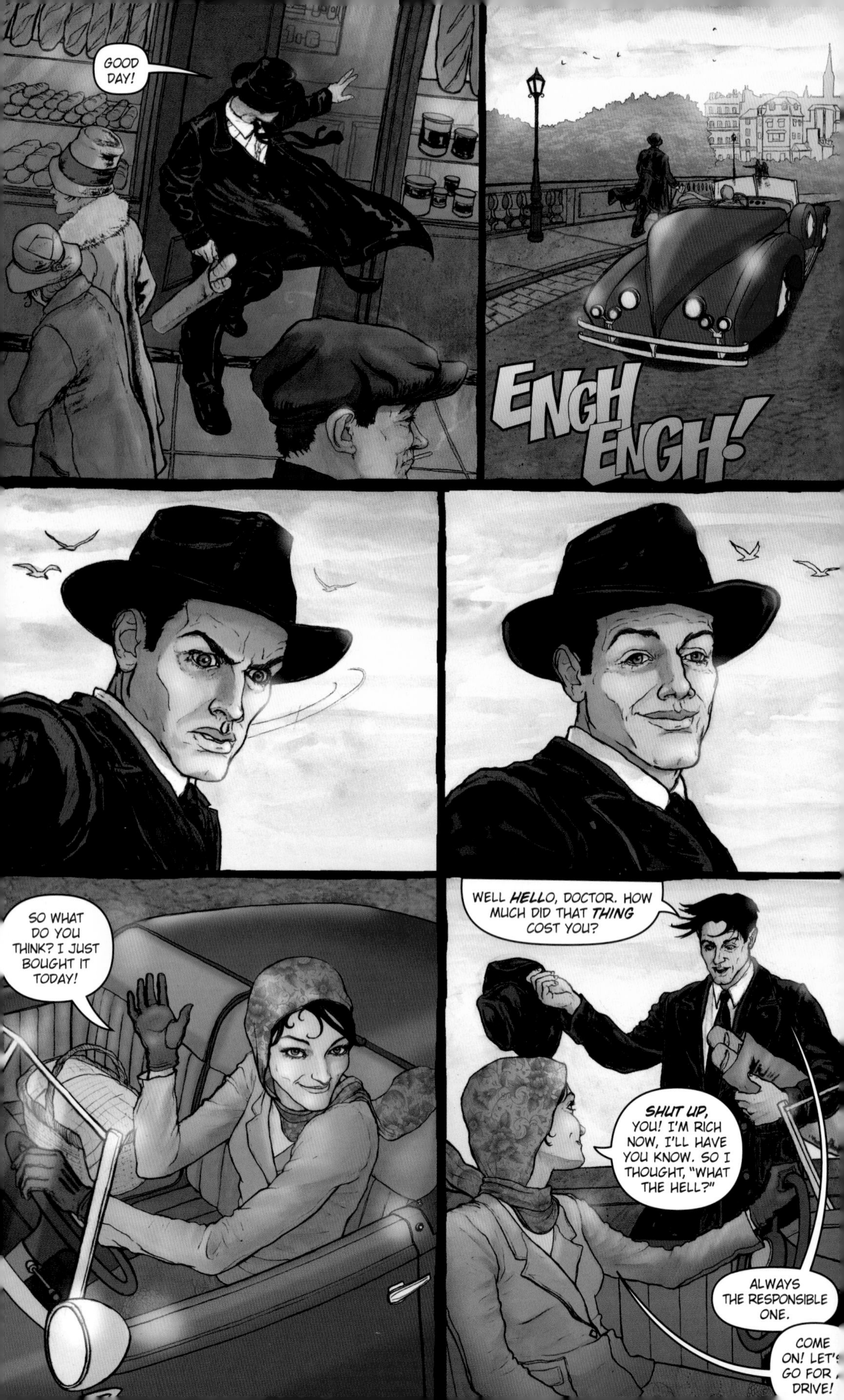
GOOD DAY!
ENGH ENGH!
SO WHAT DO YOU THINK? I JUST BOUGHT IT TODAY!
WELL HELLO, DOCTOR. HOW MUCH DID THAT THING COST YOU?
SHUT UP, YOU! I'M RICH NOW, I'LL HAVE YOU KNOW. SO I THOUGHT, "WHAT THE HELL?"
ALWAYS THE RESPONSIBLE ONE.
COME ON! LET'S GO FOR A DRIVE!

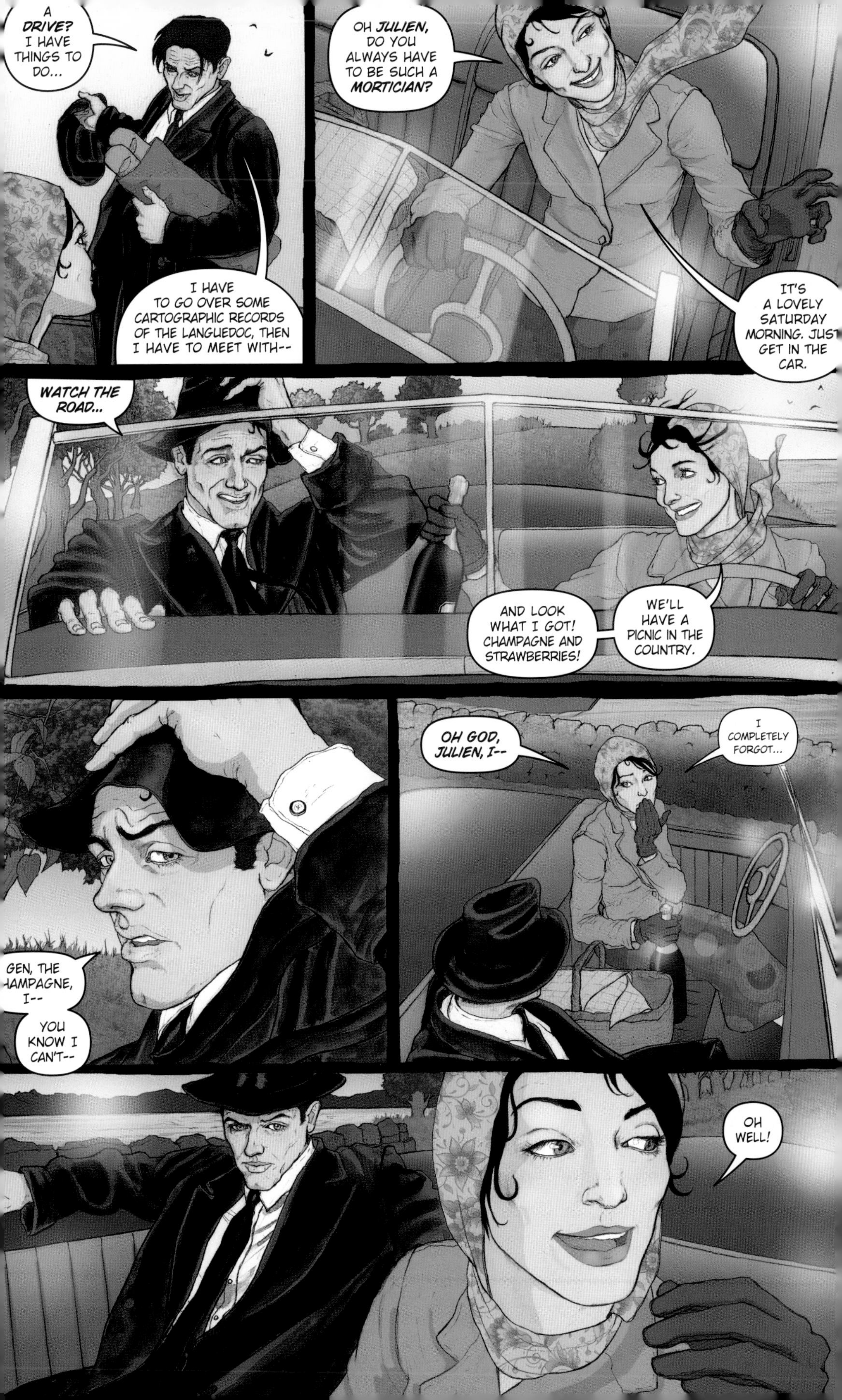
A DRIVE? I HAVE THINGS TO DO...
I HAVE TO GO OVER SOME CARTOGRAPHIC RECORDS OF THE LANGUEDOC, THEN I HAVE TO MEET WITH--
OH JULIEN, DO YOU ALWAYS HAVE TO BE SUCH A MORTICIAN?
IT'S A LOVELY SATURDAY MORNING. JUST GET IN THE CAR.
WATCH THE ROAD...
WE'LL HAVE A PICNIC IN THE COUNTRY.
AND LOOK WHAT I GOT! CHAMPAGNE AND STRAWBERRIES!
GEN, THE HAMPAGNE, I--
YOU KNOW I CAN'T--
OH GOD, JULIEN, I--
I COMPLETELY FORGOT...
OH WELL!

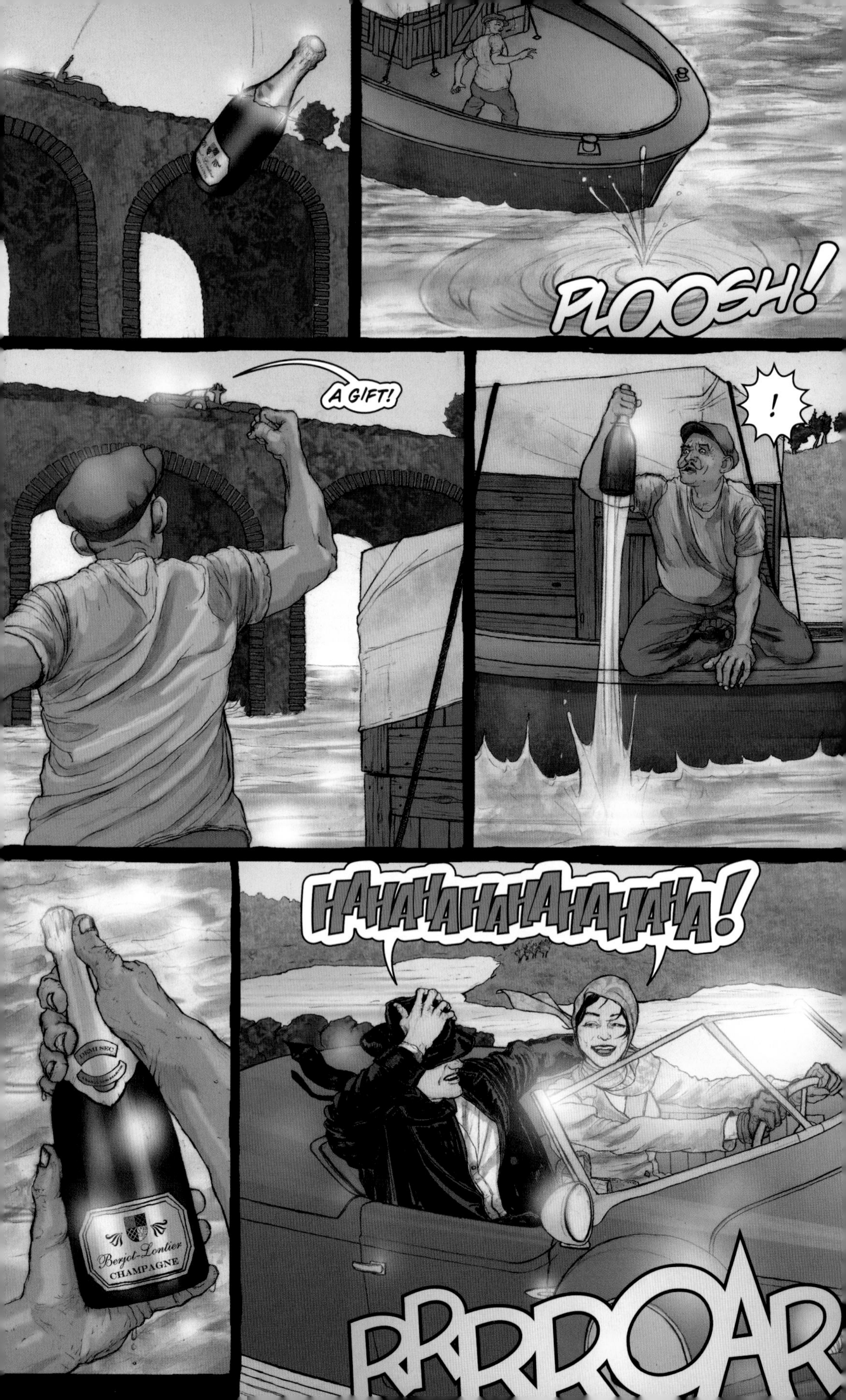
PLOOSH!
A GIFT!
!
DEMI SEC
Berjot-Lontier
CHAMPAGNE
HAHAHAHAHAHAHAHA!
RRRROAR

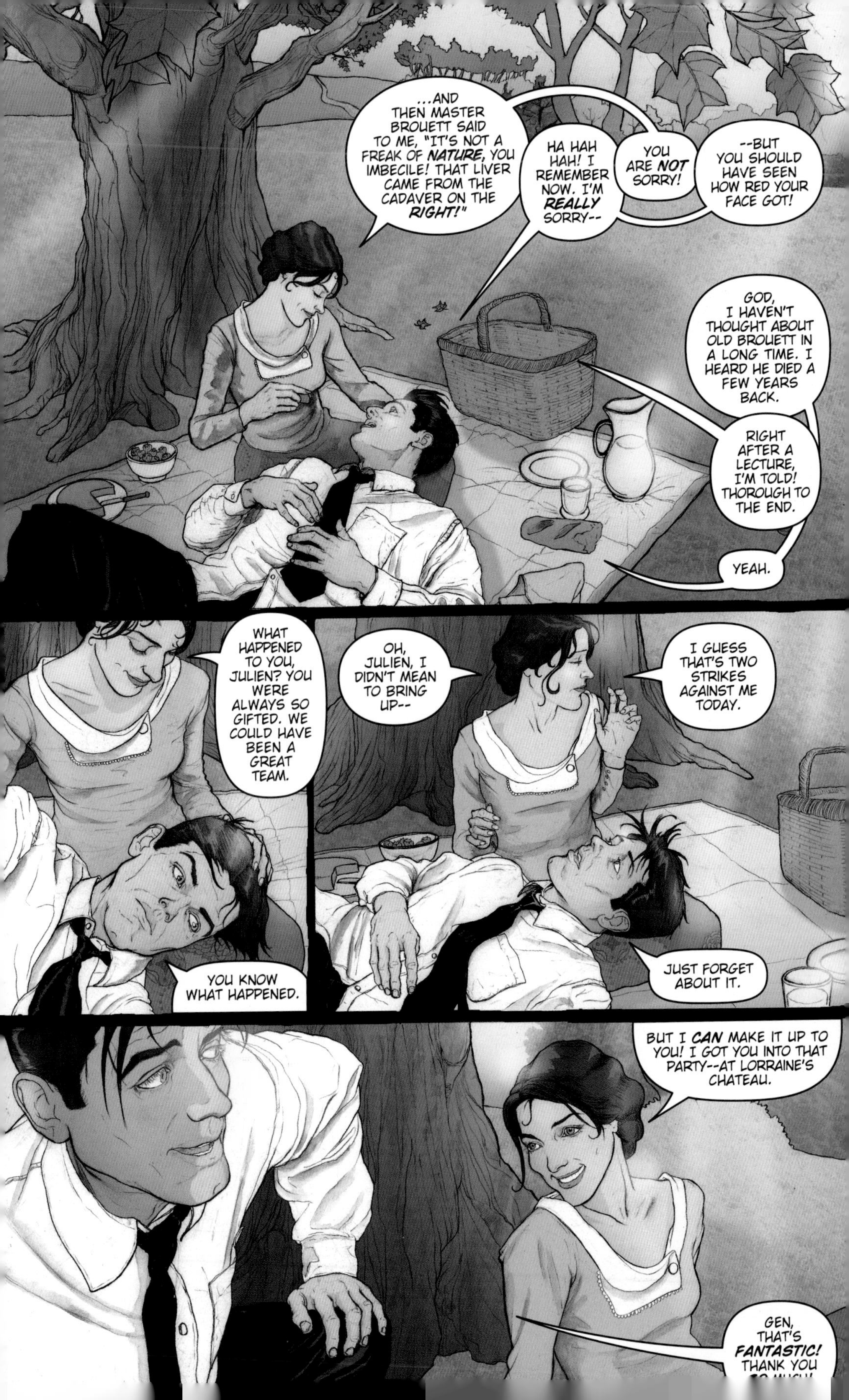
...AND THEN MASTER BROUETT SAID TO ME, "IT'S NOT A FREAK OF NATURE, YOU IMBECILE! THAT LIVER CAME FROM THE CADAVER ON THE RIGHT!"
HA HAH HAH! I REMEMBER NOW. I'M REALLY SORRY--
YOU ARE NOT SORRY!
--BUT YOU SHOULD HAVE SEEN HOW RED YOUR FACE GOT!
GOD, I HAVEN'T THOUGHT ABOUT OLD BROUETT IN A LONG TIME. I HEARD HE DIED A FEW YEARS BACK.
RIGHT AFTER A LECTURE, I'M TOLD! THOROUGH TO THE END.
YEAH.
WHAT HAPPENED TO YOU, JULIEN? YOU WERE ALWAYS SO GIFTED. WE COULD HAVE BEEN A GREAT TEAM.
YOU KNOW WHAT HAPPENED.
OH, JULIEN, I DIDN'T MEAN TO BRING UP--
I GUESS THAT'S TWO STRIKES AGAINST ME TODAY.
JUST FORGET ABOUT IT.
BUT I CAN MAKE IT UP TO YOU! I GOT YOU INTO THAT PARTY--AT LORRAINE'S CHATEAU.
GEN, THAT'S FANTASTIC! THANK YOU

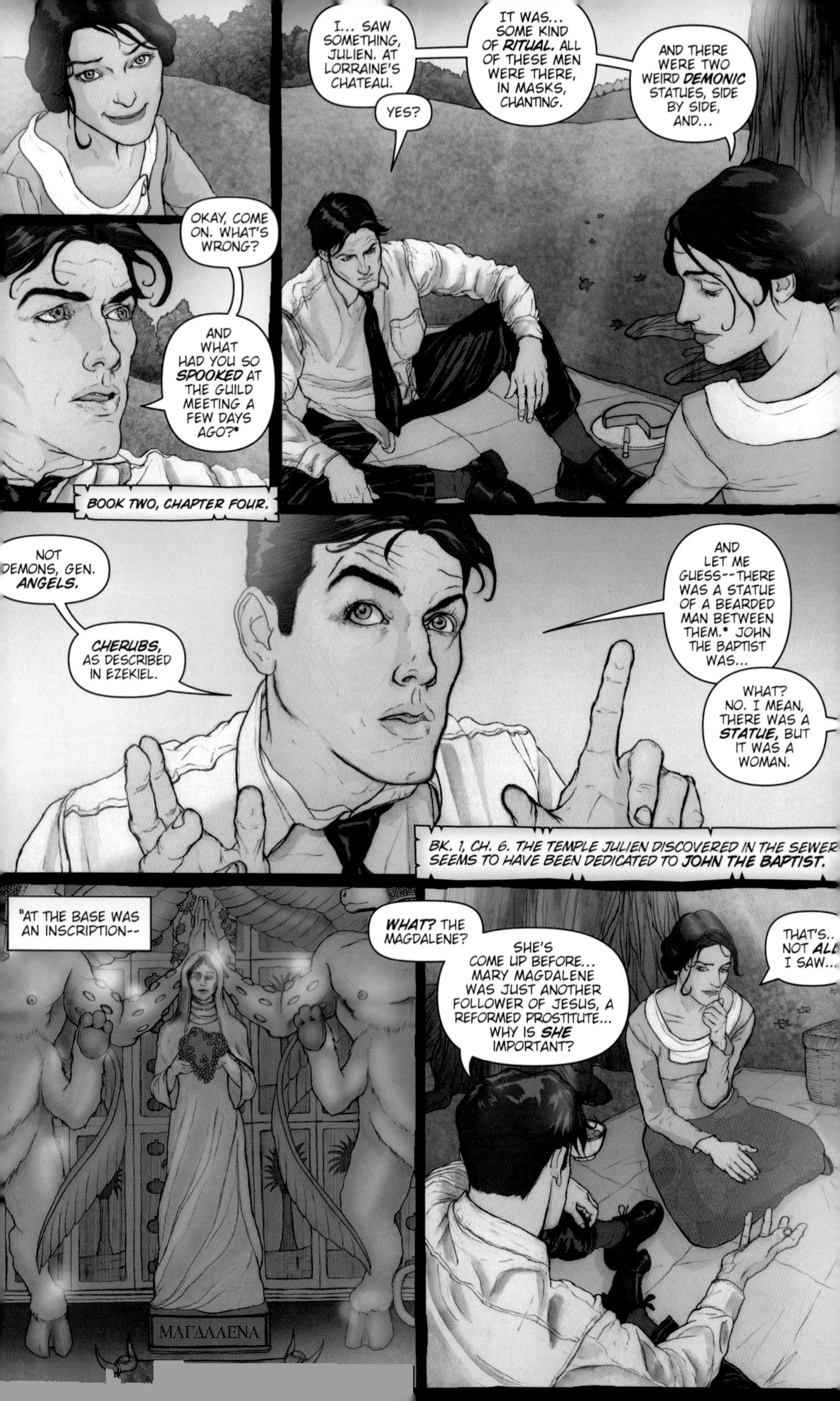
I... SAW SOMETHING, JULIEN. AT LORRAINE'S CHATEAU.
YES?
IT WAS... SOME KIND OF RITUAL. ALL OF THESE MEN WERE THERE, IN MASKS, CHANTING.
AND THERE WERE TWO WEIRD DEMONIC STATUES, SIDE BY SIDE, AND...
OKAY, COME ON. WHAT'S WRONG?
AND WHAT HAD YOU SO SPOOKED AT THE GUILD MEETING A FEW DAYS AGO?*
BOOK TWO, CHAPTER FOUR.
NOT DEMONS, GEN. ANGELS.
CHERUBS, AS DESCRIBED IN EZEKIEL.
AND LET ME GUESS--THERE WAS A STATUE OF A BEARDED MAN BETWEEN THEM.* JOHN THE BAPTIST WAS...
WHAT? NO. I MEAN, THERE WAS A STATUE, BUT IT WAS A WOMAN.
BK. 1, CH. 6. THE TEMPLE JULIEN DISCOVERED IN THE SEWER SEEMS TO HAVE BEEN DEDICATED TO JOHN THE BAPTIST.
"AT THE BASE WAS AN INSCRIPTION--
ΜΑΓΔΑΛΕΝΑ
WHAT? THE MAGDALENE?
SHE'S COME UP BEFORE... MARY MAGDALENE WAS JUST ANOTHER FOLLOWER OF JESUS, A REFORMED PROSTITUTE... WHY IS SHE IMPORTANT?
THAT'S... NOT ALL I SAW...

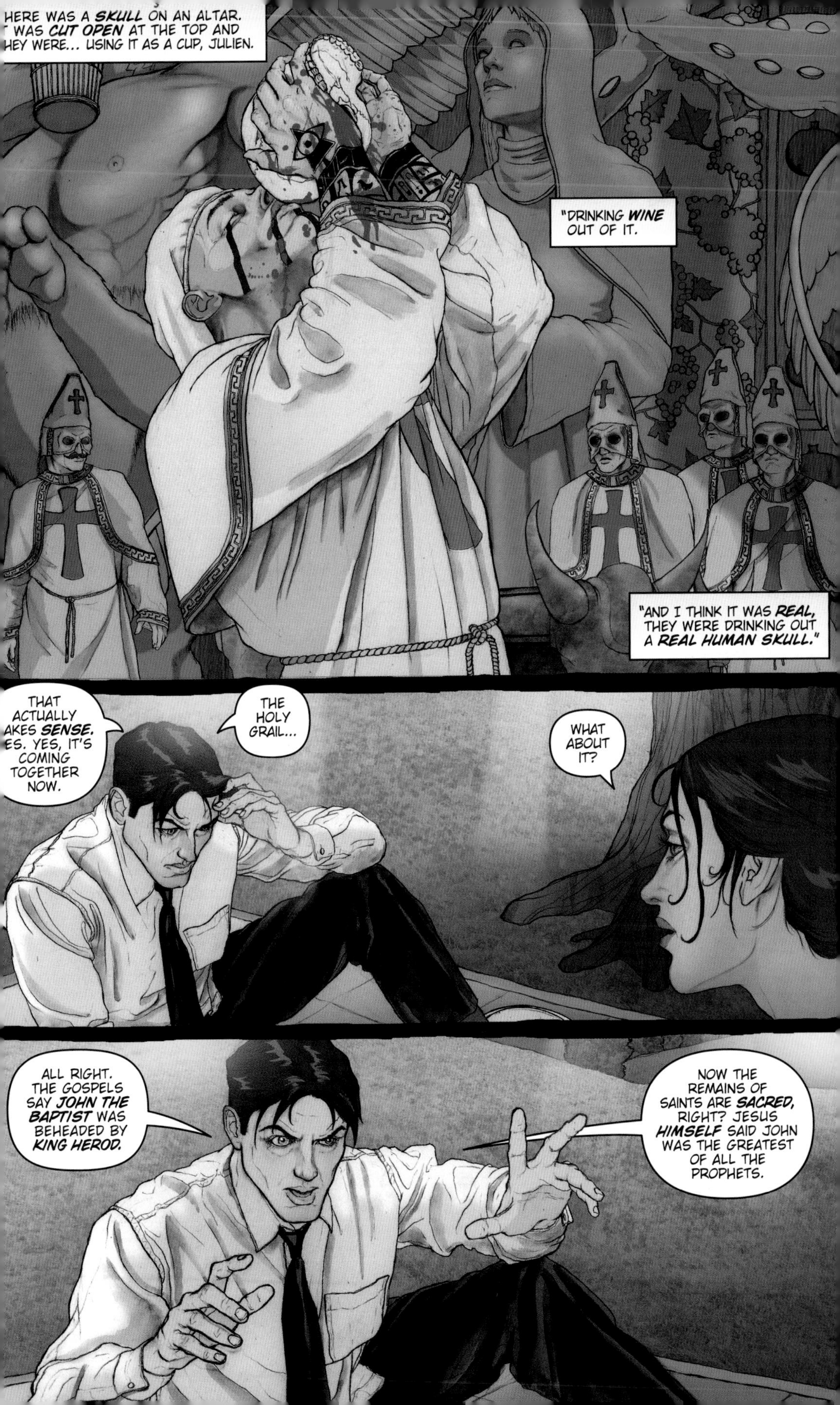
HERE WAS A SKULL ON AN ALTAR.
T WAS CUT OPEN AT THE TOP AND
HEY WERE... USING IT AS A CUP, JULIEN.
"DRINKING WINE OUT OF IT.
"AND I THINK IT WAS REAL, THEY WERE DRINKING OUT A REAL HUMAN SKULL."
THAT ACTUALLY AKES SENSE. ES. YES, IT'S COMING TOGETHER NOW.
THE HOLY GRAIL...
WHAT ABOUT IT?
ALL RIGHT. THE GOSPELS SAY JOHN THE BAPTIST WAS BEHEADED BY KING HEROD.
NOW THE REMAINS OF SAINTS ARE SACRED, RIGHT? JESUS HIMSELF SAID JOHN WAS THE GREATEST OF ALL THE PROPHETS.

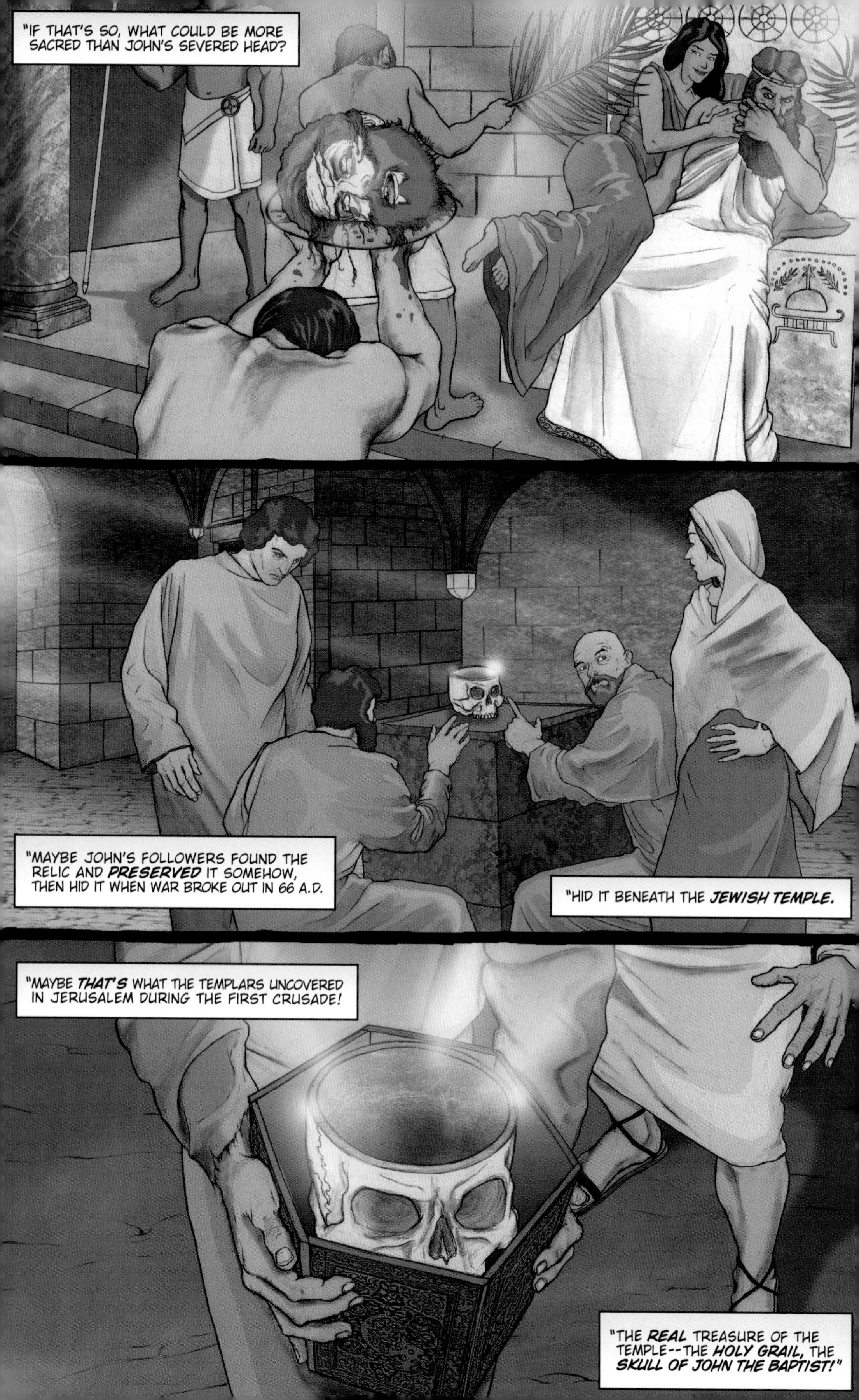
"IF THAT'S SO, WHAT COULD BE MORE SACRED THAN JOHN'S SEVERED HEAD?
"MAYBE JOHN'S FOLLOWERS FOUND THE RELIC AND PRESERVED IT SOMEHOW, THEN HID IT WHEN WAR BROKE OUT IN 66 A.D.
"HID IT BENEATH THE JEWISH TEMPLE.
"MAYBE THAT'S WHAT THE TEMPLARS UNCOVERED IN JERUSALEM DURING THE FIRST CRUSADE!
"THE REAL TREASURE OF THE TEMPLE--THE HOLY GRAIL, THE SKULL OF JOHN THE BAPTIST!"

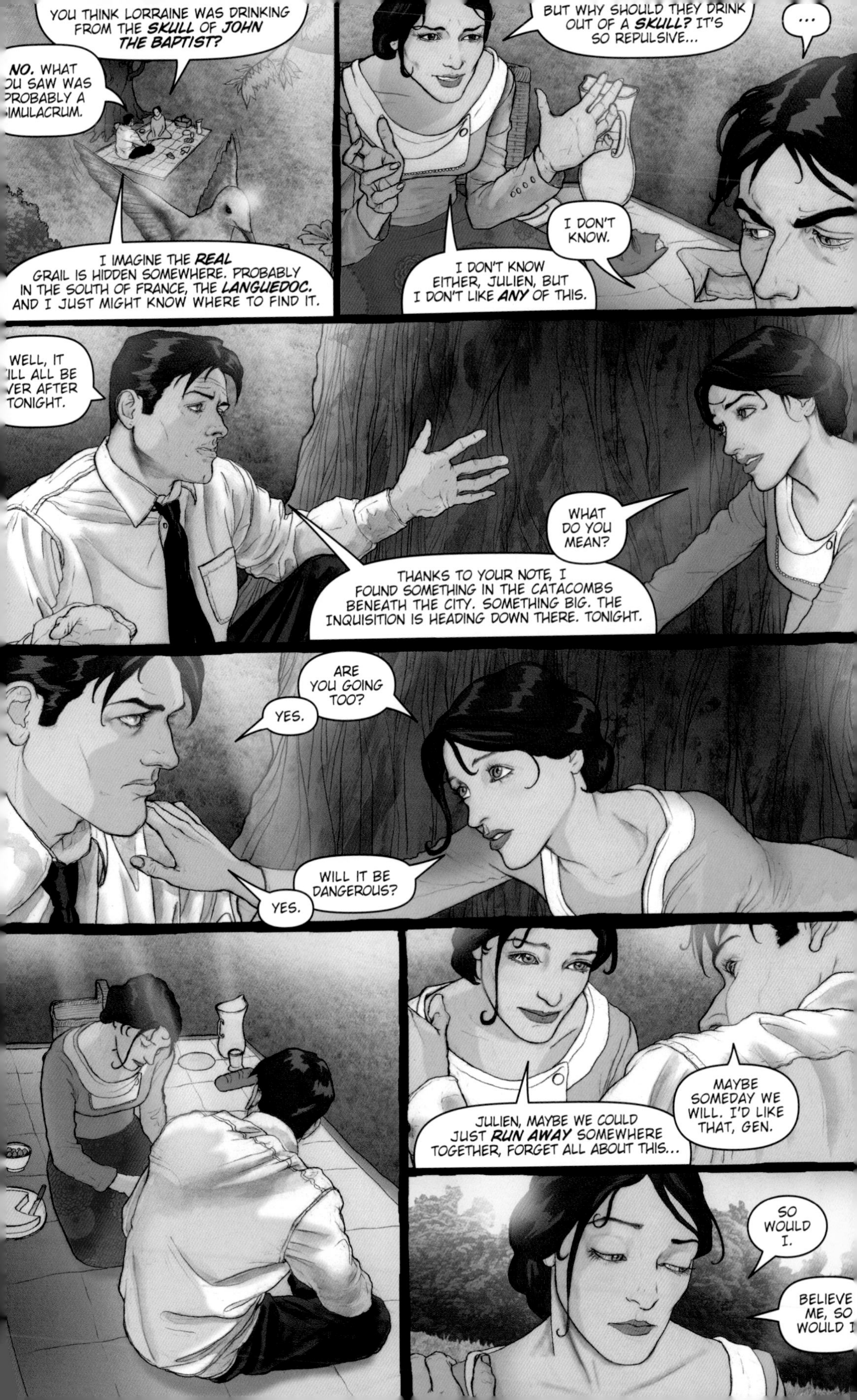

YOU THINK LORRAINE WAS DRINKING FROM THE SKULL OF JOHN THE BAPTIST?
NO. WHAT OU SAW WAS PROBABLY A IMULACRUM.
I IMAGINE THE REAL GRAIL IS HIDDEN SOMEWHERE. PROBABLY IN THE SOUTH OF FRANCE, THE LANGUEDOC. AND I JUST MIGHT KNOW WHERE TO FIND IT.
BUT WHY SHOULD THEY DRINK OUT OF A SKULL? IT'S SO REPULSIVE...
...
I DON'T KNOW.
I DON'T KNOW EITHER, JULIEN, BUT I DON'T LIKE ANY OF THIS.
WELL, IT ILL ALL BE VER AFTER TONIGHT.
WHAT DO YOU MEAN?
THANKS TO YOUR NOTE, I FOUND SOMETHING IN THE CATACOMBS BENEATH THE CITY. SOMETHING BIG. THE INQUISITION IS HEADING DOWN THERE. TONIGHT.
ARE YOU GOING TOO?
YES.
WILL IT BE DANGEROUS?
YES.
JULIEN, MAYBE WE COULD JUST RUN AWAY SOMEWHERE TOGETHER, FORGET ALL ABOUT THIS...
MAYBE SOMEDAY WE WILL. I'D LIKE THAT, GEN.
SO WOULD I.
BELIEVE ME, SO WOULD I

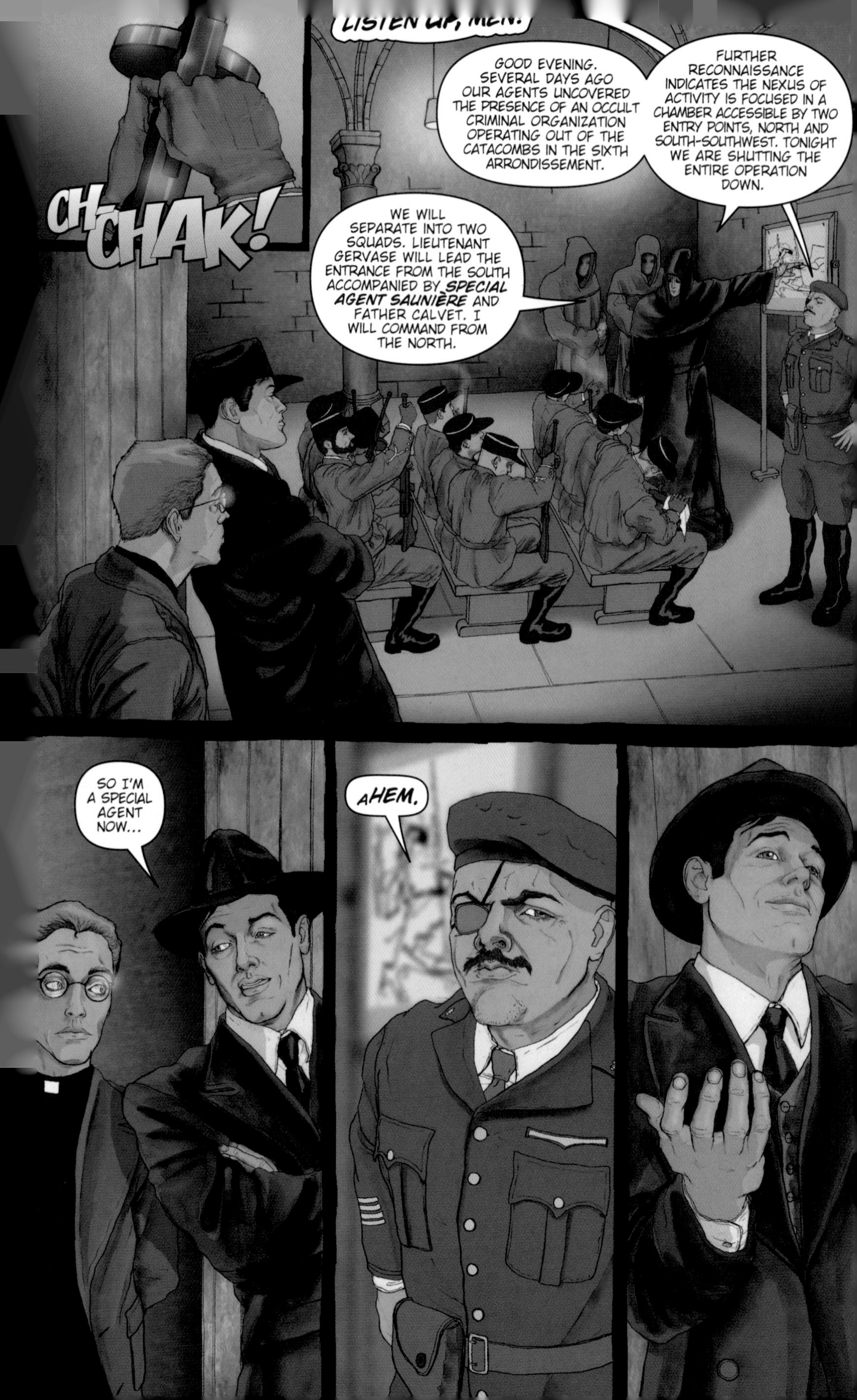

LISTEN UP, MEN!
CH-CHAK!
GOOD EVENING. SEVERAL DAYS AGO OUR AGENTS UNCOVERED THE PRESENCE OF AN OCCULT CRIMINAL ORGANIZATION OPERATING OUT OF THE CATACOMBS IN THE SIXTH ARRONDISSEMENT.
FURTHER RECONNAISSANCE INDICATES THE NEXUS OF ACTIVITY IS FOCUSED IN A CHAMBER ACCESSIBLE BY TWO ENTRY POINTS, NORTH AND SOUTH-SOUTHWEST. TONIGHT WE ARE SHUTTING THE ENTIRE OPERATION DOWN.
WE WILL SEPARATE INTO TWO SQUADS. LIEUTENANT GERVASE WILL LEAD THE ENTRANCE FROM THE SOUTH ACCOMPANIED BY SPECIAL AGENT SAUNIÈRE AND FATHER CALVET. I WILL COMMAND FROM THE NORTH.
SO I'M A SPECIAL AGENT NOW...
AHEM.

IF ALL GOES WELL THERE SHOULD BE NO EXCHANGE OF FIRE, BUT BE READY FOR ANYTHING.

REPORTS INDICATE THE SUSPECTS ARE HEAVILY ARMED, AND WE HAVE REASON TO BELIEVE SOME OR ALL MAY BE OCCULT PRACTITIONERS.

EACH SQUAD WILL ASSAULT THE CHAMBER SIMULTANEOUSLY, TO MAXIMIZE INITIATIVE.

SILENCE IS AT A PREMIUM HERE--SAFETIES *ON* UNTIL MY OR BROTHER MORICANT'S COMMAND.

WATCH THE ENTRY POINTS--WE DON'T WANT TO GET VENTILATED BY OUR OWN CROSSFIRE. ARE THERE ANY QUESTIONS?

GOOD. IT IS EXACTLY *TEN O'CLOCK.* THE RAID WILL COMMENCE *ONE HOUR* FROM NOW.

THIS MISSION IS OF EXTREME INTEREST TO THE ARCHBISHOP, GENTLEMEN. AND TO THE *HOLY FATHER* HIMSELF. FOLLOW OUR LEAD, AND DO NOT FAIL.

BLESS YOU ALL, AND MAY YOU RETURN SAFELY.

IN CHRIST'S NAME, AMEN.

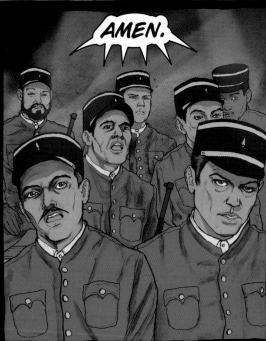

AMEN.

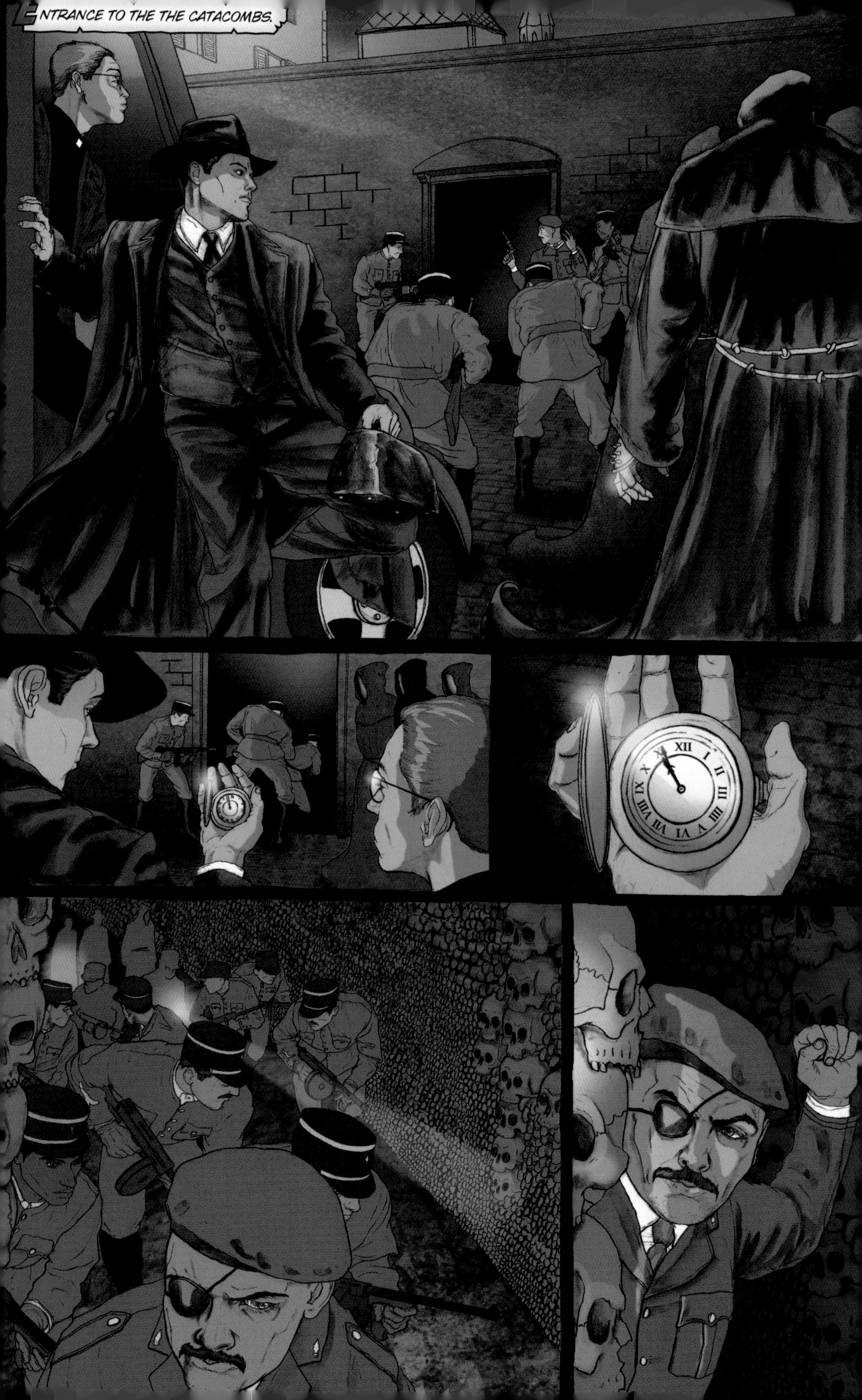
ENTRANCE TO THE THE CATACOMBS.

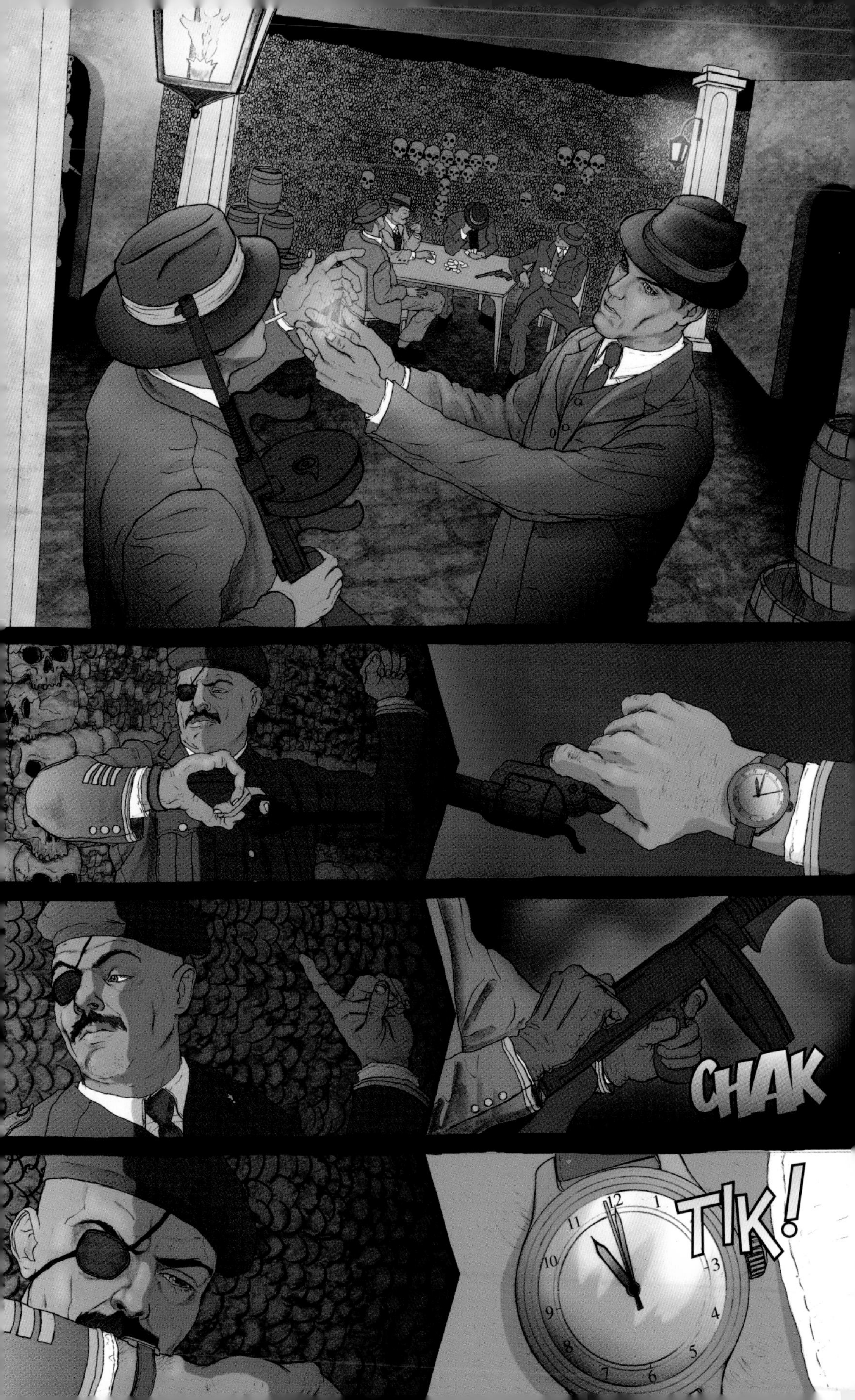
CHAK
TIK!

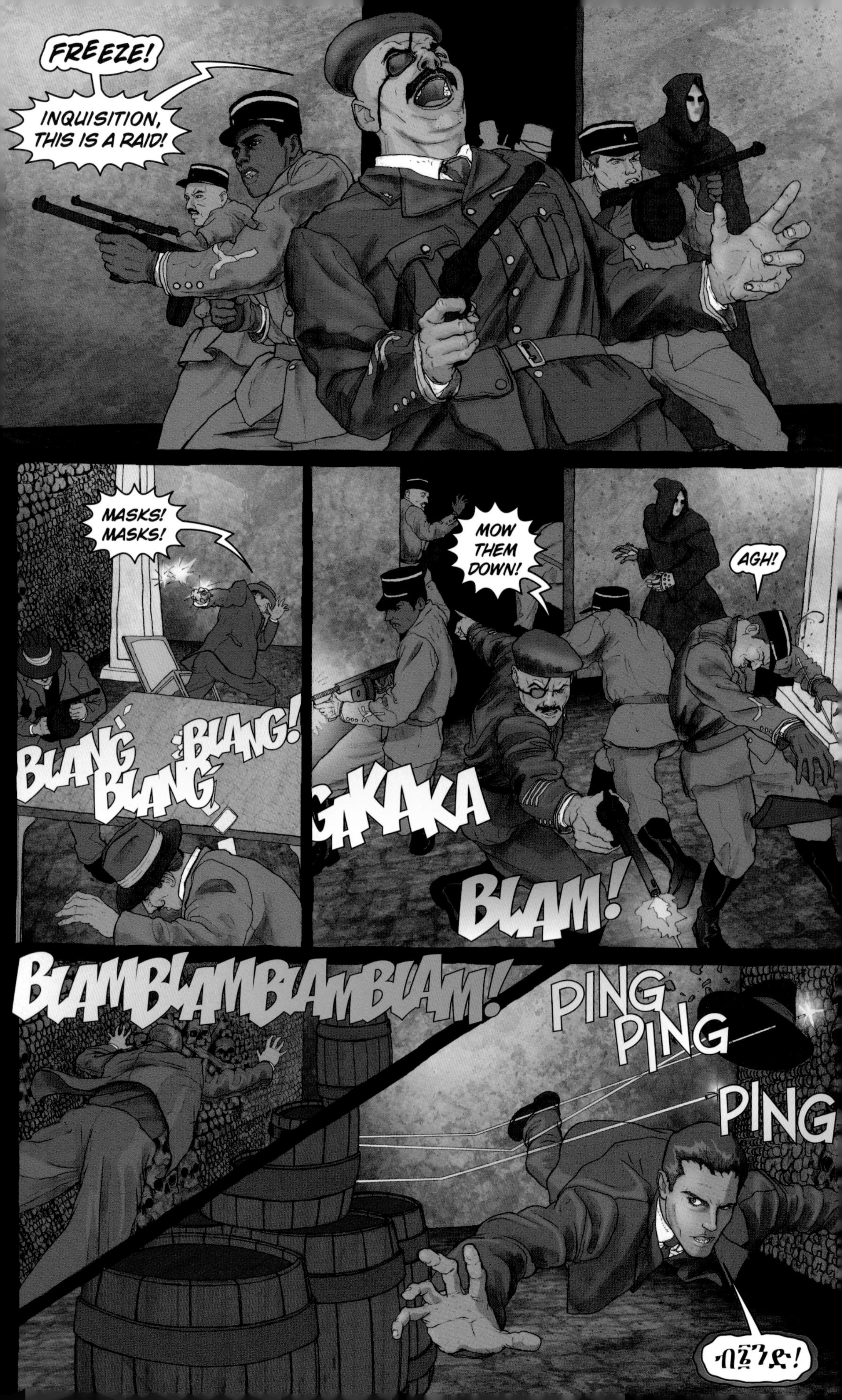
FREEZE!
INQUISITION, THIS IS A RAID!
MASKS! MASKS!
BLANG BLANG BLANG!
MOW THEM DOWN!
AGH!
GAKAKA
BLAM!
BLAMBLAMBLAMBLAM!
PING PING
PING
ብሺንድ!

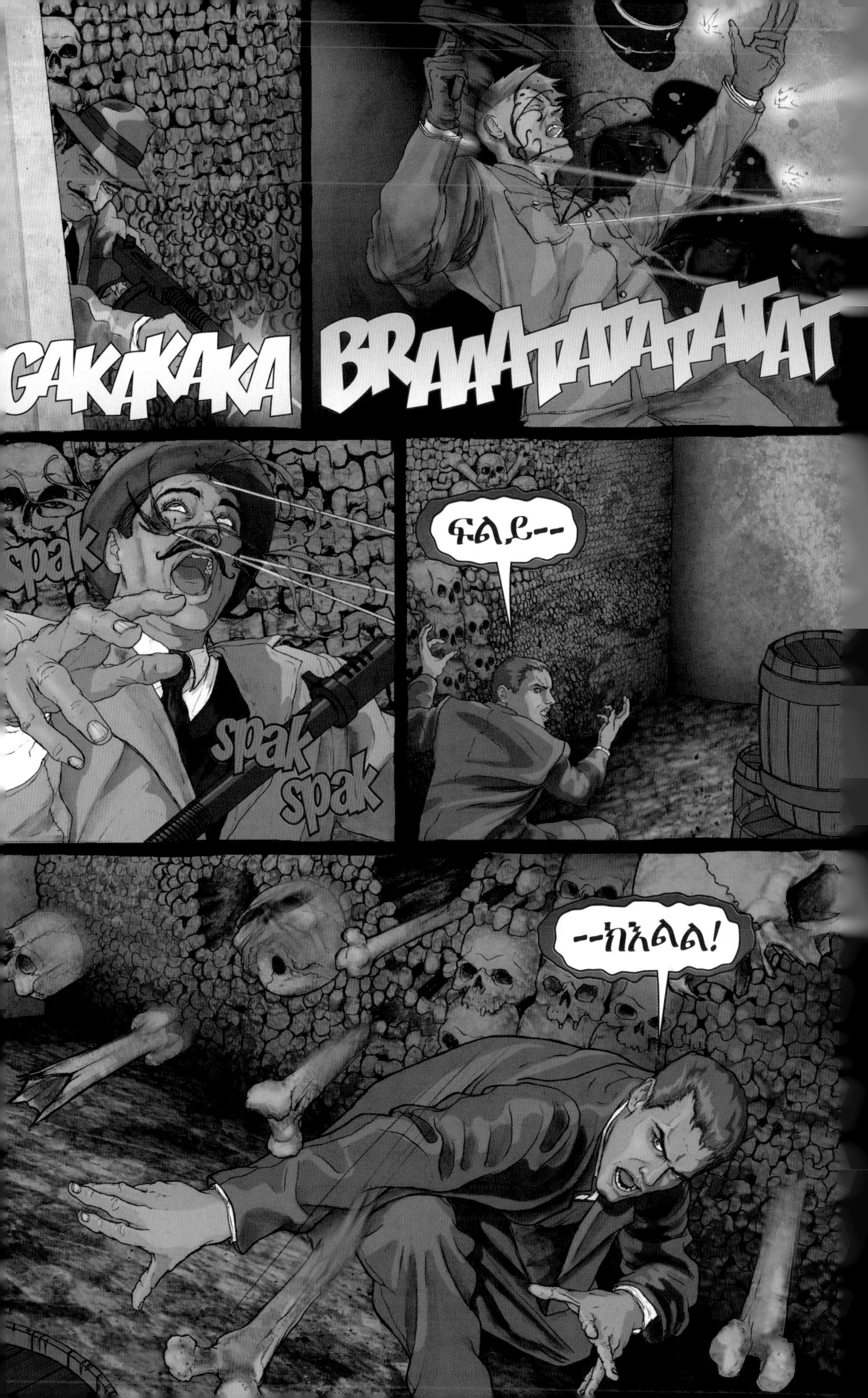
GAKAKAKA
BRAAATATATATATAT
spak
spak
spak
ፍልይ--
--ክእልል!

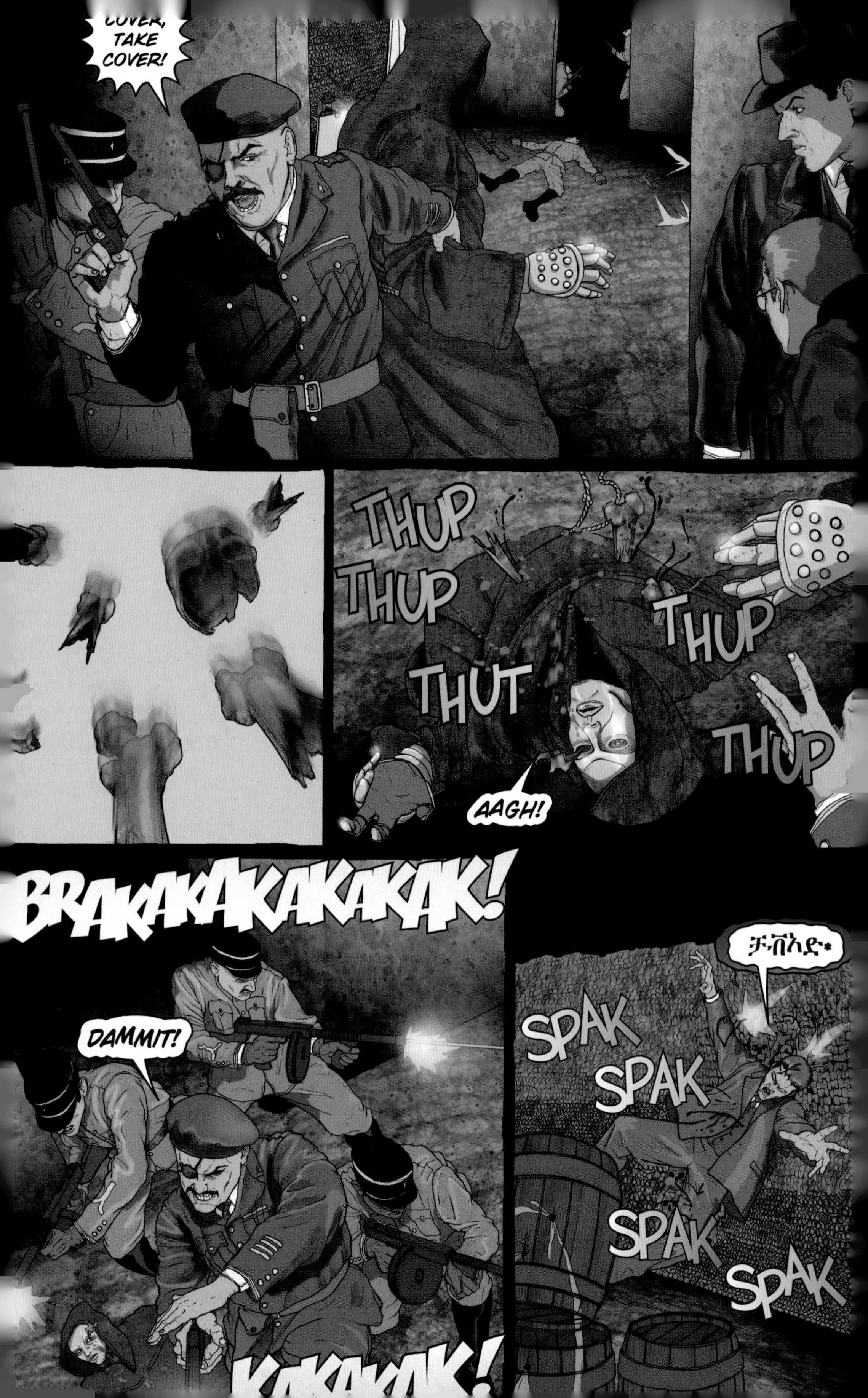
COVER, TAKE COVER!
THUP
THUP
THUP
THUT
THUP
AAGH!
BRAKAKAKAKAKAK!
DAMMIT!
ቻቨአድ*
SPAK
SPAK
SPAK
SPAK
KAKAKAK!

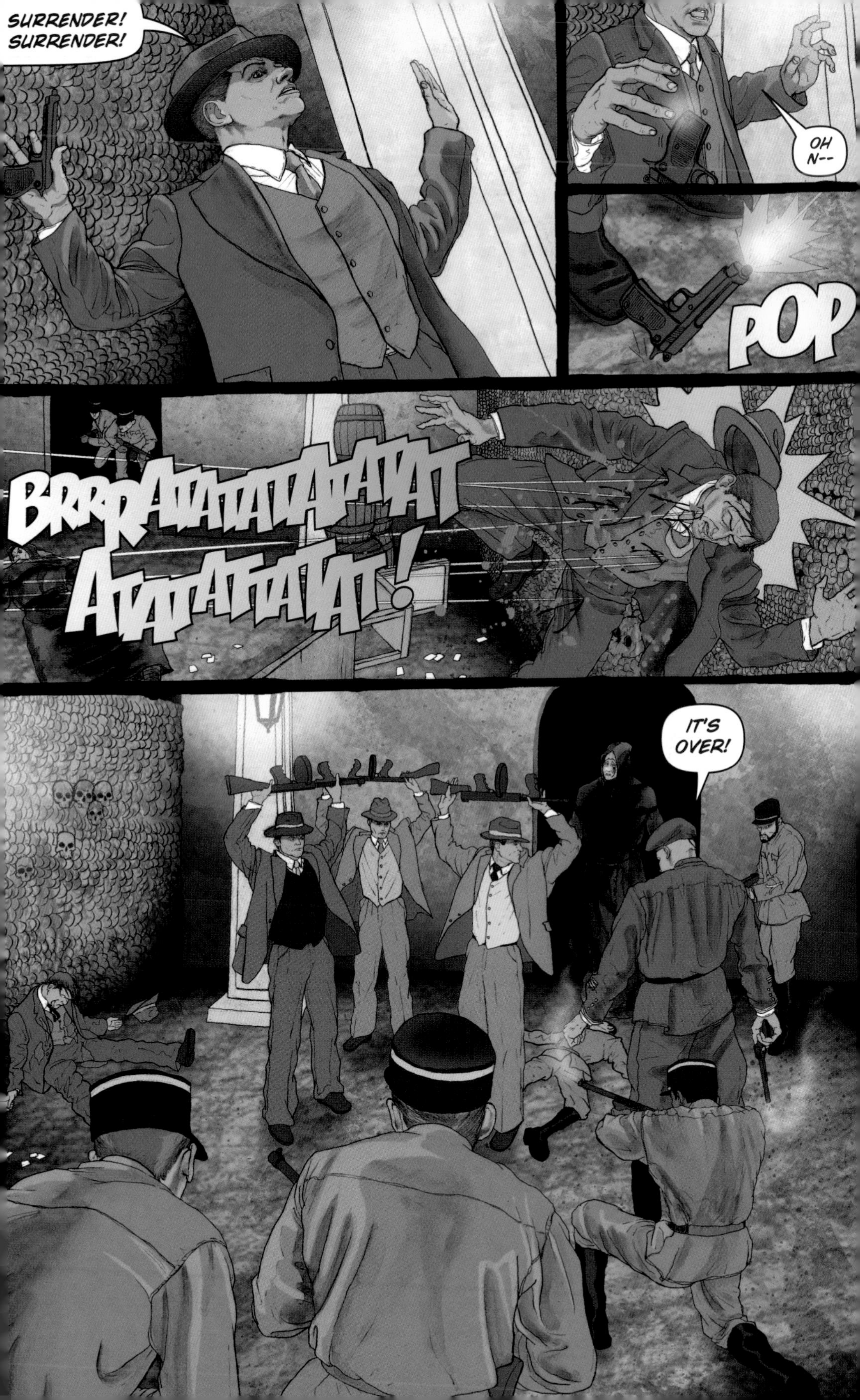
SURRENDER! SURRENDER!
OH N--
POP
BRRRATATATATATAT ATATATATATAT!
IT'S OVER!

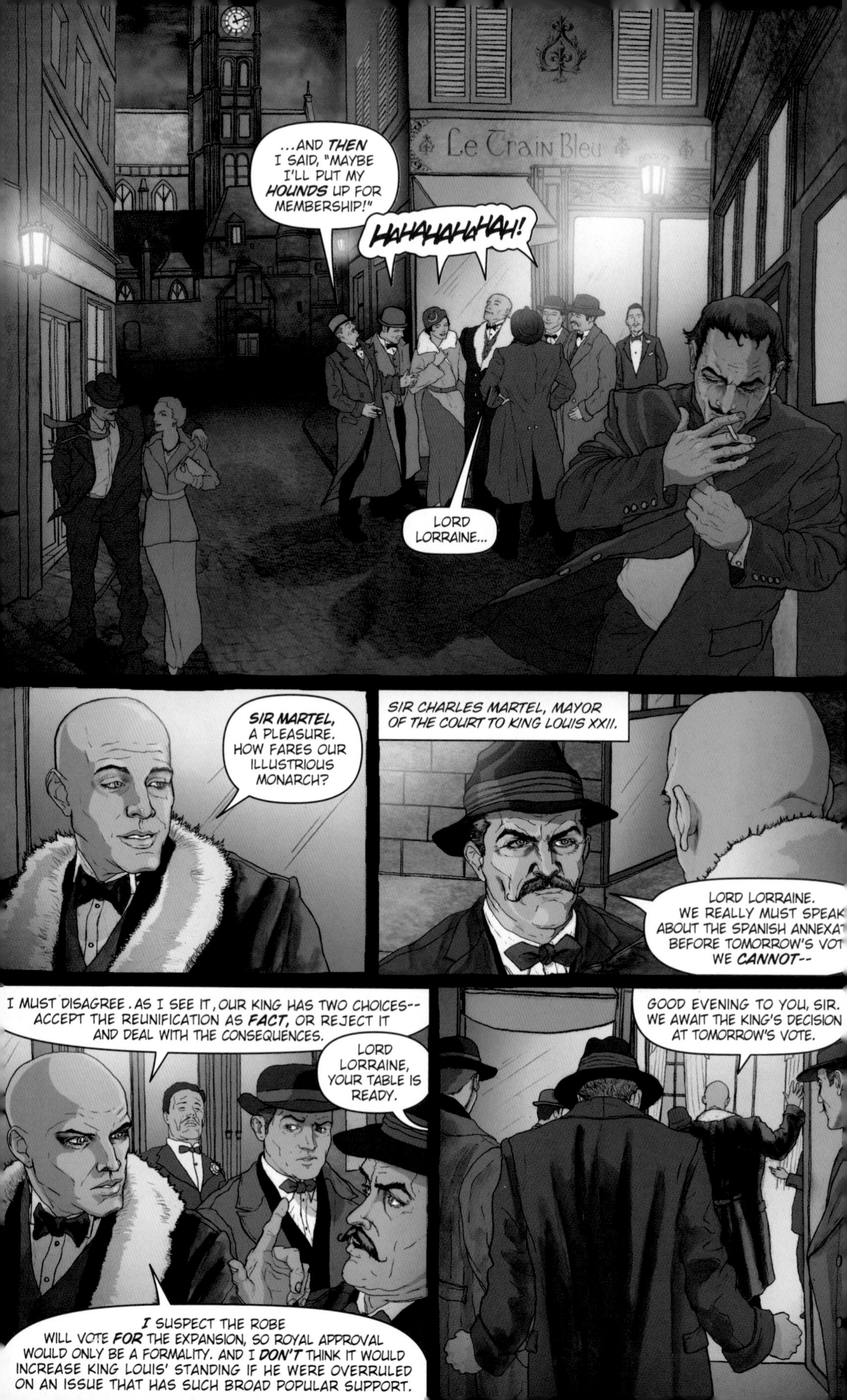

Le Train Bleu
...AND **THEN** I SAID, "MAYBE I'LL PUT MY **HOUNDS** UP FOR MEMBERSHIP!"
HAHAHAHAHAH!
LORD LORRAINE...
SIR MARTEL, A PLEASURE. HOW FARES OUR ILLUSTRIOUS MONARCH?
SIR CHARLES MARTEL, MAYOR OF THE COURT TO KING LOUIS XXII.
LORD LORRAINE. WE REALLY MUST SPEAK ABOUT THE SPANISH ANNEXAT BEFORE TOMORROW'S VOT WE **CANNOT**--
I MUST DISAGREE. AS I SEE IT, OUR KING HAS TWO CHOICES-- ACCEPT THE REUNIFICATION AS **FACT**, OR REJECT IT AND DEAL WITH THE CONSEQUENCES.
LORD LORRAINE, YOUR TABLE IS READY.
I SUSPECT THE ROBE WILL VOTE ***FOR*** THE EXPANSION, SO ROYAL APPROVAL WOULD ONLY BE A FORMALITY. AND I ***DON'T*** THINK IT WOULD INCREASE KING LOUIS' STANDING IF HE WERE OVERRULED ON AN ISSUE THAT HAS SUCH BROAD POPULAR SUPPORT.
GOOD EVENING TO YOU, SIR. WE AWAIT THE KING'S DECISION AT TOMORROW'S VOTE.

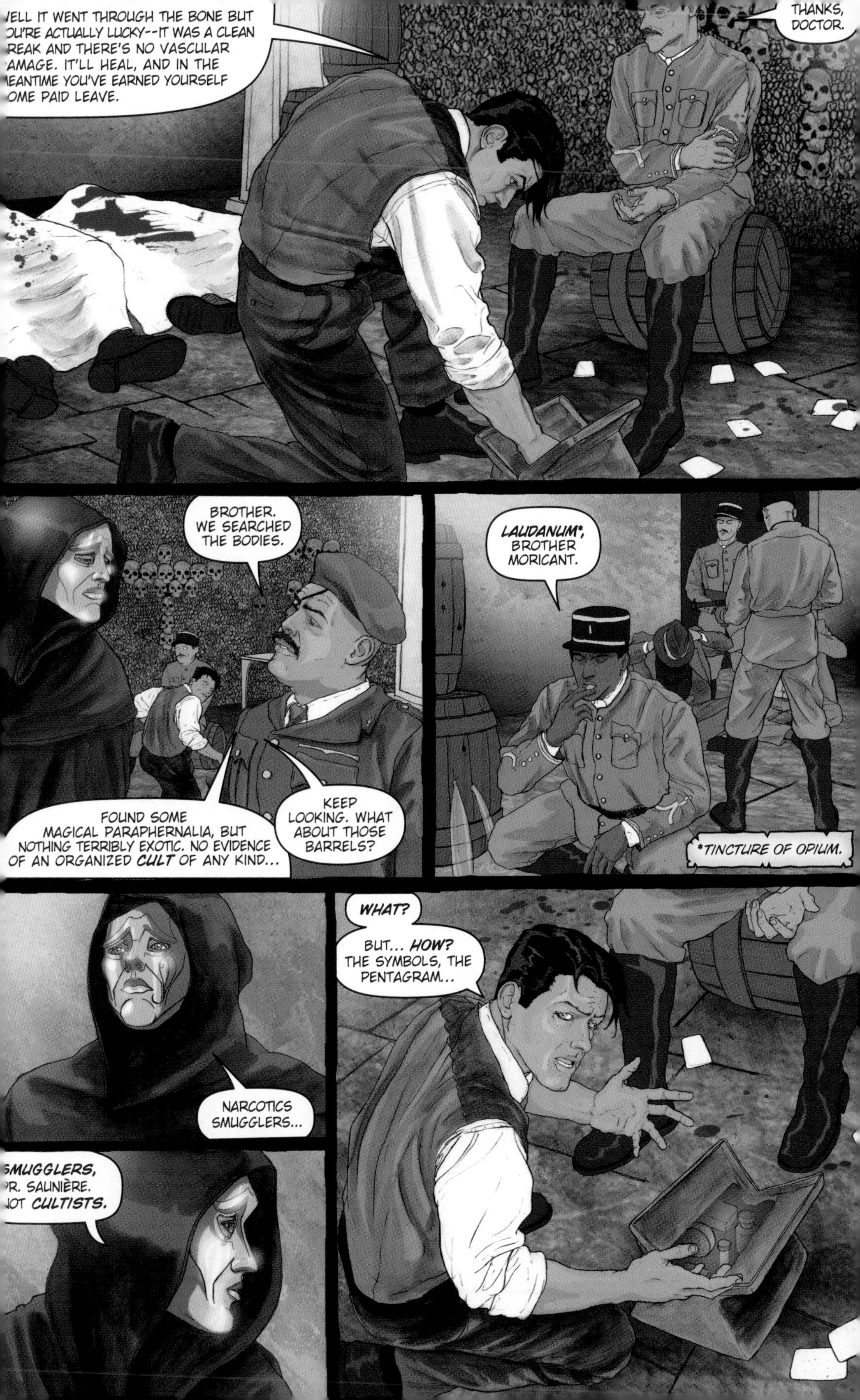
VELL IT WENT THROUGH THE BONE BUT OU'RE ACTUALLY LUCKY--IT WAS A CLEAN REAK AND THERE'S NO VASCULAR AMAGE. IT'LL HEAL, AND IN THE EANTIME YOU'VE EARNED YOURSELF OME PAID LEAVE.
THANKS, DOCTOR.
BROTHER. WE SEARCHED THE BODIES.
FOUND SOME MAGICAL PARAPHERNALIA, BUT NOTHING TERRIBLY EXOTIC. NO EVIDENCE OF AN ORGANIZED ***CULT*** OF ANY KIND...
KEEP LOOKING. WHAT ABOUT THOSE BARRELS?
LAUDANUM*, BROTHER MORICANT.
**TINCTURE OF OPIUM.*
NARCOTICS SMUGGLERS...
WHAT?
BUT... ***HOW?*** THE SYMBOLS, THE PENTAGRAM...
SMUGGLERS, R. SAUNIÈRE. OT ***CULTISTS.***

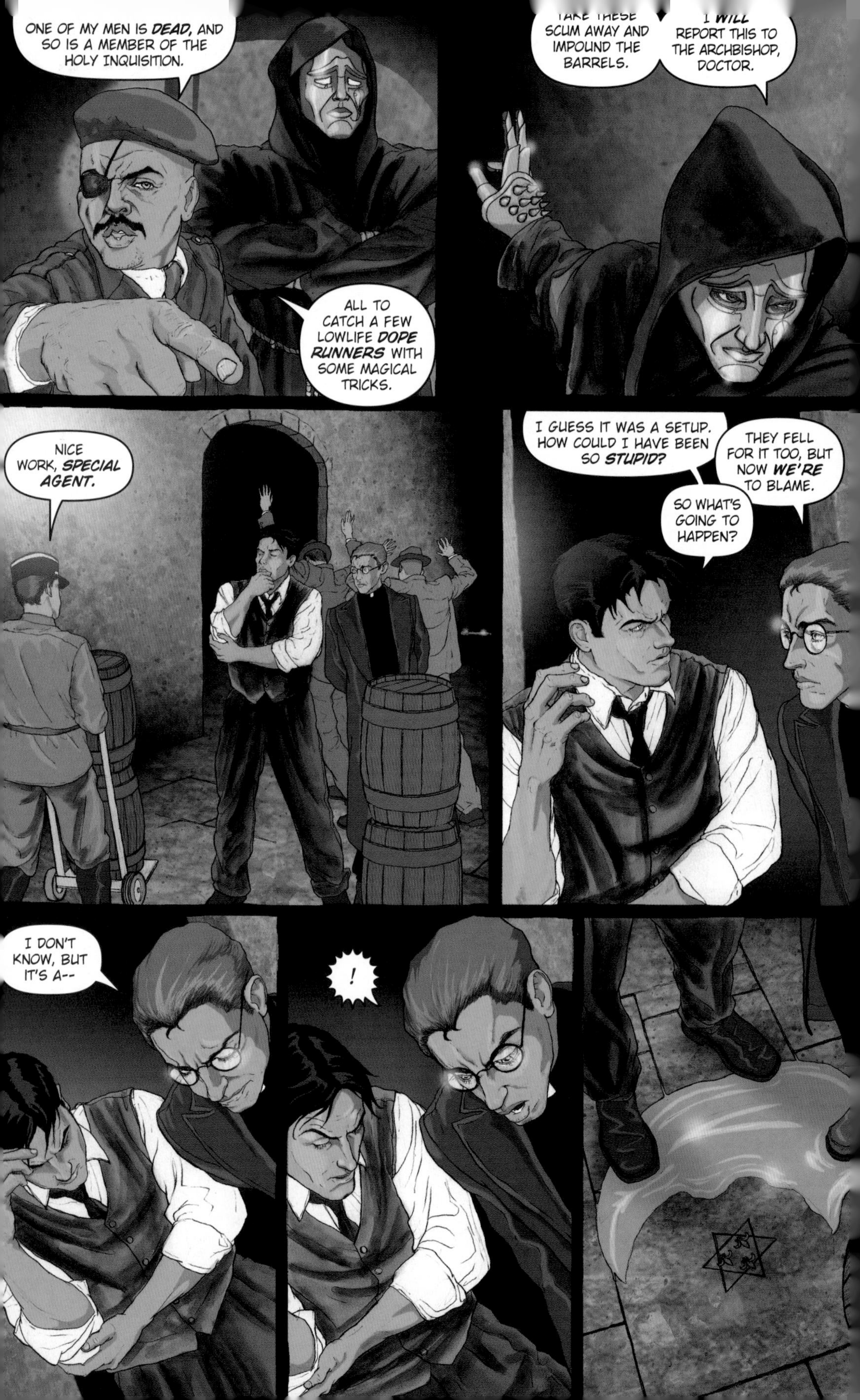
ONE OF MY MEN IS DEAD, AND SO IS A MEMBER OF THE HOLY INQUISITION.
ALL TO CATCH A FEW LOWLIFE DOPE RUNNERS WITH SOME MAGICAL TRICKS.
TAKE THESE SCUM AWAY AND IMPOUND THE BARRELS.
I WILL REPORT THIS TO THE ARCHBISHOP, DOCTOR.
NICE WORK, SPECIAL AGENT.
I GUESS IT WAS A SETUP. HOW COULD I HAVE BEEN SO STUPID?
THEY FELL FOR IT TOO, BUT NOW WE'RE TO BLAME.
SO WHAT'S GOING TO HAPPEN?
I DON'T KNOW, BUT IT'S A--
!

Le Journal de la Liberté

Paris' leading anglophone newspaper • vol. 205, no. 98 • Oct. 31, MCMXXXIII

Editors in Chief: M. Tait Bergstrom, M. Matthew Pasteris. **Story Editor:** M. Arvid Nelson.
Art Editor: M. James Di Bartolo. **Photography Editor:** M. Alexander Waldman.
Layout Supervisor: M. William Kartalopoulos. **Editors Emeritus:** M. Clark A. Smith,
M. Howard P. Lovecraft, M. Robert E. Howard. Redacted by the Holy Inquisition under the direction
of His Excellency Archbishop Emile-Jean Ireneaux. Le Journal de la Liberté is printed under the benign
auspices of his most puissant majesty KING LOUIS XXII of FRANCE. GOD SAVE THE KING.

Papal seal

of Approval

Raiders from Maine Demolish Two Québec Homesteads

Governor Blames 'Indian Raiders,' Eyewitness Reports Conflict with Official Account

Lac Frontière, Québec – Raiders from Maine pillaged two French homesteads yesterday, killing three people and capturing five others in a brazen daylight attack.

The raid occurred on a frontier settlement between the French colony of Québec and the federal Republic of America.

"The motive for the attack seems to have been greed, plain and simple," Georges Depuy-Maréchal, the viceroy of Québec, said. "The men were slain and the womenfolk and children captured, most likely for slavery."

Jim McCarter, the governor of Maine, was quick to blame "Indian savages" for the outrage.

"This bears all the hallmarks of an attack by heathen malcontents," McCarter said. "Sadly, there is little we can do to curb a population of people who are nomadic and lawless by nature."

Officials of the French Viceroyalty were not convinced, citing eyewitness reports the attackers were white.

"We call upon the FRA to investigate this crime and punish those responsible," he said. "We demand that they put an end to these wanton attacks on innocent subjects of the French crown."

Indian attacks, while infrequent, especially in the past ten years, are not unheard of. But Québec officials have long charged that brigands attack vulnerable French settlers with the tacit approval of the FRA.

continued on page A9

⊹ INSIDE ⊹

Unite Behind our King: The addition of the Spanish Marches is a dangerous move, say our political analysts ⋯ **D1**

Plus commentary by eds. A. Nelson and J. Di Bartolo ⋯⋯ **E1**

MARQUIS OF NAVARRE DIES IN HUNTING ACCIDENT, CEDES LANDS TO FRANCE; SURVIVING SPANISH LORDS PLEDGE SAME

Paris, the Assemblée Nationale – The Marquis of Navarre died yesterday afternoon in a hunting accident in the French countryside. His death came as a surprise to everyone who knew him.

But an even greater surprise awaited the members of the Assemblée Nationale this morning, when they learned the late Marquis had donated all of his lands to the French crown.

Navarre has cultural and political ties to France that extend back to the days of Charlemagne, but the Marquises have always guarded their independence jealously.

"It's something of a surprise, yes," the Duke of Nevers said. "But times have changed. There is a growing realization that the French people and the Christian peoples of the Spanish Marches are one. Navarre realized that."

Nevers is one of the staunchest supporters of the Duke of Lorraine, who has come to embody the "Greater France" movement of French expansion and colonialism.

Lorraine's cause received an even bigger boost from the two remaining Spanish Lords, the Marquises of Aragon and Catalonia, who spoke before the Assembly today.

The Duke of Lorraine speaking before parliament earlier today. At his side stood the surviving Spanish marquises, the lords of Aragon and Catalonia.

Citing Navarre as a "noble example," They together pledged their lands to the French crown as well.

The members of the Assemblée were shocked into silence for several moments, but Aragon and Catalonia's speech eventually drew thunderous cheers from Lorraine's supporters.

In recent months Lorraine has won over more and more members of the Hall of the Robe, traditionally the King's power base, over to his side.

The most notable defec-

The late Marquis of Navarre

tor to date is Baronet Charles deMandeville, Speaker for the Hall of the Robe and formerly King Louis' staunchest ally. In fact, it was deMandeville who put forward the resolution to bring the "reunification" to a vote tomorrow.

Although King Louis would stand to gain tremendous power from the annexation, if it goes forward, it would also weaken him politically. He has stated time and again that he op-

continued on page A2

SPANISH ANNEXATION SETS STAGE SET FOR CONFRONTATION IN PARLIAMENT TOMORROW
Lorraine, Supporters Eye Much More Than Iberia; Crown Vows Defeat of "Upstarts"

Versailles – The news in the Assemblée Nationale of the proposed Spanish annexation today was a "shocking wake-up call" for the King and his supporters, according to a source close to the crown. King Louis bitterly opposes the addition of new territories to France.

"It would mean war. It would be a disaster," Sir Charles Martel, King Louis' Mayor of the Court, said. King Louis is rallying his allies for a showdown tomorrow

against the forces of the Duke of Lorraine.

The stakes could not be higher. The King's hold on the Hall of the Robe, his traditional power base, has weakened over the past few years. More and more Robe constituents are flocking to the cause of the Duke of Lorraine.

The King was recently voted down by both houses of the Assemblée on a minor piece of legislation. According to some, it's a sign the King needs to reassert

his control over the Robe.

King Louis is confident he will do just that tomorrow.

"We trust the members of the Robe will reject this foolish and misguided annexation," the King declared in a written statement.

"With all due respect, Lord Lorraine and his supporters are upstarts," said the Count of Montfort, one of Louis' advisors Robe. "We have the votes to defeat this."

continued on page A2

LES ARMÉES DES SATAN

Et in Arcadia ego...

ER NOSTER QUI EST IN COEL

CHAPTER FOUR

MOST BELOVED

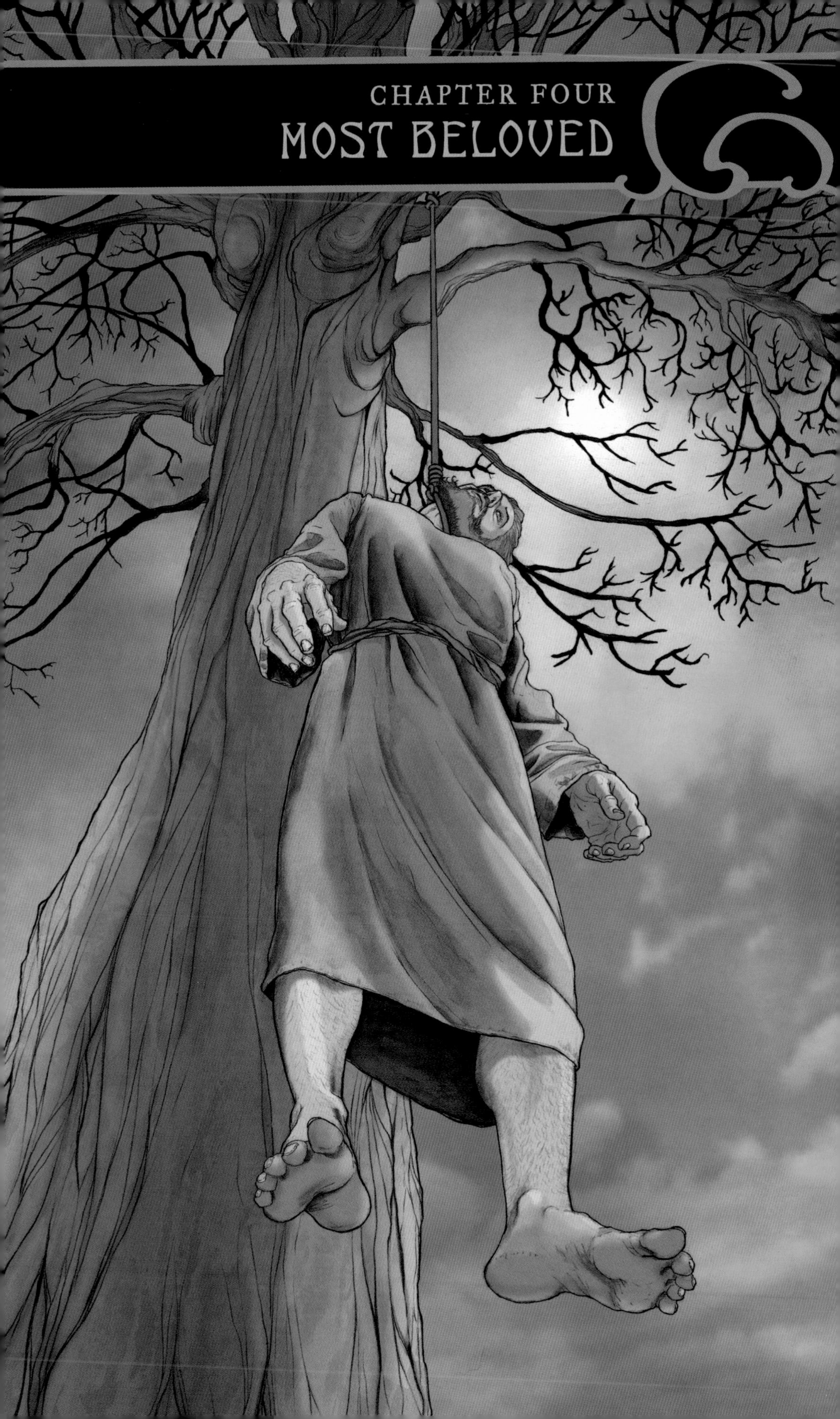

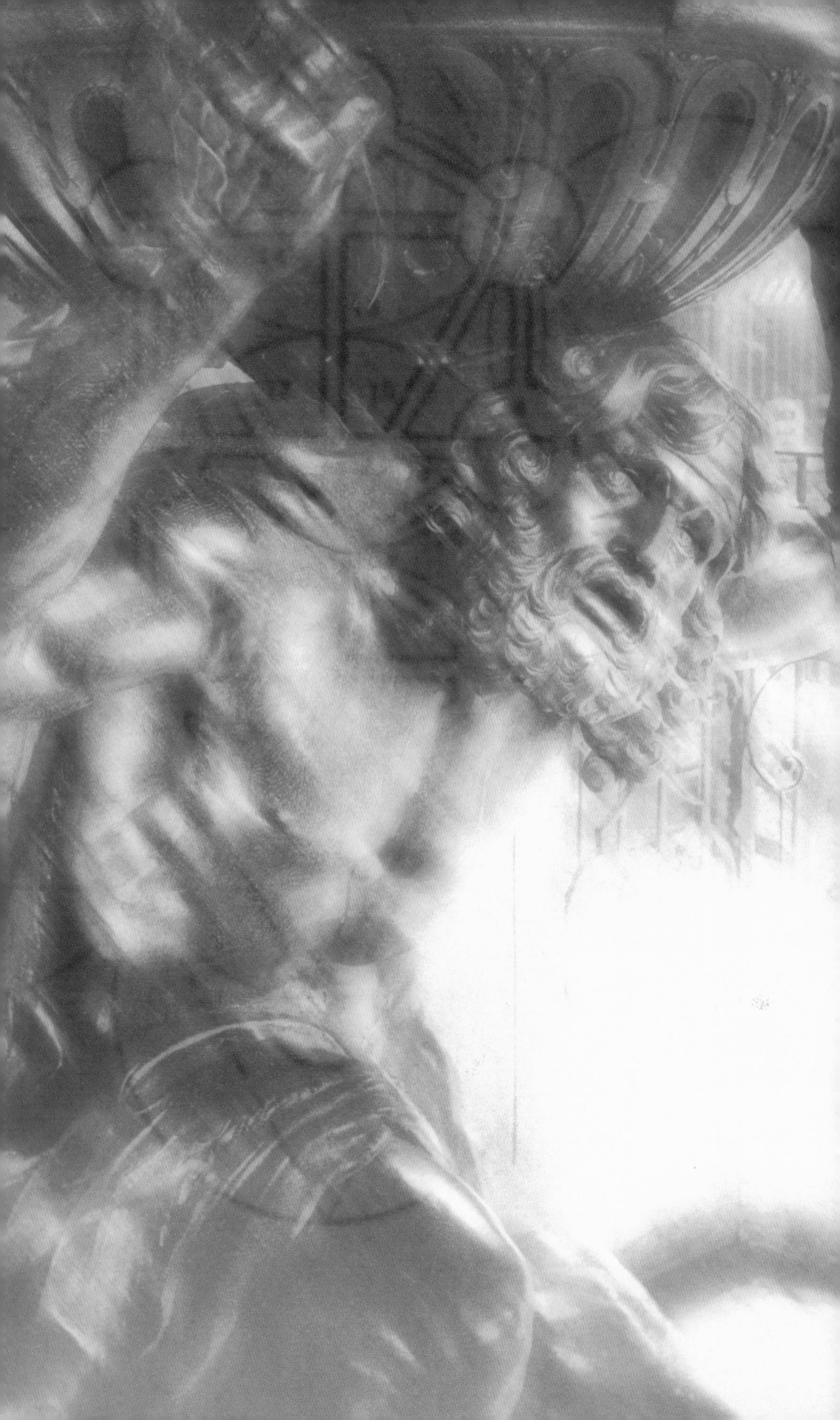

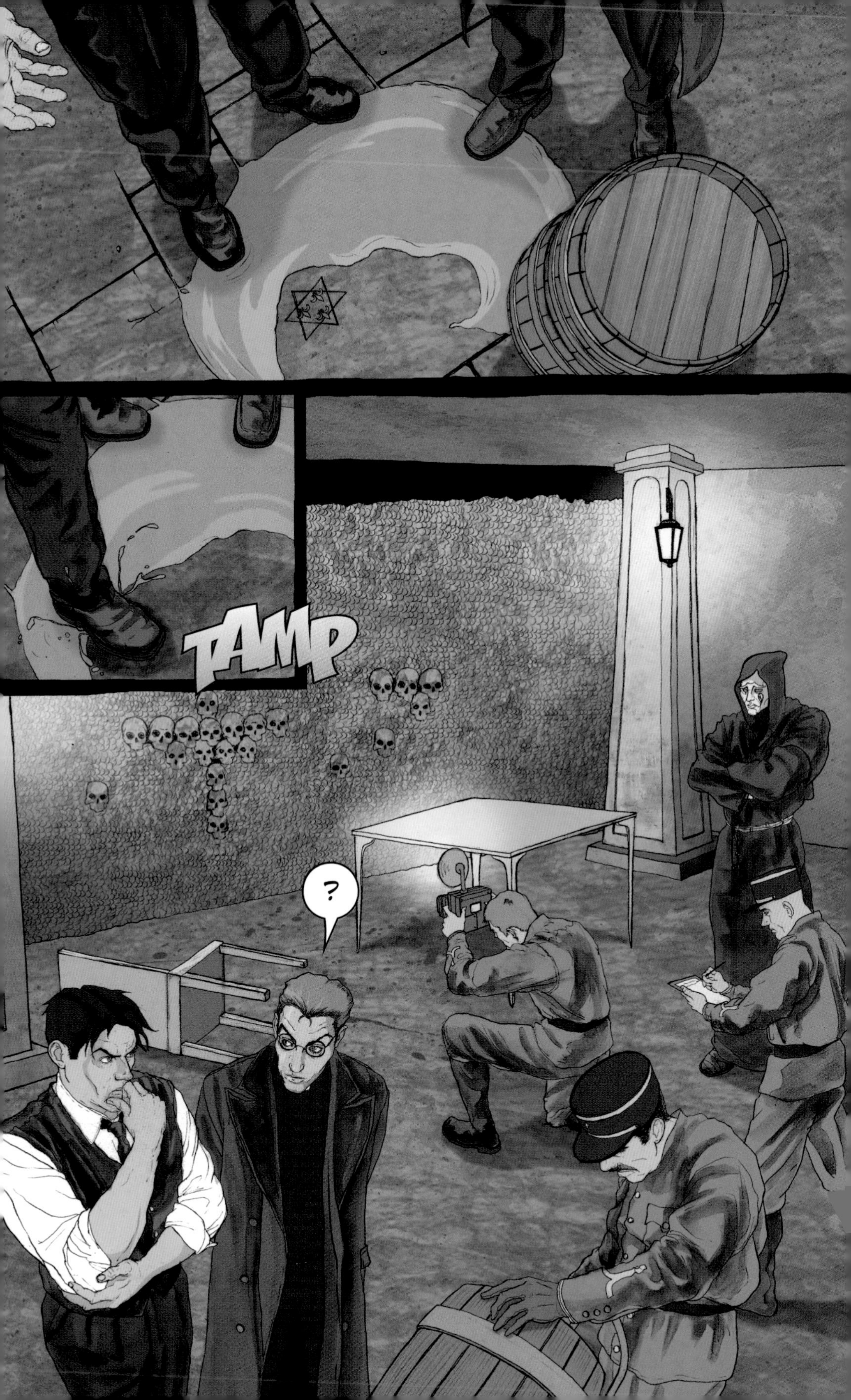
TAMP
?

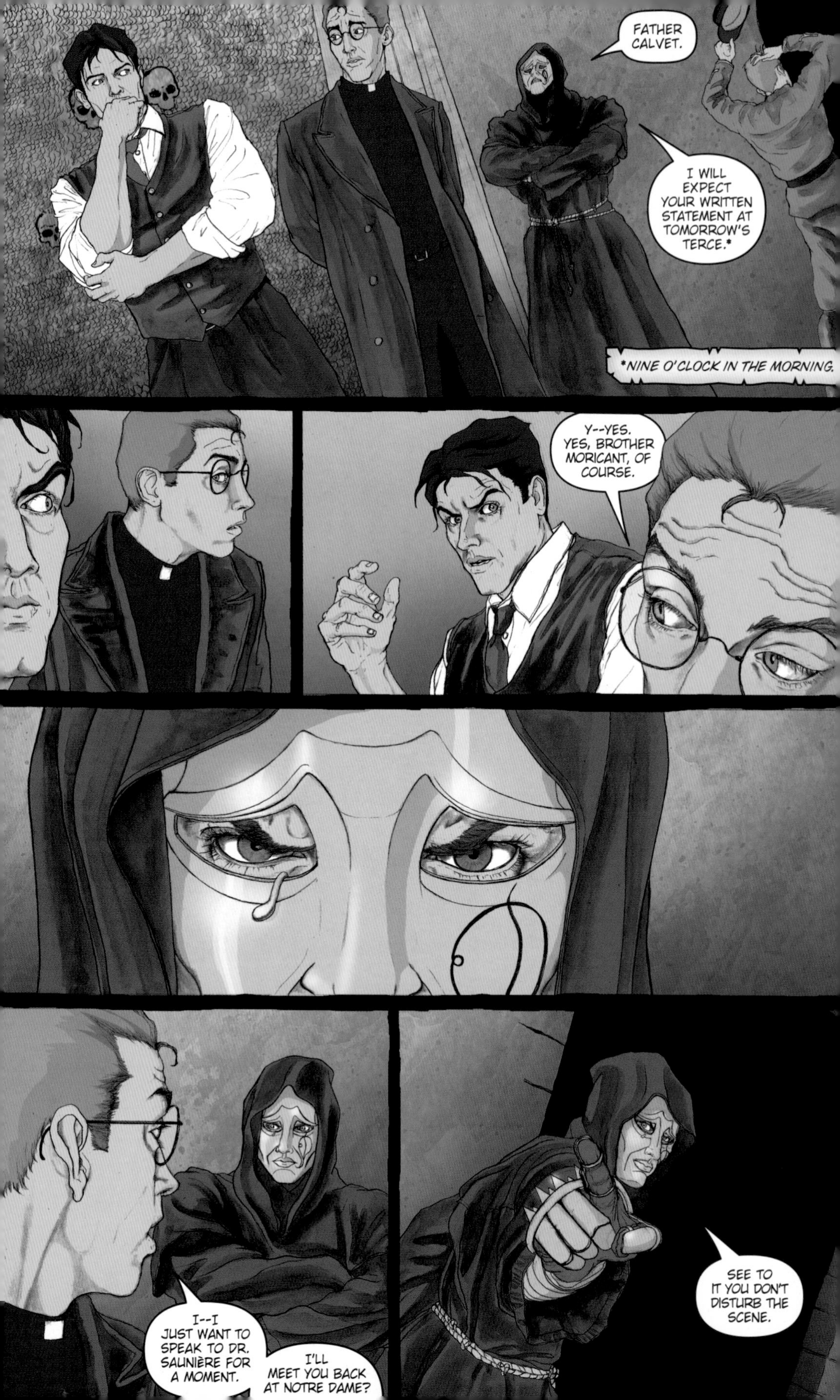
FATHER CALVET.
I WILL EXPECT YOUR WRITTEN STATEMENT AT TOMORROW'S TERCE.*
*NINE O'CLOCK IN THE MORNING.
Y--YES. YES, BROTHER MORICANT, OF COURSE.
I--I JUST WANT TO SPEAK TO DR. SAUNIÈRE FOR A MOMENT.
I'LL MEET YOU BACK AT NOTRE DAME?
SEE TO IT YOU DON'T DISTURB THE SCENE.

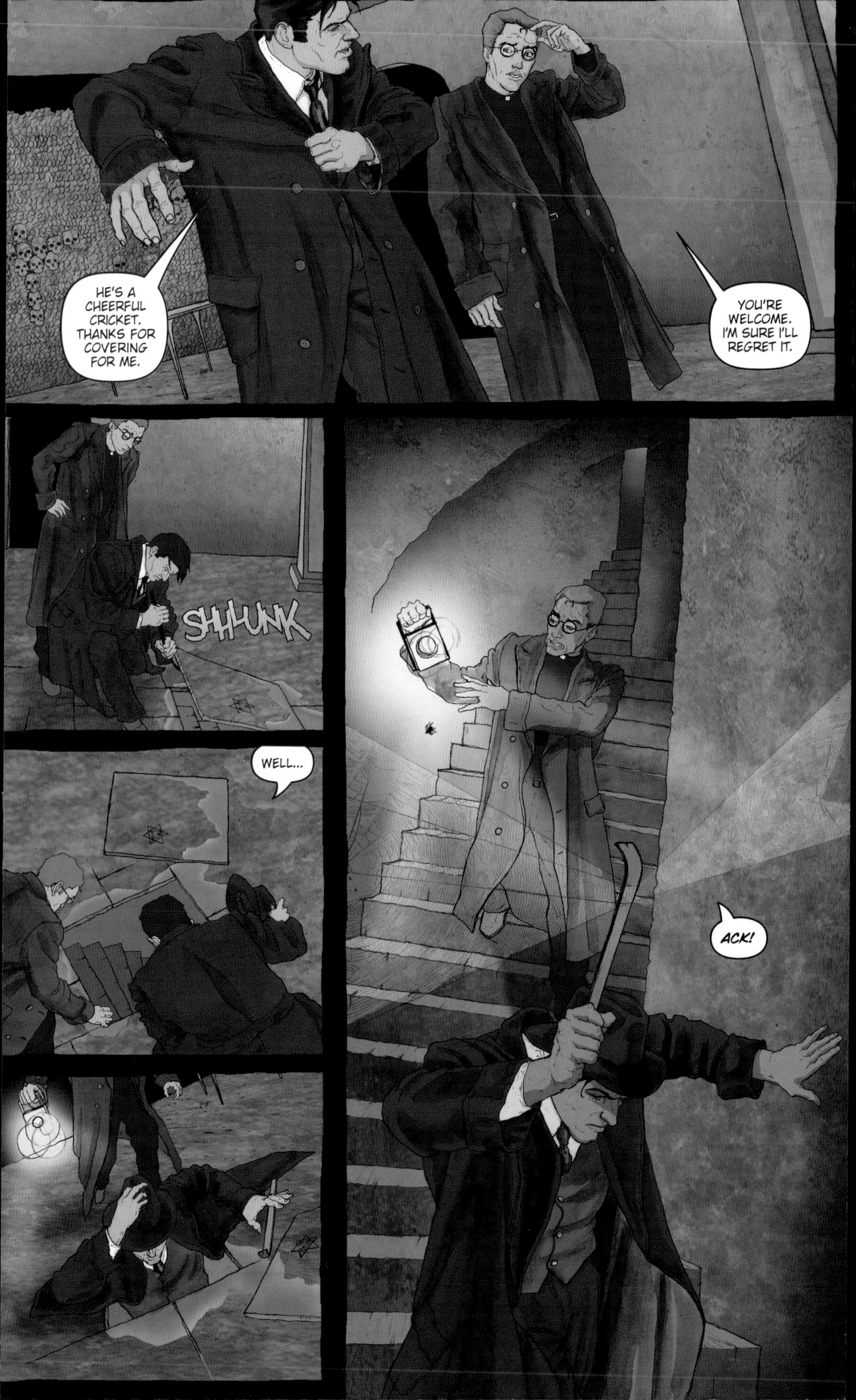
HE'S A CHEERFUL CRICKET. THANKS FOR COVERING FOR ME.
YOU'RE WELCOME. I'M SURE I'LL REGRET IT.
SHHLUNK
WELL...
ACK!

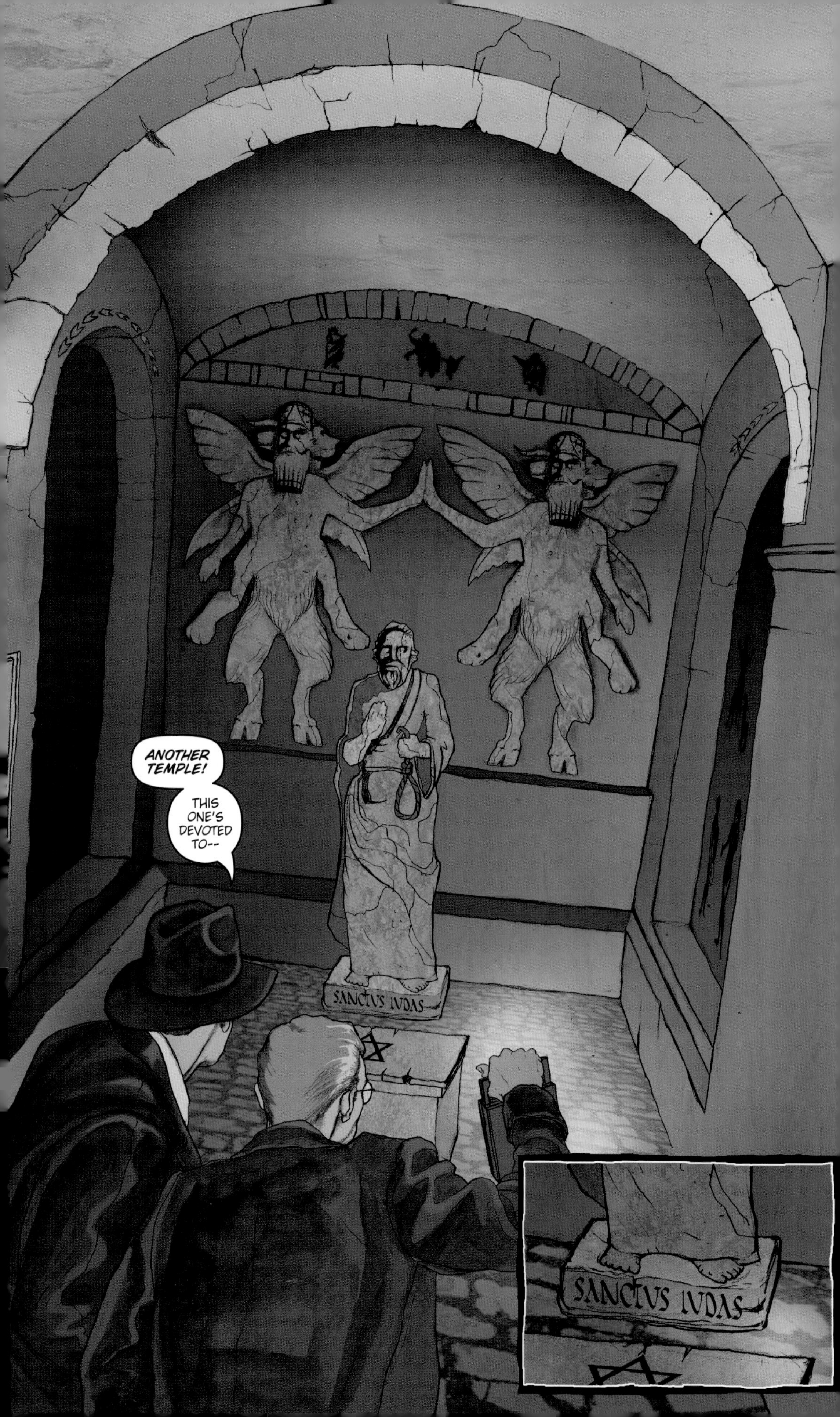
ANOTHER TEMPLE!
THIS ONE'S DEVOTED TO--
SANCTUS IUDAS
SANCTUS IUDAS

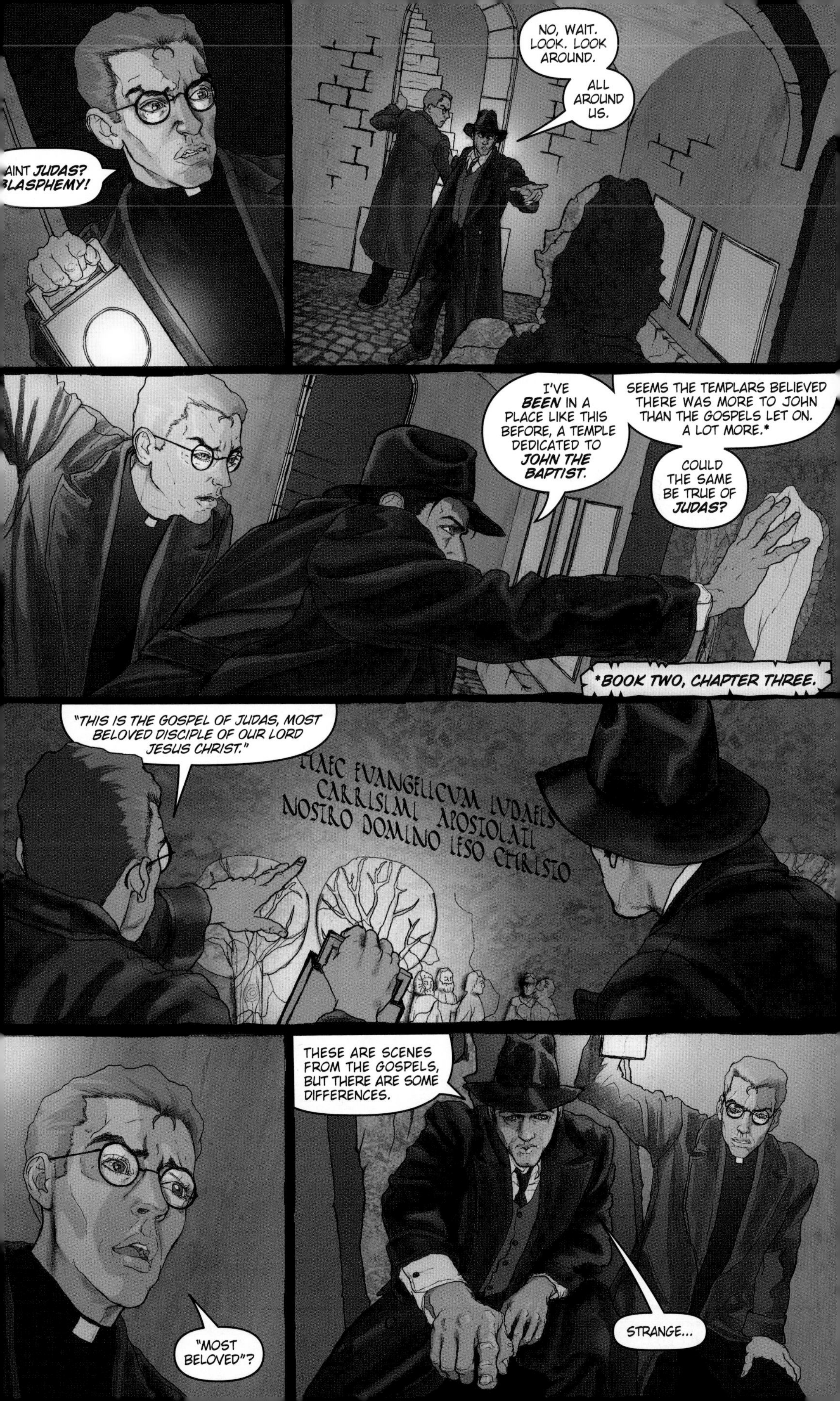

AINT JUDAS? BLASPHEMY!
NO, WAIT. LOOK. LOOK AROUND.
ALL AROUND US.
I'VE BEEN IN A PLACE LIKE THIS BEFORE, A TEMPLE DEDICATED TO JOHN THE BAPTIST.
SEEMS THE TEMPLARS BELIEVED THERE WAS MORE TO JOHN THAN THE GOSPELS LET ON. A LOT MORE.*
COULD THE SAME BE TRUE OF JUDAS?
*BOOK TWO, CHAPTER THREE.
"THIS IS THE GOSPEL OF JUDAS, MOST BELOVED DISCIPLE OF OUR LORD JESUS CHRIST."
HAEC EVANGELICUM IUDAEIS CARRISIMI APOSTOLATI NOSTRO DOMINO IESO CHRISTO
"MOST BELOVED"?
THESE ARE SCENES FROM THE GOSPELS, BUT THERE ARE SOME DIFFERENCES.
STRANGE...

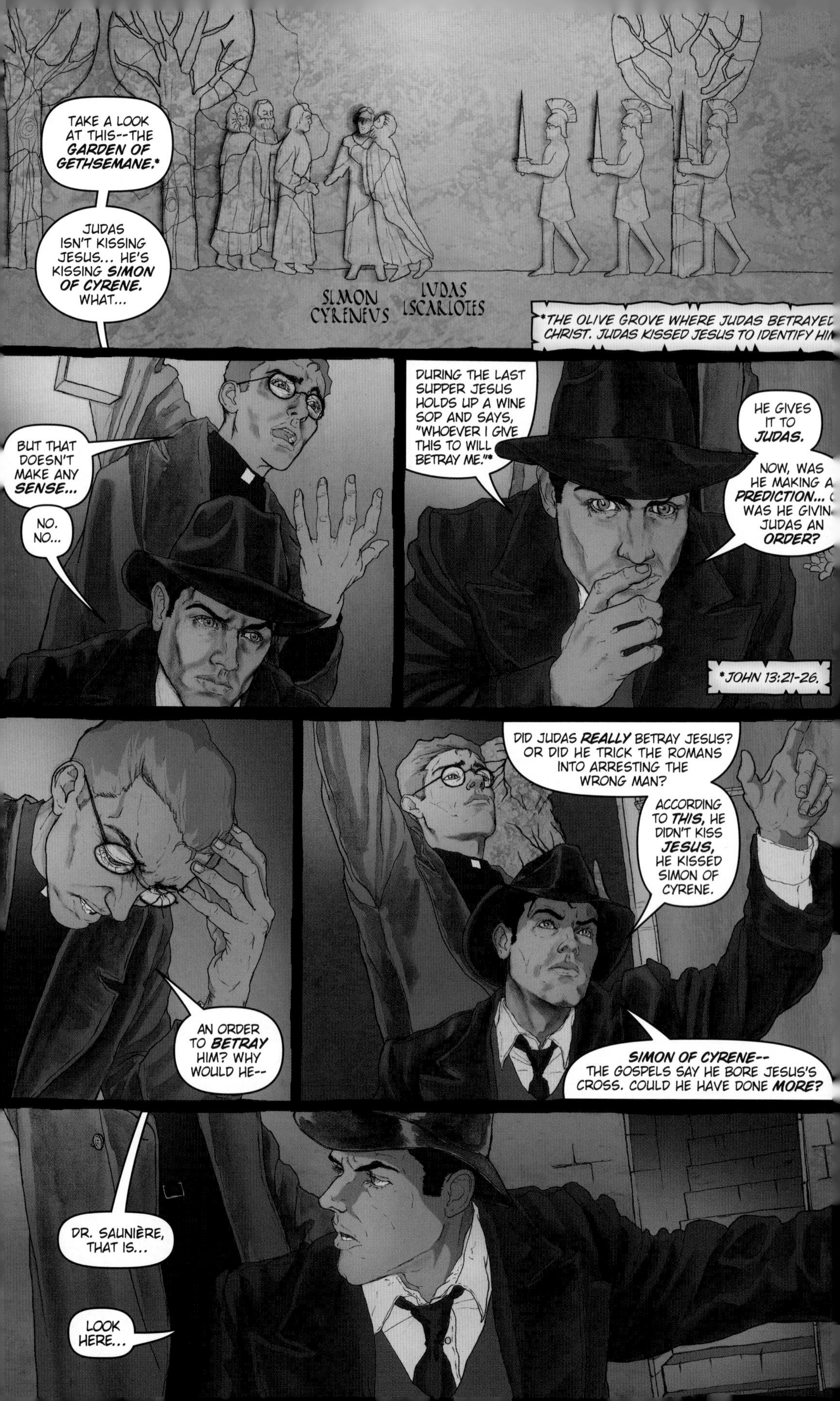

TAKE A LOOK AT THIS--THE GARDEN OF GETHSEMANE.*
JUDAS ISN'T KISSING JESUS... HE'S KISSING SIMON OF CYRENE. WHAT...
SIMON CYRENEVS
IVDAS ISCARIOTES
*THE OLIVE GROVE WHERE JUDAS BETRAYED CHRIST. JUDAS KISSED JESUS TO IDENTIFY HIM
BUT THAT DOESN'T MAKE ANY SENSE...
NO. NO...
DURING THE LAST SUPPER JESUS HOLDS UP A WINE SOP AND SAYS, "WHOEVER I GIVE THIS TO WILL BETRAY ME."*
HE GIVES IT TO JUDAS.
NOW, WAS HE MAKING A PREDICTION... OR WAS HE GIVING JUDAS AN ORDER?
*JOHN 13:21-26.
AN ORDER TO BETRAY HIM? WHY WOULD HE--
DID JUDAS REALLY BETRAY JESUS? OR DID HE TRICK THE ROMANS INTO ARRESTING THE WRONG MAN?
ACCORDING TO THIS, HE DIDN'T KISS JESUS, HE KISSED SIMON OF CYRENE.
SIMON OF CYRENE-- THE GOSPELS SAY HE BORE JESUS'S CROSS. COULD HE HAVE DONE MORE?
DR. SAUNIÈRE, THAT IS...
LOOK HERE...

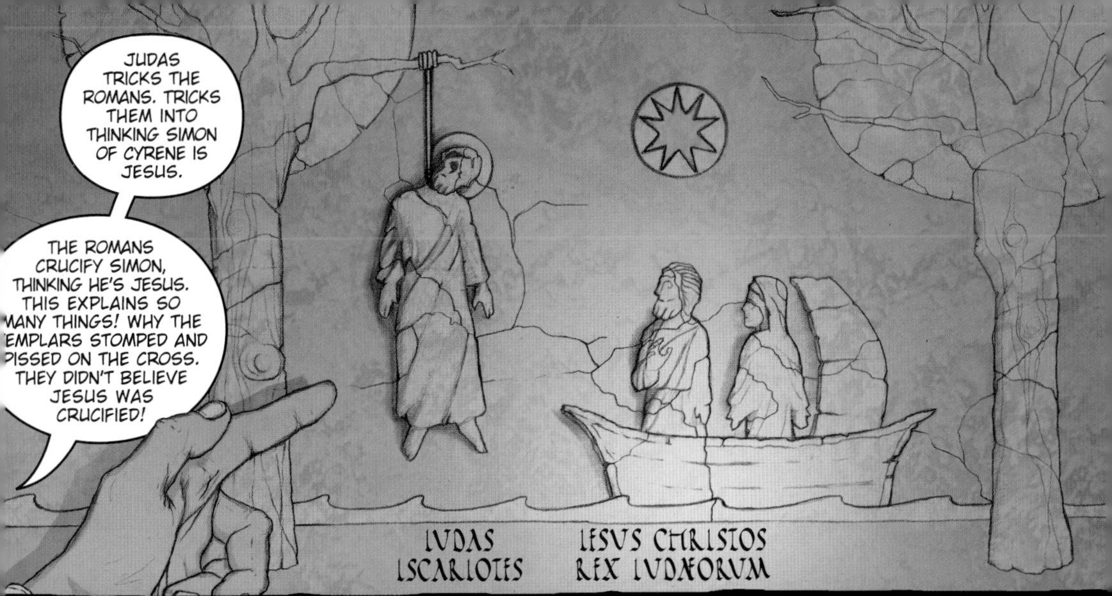
JUDAS TRICKS THE ROMANS. TRICKS THEM INTO THINKING SIMON OF CYRENE IS JESUS.
THE ROMANS CRUCIFY SIMON, THINKING HE'S JESUS. THIS EXPLAINS SO MANY THINGS! WHY THE TEMPLARS STOMPED AND PISSED ON THE CROSS. THEY DIDN'T BELIEVE JESUS WAS CRUCIFIED!
IVDAS ISCARIOTES
IESVS CHRISTOS REX IVDÆORVM

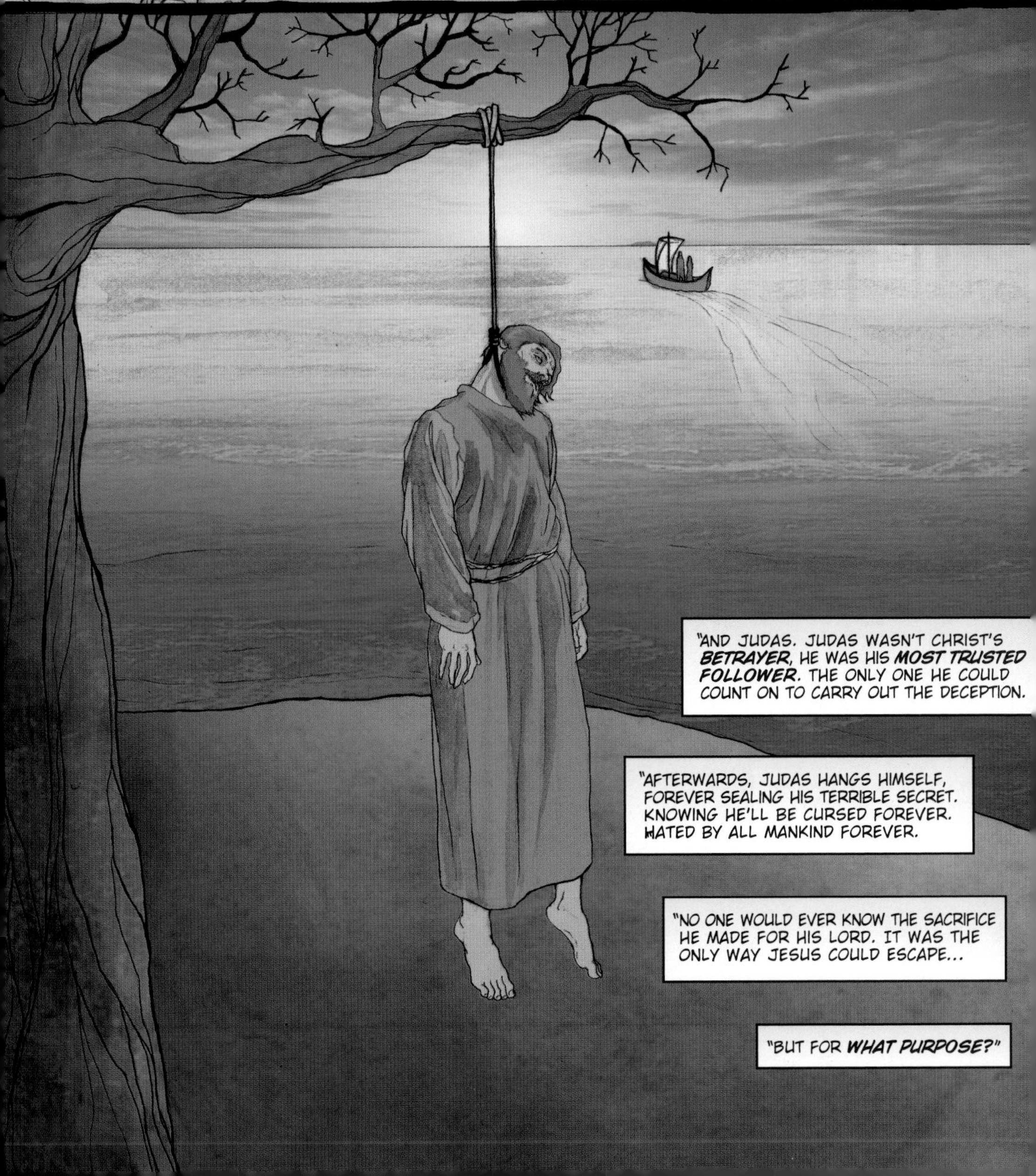
"AND JUDAS. JUDAS WASN'T CHRIST'S ***BETRAYER***, HE WAS HIS ***MOST TRUSTED FOLLOWER***. THE ONLY ONE HE COULD COUNT ON TO CARRY OUT THE DECEPTION.
"AFTERWARDS, JUDAS HANGS HIMSELF, FOREVER SEALING HIS TERRIBLE SECRET. KNOWING HE'LL BE CURSED FOREVER. HATED BY ALL MANKIND FOREVER.
"NO ONE WOULD EVER KNOW THE SACRIFICE HE MADE FOR HIS LORD. IT WAS THE ONLY WAY JESUS COULD ESCAPE...
"BUT FOR ***WHAT PURPOSE?***"

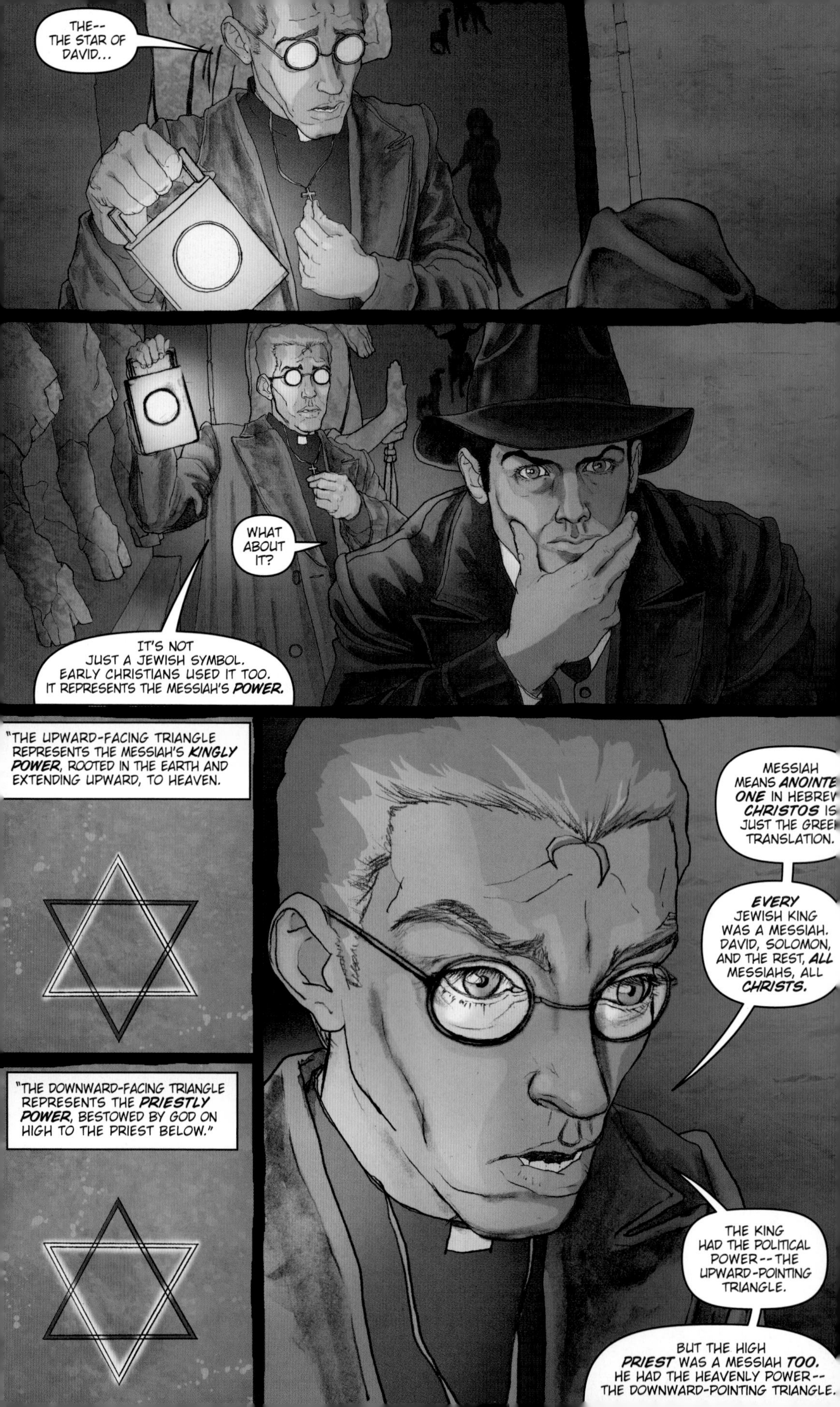

THE-- THE STAR OF DAVID...
WHAT ABOUT IT?
IT'S NOT JUST A JEWISH SYMBOL. EARLY CHRISTIANS USED IT TOO. IT REPRESENTS THE MESSIAH'S *POWER.*
"THE UPWARD-FACING TRIANGLE REPRESENTS THE MESSIAH'S *KINGLY POWER*, ROOTED IN THE EARTH AND EXTENDING UPWARD, TO HEAVEN.
MESSIAH MEANS *ANOINTE ONE* IN HEBREV *CHRISTOS* IS JUST THE GREE TRANSLATION.
EVERY JEWISH KING WAS A MESSIAH. DAVID, SOLOMON, AND THE REST, *ALL* MESSIAHS, ALL *CHRISTS.*
"THE DOWNWARD-FACING TRIANGLE REPRESENTS THE *PRIESTLY POWER*, BESTOWED BY GOD ON HIGH TO THE PRIEST BELOW."
THE KING HAD THE POLITICAL POWER--THE UPWARD-POINTING TRIANGLE.
BUT THE HIGH *PRIEST* WAS A MESSIAH *TOO.* HE HAD THE HEAVENLY POWER-- THE DOWNWARD-POINTING TRIANGLE.

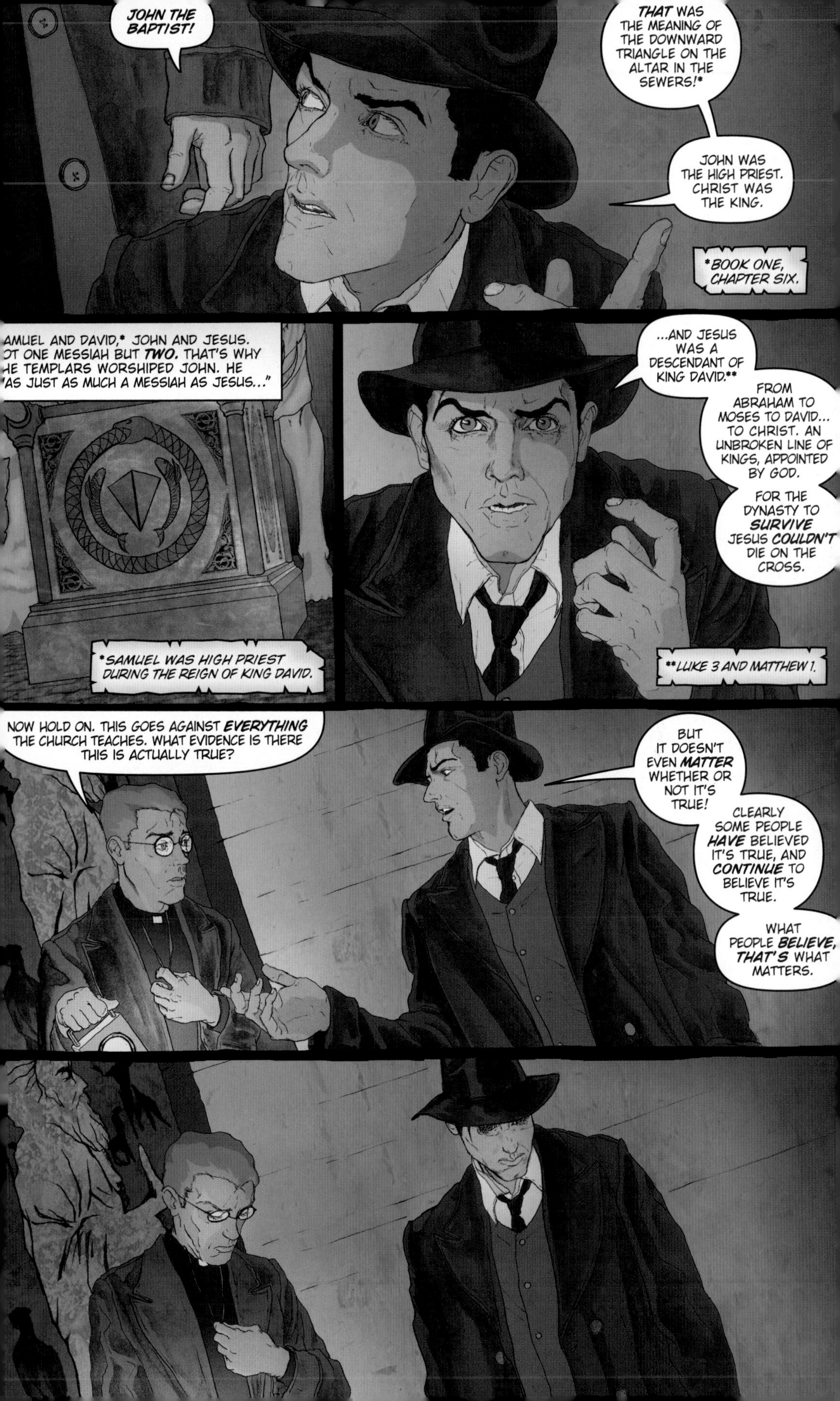

JOHN THE BAPTIST!
THAT WAS THE MEANING OF THE DOWNWARD TRIANGLE ON THE ALTAR IN THE SEWERS!*
JOHN WAS THE HIGH PRIEST. CHRIST WAS THE KING.
*BOOK ONE, CHAPTER SIX.
AMUEL AND DAVID,* JOHN AND JESUS. OT ONE MESSIAH BUT TWO. THAT'S WHY HE TEMPLARS WORSHIPED JOHN. HE AS JUST AS MUCH A MESSIAH AS JESUS..."
*SAMUEL WAS HIGH PRIEST DURING THE REIGN OF KING DAVID.
...AND JESUS WAS A DESCENDANT OF KING DAVID.**
FROM ABRAHAM TO MOSES TO DAVID... TO CHRIST. AN UNBROKEN LINE OF KINGS, APPOINTED BY GOD.
FOR THE DYNASTY TO SURVIVE JESUS COULDN'T DIE ON THE CROSS.
**LUKE 3 AND MATTHEW 1.
NOW HOLD ON. THIS GOES AGAINST EVERYTHING THE CHURCH TEACHES. WHAT EVIDENCE IS THERE THIS IS ACTUALLY TRUE?
BUT IT DOESN'T EVEN MATTER WHETHER OR NOT IT'S TRUE!
CLEARLY SOME PEOPLE HAVE BELIEVED IT'S TRUE, AND CONTINUE TO BELIEVE IT'S TRUE.
WHAT PEOPLE BELIEVE, THAT'S WHAT MATTERS.

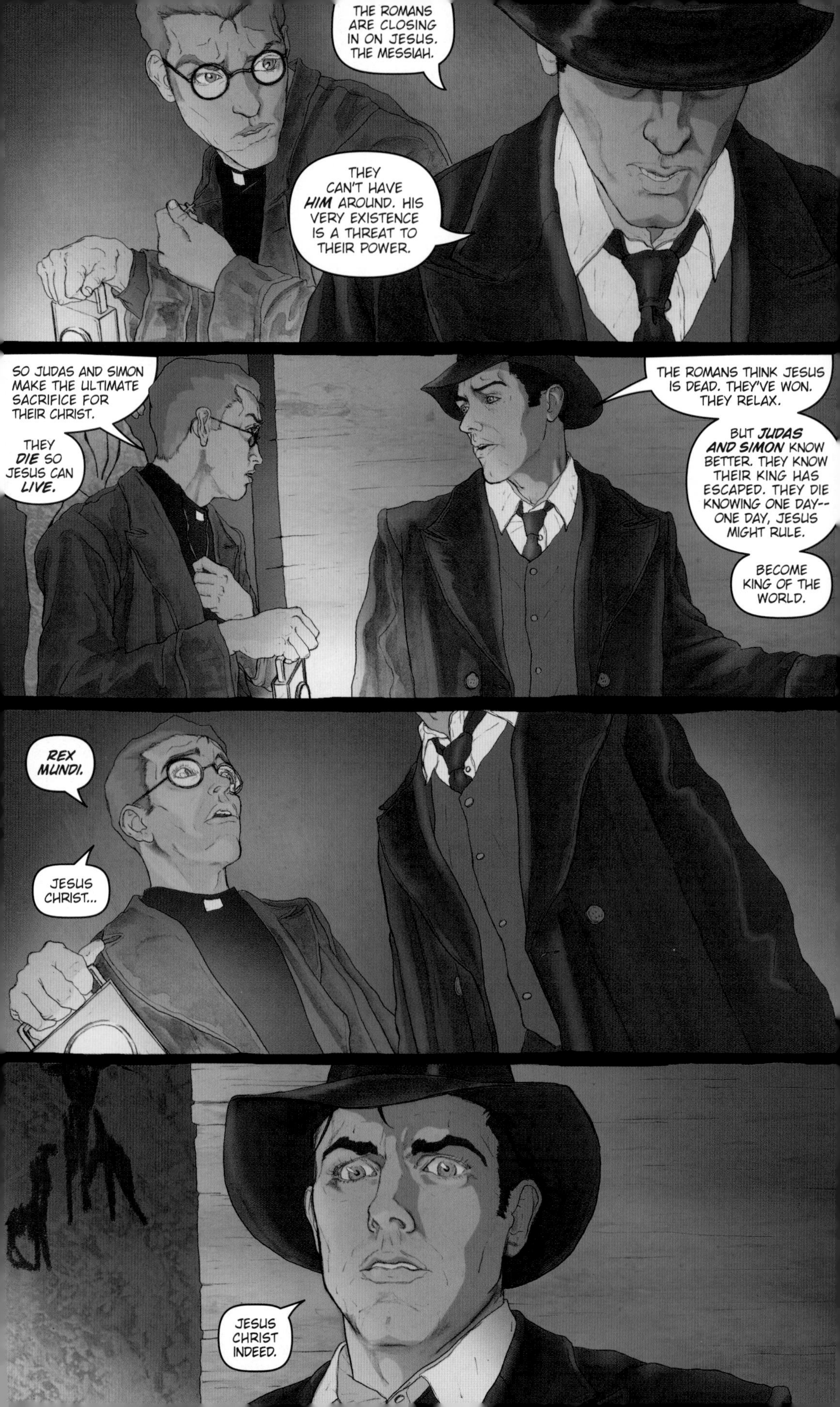
THE ROMANS ARE CLOSING IN ON JESUS. THE MESSIAH.
THEY CAN'T HAVE **HIM** AROUND. HIS VERY EXISTENCE IS A THREAT TO THEIR POWER.
SO JUDAS AND SIMON MAKE THE ULTIMATE SACRIFICE FOR THEIR CHRIST.
THEY **DIE** SO JESUS CAN **LIVE.**
THE ROMANS THINK JESUS IS DEAD. THEY'VE WON. THEY RELAX.
BUT **JUDAS AND SIMON** KNOW BETTER. THEY KNOW THEIR KING HAS ESCAPED. THEY DIE KNOWING ONE DAY-- ONE DAY, JESUS MIGHT RULE.
BECOME KING OF THE WORLD.
REX MUNDI.
JESUS CHRIST...
JESUS CHRIST INDEED.

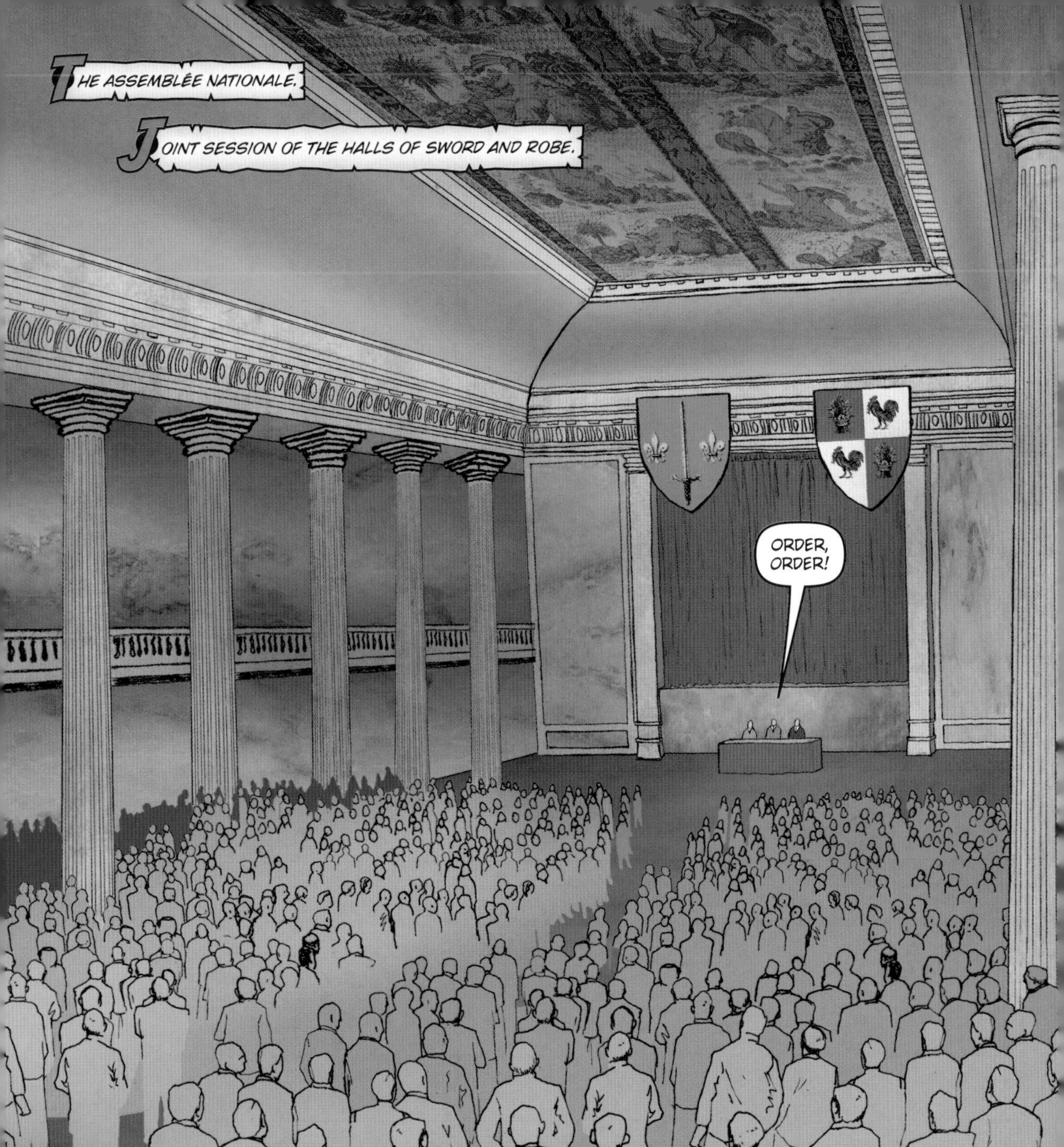
THE ASSEMBLÉE NATIONALE.
JOINT SESSION OF THE HALLS OF SWORD AND ROBE.
ORDER, ORDER!

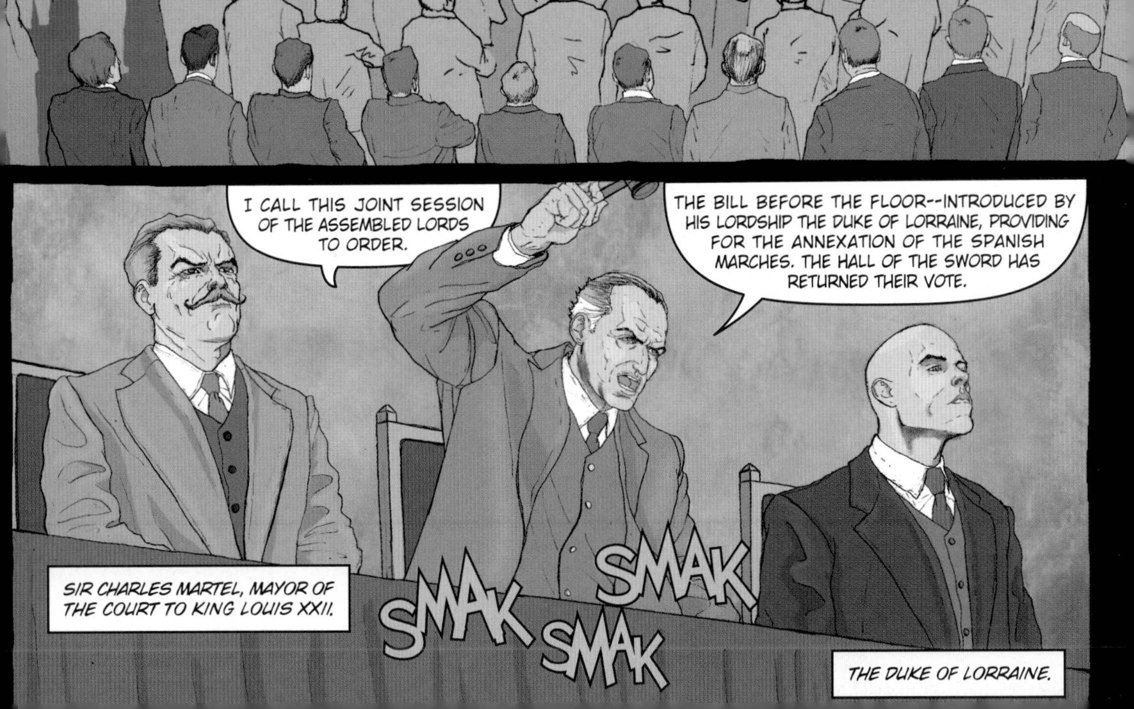
I CALL THIS JOINT SESSION OF THE ASSEMBLED LORDS TO ORDER.
THE BILL BEFORE THE FLOOR--INTRODUCED BY HIS LORDSHIP THE DUKE OF LORRAINE, PROVIDING FOR THE ANNEXATION OF THE SPANISH MARCHES. THE HALL OF THE SWORD HAS RETURNED THEIR VOTE.
SIR CHARLES MARTEL, MAYOR OF THE COURT TO KING LOUIS XXII.
SMAK
SMAK
SMAK
THE DUKE OF LORRAINE.

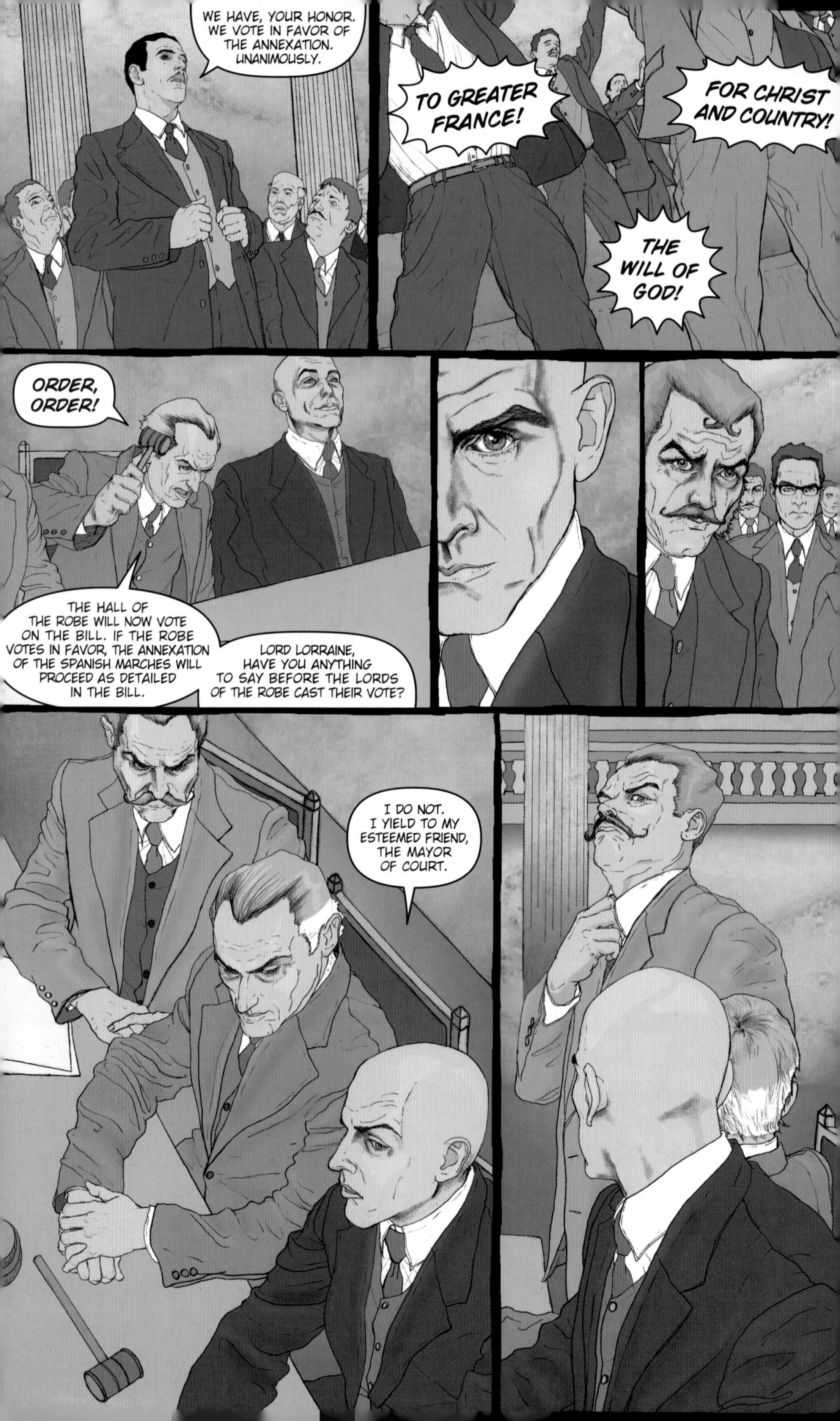
WE HAVE, YOUR HONOR. WE VOTE IN FAVOR OF THE ANNEXATION. UNANIMOUSLY.
TO GREATER FRANCE!
FOR CHRIST AND COUNTRY!
THE WILL OF GOD!
ORDER, ORDER!
THE HALL OF THE ROBE WILL NOW VOTE ON THE BILL. IF THE ROBE VOTES IN FAVOR, THE ANNEXATION OF THE SPANISH MARCHES WILL PROCEED AS DETAILED IN THE BILL.
LORD LORRAINE, HAVE YOU ANYTHING TO SAY BEFORE THE LORDS OF THE ROBE CAST THEIR VOTE?
I DO NOT. I YIELD TO MY ESTEEMED FRIEND, THE MAYOR OF COURT.

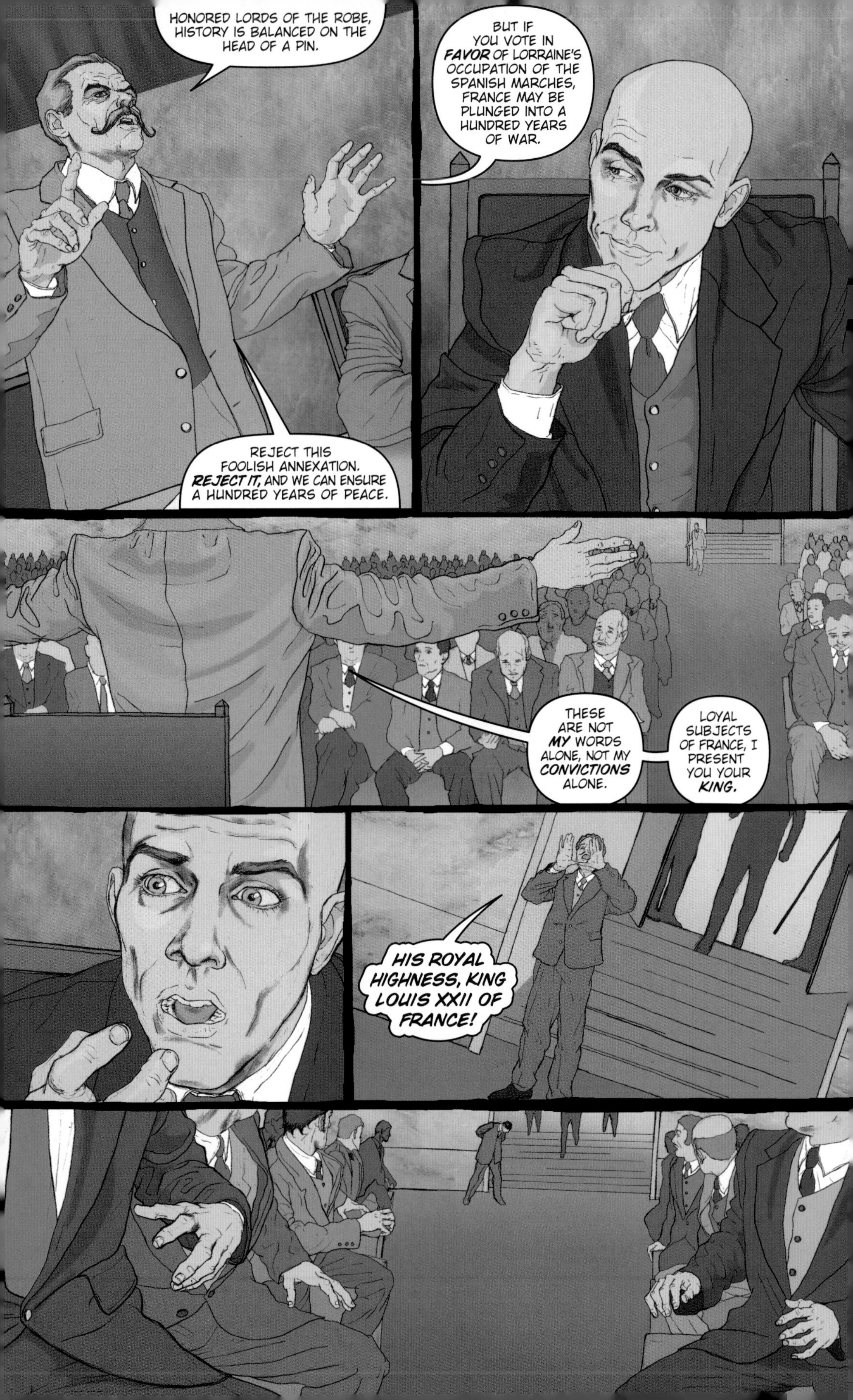
HONORED LORDS OF THE ROBE, HISTORY IS BALANCED ON THE HEAD OF A PIN.
REJECT THIS FOOLISH ANNEXATION. REJECT IT, AND WE CAN ENSURE A HUNDRED YEARS OF PEACE.
BUT IF YOU VOTE IN FAVOR OF LORRAINE'S OCCUPATION OF THE SPANISH MARCHES, FRANCE MAY BE PLUNGED INTO A HUNDRED YEARS OF WAR.
THESE ARE NOT MY WORDS ALONE, NOT MY CONVICTIONS ALONE.
LOYAL SUBJECTS OF FRANCE, I PRESENT YOU YOUR KING.
HIS ROYAL HIGHNESS, KING LOUIS XXII OF FRANCE!

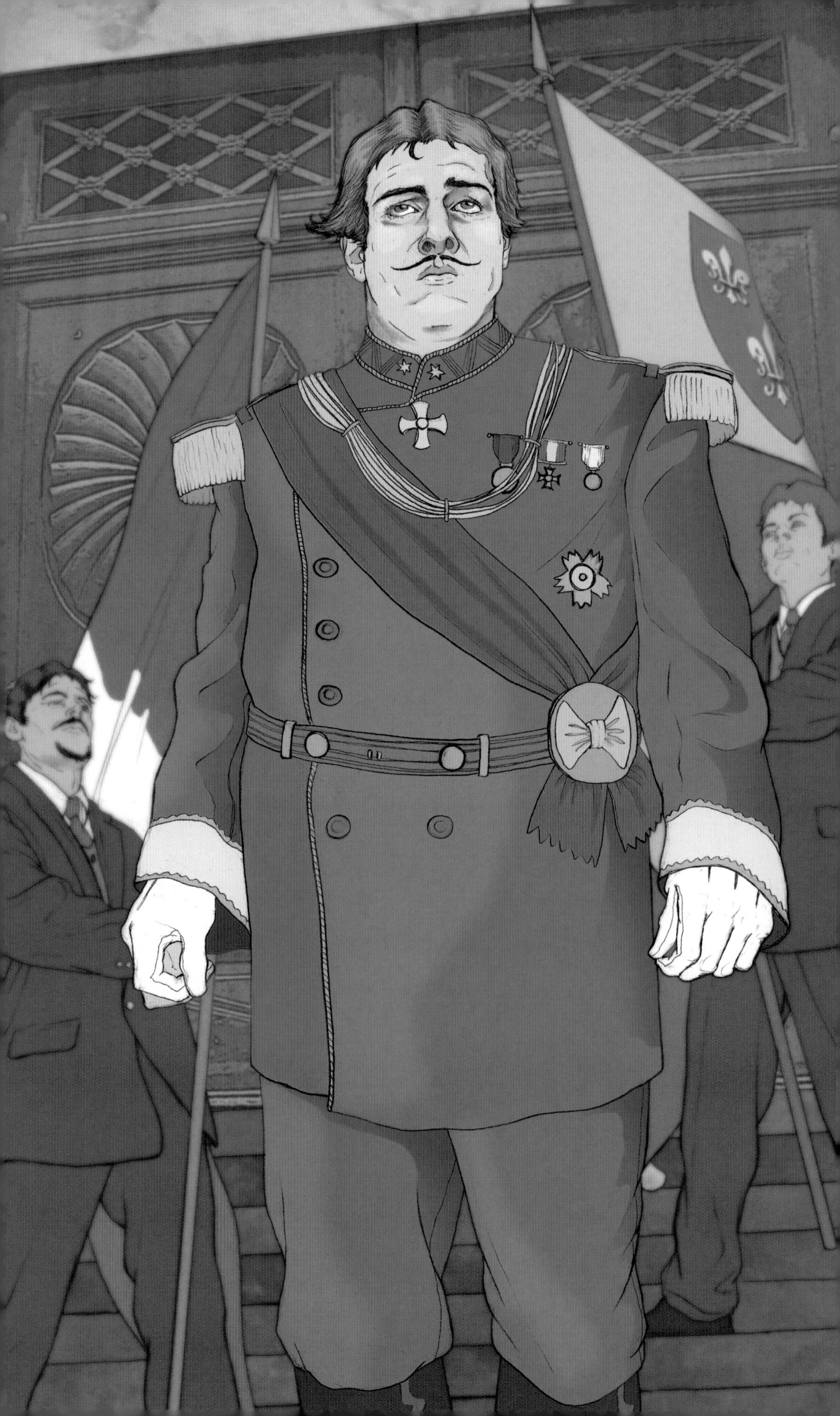

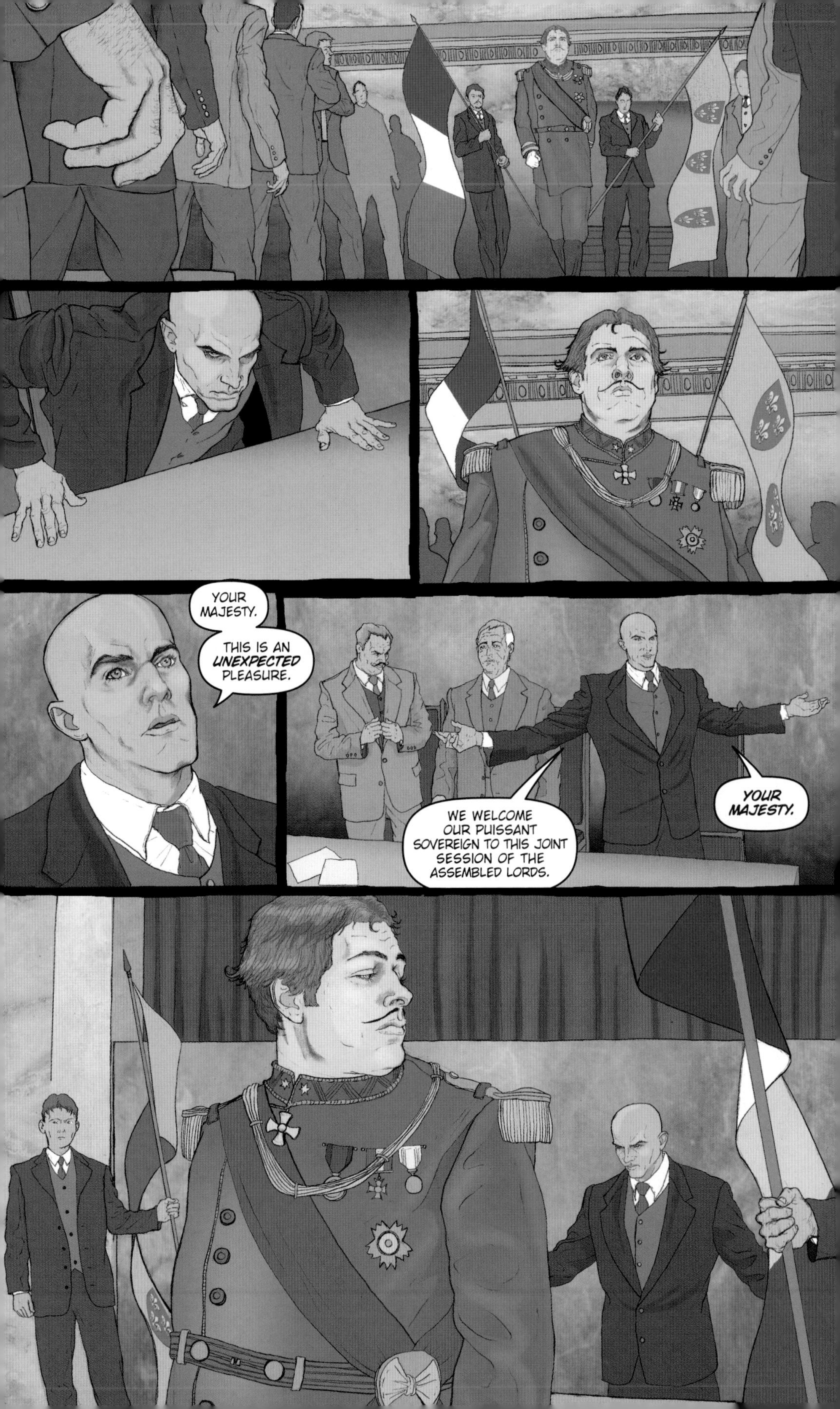
YOUR MAJESTY.
THIS IS AN *UNEXPECTED* PLEASURE.
WE WELCOME OUR PUISSANT SOVEREIGN TO THIS JOINT SESSION OF THE ASSEMBLED LORDS.
YOUR MAJESTY.

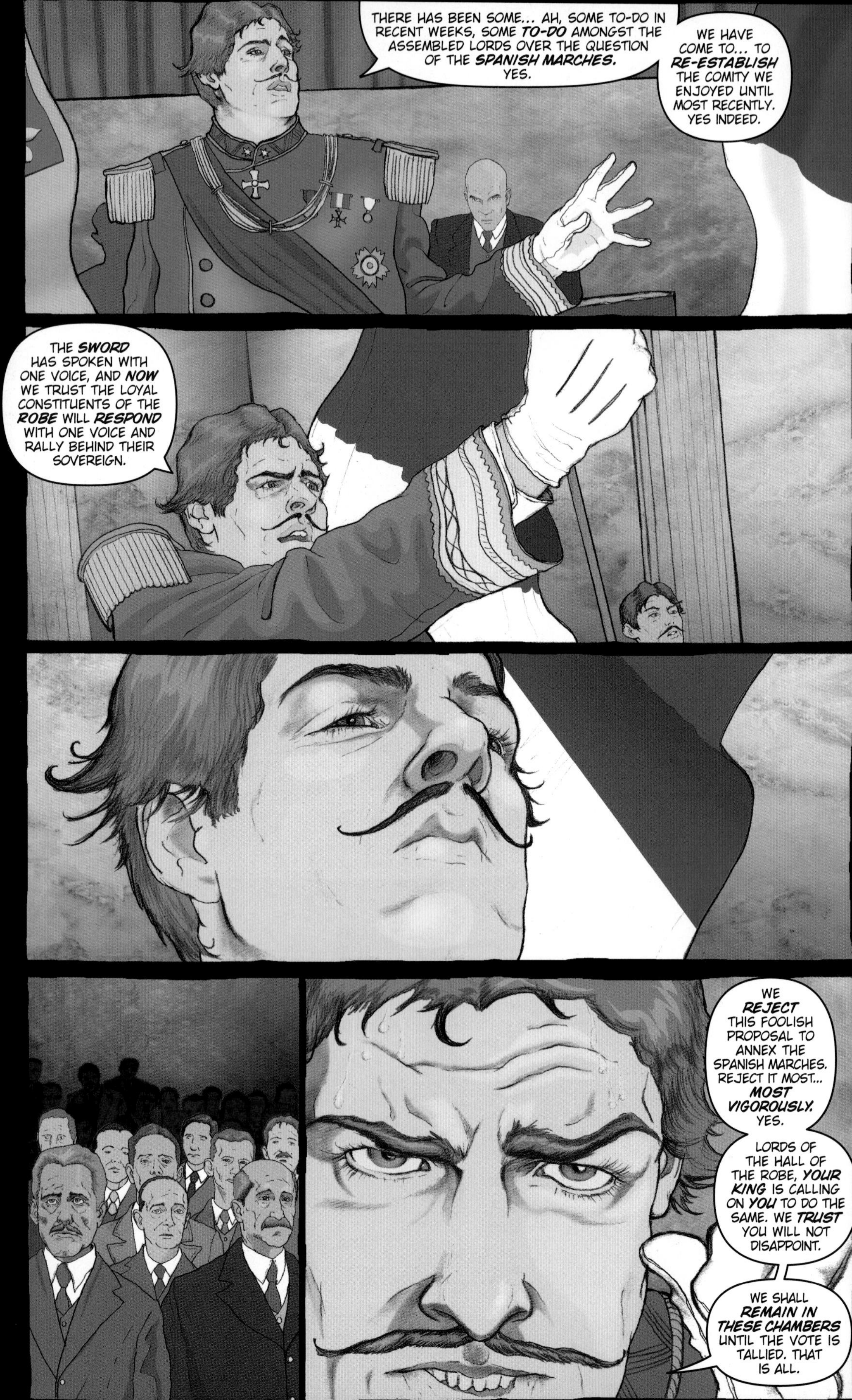

THERE HAS BEEN SOME... AH, SOME TO-DO IN RECENT WEEKS, SOME TO-DO AMONGST THE ASSEMBLED LORDS OVER THE QUESTION OF THE SPANISH MARCHES. YES.
WE HAVE COME TO... TO RE-ESTABLISH THE COMITY WE ENJOYED UNTIL MOST RECENTLY. YES INDEED.
THE SWORD HAS SPOKEN WITH ONE VOICE, AND NOW WE TRUST THE LOYAL CONSTITUENTS OF THE ROBE WILL RESPOND WITH ONE VOICE AND RALLY BEHIND THEIR SOVEREIGN.
WE REJECT THIS FOOLISH PROPOSAL TO ANNEX THE SPANISH MARCHES. REJECT IT MOST... MOST VIGOROUSLY. YES.
LORDS OF THE HALL OF THE ROBE, YOUR KING IS CALLING ON YOU TO DO THE SAME. WE TRUST YOU WILL NOT DISAPPOINT.
WE SHALL REMAIN IN THESE CHAMBERS UNTIL THE VOTE IS TALLIED. THAT IS ALL.

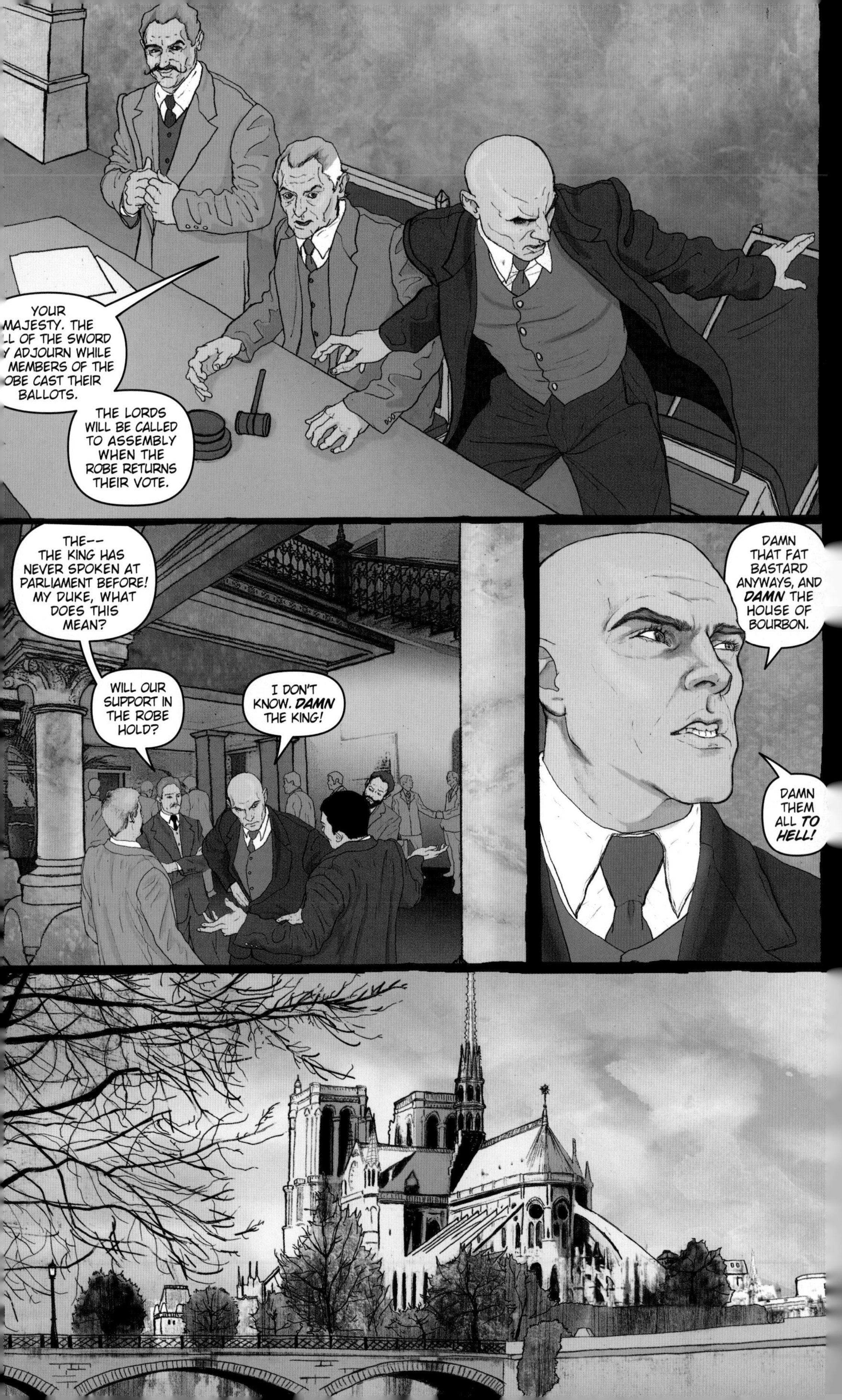

YOUR MAJESTY. THE L OF THE SWORD Y ADJOURN WHILE MEMBERS OF THE OBE CAST THEIR BALLOTS.
THE LORDS WILL BE CALLED TO ASSEMBLY WHEN THE ROBE RETURNS THEIR VOTE.
THE-- THE KING HAS NEVER SPOKEN AT PARLIAMENT BEFORE! MY DUKE, WHAT DOES THIS MEAN?
WILL OUR SUPPORT IN THE ROBE HOLD?
I DON'T KNOW. DAMN THE KING!
DAMN THAT FAT BASTARD ANYWAYS, AND DAMN THE HOUSE OF BOURBON.
DAMN THEM ALL TO HELL!

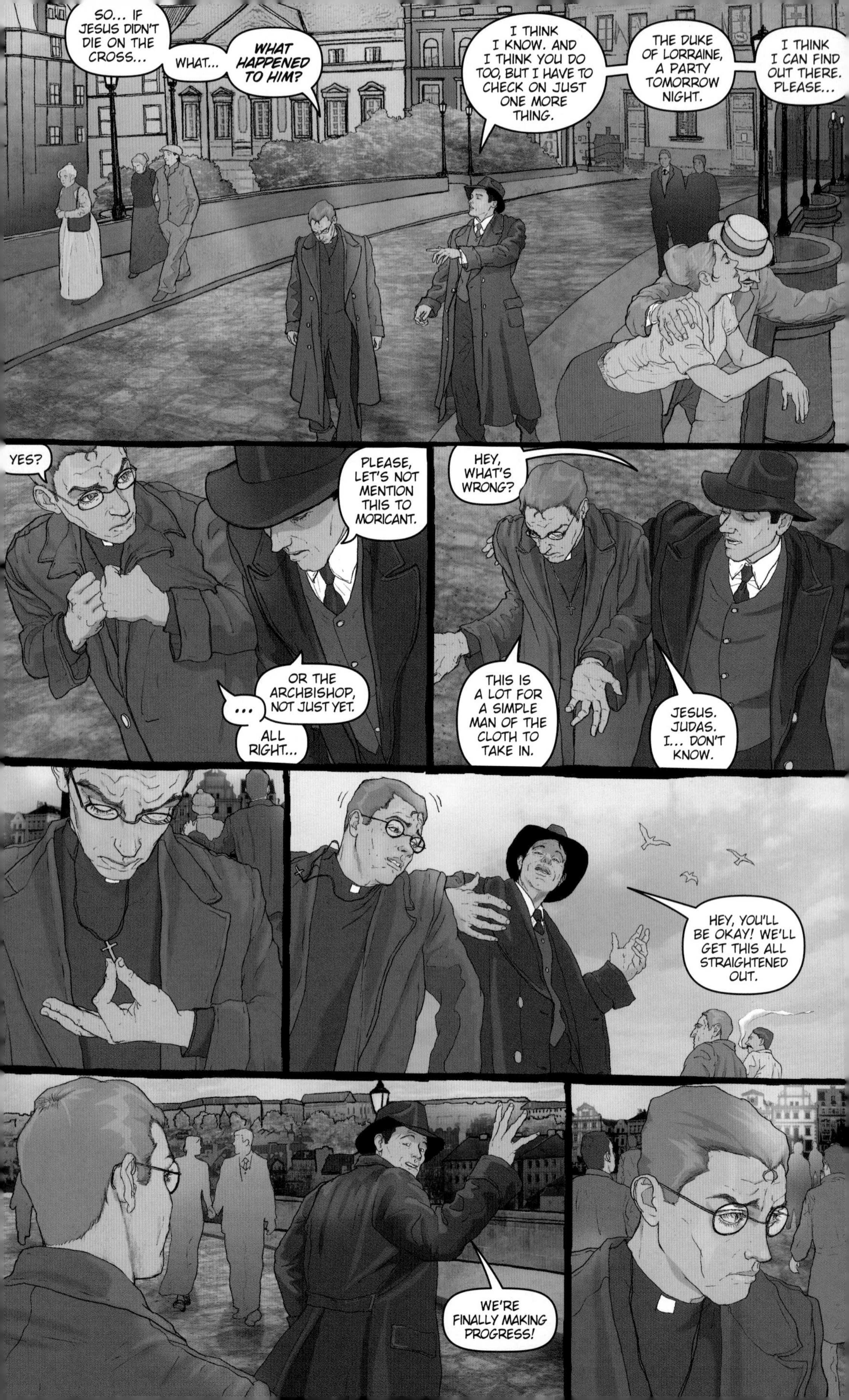
SO... IF JESUS DIDN'T DIE ON THE CROSS...
WHAT...
WHAT HAPPENED TO HIM?
I THINK I KNOW. AND I THINK YOU DO TOO, BUT I HAVE TO CHECK ON JUST ONE MORE THING.
THE DUKE OF LORRAINE, A PARTY TOMORROW NIGHT.
I THINK I CAN FIND OUT THERE. PLEASE...
YES?
PLEASE, LET'S NOT MENTION THIS TO MORICANT.
OR THE ARCHBISHOP, NOT JUST YET.
...
ALL RIGHT...
HEY, WHAT'S WRONG?
THIS IS A LOT FOR A SIMPLE MAN OF THE CLOTH TO TAKE IN.
JESUS. JUDAS. I... DON'T KNOW.
HEY, YOU'LL BE OKAY! WE'LL GET THIS ALL STRAIGHTENED OUT.
WE'RE FINALLY MAKING PROGRESS!

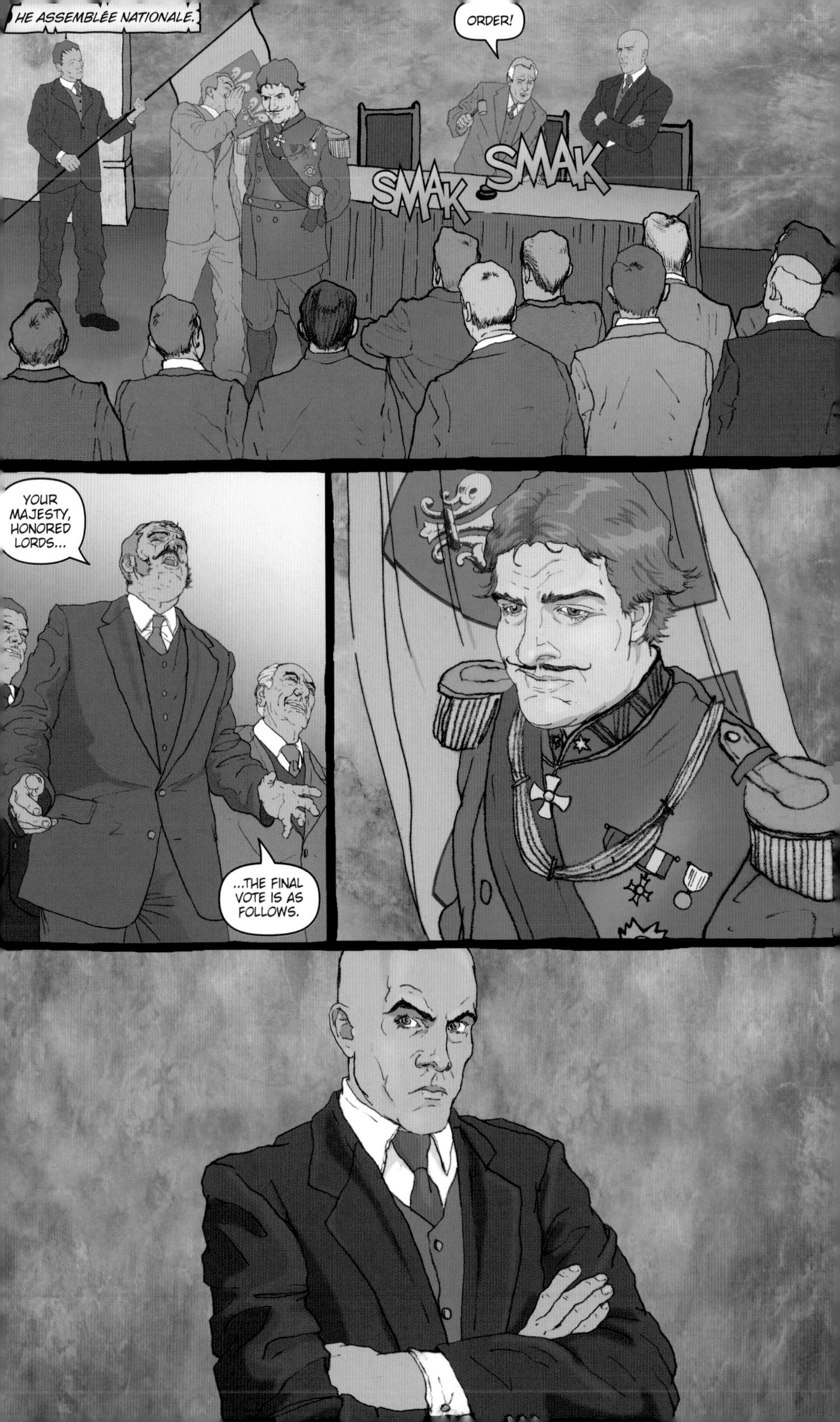
HE ASSEMBLÉE NATIONALE.
ORDER!
SMAK
SMAK
YOUR MAJESTY, HONORED LORDS...
...THE FINAL VOTE IS AS FOLLOWS.

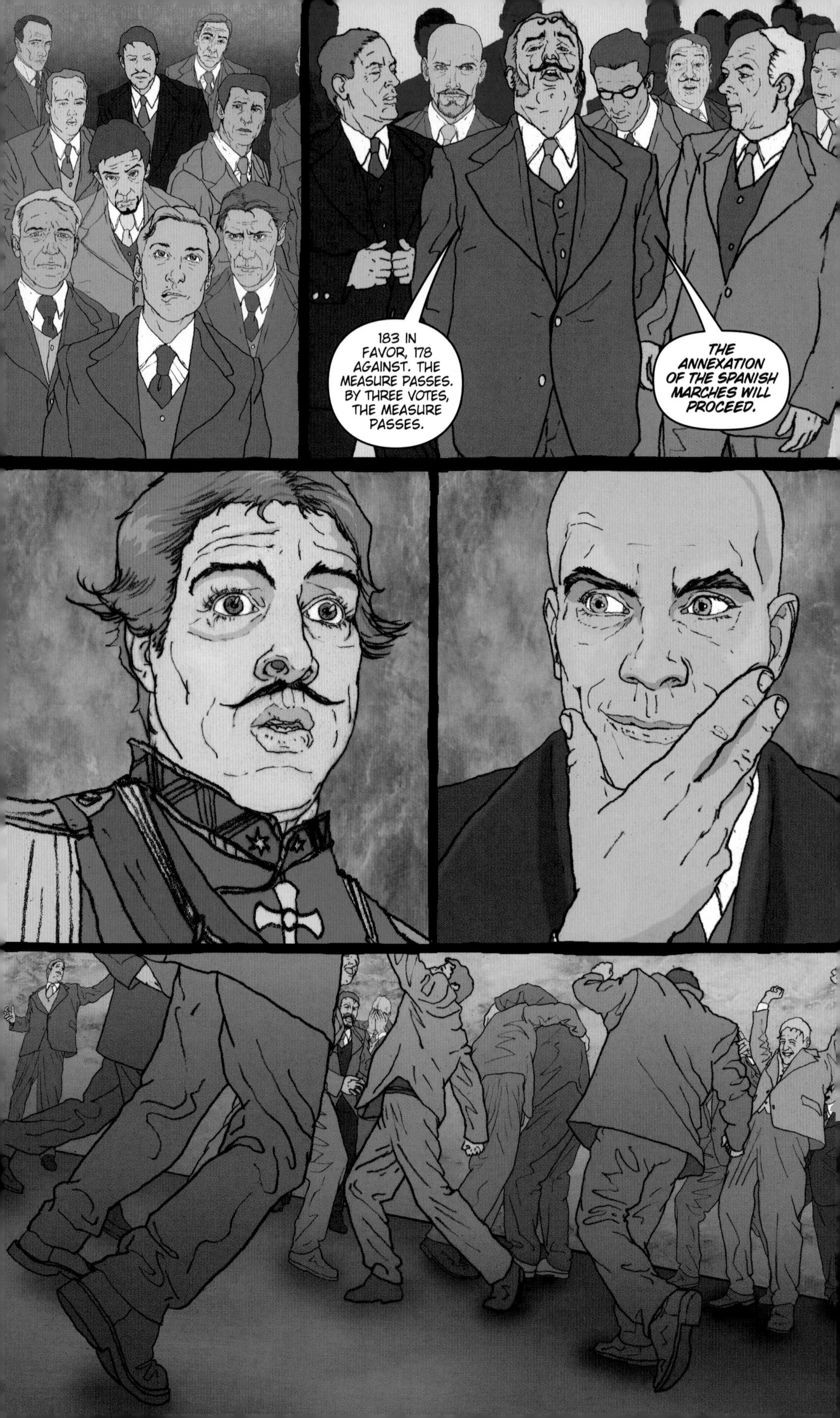
183 IN FAVOR, 178 AGAINST. THE MEASURE PASSES. BY THREE VOTES, THE MEASURE PASSES.
THE ANNEXATION OF THE SPANISH MARCHES WILL PROCEED.

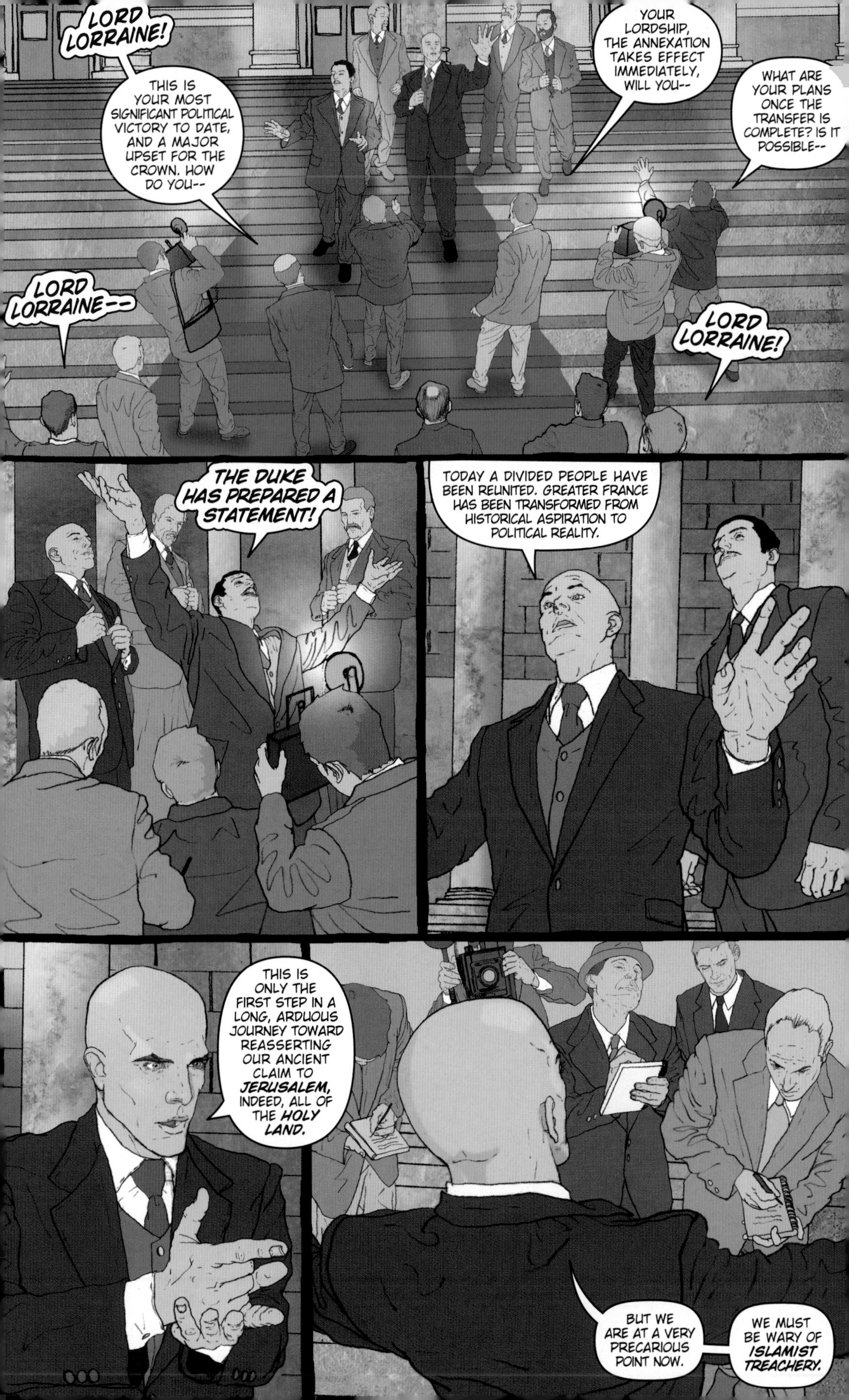
LORD LORRAINE!
THIS IS YOUR MOST SIGNIFICANT POLITICAL VICTORY TO DATE, AND A MAJOR UPSET FOR THE CROWN. HOW DO YOU--
YOUR LORDSHIP, THE ANNEXATION TAKES EFFECT IMMEDIATELY, WILL YOU--
WHAT ARE YOUR PLANS ONCE THE TRANSFER IS COMPLETE? IS IT POSSIBLE--
LORD LORRAINE--
LORD LORRAINE!
THE DUKE HAS PREPARED A STATEMENT!
TODAY A DIVIDED PEOPLE HAVE BEEN REUNITED. GREATER FRANCE HAS BEEN TRANSFORMED FROM HISTORICAL ASPIRATION TO POLITICAL REALITY.
THIS IS ONLY THE FIRST STEP IN A LONG, ARDUOUS JOURNEY TOWARD REASSERTING OUR ANCIENT CLAIM TO JERUSALEM, INDEED, ALL OF THE HOLY LAND.
BUT WE ARE AT A VERY PRECARIOUS POINT NOW.
WE MUST BE WARY OF ISLAMIST TREACHERY.

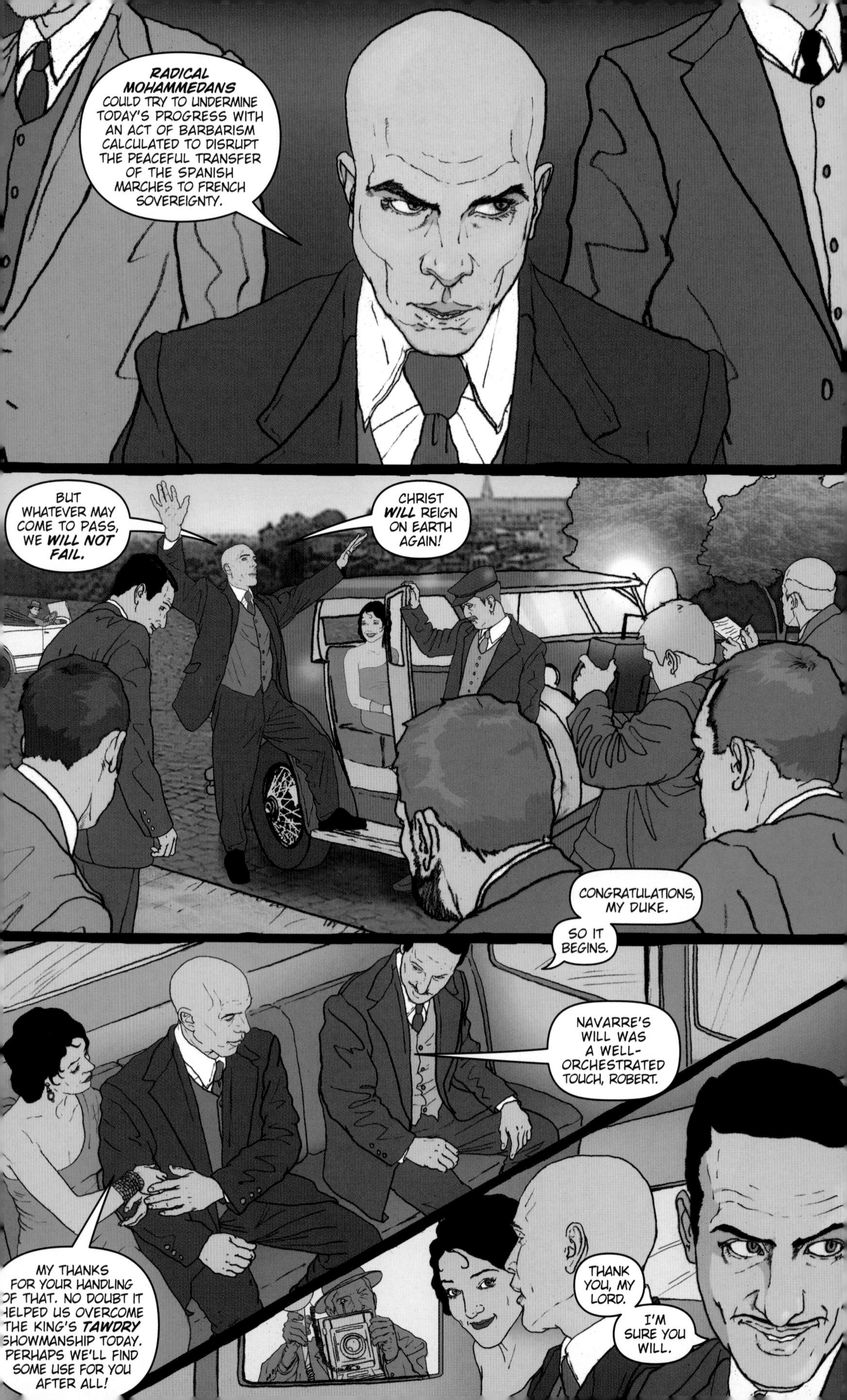
RADICAL MOHAMMEDANS COULD TRY TO UNDERMINE TODAY'S PROGRESS WITH AN ACT OF BARBARISM CALCULATED TO DISRUPT THE PEACEFUL TRANSFER OF THE SPANISH MARCHES TO FRENCH SOVEREIGNTY.
BUT WHATEVER MAY COME TO PASS, WE WILL NOT FAIL.
CHRIST WILL REIGN ON EARTH AGAIN!
CONGRATULATIONS, MY DUKE.
SO IT BEGINS.
NAVARRE'S WILL WAS A WELL-ORCHESTRATED TOUCH, ROBERT.
MY THANKS FOR YOUR HANDLING OF THAT. NO DOUBT IT HELPED US OVERCOME THE KING'S TAWDRY SHOWMANSHIP TODAY. PERHAPS WE'LL FIND SOME USE FOR YOU AFTER ALL!
THANK YOU, MY LORD.
I'M SURE YOU WILL.

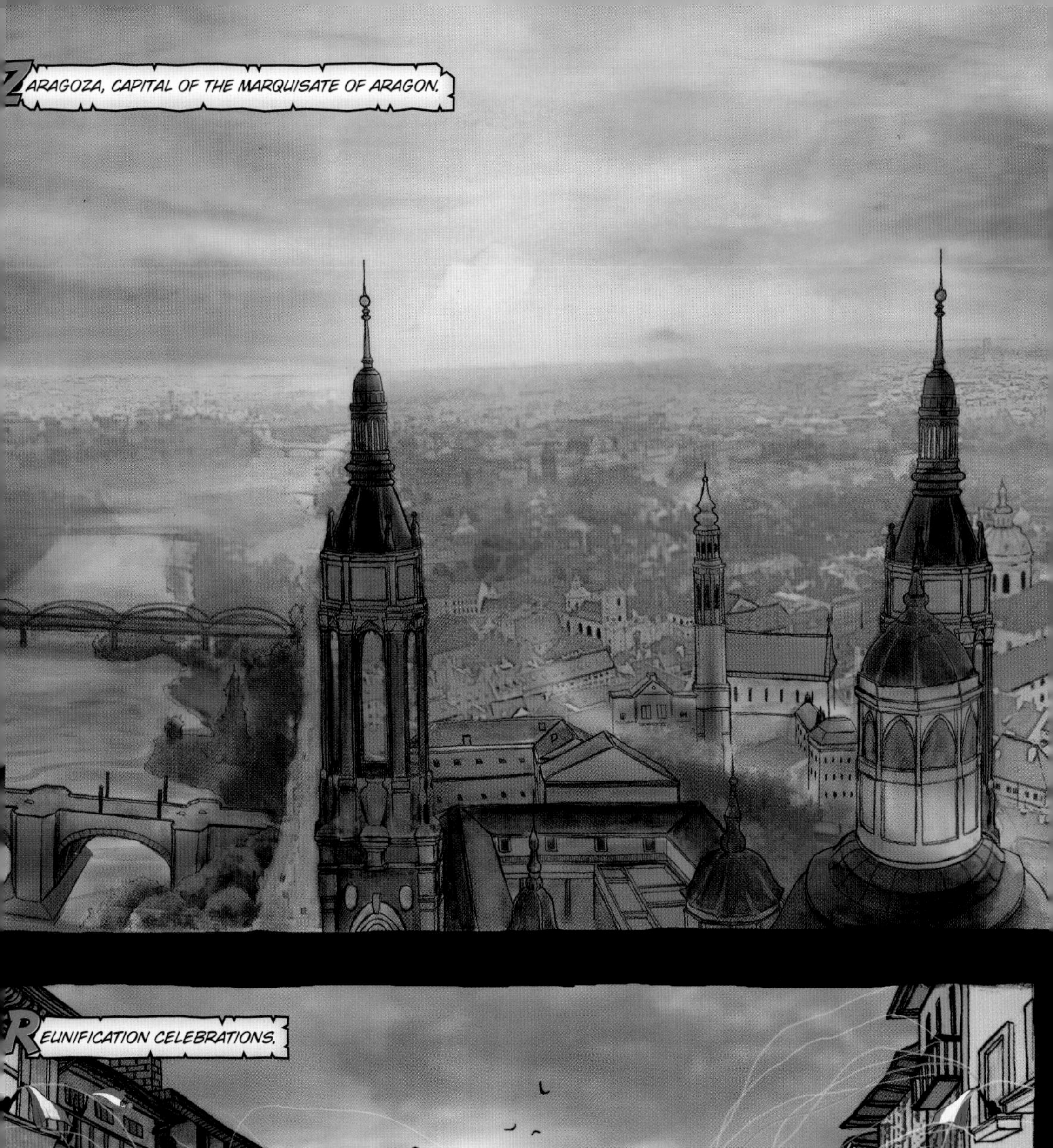
ZARAGOZA, CAPITAL OF THE MARQUISATE OF ARAGON.

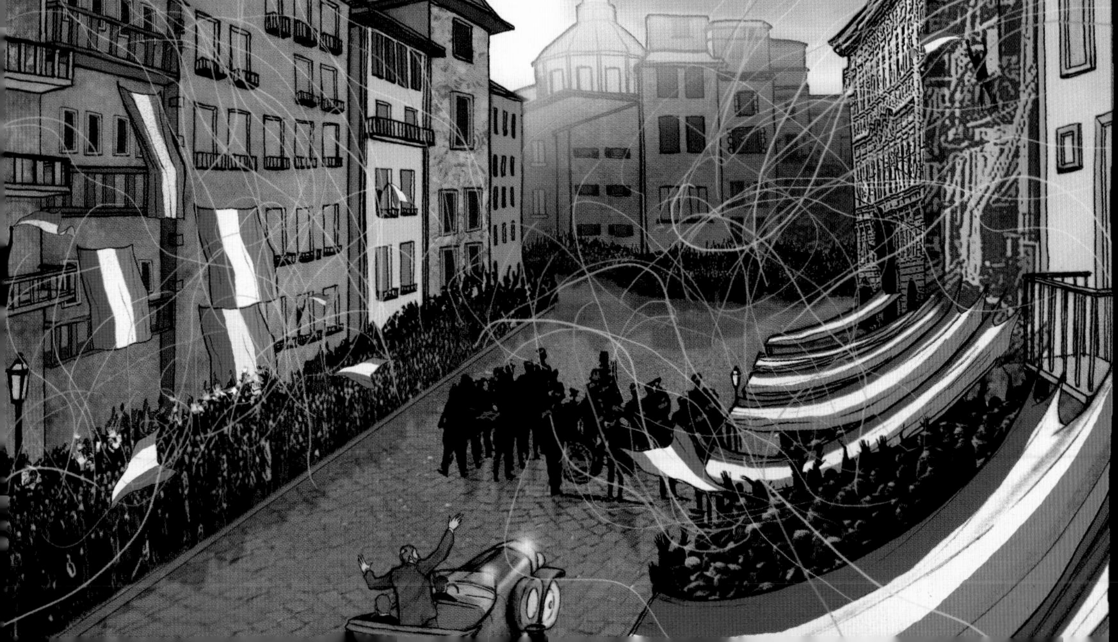
REUNIFICATION CELEBRATIONS.

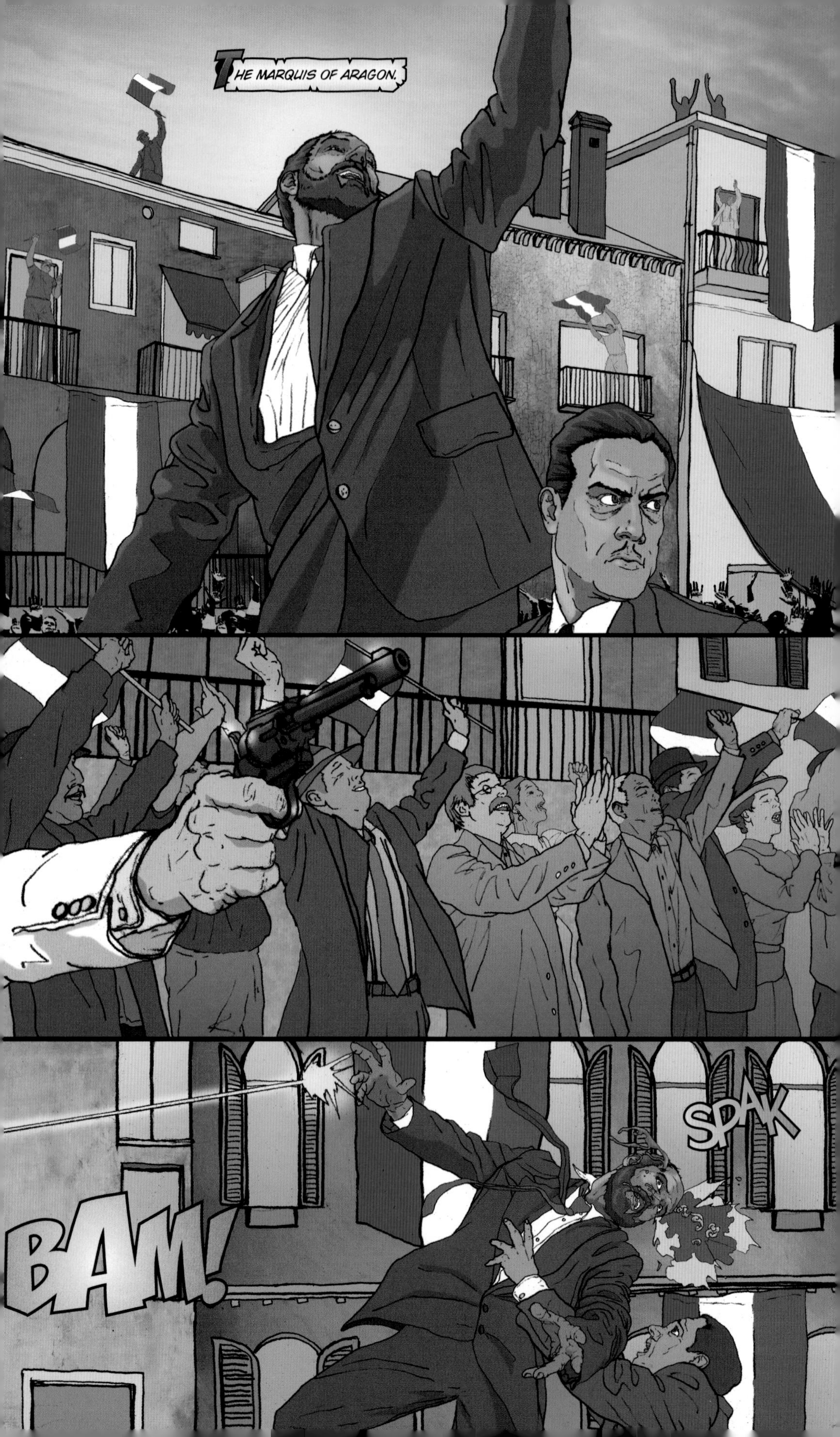
THE MARQUIS OF ARAGON.
SPAK
BAM!

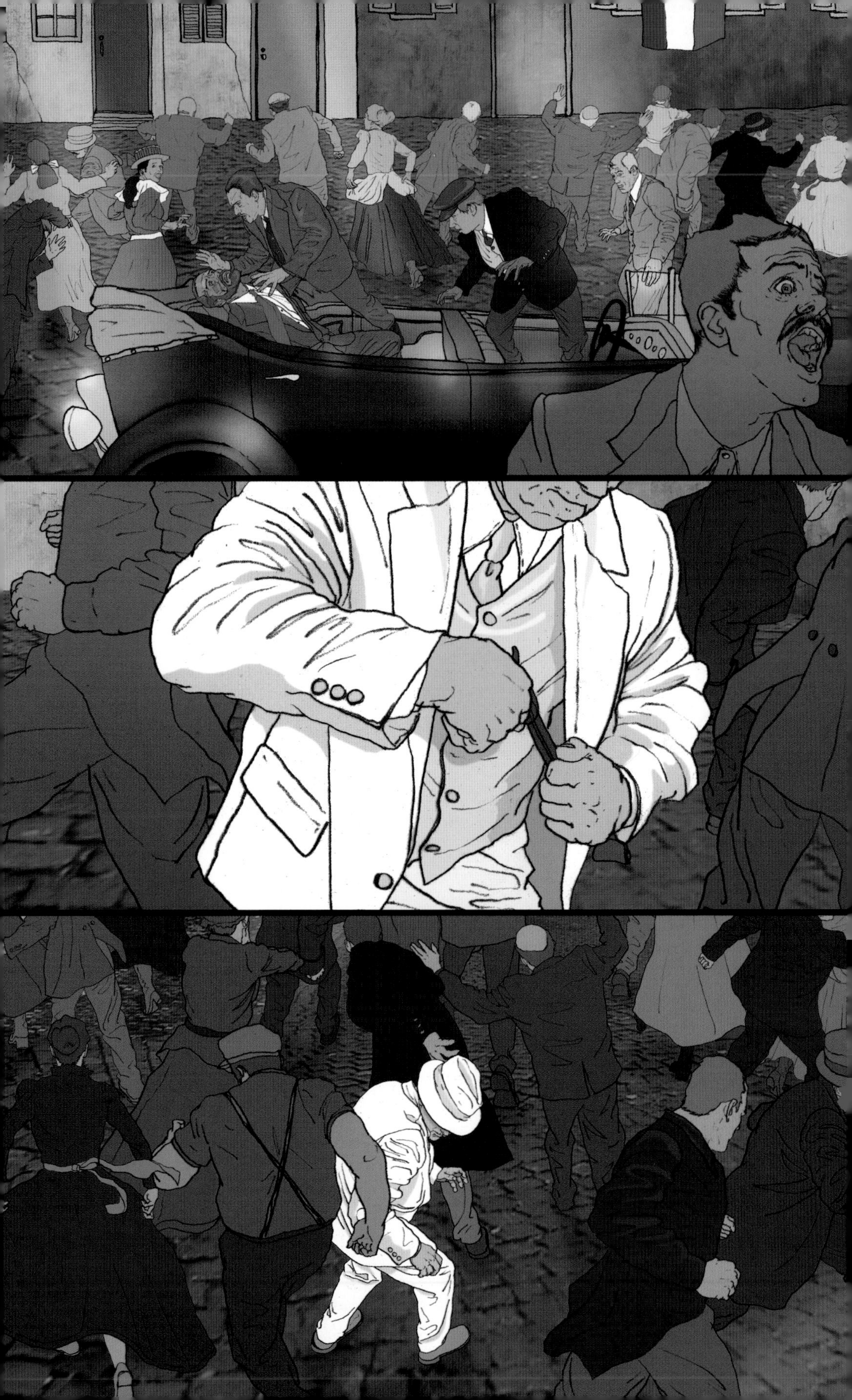

Le Journal de la Libert

Paris' leading anglophone newspaper • vol. 205, no. 98 • Oct. 31, MCMXXXIII

apal seal

Editors in Chief: M. Tait Bergstrom, M. Matthew Pasteris. **Story Editor:** M. Arvid Nelson. **Art Editor:** M. James Di Bartolo. **Photography Editor:** M. Alexander Waldman. **Layout Supervisor:** M. William Kartalopoulos. **Editors Emeritus:** M. Clark A. Smith, M. Howard P. Lovecraft, M. Robert E. Howard. Redacted by the Holy Inquisition under the direction of His Excellency Archbishop Emile-Jean Ireneaux. Le Journal de la Liberté is printed under the benign auspices of his most puissant majesty KING LOUIS XXII of FRANCE. GOD SAVE THE KING.

of Approv

MARQUIS OF ARAGO ASSASSINATED

ANCE WITHDRAWS DIPLOMATIC TIES WITH CORDOVA; WAR MAY BE EMINENT • SECOND DEATH OF POWERFUL SPANISH LORD IN AS MANY WEE

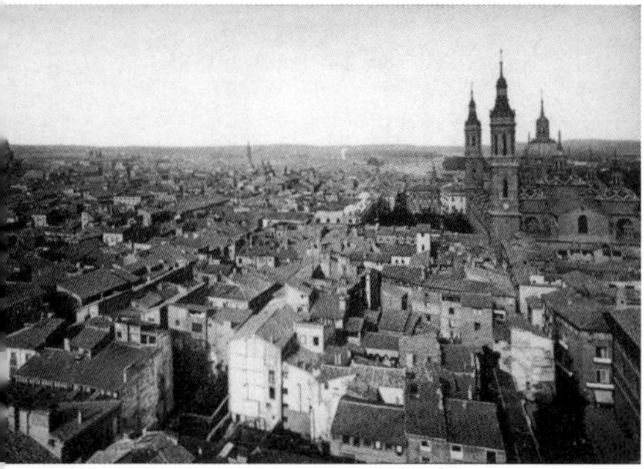

he capital, Zaragoza, was eerily quiet after riots yesterday. "Things are tense here. They could still explode any minute," one resident said.

Zaragoza, France – The rquis of Aragon was fatally shot ne head by an assassin yesterday. death has thrown the Spanish rches in chaos. Tensions run n between France and the rdovan Emirate, suspected of ting the assassination.

France may soon be at war h her southern neighbor. g Louis has responded to ssure from parliament and hdrawn France's ambassador n Cordova.

Islamic militants in the employ he Emir are suspected of the tical slaying because of chron- iolence against Christians liv- in the Cordovan Emirate.

Over the last decade, Mus- radicals have largely emptied rdova of its minority Chris- population.

There is widespread concern ar could ignite a larger con- , large enough to engulf all urope.

INSIDE

ore coverage of Aragon's ssassination, plus commentary by . Nelson and James Di Bartolo

The marquis was shot with a small-caliber weapon which has not been recovered. Inquisition officials have not apprehended any suspects.

Anti-Muslim crowds rioted in the Arab quarter of Zaragoza several hours after the assassination, attacking residents, looting, and destroying buildings. Unconfirmed accounts of several dozen deaths, mostly Arab, have been reported.

In France the mood was also dire. The Duke of Lorraine issued an ultimatum to Cordova in an emergency joint session of parliament.

"Our military must have complete and unrestricted access to Cordovan lands so we can do what the Emir could not or would not do: eradicate Islamic extremism," Lorraine said in a speech that drew thunderous applause. "If the Emir does not acquiesce to this demand in 48 hours, we shall declare war."

The ultimatum passed by a wide margin. It went into effect last evening.

Until recently, such a statement by any man other than the king would have been unthinkable. But King Louis XXII's political support in the Assemblée disintegrated four days earlier.

Members of the Hall Robe defected from their King en masse to pass a bill sponsored by Lorraine. The bill provided for the annexation of the Spanish Marches, the very scene of today's chaos.

As a consequence, the Crown finds itself wounded and on the defensive, but King Louis' mayor of the court Charles Martel denies the King is "bleeding to death politically."

Martel also dismissed claims he is secretly in contact with Cordovan officials, although ties are officially broken.

"Nothing of the sort," Martel said. "The assassination of Aragon comes as a great shock to all of us, but now is the time for calmness and deliberation."

Nonetheless, if the Cordovans do not accept Lorraine's terms, the King may find himself further marginalized.

Mohammed Al-Rashid, vizier to the Cordovan Emir Suleiman

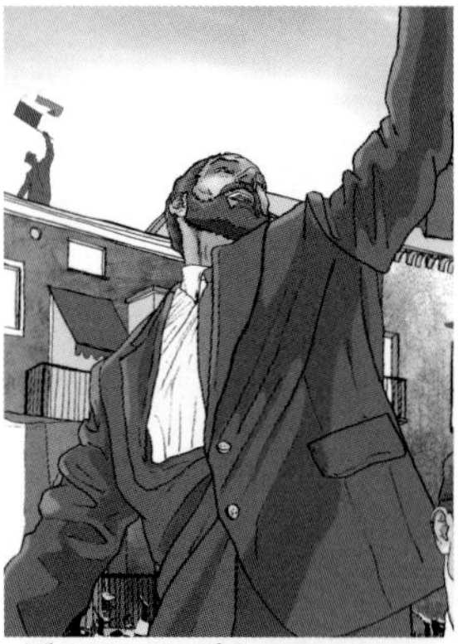

The Marquis of Aragon, moments

IV, vigorously denied responsib ity for Aragon's assassination.

"The claim the murde was an agent of my governme is entirely unfounded. Whe where is the evidence?" he sa "We share France's shock o Aragon's death, but there is way we can accept Lorrain ultimatum. Unrestricted access Cordovan lands? It's tantamou to occupation."

If Cordova does not acce the terms, there are wider i plications.

Prussian Chancellor Aug Karl von Haugwitz issued warning from the Reichscha cellory yesterday.

"Prussia and her allies abs lutely will not tolerate a Ga invasion of Iberia," he said. " will consider any such acti a declaration of war on Prus herself." Ferdinand Beust, Fo eign Minister of the Holy R man Empire, expressed Empe Rudolf's solidarity with Prussi

England, meanwhile, has d clared her support for France.

"The time is long overdue us to draw together as Christia and drive the Moor back acr the Strait of Gibraltar," Sir Wi ston Churchill, first lord of t British Admiralty and member the House of Lords, said.

The situation in France mains tense. The next twenty-fo hours could prove decisive for t future of the House of Bourb and for the House of Lorraine.

"If it comes to war, the Du of Lorraine will see his p sition further strengthened, King Louis' expense," a meml of the Hall of the Robe sa "Many of us are still on t fence, but Lorraine's performan yesterday was quite impressi

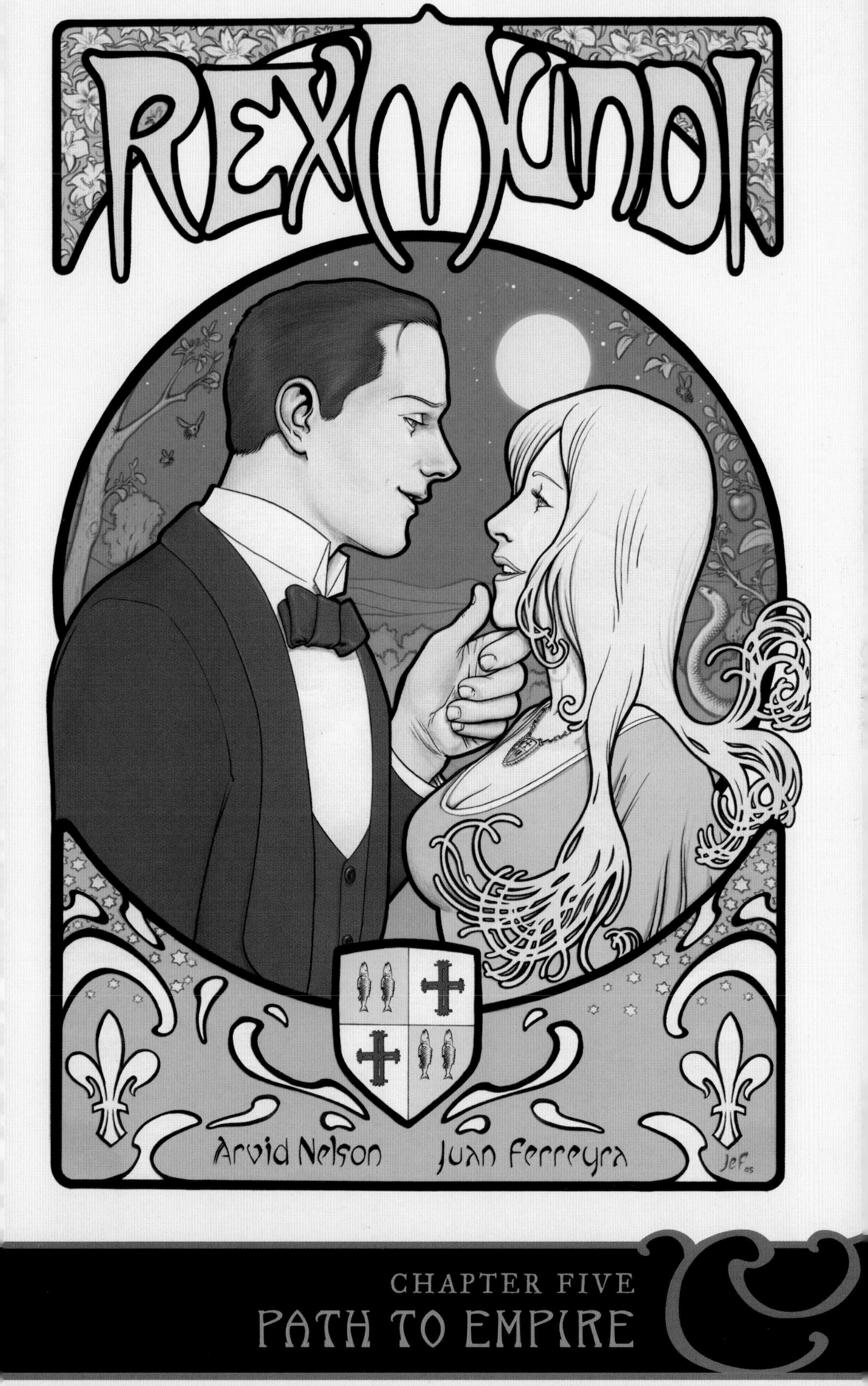
REX MUNDI
Arvid Nelson
Juan Ferreyra
JeF 05

CHAPTER FIVE

PATH TO EMPIRE

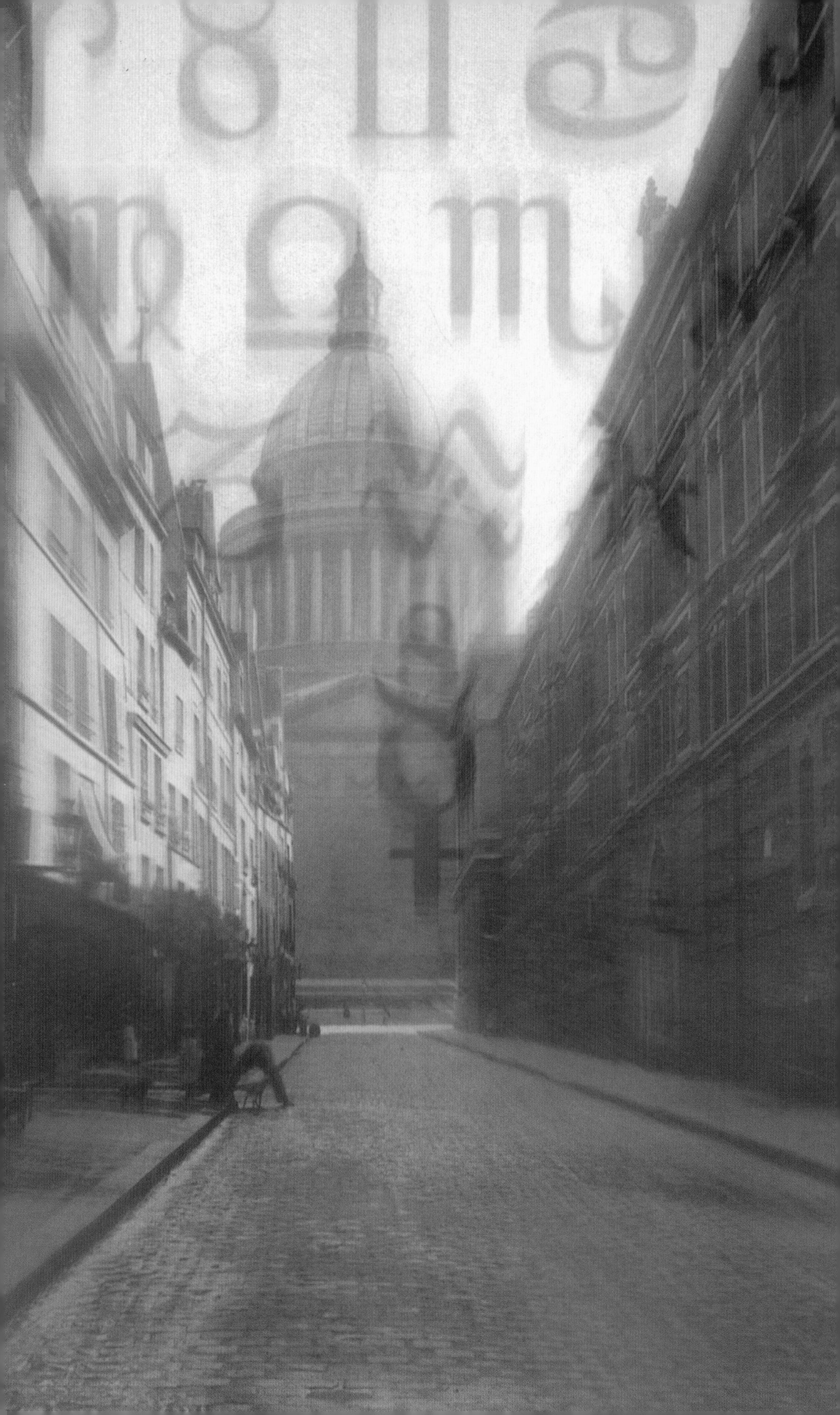

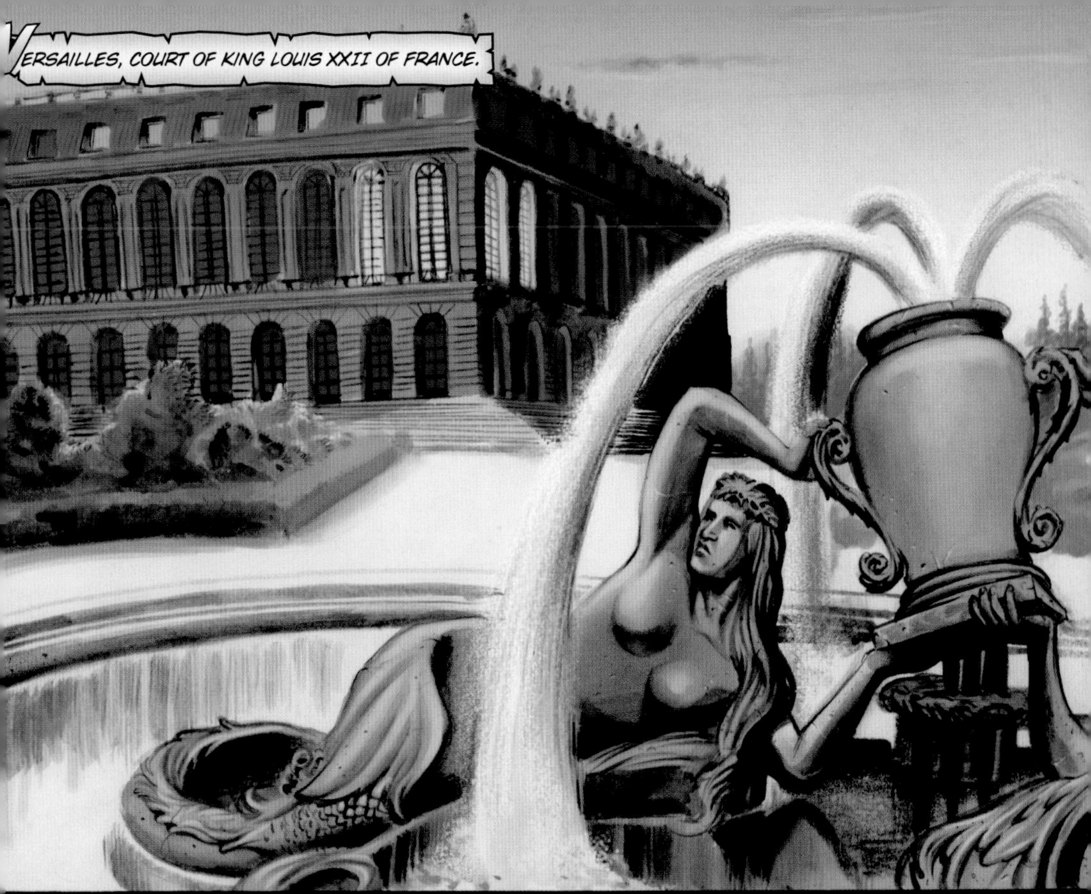
VERSAILLES, COURT OF KING LOUIS XXII OF FRANCE.

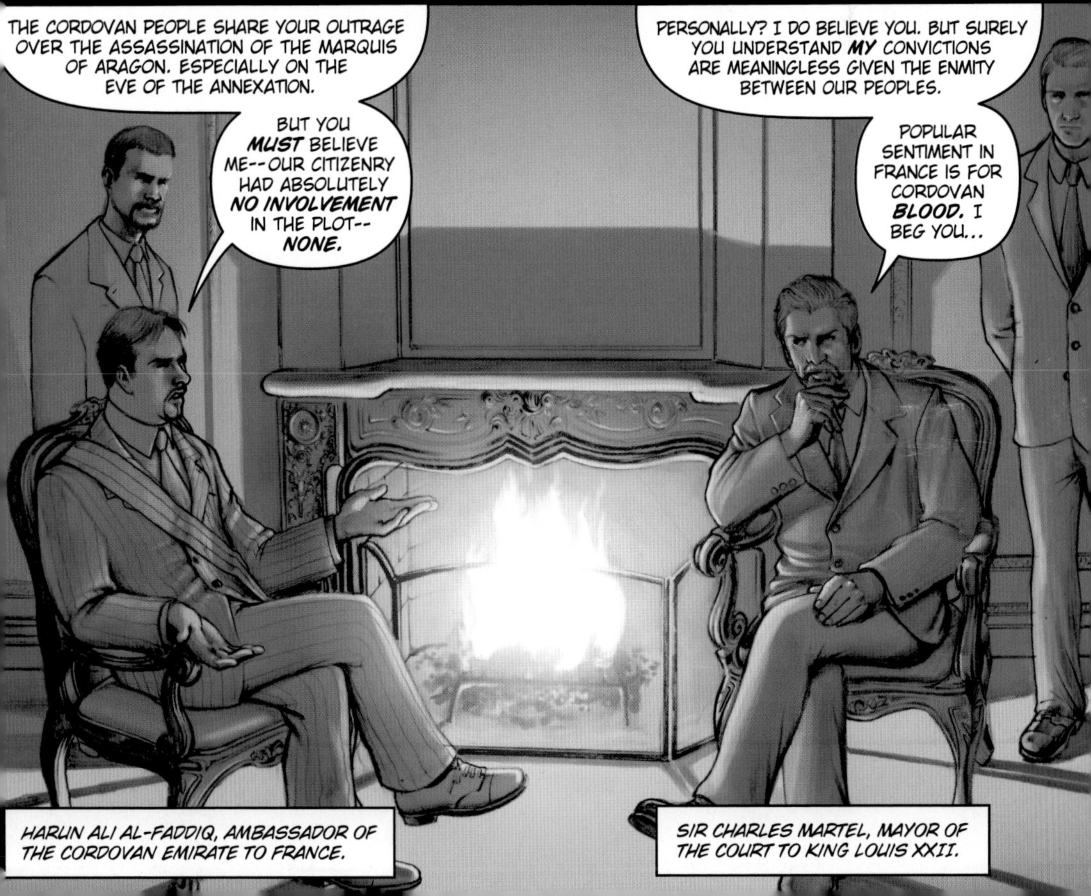
THE CORDOVAN PEOPLE SHARE YOUR OUTRAGE OVER THE ASSASSINATION OF THE MARQUIS OF ARAGON. ESPECIALLY ON THE EVE OF THE ANNEXATION.
BUT YOU MUST BELIEVE ME--OUR CITIZENRY HAD ABSOLUTELY NO INVOLVEMENT IN THE PLOT-- NONE.
PERSONALLY? I DO BELIEVE YOU. BUT SURELY YOU UNDERSTAND MY CONVICTIONS ARE MEANINGLESS GIVEN THE ENMITY BETWEEN OUR PEOPLES.
POPULAR SENTIMENT IN FRANCE IS FOR CORDOVAN BLOOD. I BEG YOU...
HARUN ALI AL-FADDIQ, AMBASSADOR OF THE CORDOVAN EMIRATE TO FRANCE.
SIR CHARLES MARTEL, MAYOR OF THE COURT TO KING LOUIS XXII.

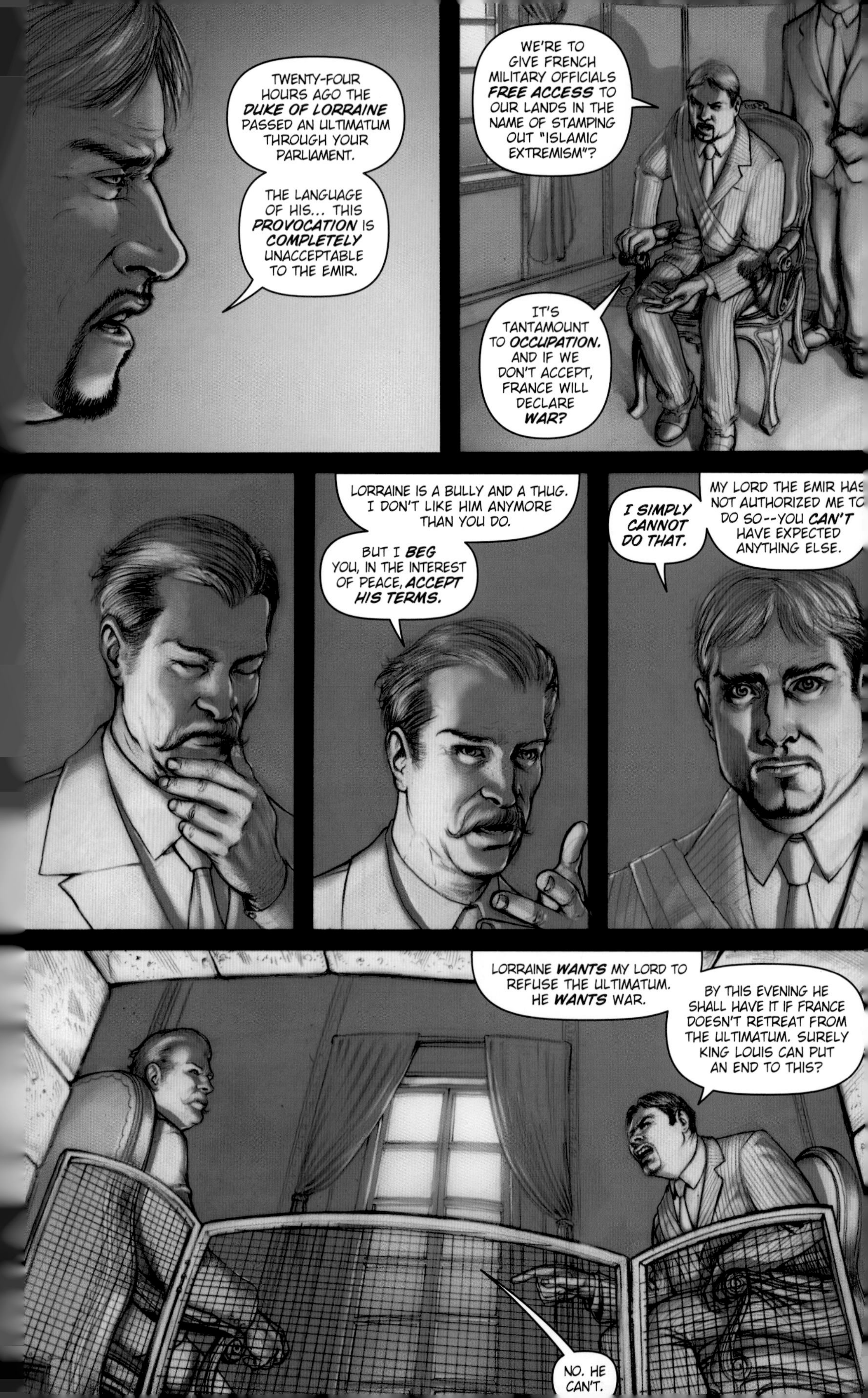
TWENTY-FOUR HOURS AGO THE DUKE OF LORRAINE PASSED AN ULTIMATUM THROUGH YOUR PARLIAMENT.
THE LANGUAGE OF HIS... THIS PROVOCATION IS COMPLETELY UNACCEPTABLE TO THE EMIR.
WE'RE TO GIVE FRENCH MILITARY OFFICIALS FREE ACCESS TO OUR LANDS IN THE NAME OF STAMPING OUT "ISLAMIC EXTREMISM"?
IT'S TANTAMOUNT TO OCCUPATION. AND IF WE DON'T ACCEPT, FRANCE WILL DECLARE WAR?
LORRAINE IS A BULLY AND A THUG. I DON'T LIKE HIM ANYMORE THAN YOU DO.
BUT I BEG YOU, IN THE INTEREST OF PEACE, ACCEPT HIS TERMS.
I SIMPLY CANNOT DO THAT.
MY LORD THE EMIR HAS NOT AUTHORIZED ME TO DO SO--YOU CAN'T HAVE EXPECTED ANYTHING ELSE.
LORRAINE WANTS MY LORD TO REFUSE THE ULTIMATUM. HE WANTS WAR.
BY THIS EVENING HE SHALL HAVE IT IF FRANCE DOESN'T RETREAT FROM THE ULTIMATUM. SURELY KING LOUIS CAN PUT AN END TO THIS?
NO. HE CAN'T.

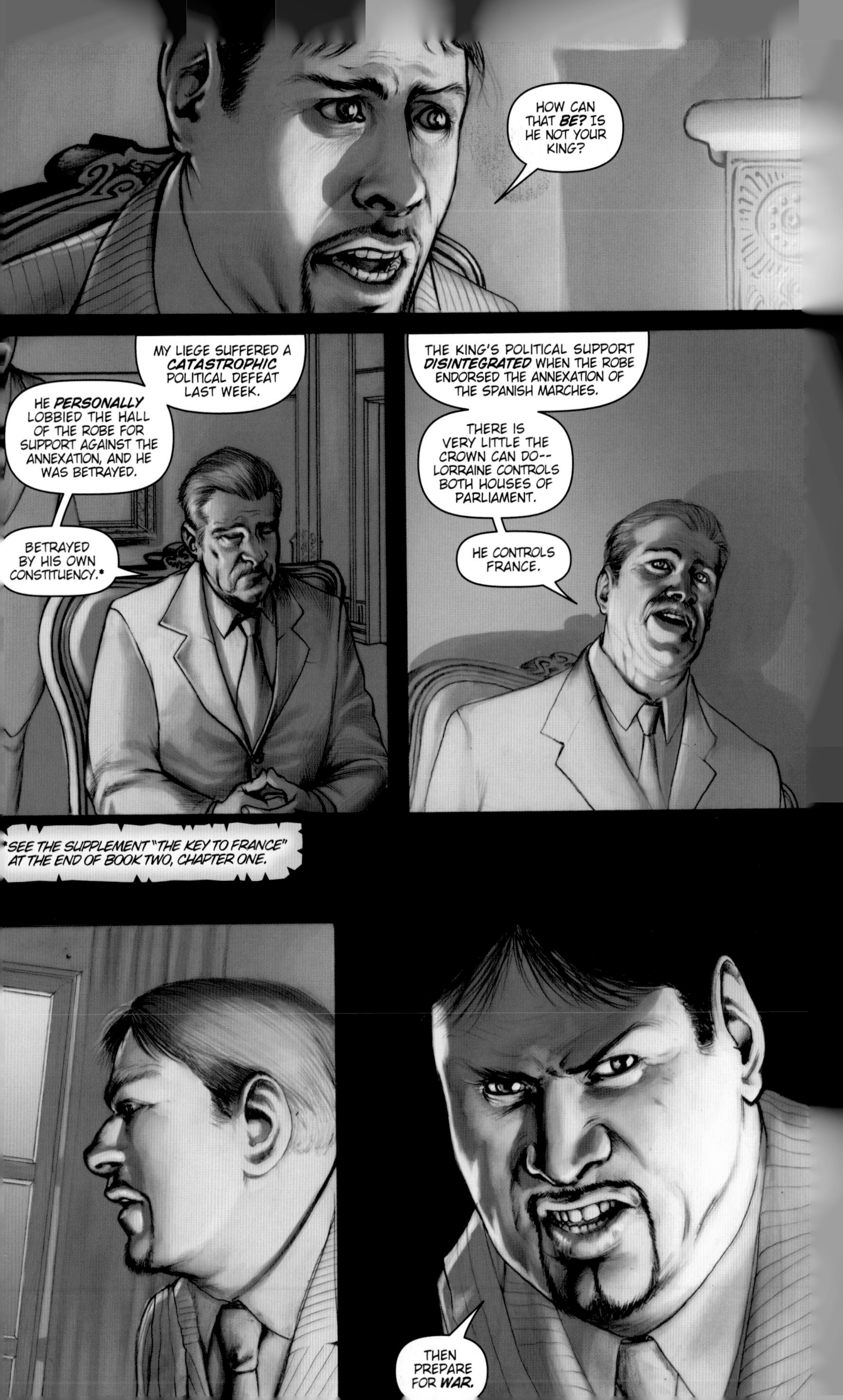
HOW CAN THAT **BE?** IS HE NOT YOUR KING?
MY LIEGE SUFFERED A **CATASTROPHIC** POLITICAL DEFEAT LAST WEEK.
HE **PERSONALLY** LOBBIED THE HALL OF THE ROBE FOR SUPPORT AGAINST THE ANNEXATION, AND HE WAS BETRAYED.
BETRAYED BY HIS OWN CONSTITUENCY.*
THE KING'S POLITICAL SUPPORT **DISINTEGRATED** WHEN THE ROBE ENDORSED THE ANNEXATION OF THE SPANISH MARCHES.
THERE IS VERY LITTLE THE CROWN CAN DO-- LORRAINE CONTROLS BOTH HOUSES OF PARLIAMENT.
HE CONTROLS FRANCE.
*SEE THE SUPPLEMENT "THE KEY TO FRANCE" AT THE END OF BOOK TWO, CHAPTER ONE.
THEN PREPARE FOR **WAR.**

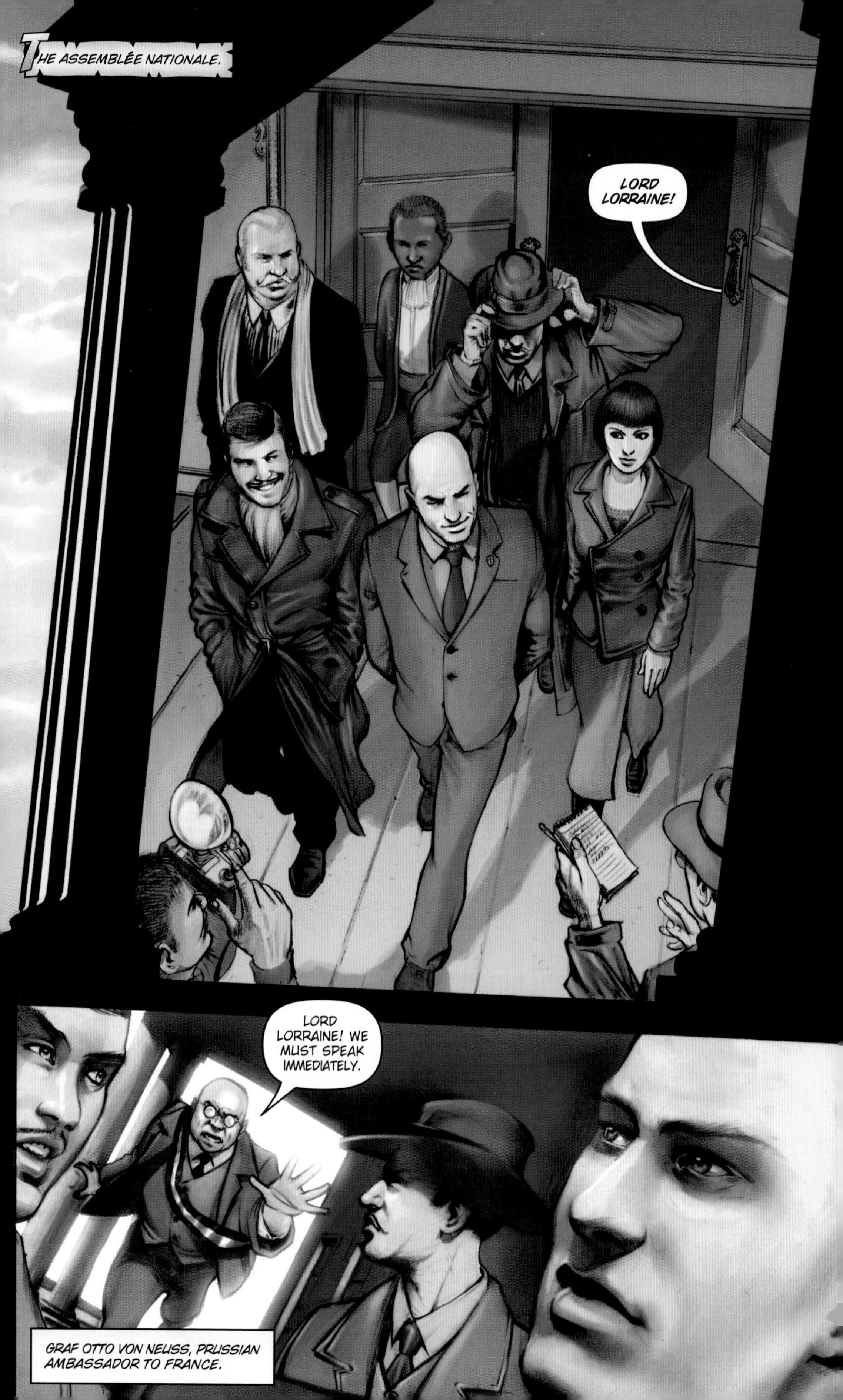
THE ASSEMBLÉE NATIONALE.
LORD LORRAINE!
LORD LORRAINE! WE MUST SPEAK IMMEDIATELY.
GRAF OTTO VON NEUSS, PRUSSIAN AMBASSADOR TO FRANCE.

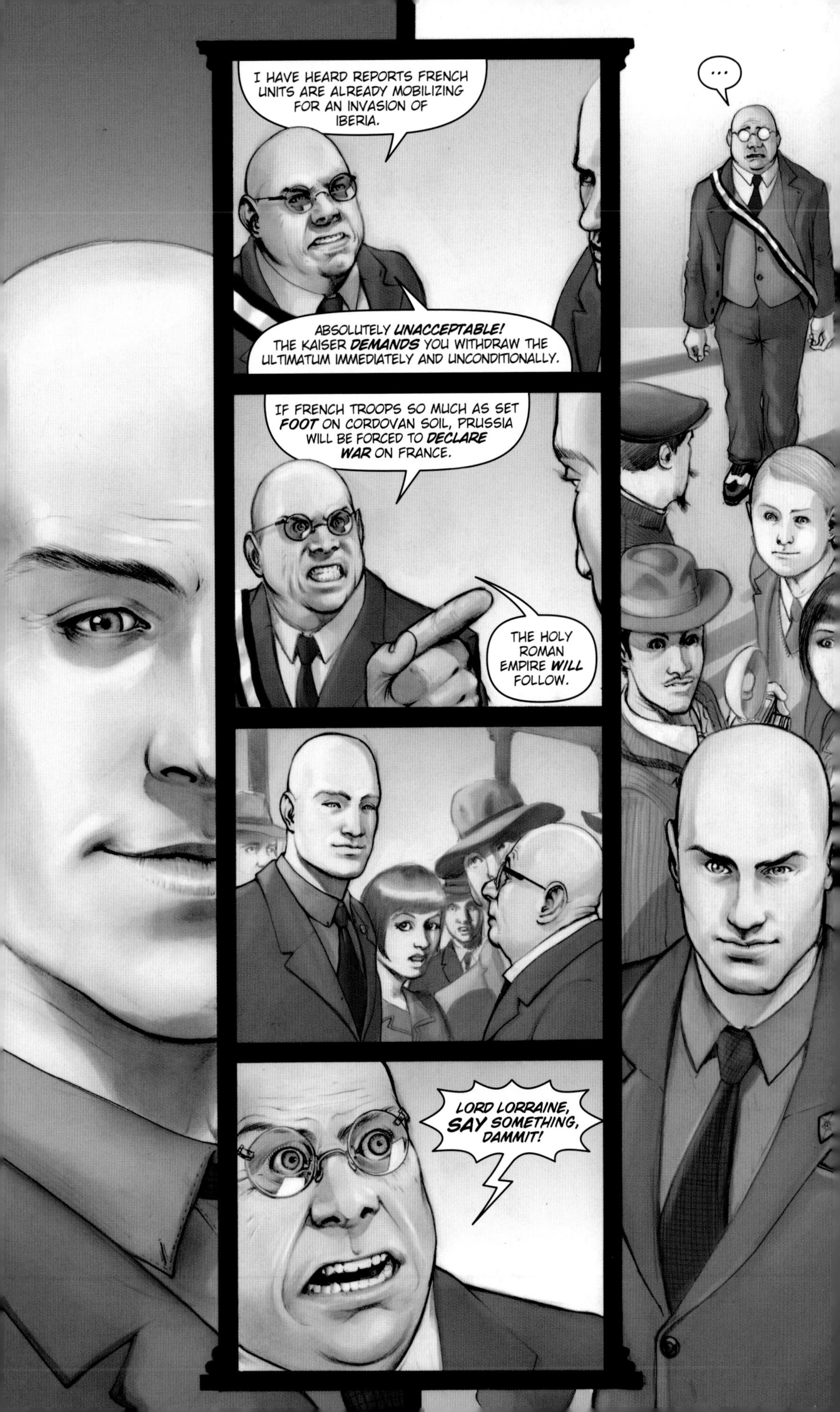
I HAVE HEARD REPORTS FRENCH UNITS ARE ALREADY MOBILIZING FOR AN INVASION OF IBERIA.
ABSOLUTELY UNACCEPTABLE! THE KAISER DEMANDS YOU WITHDRAW THE ULTIMATUM IMMEDIATELY AND UNCONDITIONALLY.
...
IF FRENCH TROOPS SO MUCH AS SET FOOT ON CORDOVAN SOIL, PRUSSIA WILL BE FORCED TO DECLARE WAR ON FRANCE.
THE HOLY ROMAN EMPIRE WILL FOLLOW.
LORD LORRAINE, SAY SOMETHING, DAMMIT!

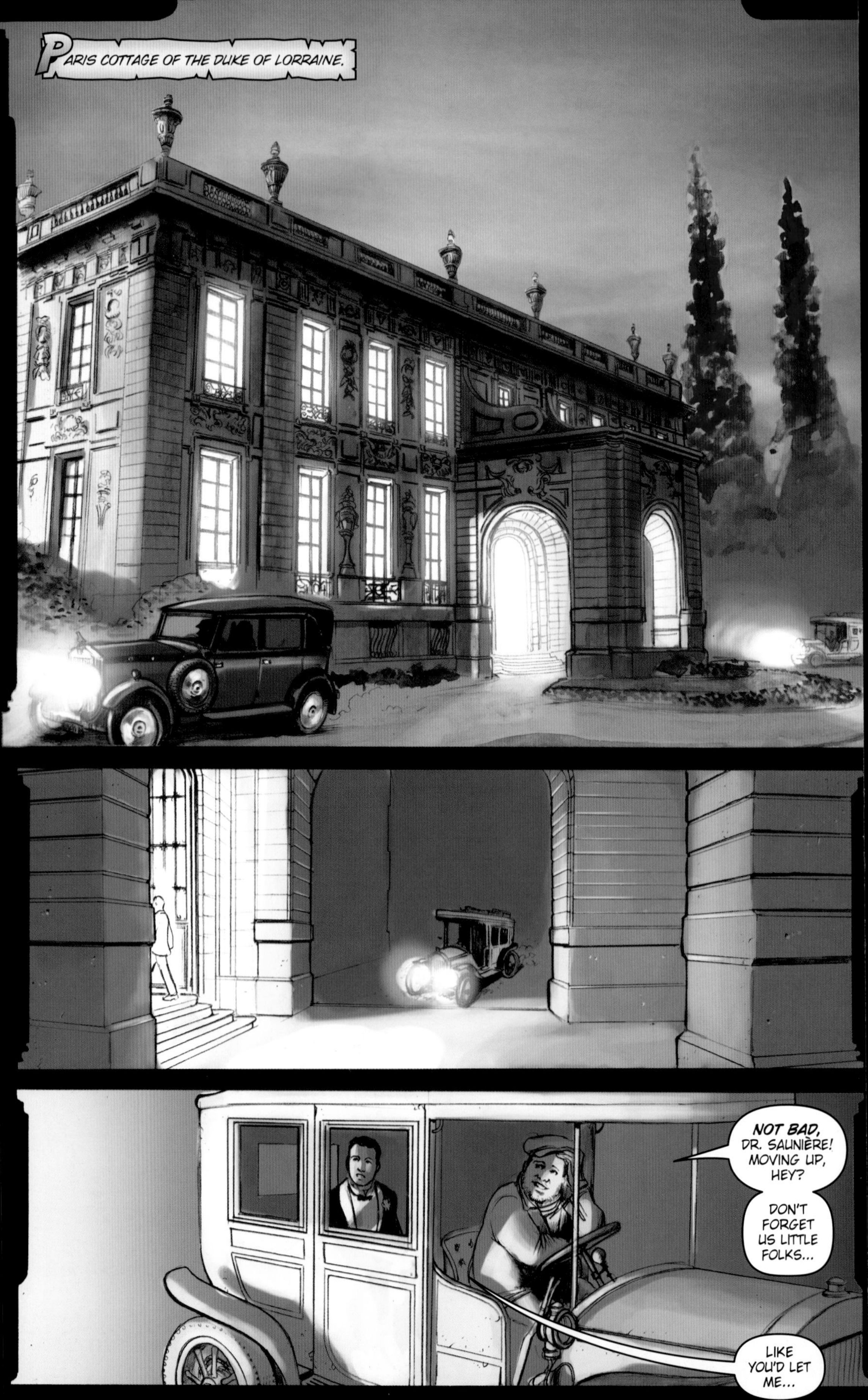
PARIS COTTAGE OF THE DUKE OF LORRAINE.
NOT BAD, DR. SAUNIÈRE! MOVING UP, HEY?
DON'T FORGET US LITTLE FOLKS...
LIKE YOU'D LET ME...

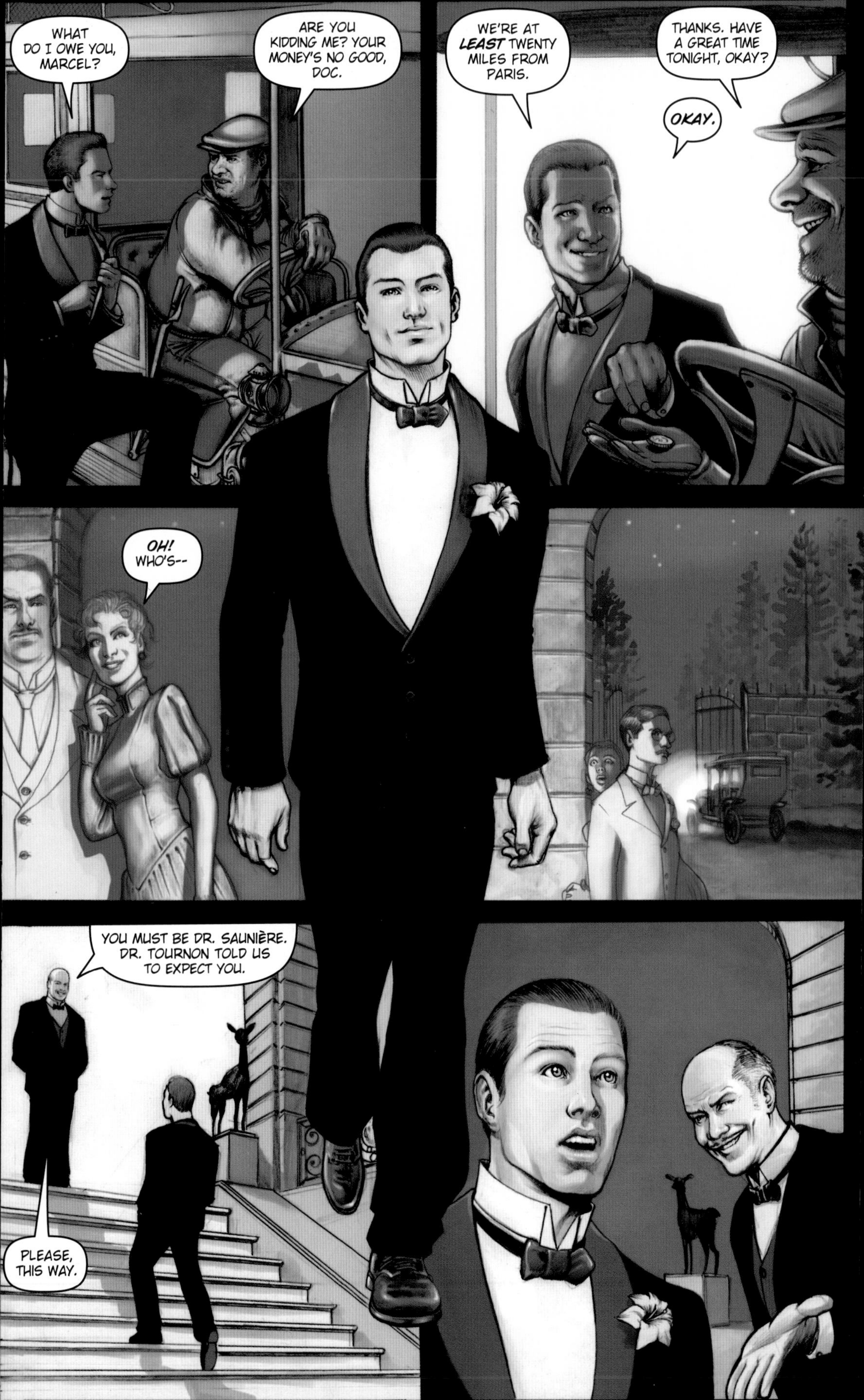
WHAT DO I OWE YOU, MARCEL?
ARE YOU KIDDING ME? YOUR MONEY'S NO GOOD, DOC.
WE'RE AT LEAST TWENTY MILES FROM PARIS.
THANKS. HAVE A GREAT TIME TONIGHT, OKAY?
OKAY.
OH! WHO'S--
YOU MUST BE DR. SAUNIÈRE. DR. TOURNON TOLD US TO EXPECT YOU.
PLEASE, THIS WAY.

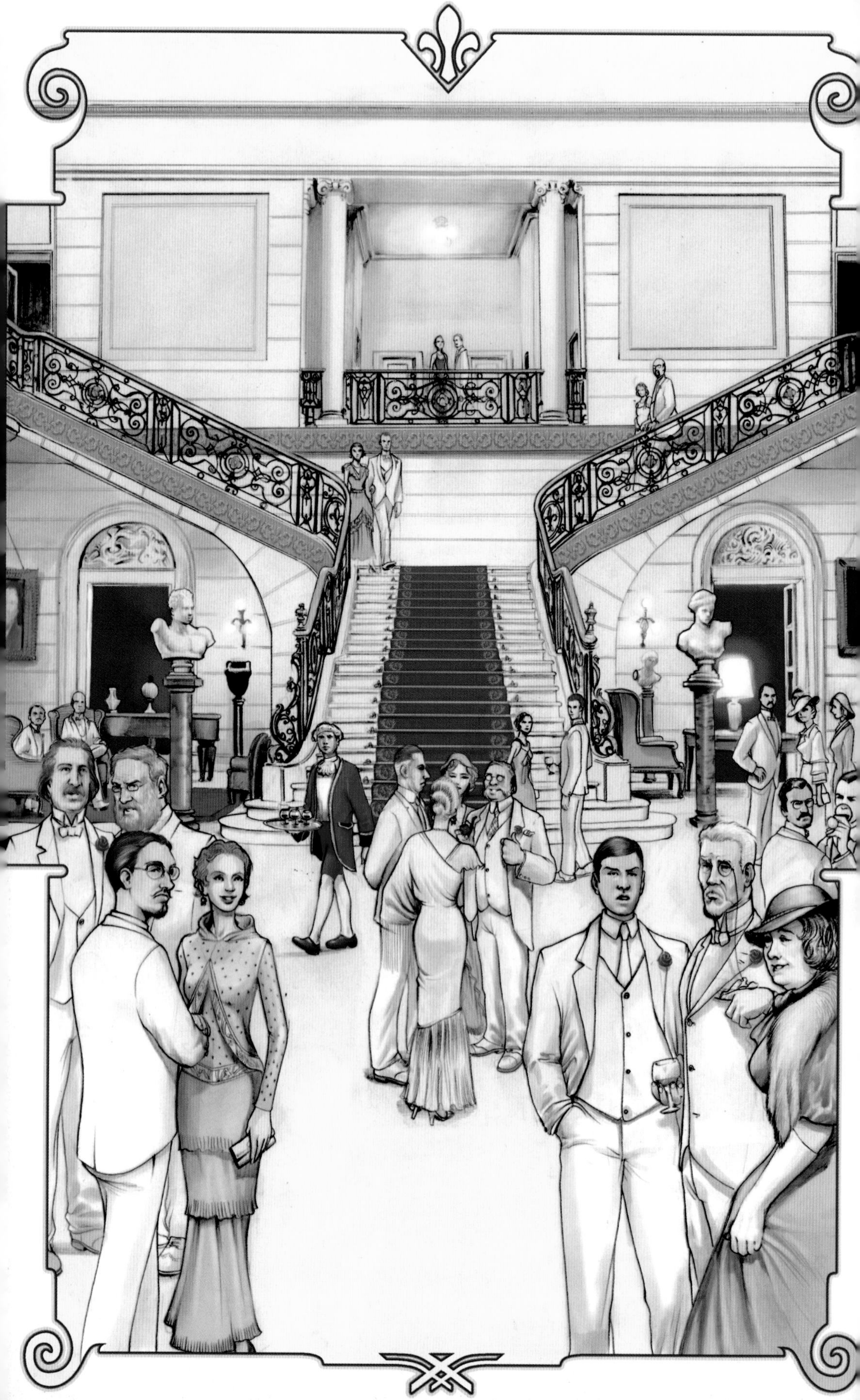

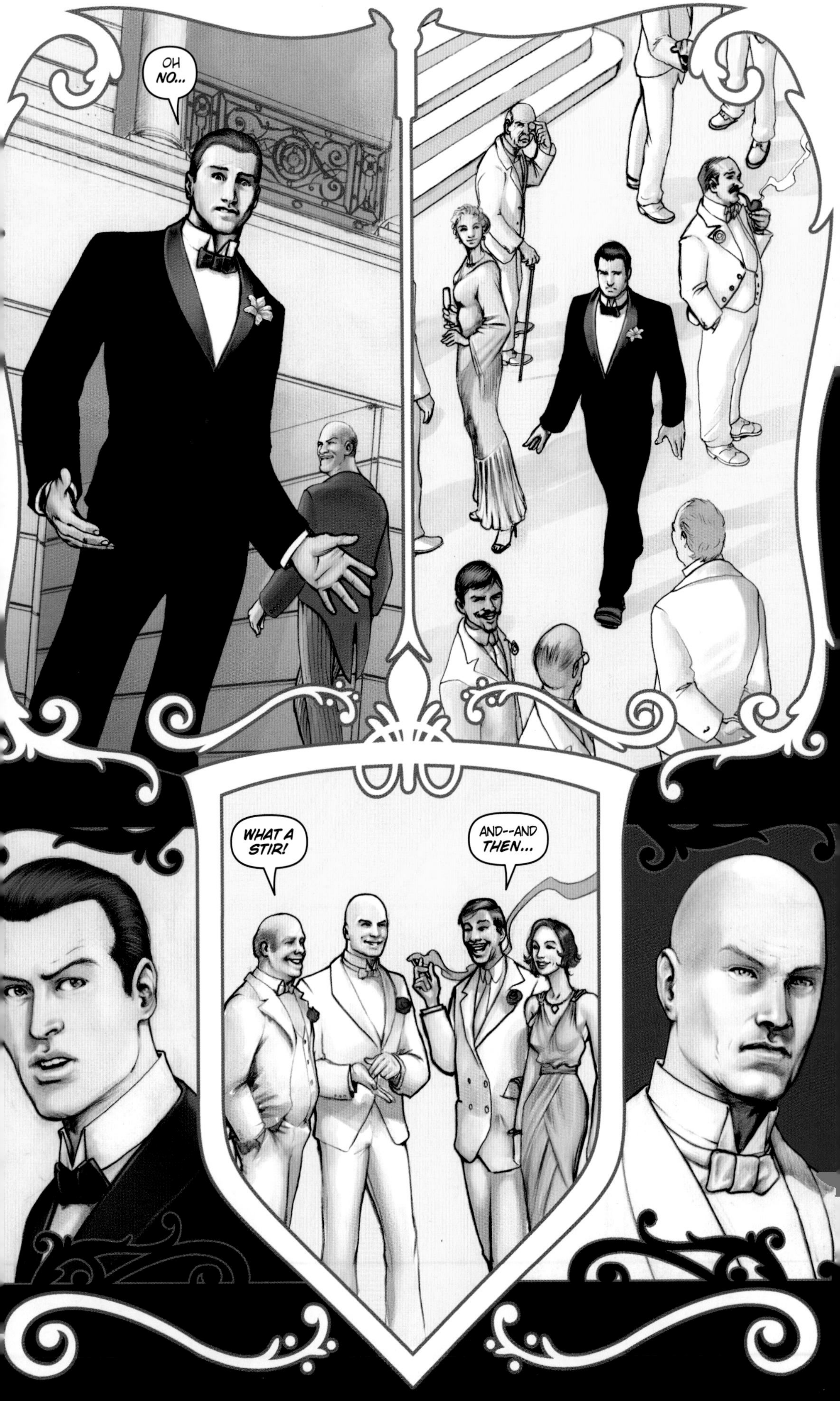
OH NO...
WHAT A STIR!
AND--AND THEN...

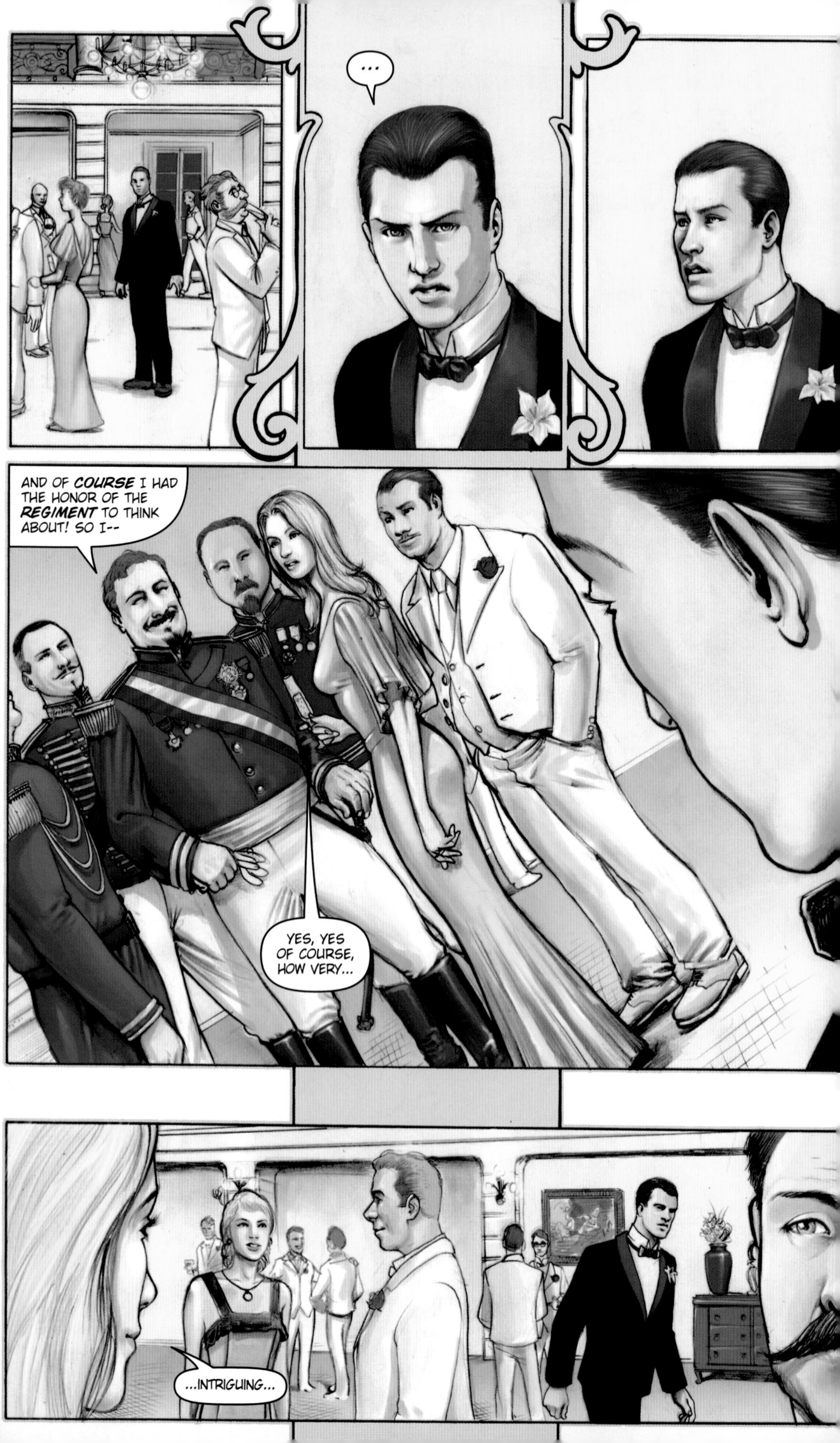
...
AND OF COURSE I HAD THE HONOR OF THE REGIMENT TO THINK ABOUT! SO I--
YES, YES OF COURSE, HOW VERY...
...INTRIGUING...

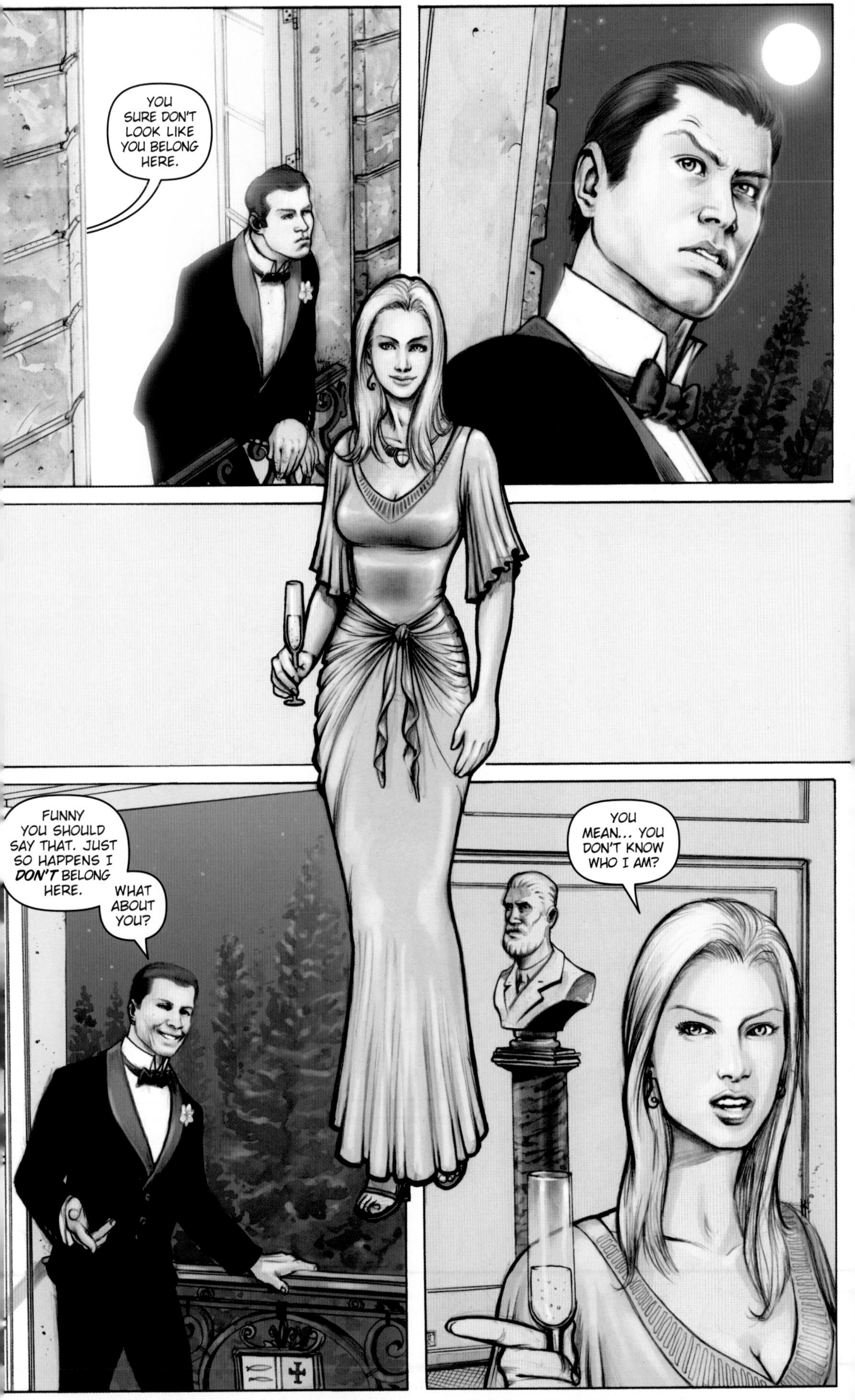
YOU SURE DON'T LOOK LIKE YOU BELONG HERE.
FUNNY YOU SHOULD SAY THAT. JUST SO HAPPENS I **DON'T** BELONG HERE.
WHAT ABOUT YOU?
YOU MEAN... YOU DON'T KNOW WHO I AM?

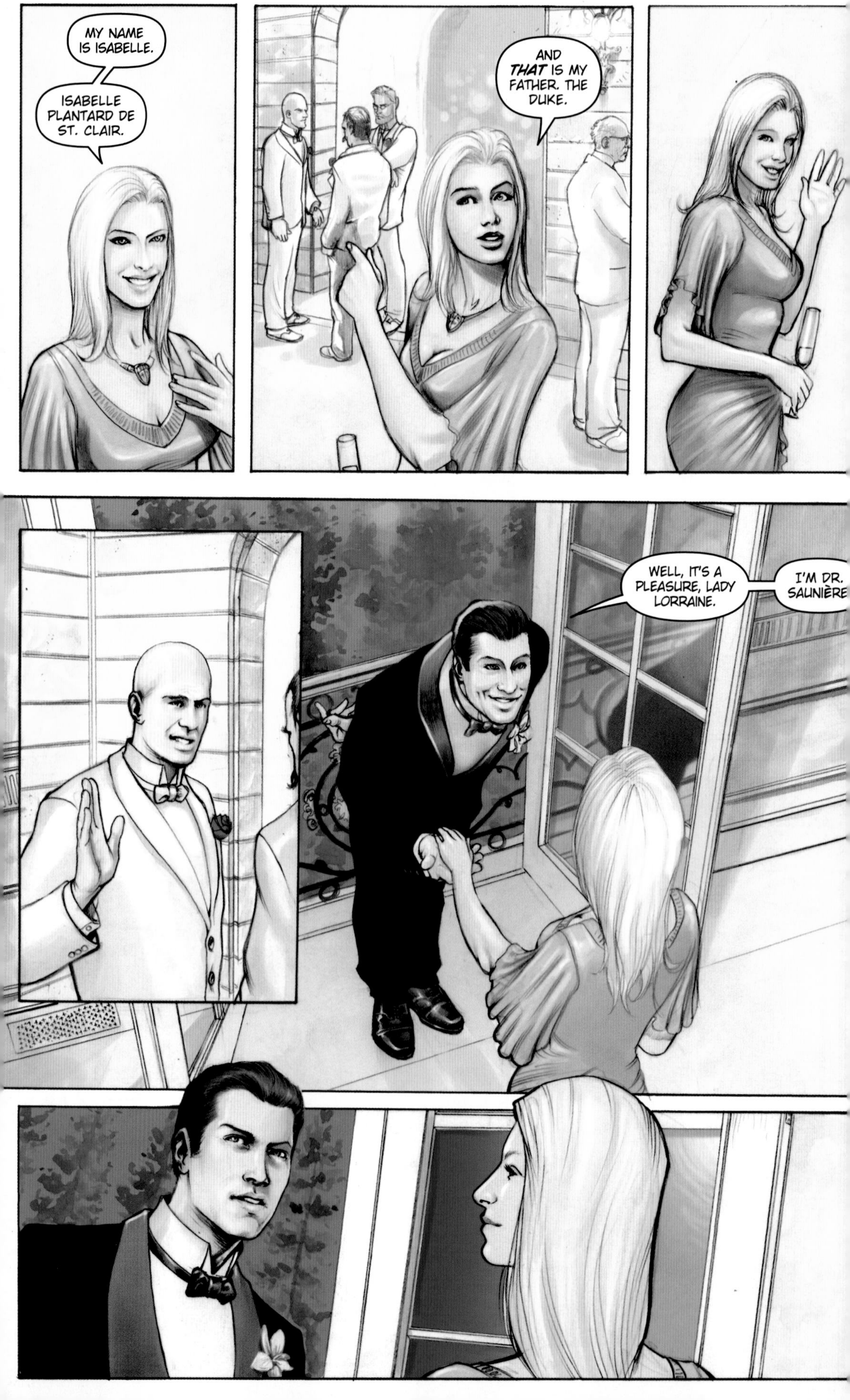
MY NAME IS ISABELLE.
ISABELLE PLANTARD DE ST. CLAIR.
AND *THAT* IS MY FATHER. THE DUKE.
WELL, IT'S A PLEASURE, LADY LORRAINE.
I'M DR. SAUNIÈRE

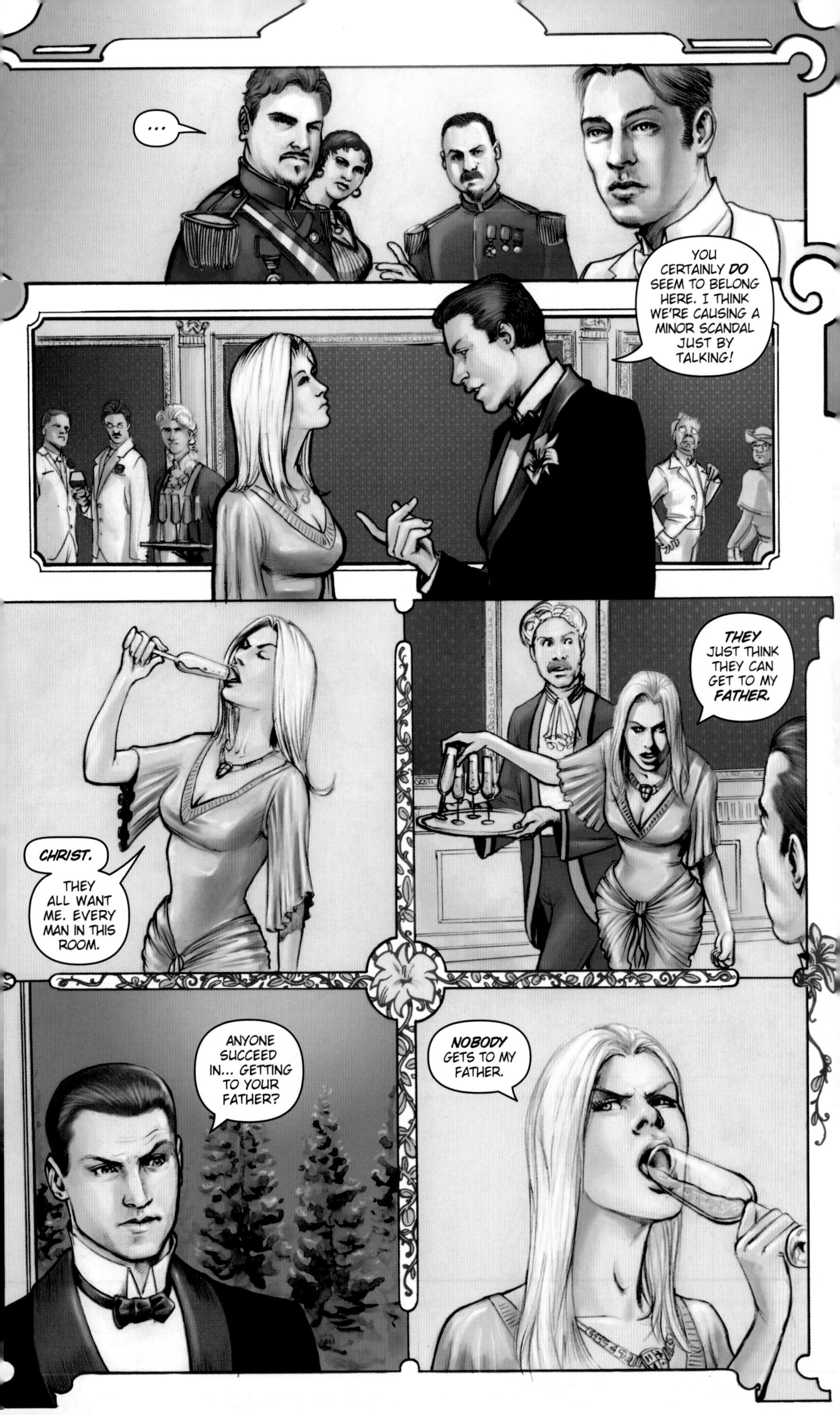
...
YOU CERTAINLY DO SEEM TO BELONG HERE. I THINK WE'RE CAUSING A MINOR SCANDAL JUST BY TALKING!
CHRIST.
THEY ALL WANT ME. EVERY MAN IN THIS ROOM.
THEY JUST THINK THEY CAN GET TO MY FATHER.
ANYONE SUCCEED IN... GETTING TO YOUR FATHER?
NOBODY GETS TO MY FATHER.

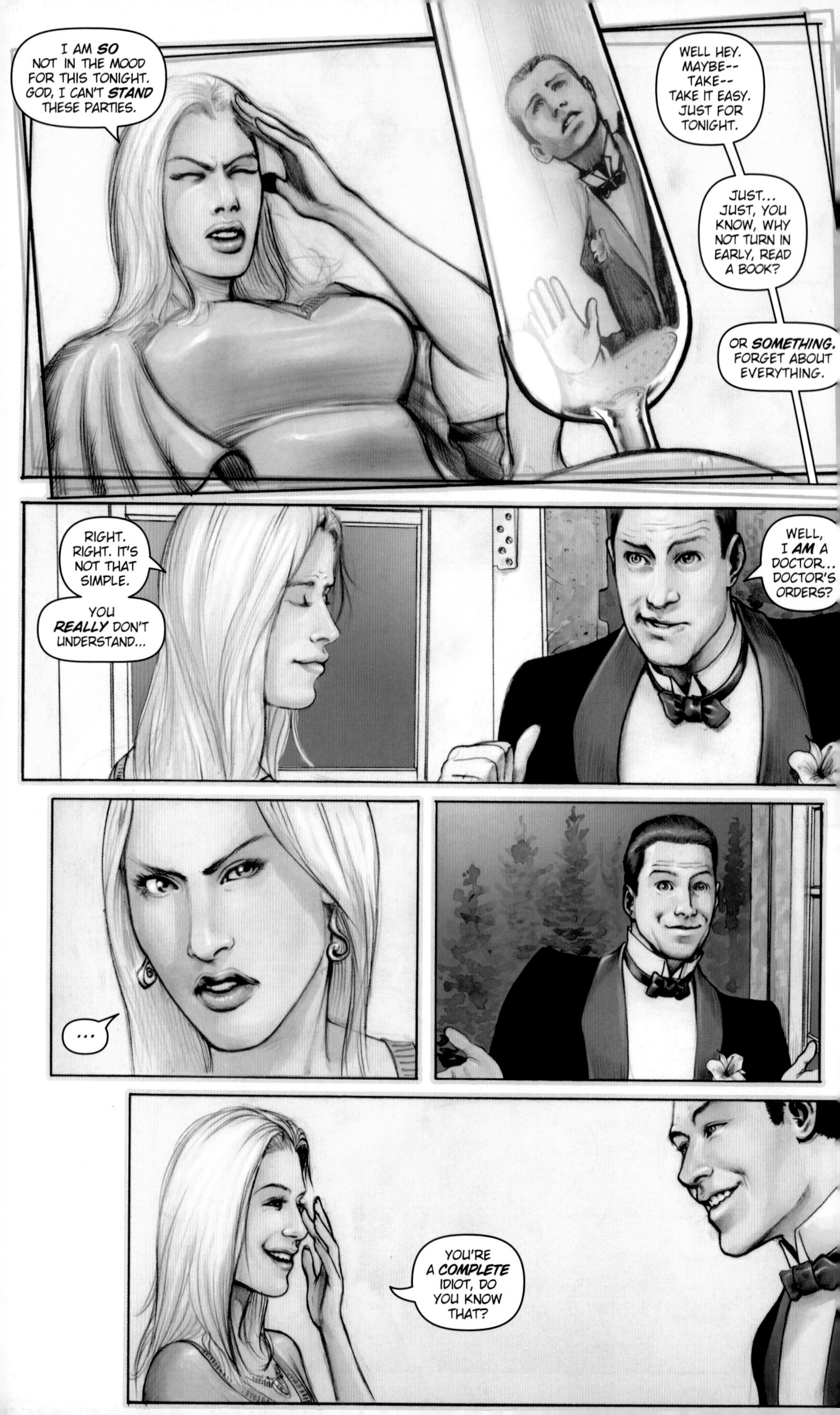
I AM **SO** NOT IN THE MOOD FOR THIS TONIGHT. GOD, I CAN'T **STAND** THESE PARTIES.
WELL HEY. MAYBE-- TAKE-- TAKE IT EASY. JUST FOR TONIGHT.
JUST... JUST, YOU KNOW, WHY NOT TURN IN EARLY, READ A BOOK?
OR **SOMETHING.** FORGET ABOUT EVERYTHING.
RIGHT. RIGHT. IT'S NOT THAT SIMPLE.
YOU **REALLY** DON'T UNDERSTAND...
WELL, I **AM** A DOCTOR... DOCTOR'S ORDERS?
...
YOU'RE A **COMPLETE** IDIOT, DO YOU KNOW THAT?

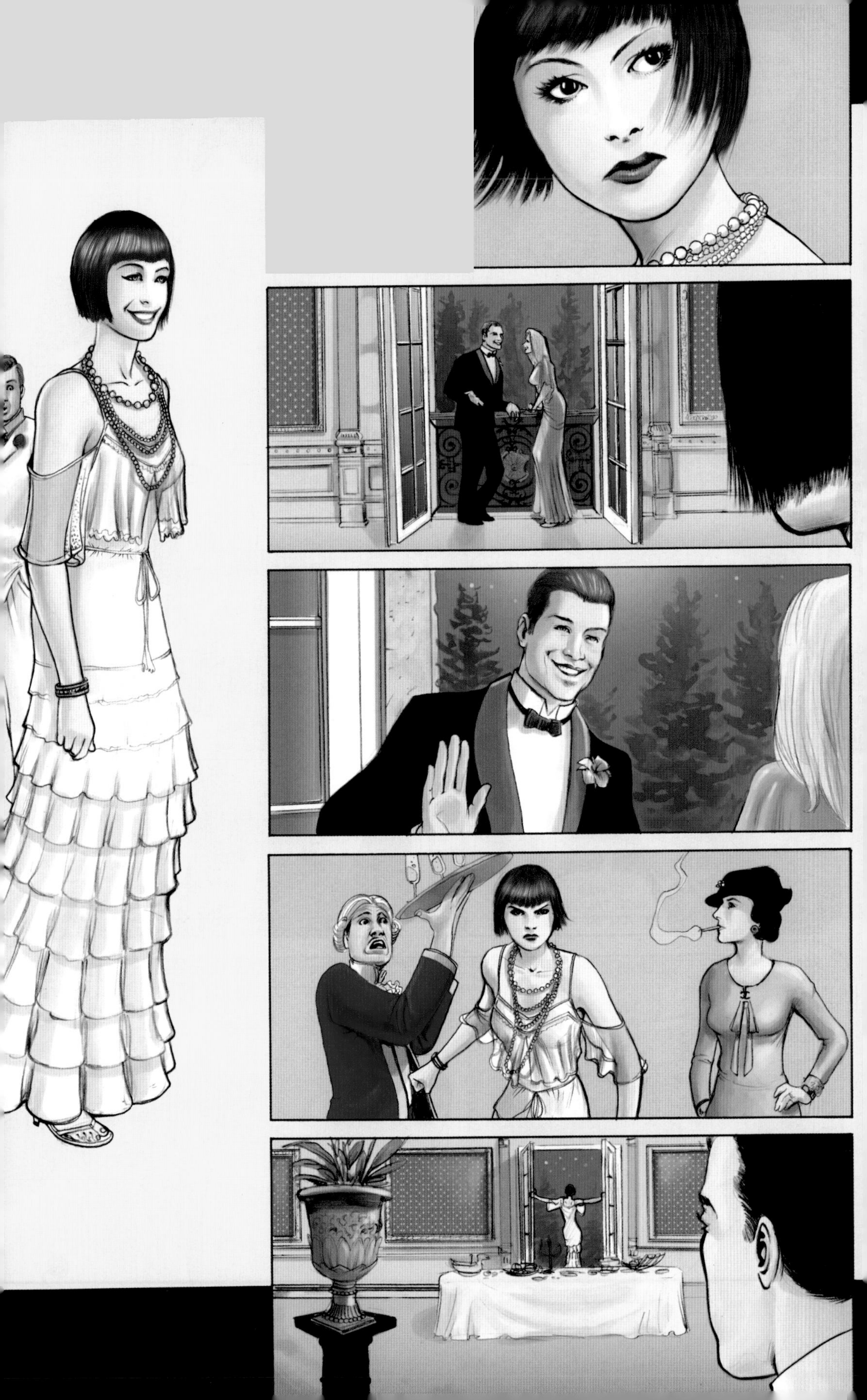

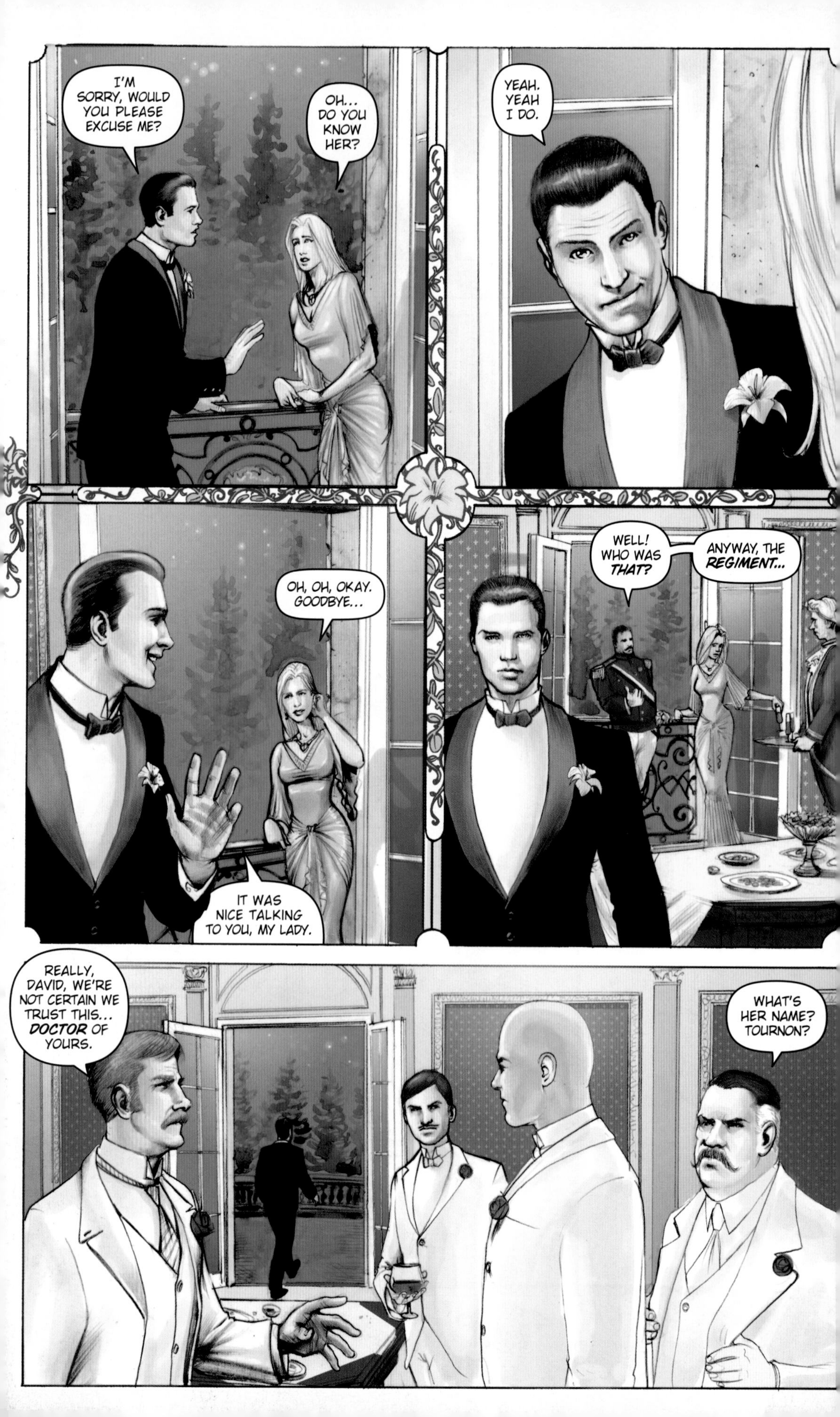
I'M SORRY, WOULD YOU PLEASE EXCUSE ME?
OH... DO YOU KNOW HER?
YEAH. YEAH I DO.
OH, OH, OKAY. GOODBYE...
IT WAS NICE TALKING TO YOU, MY LADY.
WELL! WHO WAS *THAT?*
ANYWAY, THE ***REGIMENT...***
REALLY, DAVID, WE'RE NOT CERTAIN WE TRUST THIS... ***DOCTOR*** OF YOURS.
WHAT'S HER NAME? TOURNON?

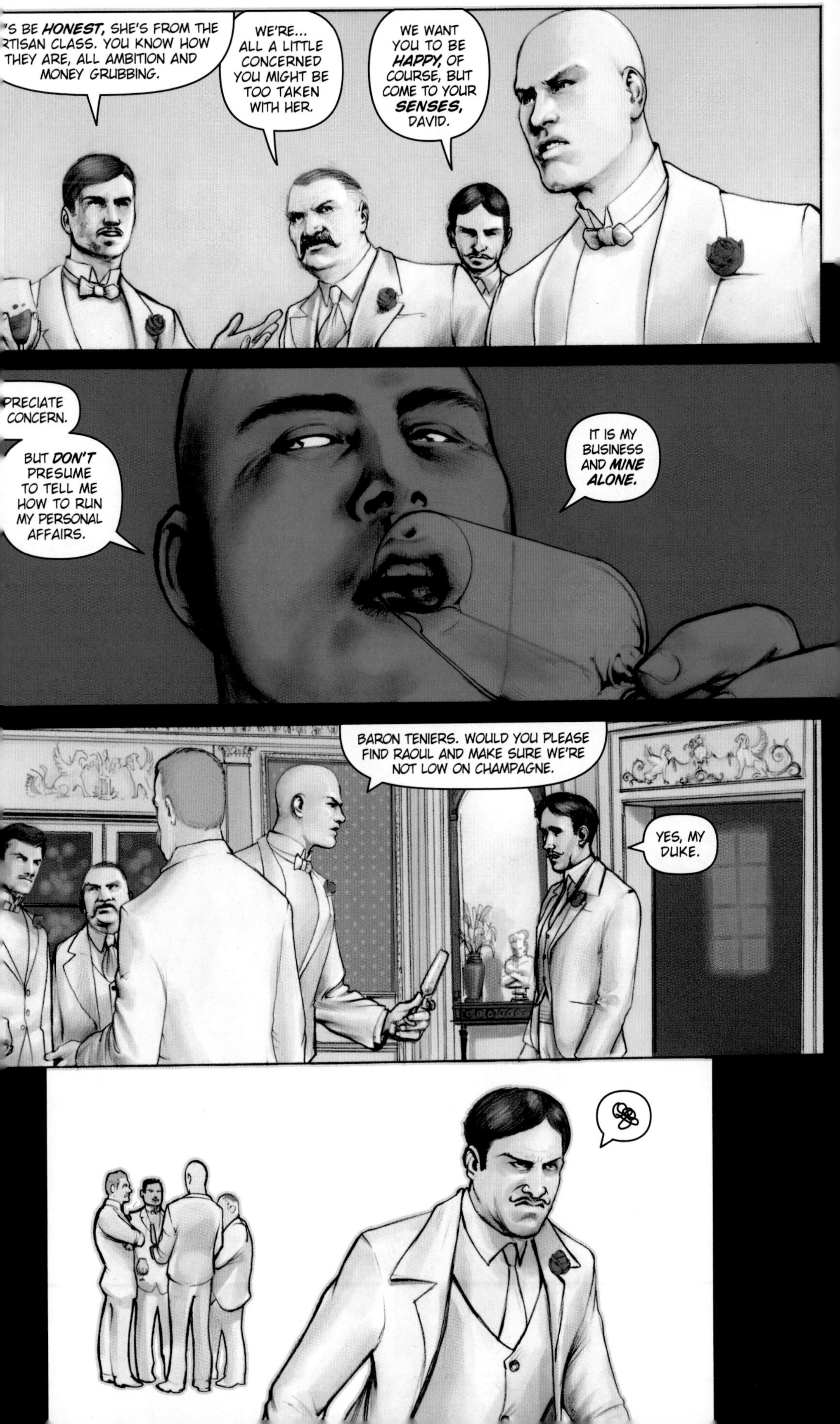
'S BE HONEST, SHE'S FROM THE RTISAN CLASS. YOU KNOW HOW THEY ARE, ALL AMBITION AND MONEY GRUBBING.
WE'RE... ALL A LITTLE CONCERNED YOU MIGHT BE TOO TAKEN WITH HER.
WE WANT YOU TO BE HAPPY, OF COURSE, BUT COME TO YOUR SENSES, DAVID.
PRECIATE CONCERN.
BUT DON'T PRESUME TO TELL ME HOW TO RUN MY PERSONAL AFFAIRS.
IT IS MY BUSINESS AND MINE ALONE.
BARON TENIERS. WOULD YOU PLEASE FIND RAOUL AND MAKE SURE WE'RE NOT LOW ON CHAMPAGNE.
YES, MY DUKE.

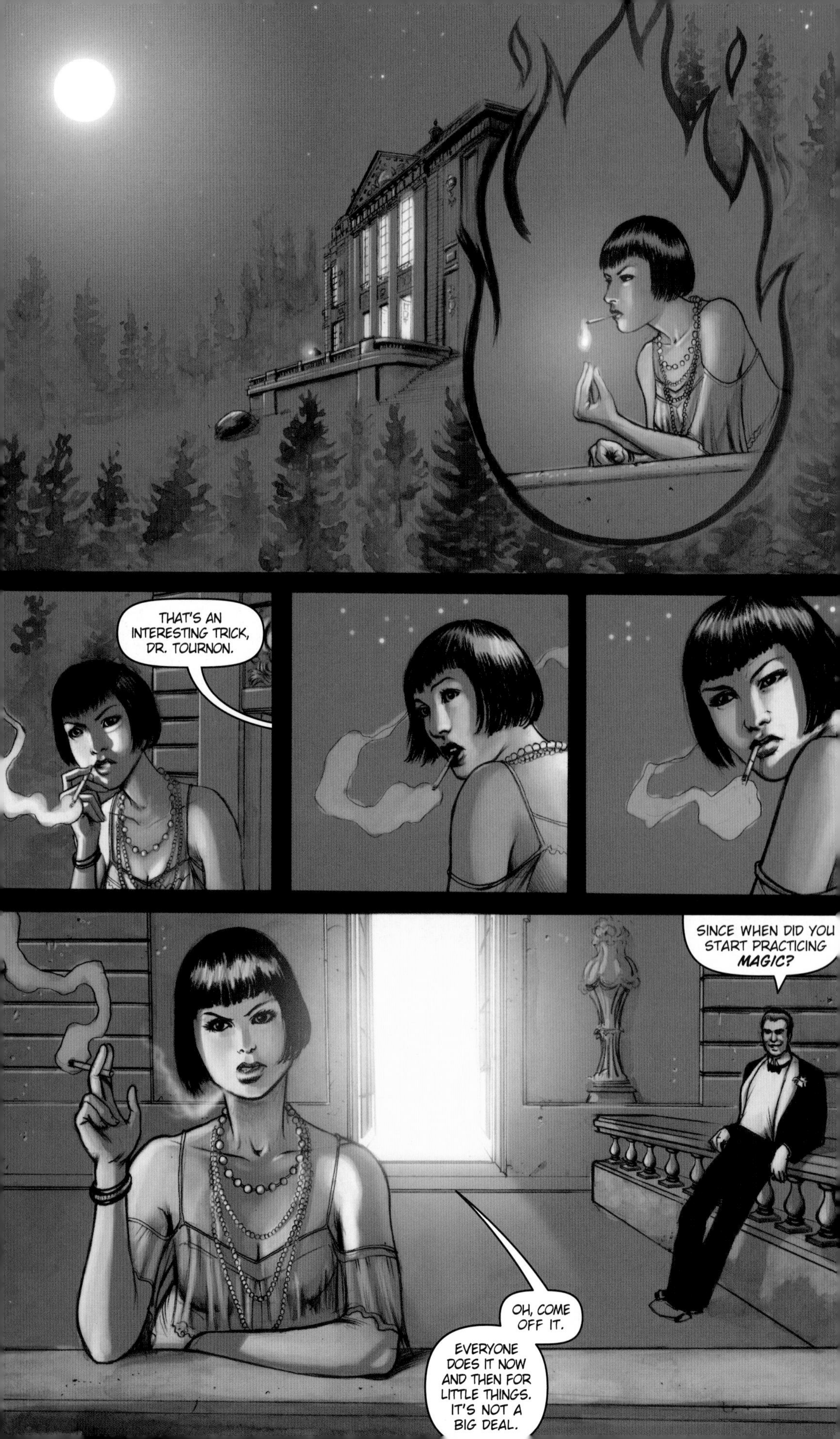
THAT'S AN INTERESTING TRICK, DR. TOURNON.
SINCE WHEN DID YOU START PRACTICING MAGIC?
OH, COME OFF IT.
EVERYONE DOES IT NOW AND THEN FOR LITTLE THINGS. IT'S NOT A BIG DEAL.

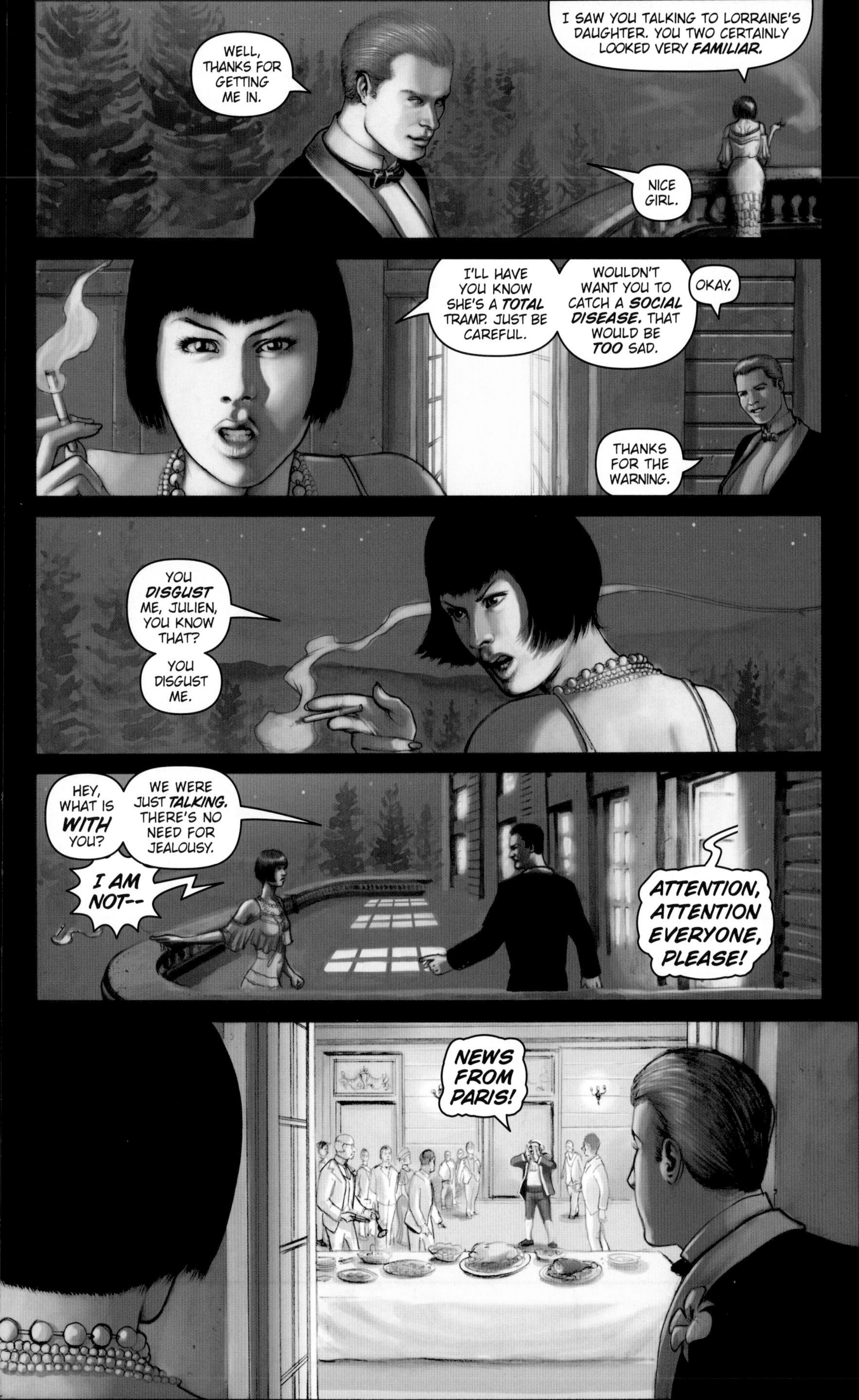
WELL, THANKS FOR GETTING ME IN.
I SAW YOU TALKING TO LORRAINE'S DAUGHTER. YOU TWO CERTAINLY LOOKED VERY FAMILIAR.
NICE GIRL.
I'LL HAVE YOU KNOW SHE'S A TOTAL TRAMP. JUST BE CAREFUL.
WOULDN'T WANT YOU TO CATCH A SOCIAL DISEASE. THAT WOULD BE TOO SAD.
OKAY.
THANKS FOR THE WARNING.
YOU DISGUST ME, JULIEN, YOU KNOW THAT?
YOU DISGUST ME.
HEY, WHAT IS WITH YOU?
WE WERE JUST TALKING. THERE'S NO NEED FOR JEALOUSY.
I AM NOT--
ATTENTION, ATTENTION EVERYONE, PLEASE!
NEWS FROM PARIS!

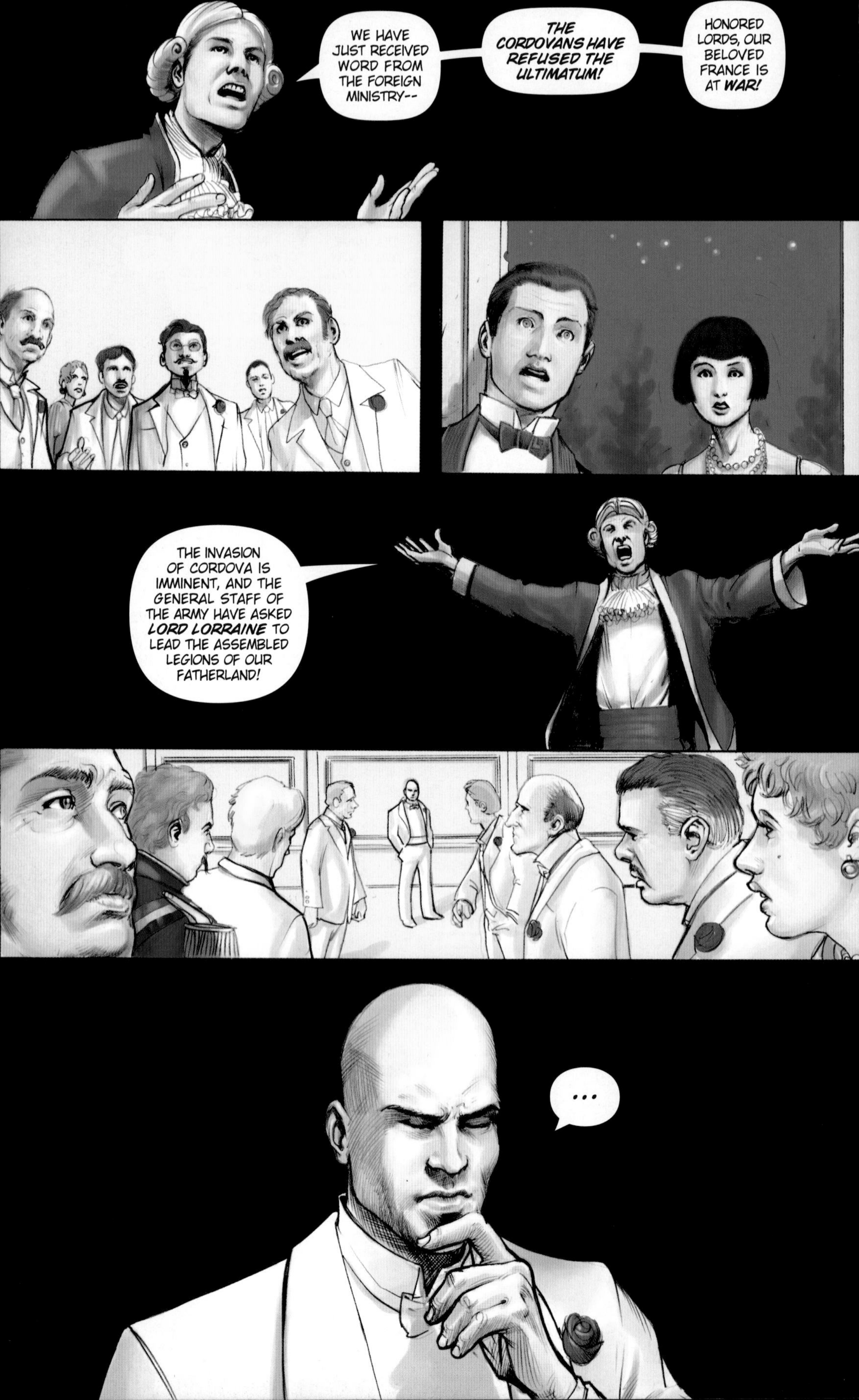
WE HAVE JUST RECEIVED WORD FROM THE FOREIGN MINISTRY--
THE CORDOVANS HAVE REFUSED THE ULTIMATUM!
HONORED LORDS, OUR BELOVED FRANCE IS AT WAR!
THE INVASION OF CORDOVA IS IMMINENT, AND THE GENERAL STAFF OF THE ARMY HAVE ASKED LORD LORRAINE TO LEAD THE ASSEMBLED LEGIONS OF OUR FATHERLAND!
...

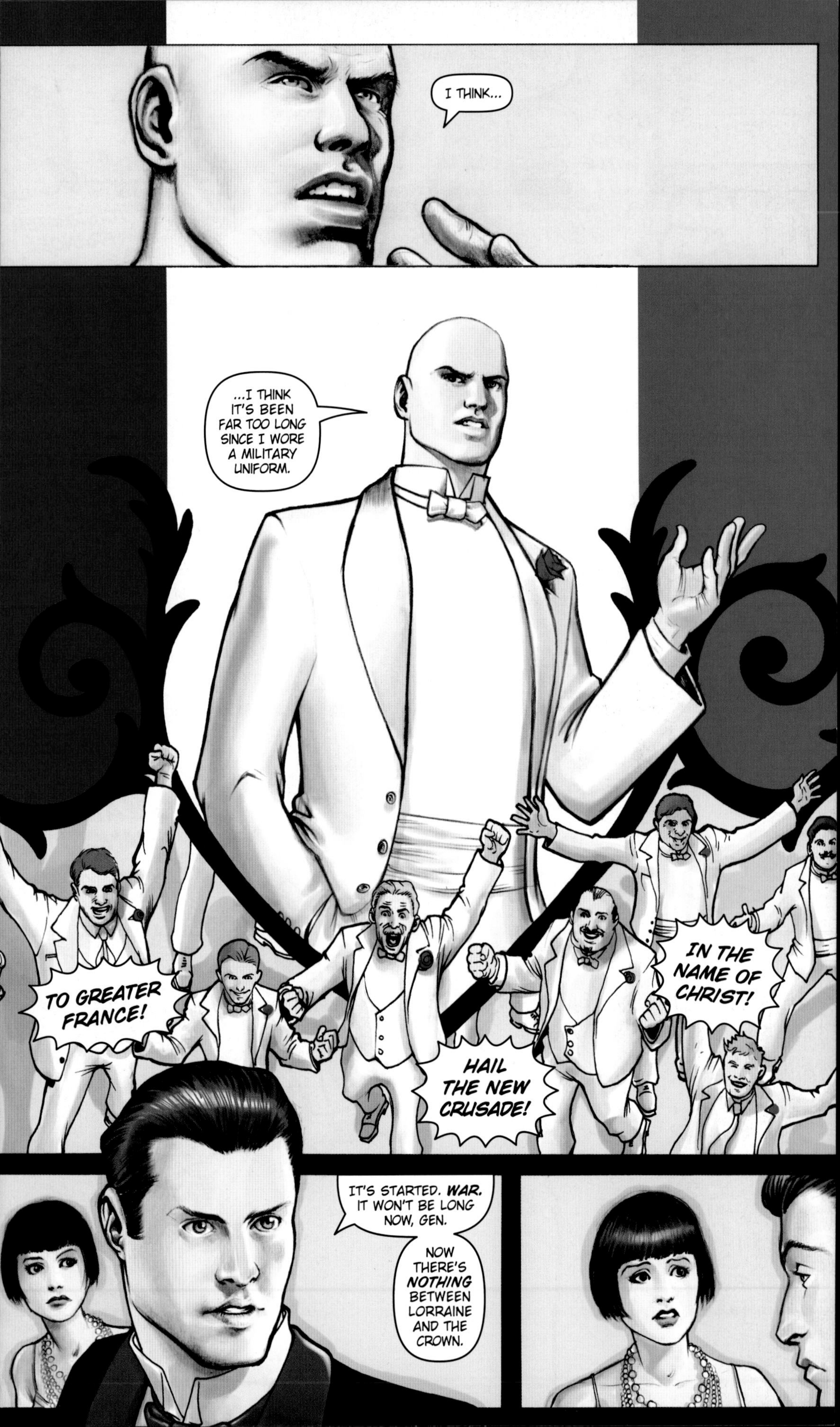
I THINK...
...I THINK IT'S BEEN FAR TOO LONG SINCE I WORE A MILITARY UNIFORM.
TO GREATER FRANCE!
HAIL THE NEW CRUSADE!
IN THE NAME OF CHRIST!
IT'S STARTED. WAR. IT WON'T BE LONG NOW, GEN.
NOW THERE'S NOTHING BETWEEN LORRAINE AND THE CROWN.

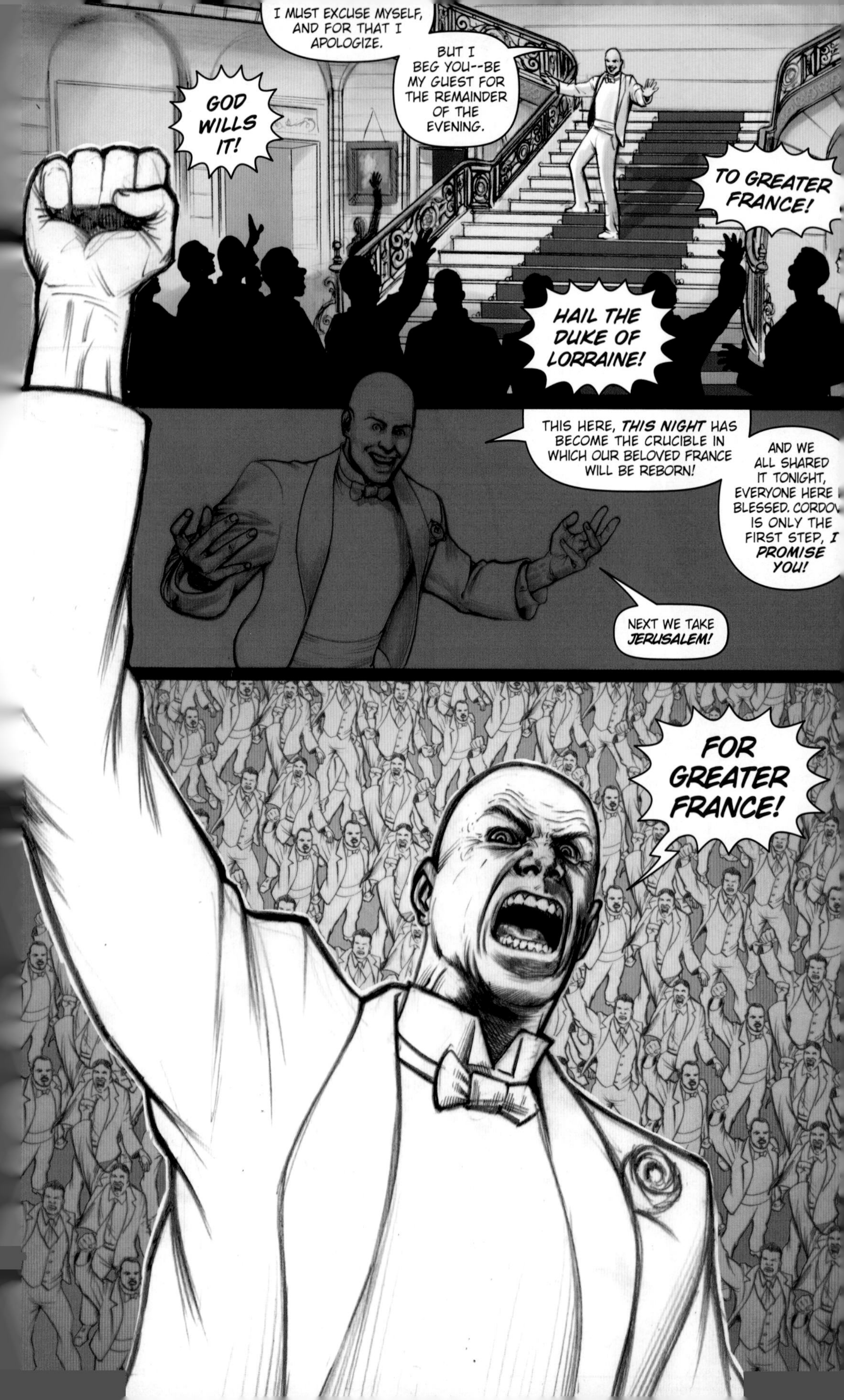
I MUST EXCUSE MYSELF, AND FOR THAT I APOLOGIZE.
BUT I BEG YOU--BE MY GUEST FOR THE REMAINDER OF THE EVENING.
GOD WILLS IT!
TO GREATER FRANCE!
HAIL THE DUKE OF LORRAINE!
THIS HERE, THIS NIGHT HAS BECOME THE CRUCIBLE IN WHICH OUR BELOVED FRANCE WILL BE REBORN!
AND WE ALL SHARED IT TONIGHT, EVERYONE HERE IS BLESSED. CORDOV IS ONLY THE FIRST STEP, I PROMISE YOU!
NEXT WE TAKE JERUSALEM!
FOR GREATER FRANCE!

Le Journal de la Liberté

Paris' leading anglophone newspaper • vol. 205, no. 101 • Nov. 4, MCMXXXIII

Editors in Chief: M. Tait Bergstrom, M. Matthew Pasteris. **Story Editor:** M. Arvid Nelson.
Art Editor: M. Juan Ferreyra. **Photography Editor:** M. Alexander Waldman.
Layout Supervisor: M. William Kartalopoulos. **Editors Emeritus:** M. Clark A. Smith,
M. Howard P. Lovecraft, M. Robert E. Howard. Redacted by the Holy Inquisition under the direction
of His Excellency Archbishop Emile-Jean Ireneaux. Le Journal de la Liberté is printed under the benign
auspices of his most puissant majesty KING LOUIS XXII of FRANCE. GOD SAVE THE KING.

Papal seal

of Approval

LORRAINE ISSUES ULTIMATUM TO CORDOVA; TWENTY-FOUR HOURS TO WAR?

The Duke of Lorraine strides confidently out of parliament following a series of stunning political victories that have pushed Europe to the brink of war.

Paris, The Assemblée Nationale – The Duke of Lorraine proposed and oversaw the passage of a harshly worded ultimatum to the Cordovan Emirate yesterday.

The ultimatum calls for "free access in Cordovan lands" for French officials, "military and otherwise" in the name of "eradicating Islamic extremism." Cordova has 48 hours to comply or France will declare war.

The Halls of the Robe and the Sword passed the ultimatum just over 24 hours ago at the time this article went to press.

French troops are massing in the newly gained territories of Navarre, Aragon and Catalonia in what the Duke of Lorraine calls a "last-ditch hope that a show of force might bring the Cordovans to accept the resolution."

But the Cordovans do not seem likely to acquiesce. Ha-run Ali Al-Faddiq, the Cordovan ambassador to France, forcefully rejected the terms.

"'Free access' is a euphemism for occupation," Al-Faddiq said. "The Emir cannot accept foreign troops on Cordovan soil. It may be Lorraine has presented my lord with these impossible demands because he wants war."

A spokesman for the Duke of Lorraine rejected that notion.

The Cordovan Emir withdrew his consulate from France last evening. Spokesmen from the French crown have not confirmed or denied rumors of desperate, eleventh-hour talks between Al-Faddiq and Sir Charles Martel, King Louis' mayor of the court.

King Louis himself voted against Lorraine's resolution but once again found himself outmaneuvered by the Duke.

The resolution passed unanimously in the Hall of the Sword but faced stern opposition in the Robe. However, the Crown's historical influence on the Robe did not hold; the Robe adopted Lorraine's ultimatum by a margin of five votes, overriding the Crown's "nay."

The ultimatum comes fast on the heels of the assassination of the Marquis of Aragon on the eve of the reunification of his lands with France.

Aragon was the second Spanish lord to have died recently – the Marquis of Navarre was killed in a hunting accident only a few days before. The deaths of the two marquises has sped up the transfer of their lands to French sovereignty, a long-time goal of the Duke of Lorraine.

There is widespread speculation Moslem extremists are responsible for Aragon's murder. Cordovan officials strongly deny the claim.

Already, sides are lining up in what looks increasingly like unavoidable armed conflict.

England has declared her support for France, while the Holy Roman Empire, The Ottoman Empire, and the Prussian Empire have forged allegiances.

Russia has long supported the Serbs living under the rule of the Hapsburg Holy Roman Emperors. It is widely believed Tzar Nicholas II is looking to expand Russia's sphere of influence westwards, and he and Austria's Emperor Rudolf are at loggerheads on the issue of Serbia.

"Russia's involvement in this war, if it will come to war, is by no means assured," a source within the Russian cabinet said.

"But it's hard to imagine Serbian nationalists wouldn't take advantage of the situation and spread the conflict all across Europe.

"The armies of the Holy Roman Empire can't fight a war on two fronts. Russia can and will capitalize on that, along with her allies England and France."

The colonial holdings of the
continued on page A2

Altercation Between Lorraine and Prussian Ambassador Raises Stakes in Showdown

Paris, The Assemblée Nationale – Otto Von Neuss, Prussia's ambassador to France, denounced the Duke of Lorraine on the front steps of the Assemblée Nationale yesterday as stark evidence of the imminence of war.

Prussia has allied herself with the Ottoman Empire, and finds herself bound by a pledge to join the Ottomans in any declaration of war.

"If the Ottomans declare war on a nation, so too does Prussia," Von Neuss said. The Ottoman Sultan, Suleiman III, has stated he would consider "any act of Christian aggression against our Cordovan brothers to be an act of war on Istanbul itself."

Prussian officials claim the Kaiser has his own reasons to be concerned.

"French colonial encroachment upon the Iberian Peninsula could be the opening salvo of a much larger campaign for domination of all Europe," a spokesman for the Prussian Kaiser said.

During the encounter at the Assemblée Nationale, the Prussian ambassador called the mobilization of French troops "unacceptable" and demanded Lorraine retract the ultimatum or Prussia would "be forced to declare war."

The Duke of Lorraine did not respond.

Later, in a press conference at his chateau outside Paris, he offered the following:

"The Prussians have made their choice, forging pacts with infidels," Lorraine said. "The Bible is very clear about what happens to those who betray Christ."

LES ARMES DES SAINTS

et in arcadia ego...

PATER NOSTER QVI EST IN COELIS

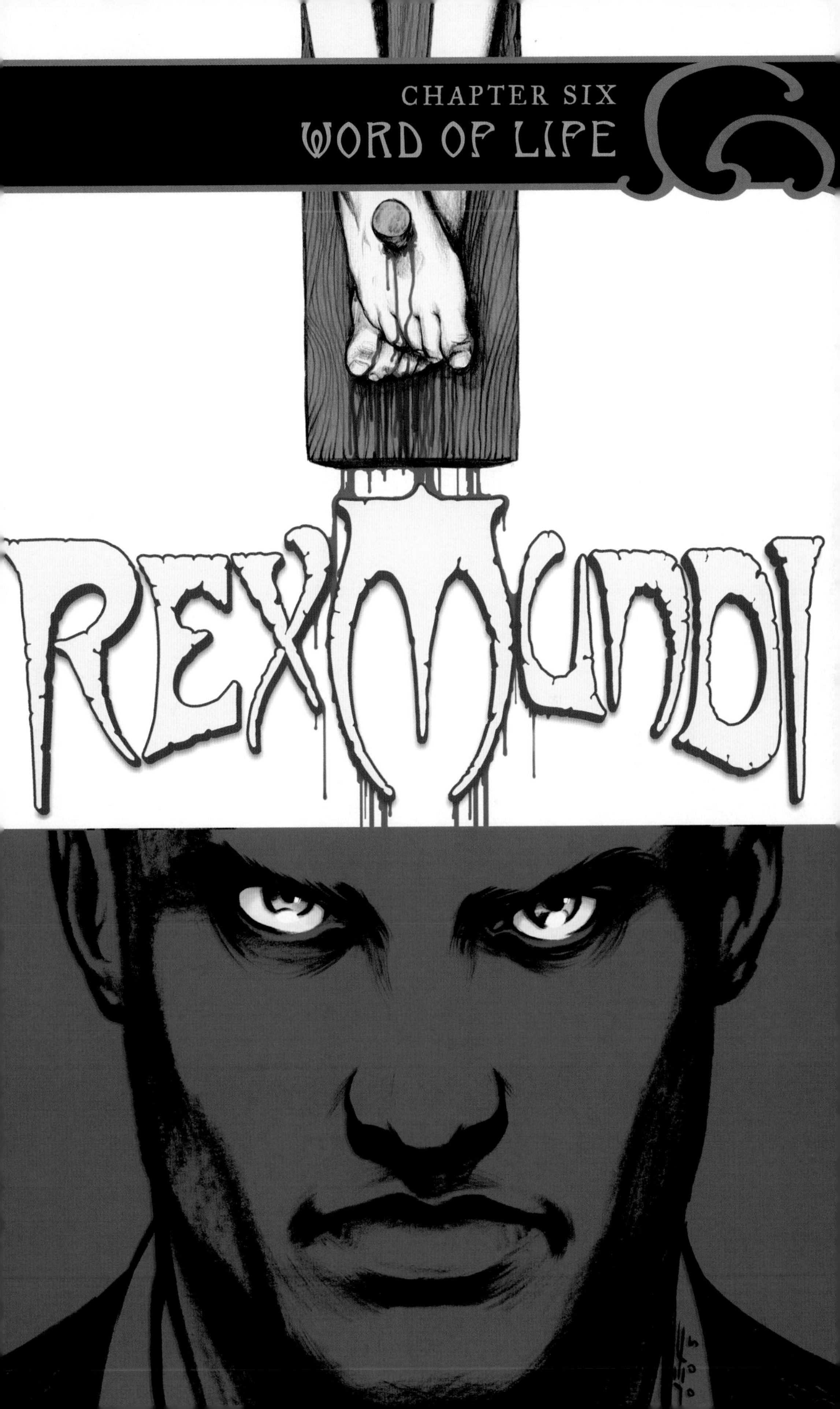

CHAPTER SIX
WORD OF LIFE
REX MUNDI

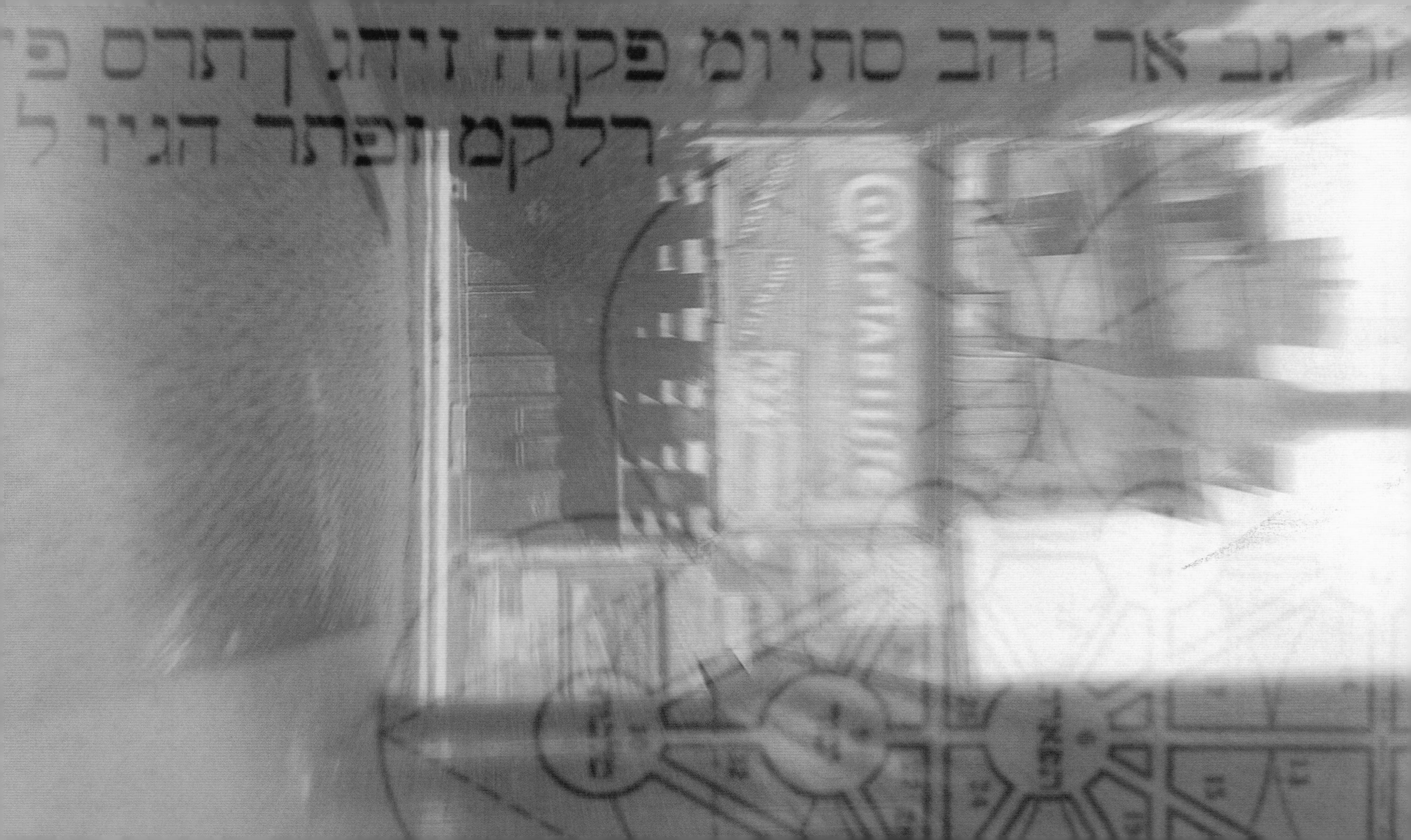
ה' גב אר והב סתיום פקוה זיהג דתרס פ'
רלקמ זפתר הגיו ל

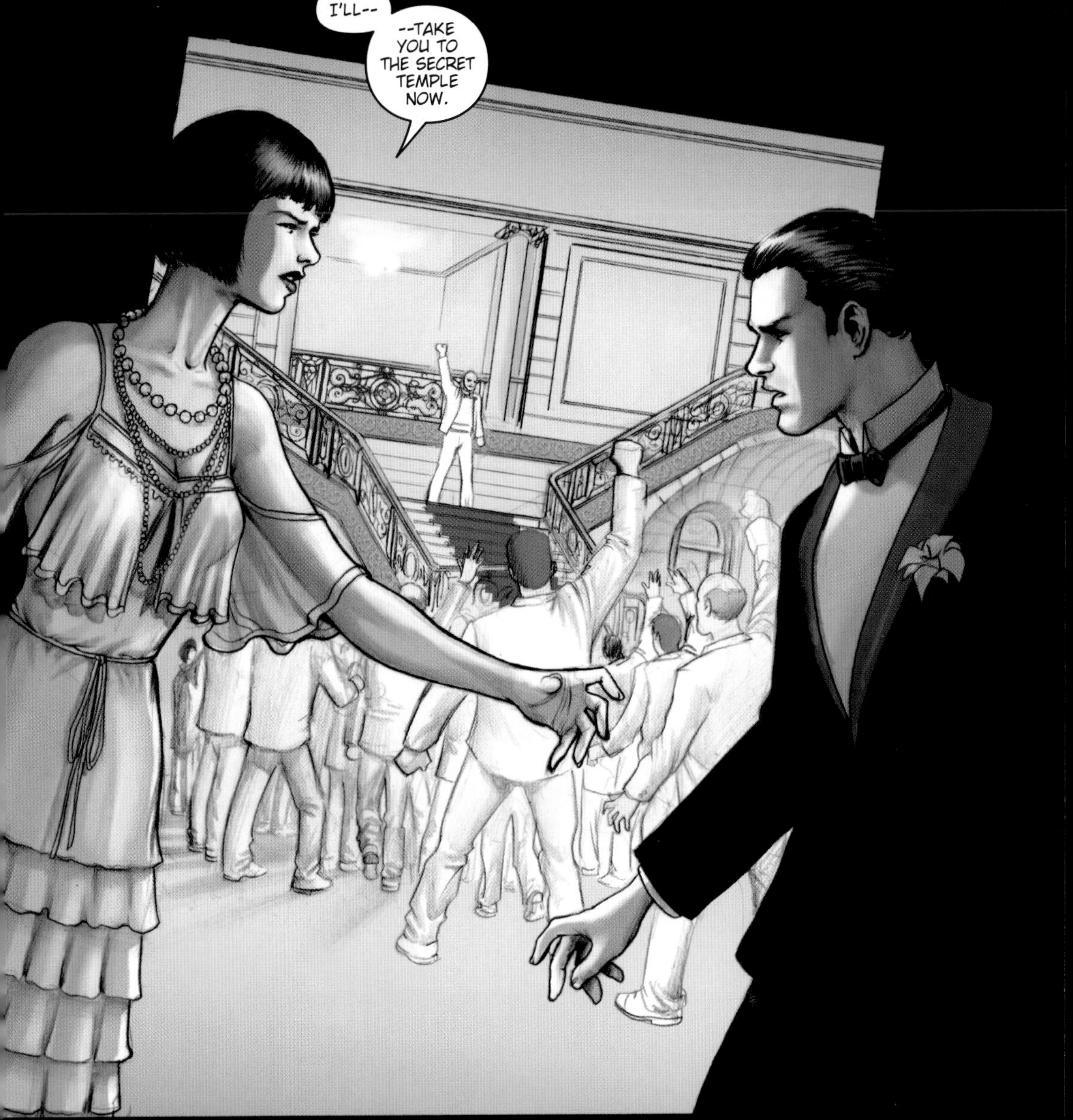
I'LL--
--TAKE YOU TO THE SECRET TEMPLE NOW.

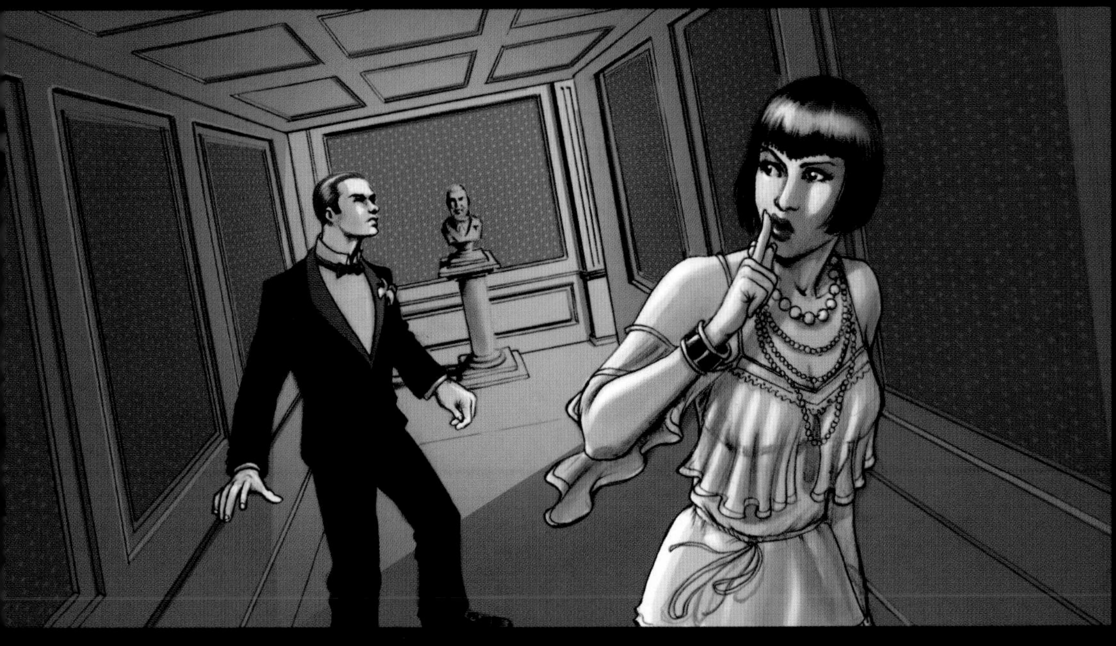

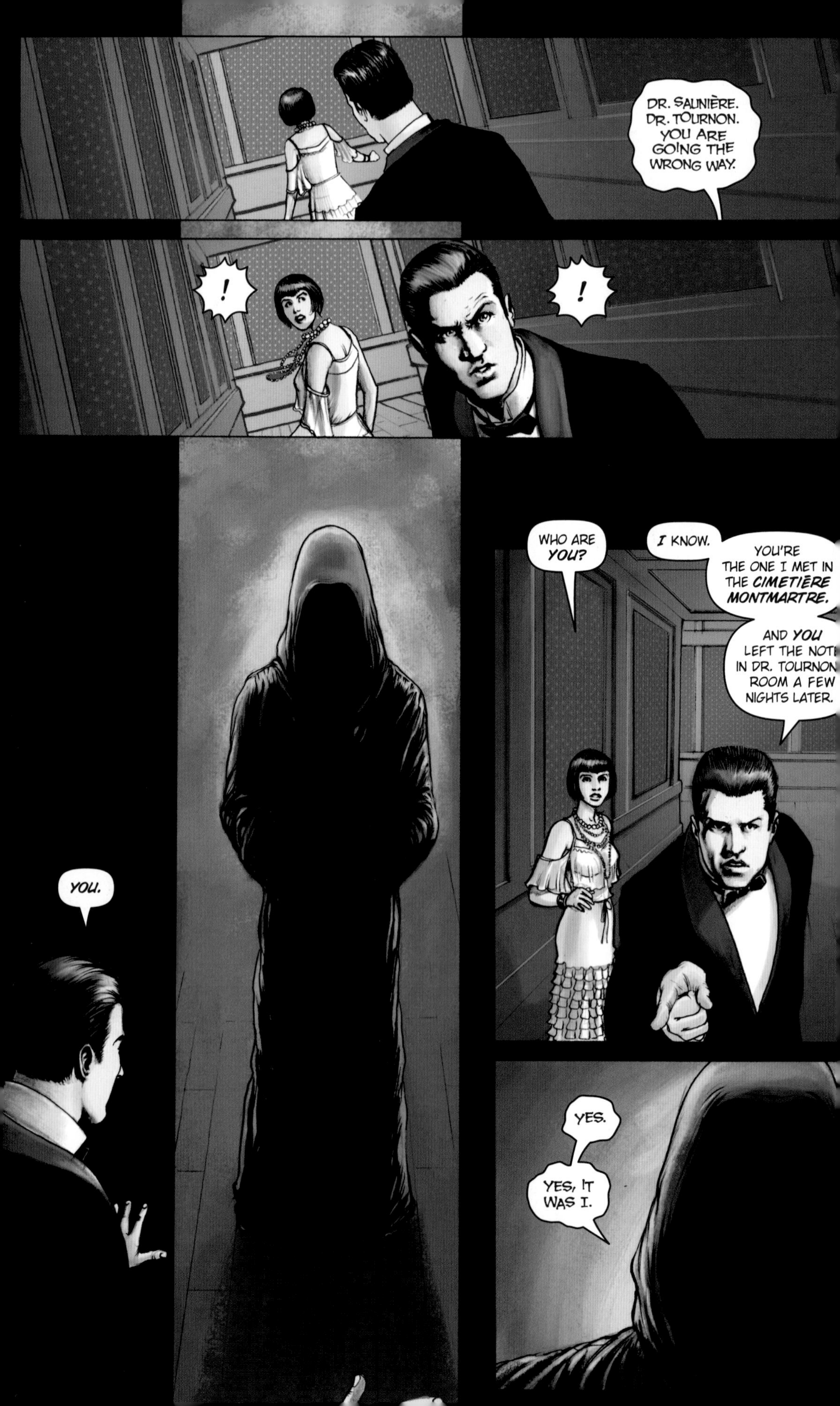
DR. SAUNIÈRE. DR. TOURNON. YOU ARE GOING THE WRONG WAY.
!
!
YOU.
WHO ARE YOU?
I KNOW.
YOU'RE THE ONE I MET IN THE CIMETIÈRE MONTMARTRE.
AND YOU LEFT THE NOT IN DR. TOURNON ROOM A FEW NIGHTS LATER.
YES.
YES, IT WAS I.

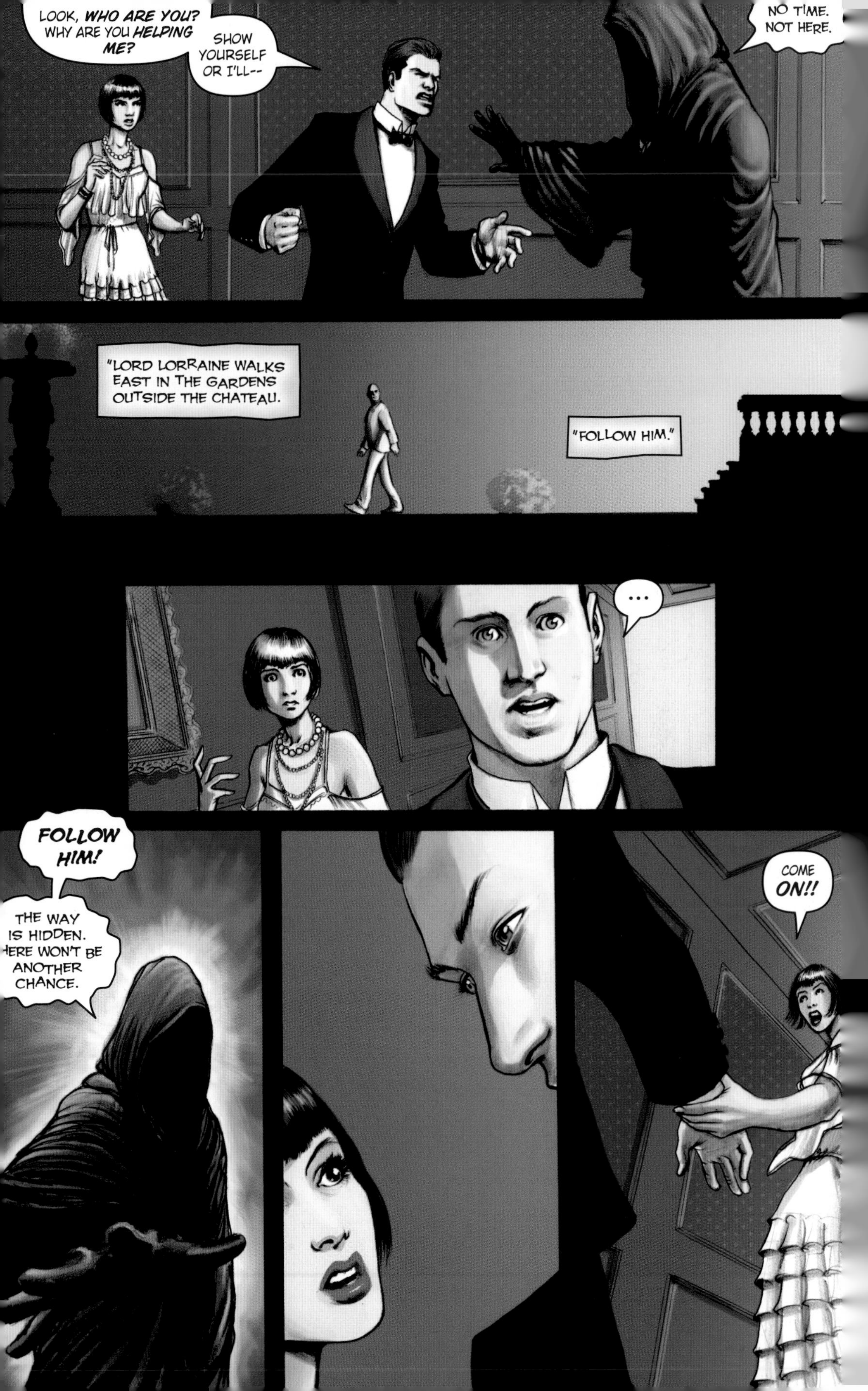
LOOK, WHO ARE YOU? WHY ARE YOU HELPING ME?
SHOW YOURSELF OR I'LL--
NO TIME. NOT HERE.
"LORD LORRAINE WALKS EAST IN THE GARDENS OUTSIDE THE CHATEAU.
"FOLLOW HIM."
...
FOLLOW HIM!
THE WAY IS HIDDEN. HERE WON'T BE ANOTHER CHANCE.
COME ON!!

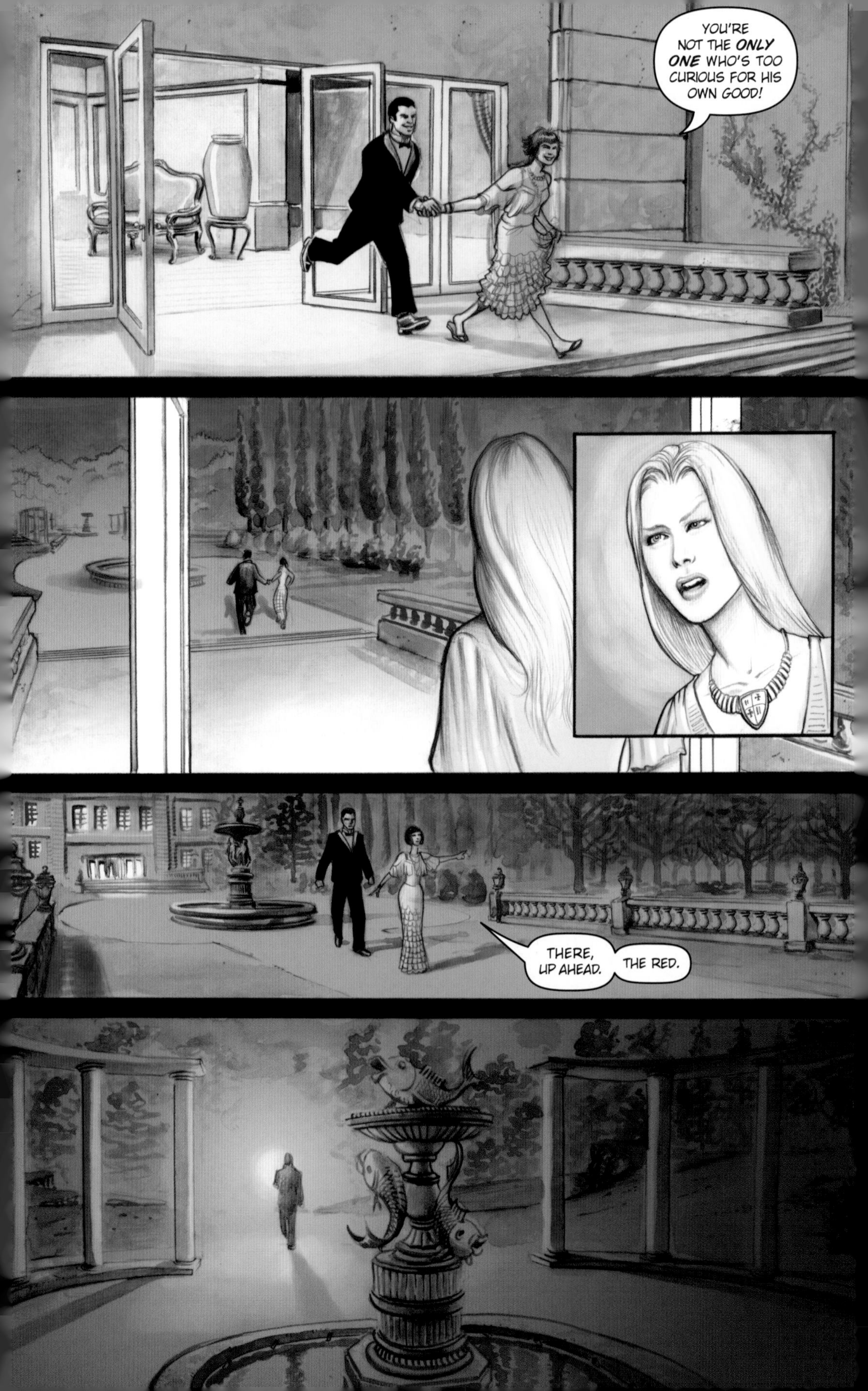
YOU'RE NOT THE ONLY ONE WHO'S TOO CURIOUS FOR HIS OWN GOOD!
THERE, UP AHEAD.
THE RED.

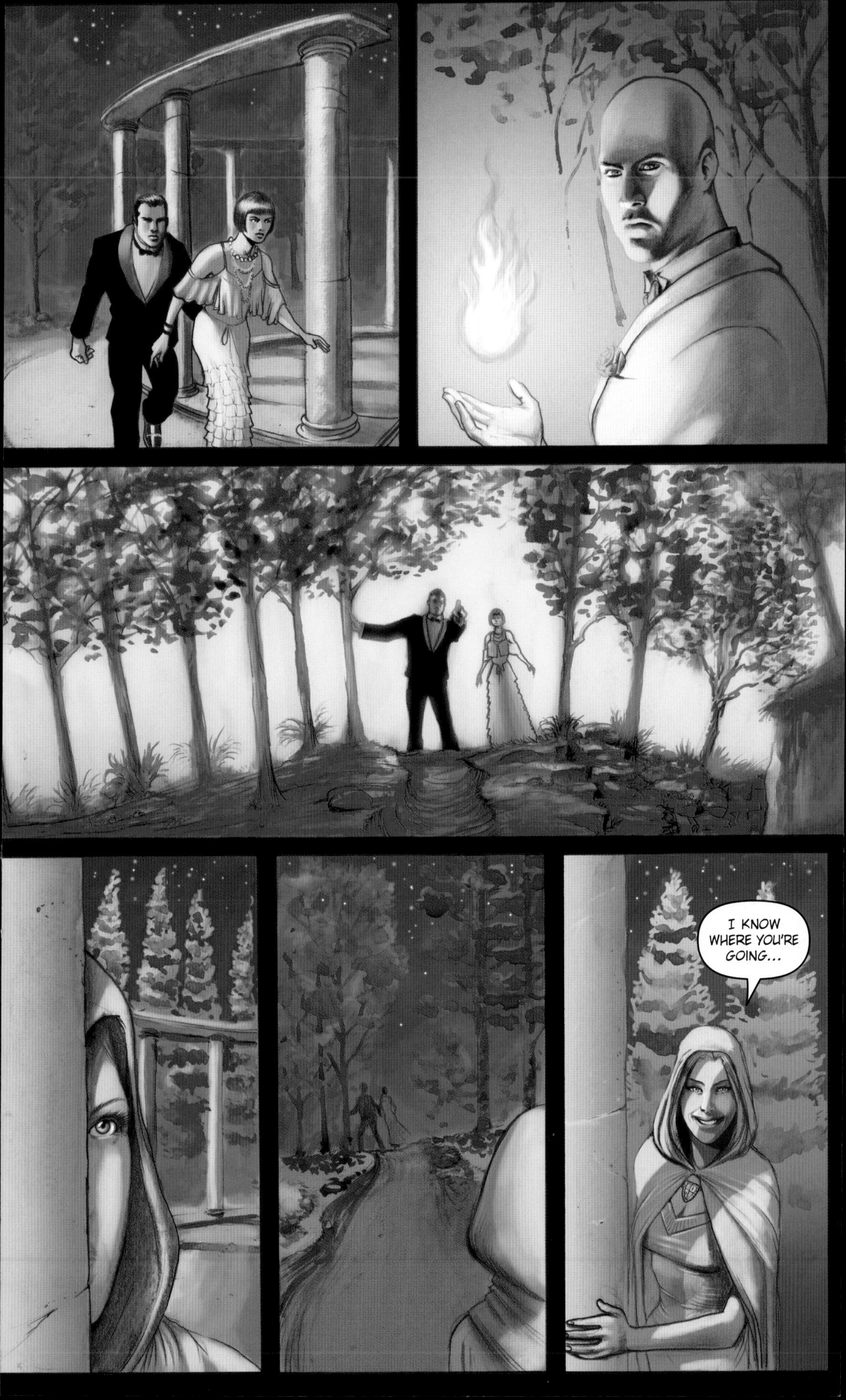
I KNOW WHERE YOU'RE GOING...

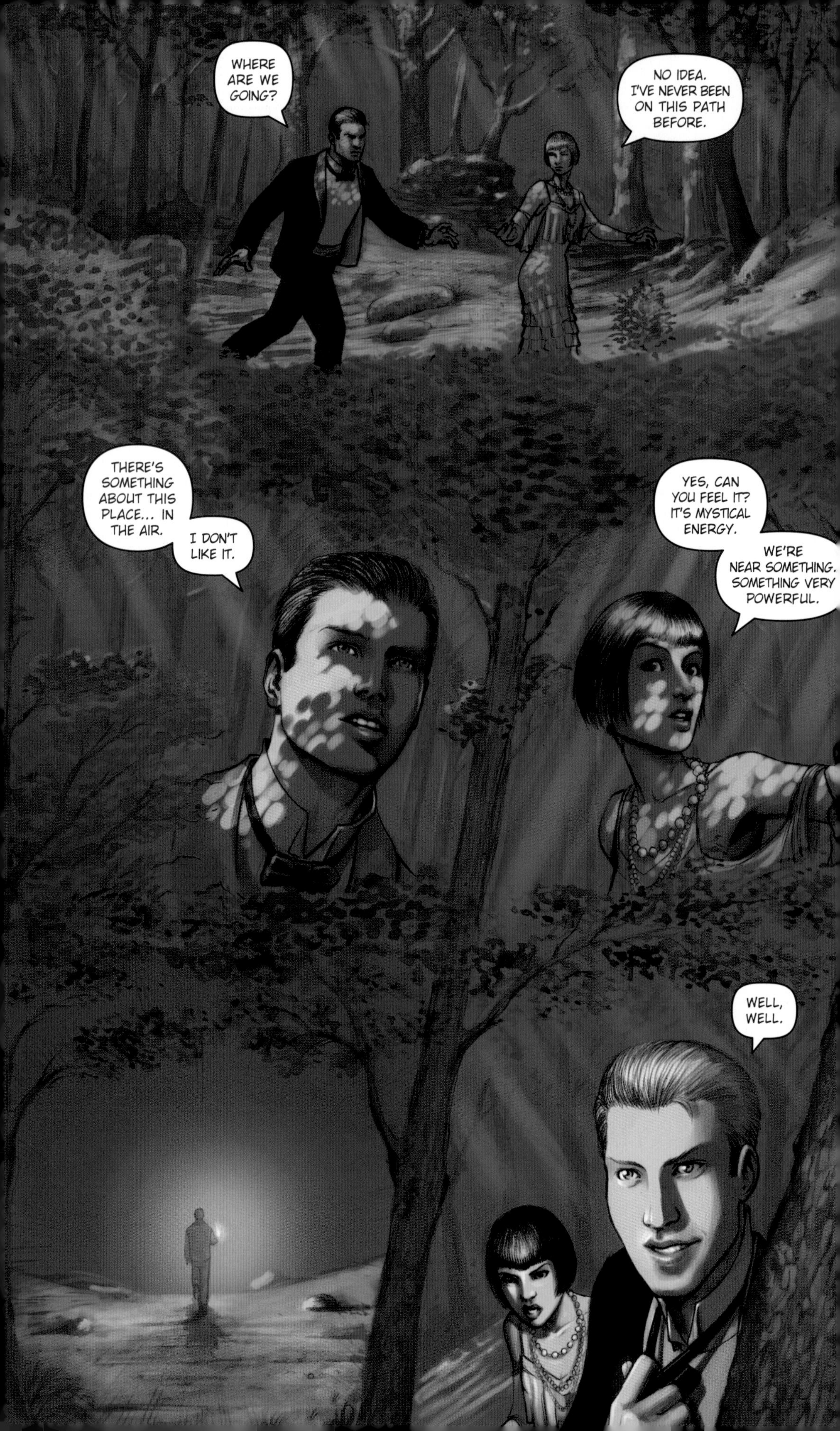
WHERE ARE WE GOING?
NO IDEA. I'VE NEVER BEEN ON THIS PATH BEFORE.
THERE'S SOMETHING ABOUT THIS PLACE... IN THE AIR.
I DON'T LIKE IT.
YES, CAN YOU FEEL IT? IT'S MYSTICAL ENERGY.
WE'RE NEAR SOMETHING. SOMETHING VERY POWERFUL.
WELL, WELL.

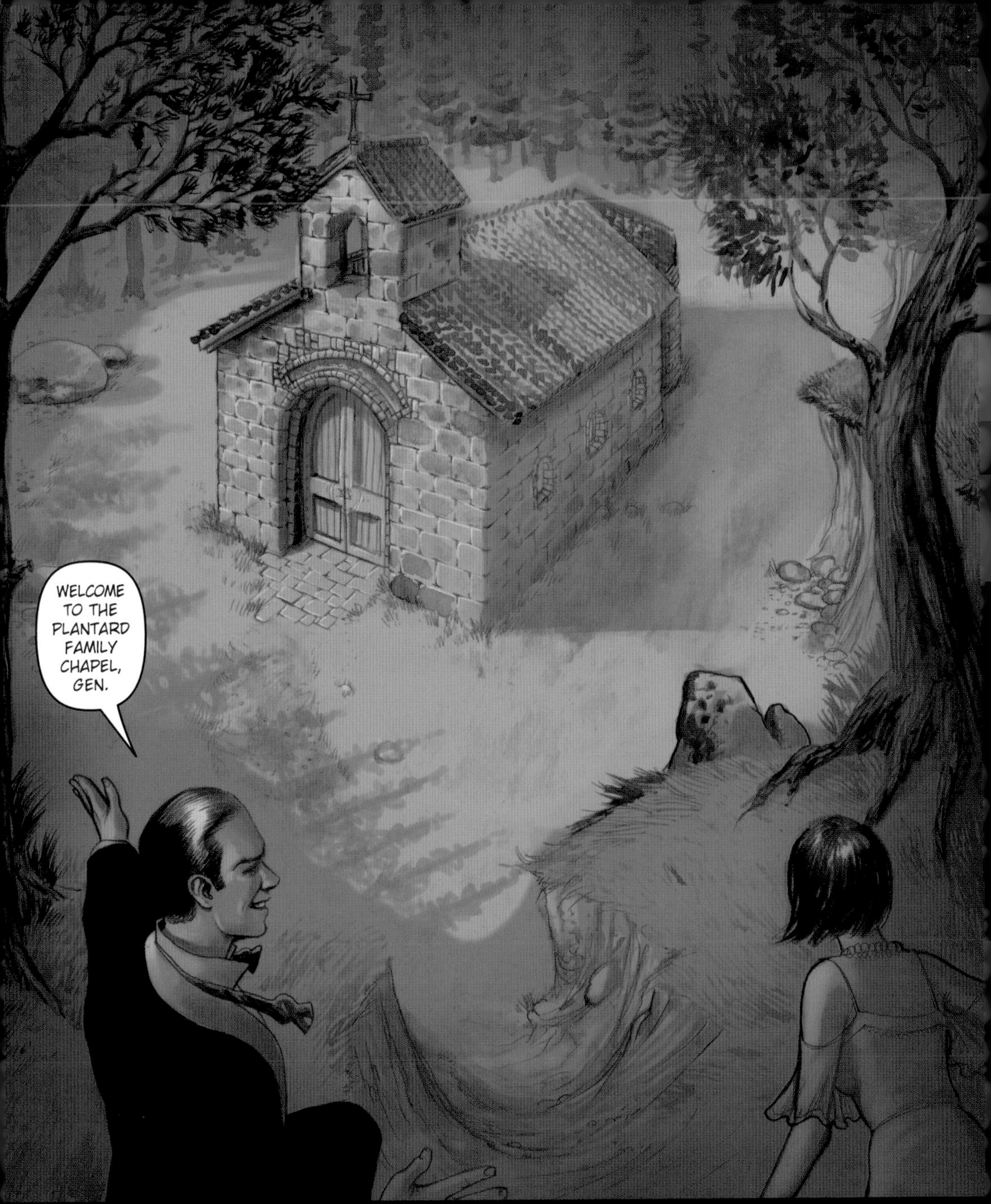
WELCOME TO THE PLANTARD FAMILY CHAPEL, GEN.

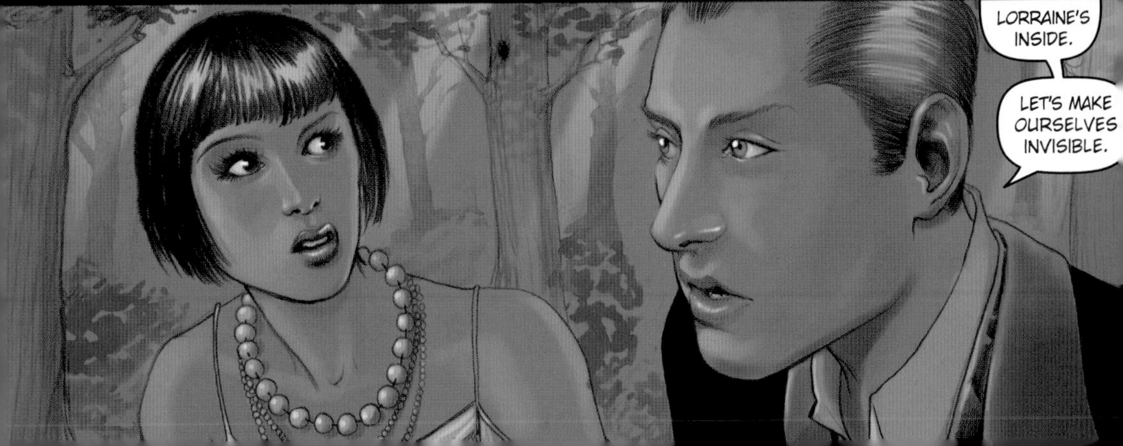
LORRAINE'S INSIDE.
LET'S MAKE OURSELVES INVISIBLE.

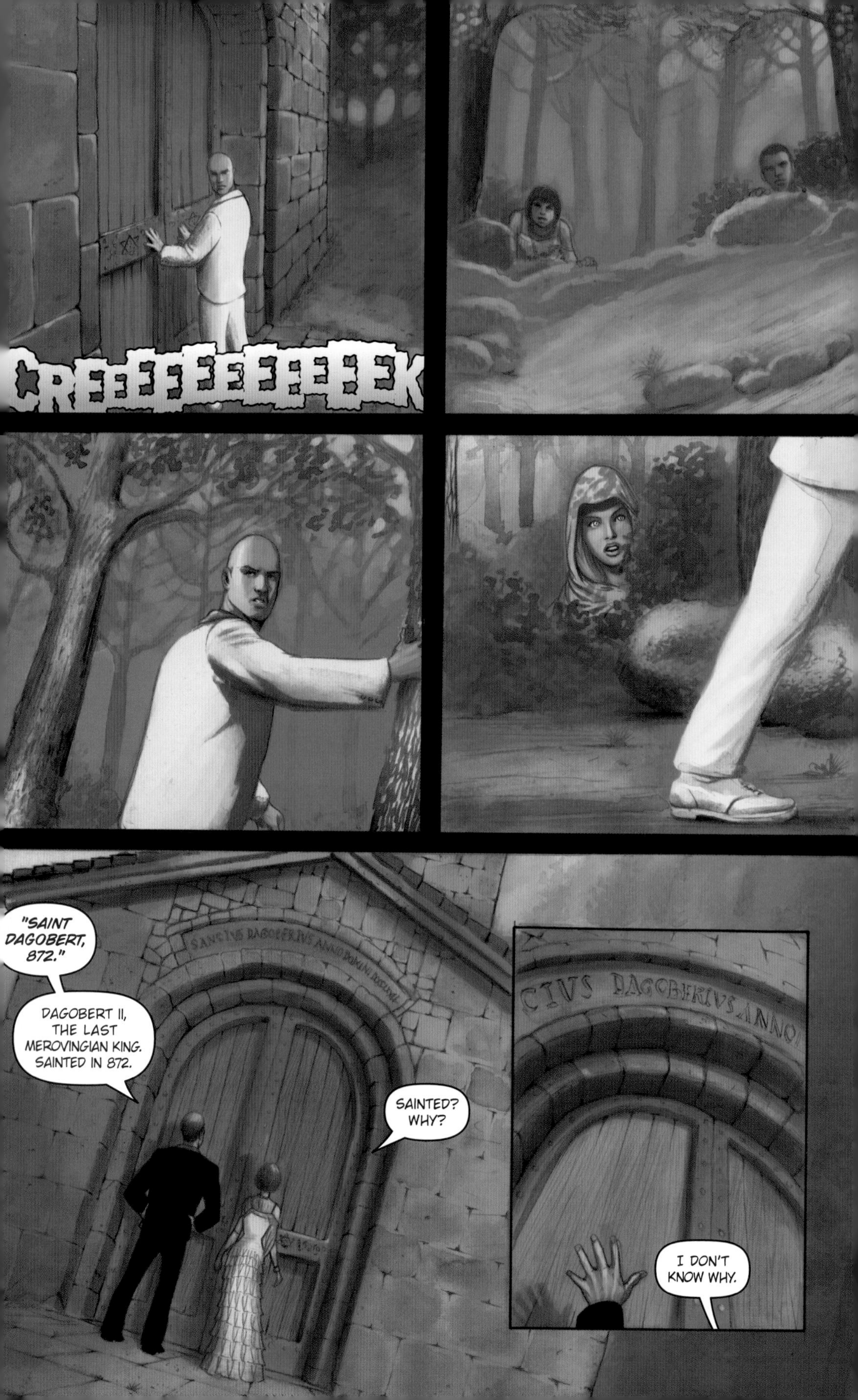
CREEEEEEEEEEEK
"SAINT DAGOBERT, 872."
DAGOBERT II, THE LAST MEROVINGIAN KING. SAINTED IN 872.
SAINTED? WHY?
I DON'T KNOW WHY.

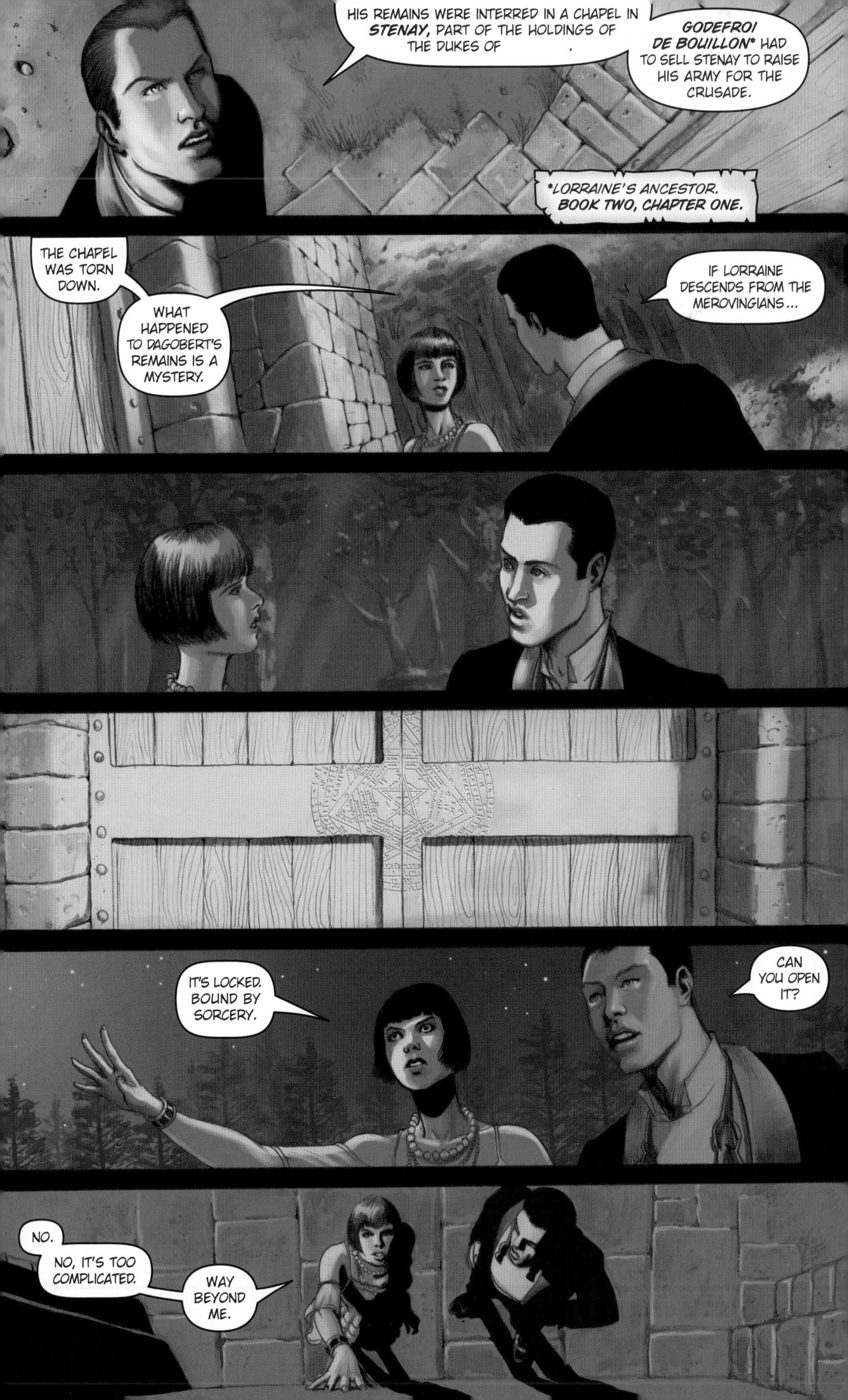
HIS REMAINS WERE INTERRED IN A CHAPEL IN STENAY, PART OF THE HOLDINGS OF THE DUKES OF .
GODEFROI DE BOUILLON* HAD TO SELL STENAY TO RAISE HIS ARMY FOR THE CRUSADE.
*LORRAINE'S ANCESTOR. BOOK TWO, CHAPTER ONE.
THE CHAPEL WAS TORN DOWN.
WHAT HAPPENED TO DAGOBERT'S REMAINS IS A MYSTERY.
IF LORRAINE DESCENDS FROM THE MEROVINGIANS...
IT'S LOCKED. BOUND BY SORCERY.
CAN YOU OPEN IT?
NO.
NO, IT'S TOO COMPLICATED.
WAY BEYOND ME.

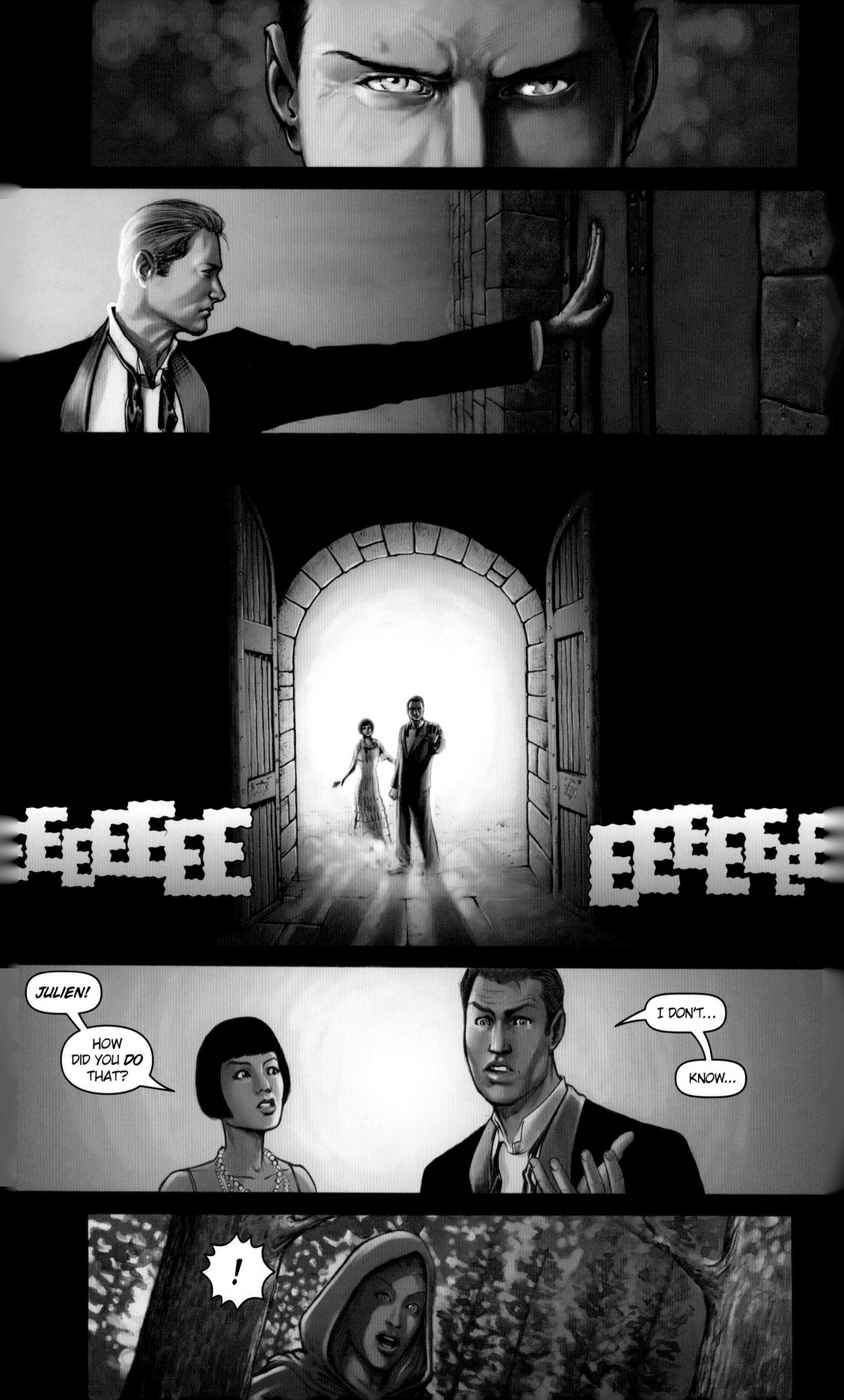
EEEEEE
EEEEEE
JULIEN!
HOW DID YOU DO THAT?
I DON'T...
KNOW...
!

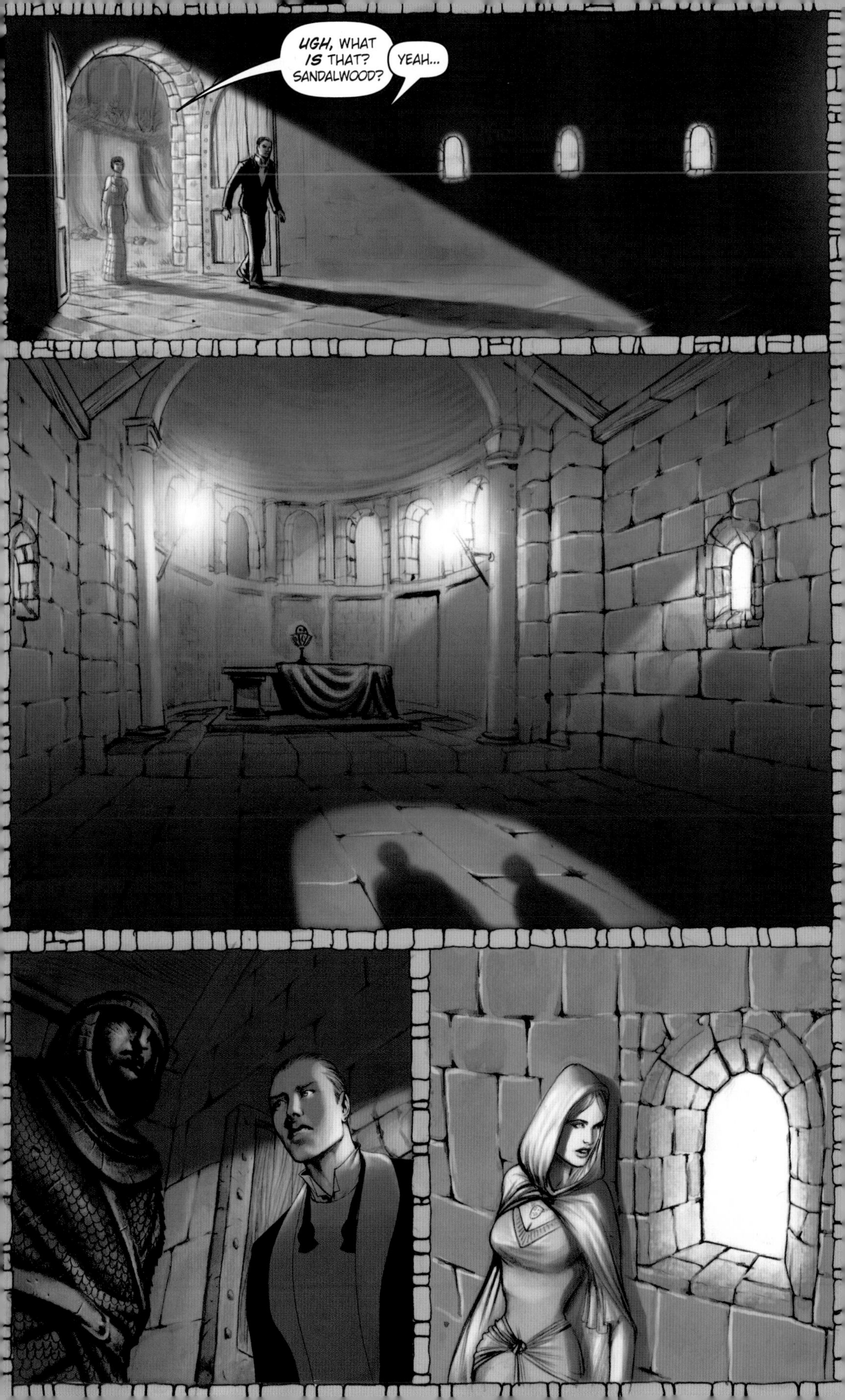
UGH, WHAT IS THAT? SANDALWOOD?
YEAH...

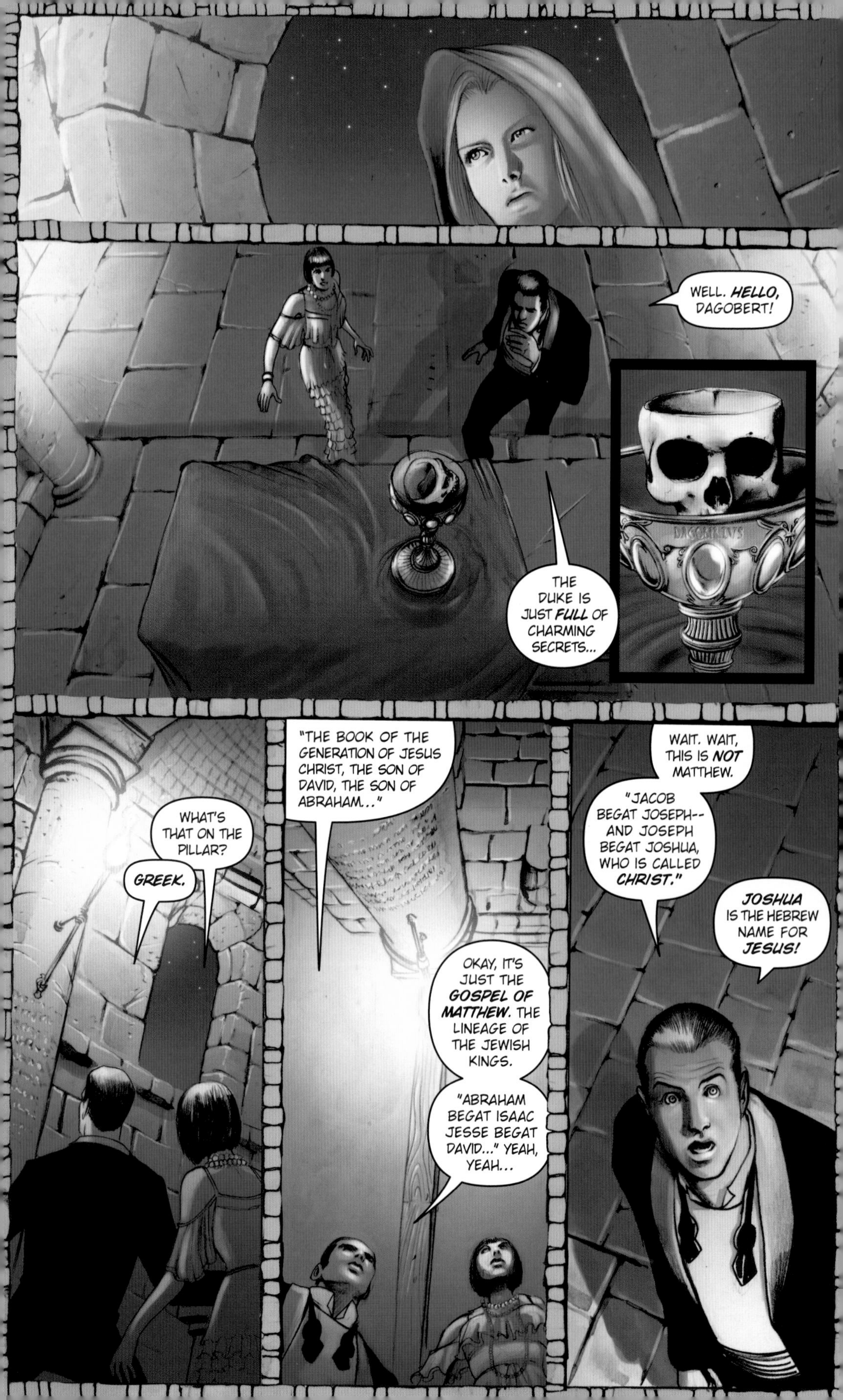
WELL. HELLO, DAGOBERT!
THE DUKE IS JUST FULL OF CHARMING SECRETS...
DAGOBERTVS
WHAT'S THAT ON THE PILLAR?
GREEK.
"THE BOOK OF THE GENERATION OF JESUS CHRIST, THE SON OF DAVID, THE SON OF ABRAHAM..."
OKAY, IT'S JUST THE GOSPEL OF MATTHEW. THE LINEAGE OF THE JEWISH KINGS.
"ABRAHAM BEGAT ISAAC JESSE BEGAT DAVID..." YEAH, YEAH...
WAIT. WAIT, THIS IS NOT MATTHEW.
"JACOB BEGAT JOSEPH-- AND JOSEPH BEGAT JOSHUA, WHO IS CALLED CHRIST."
JOSHUA IS THE HEBREW NAME FOR JESUS!

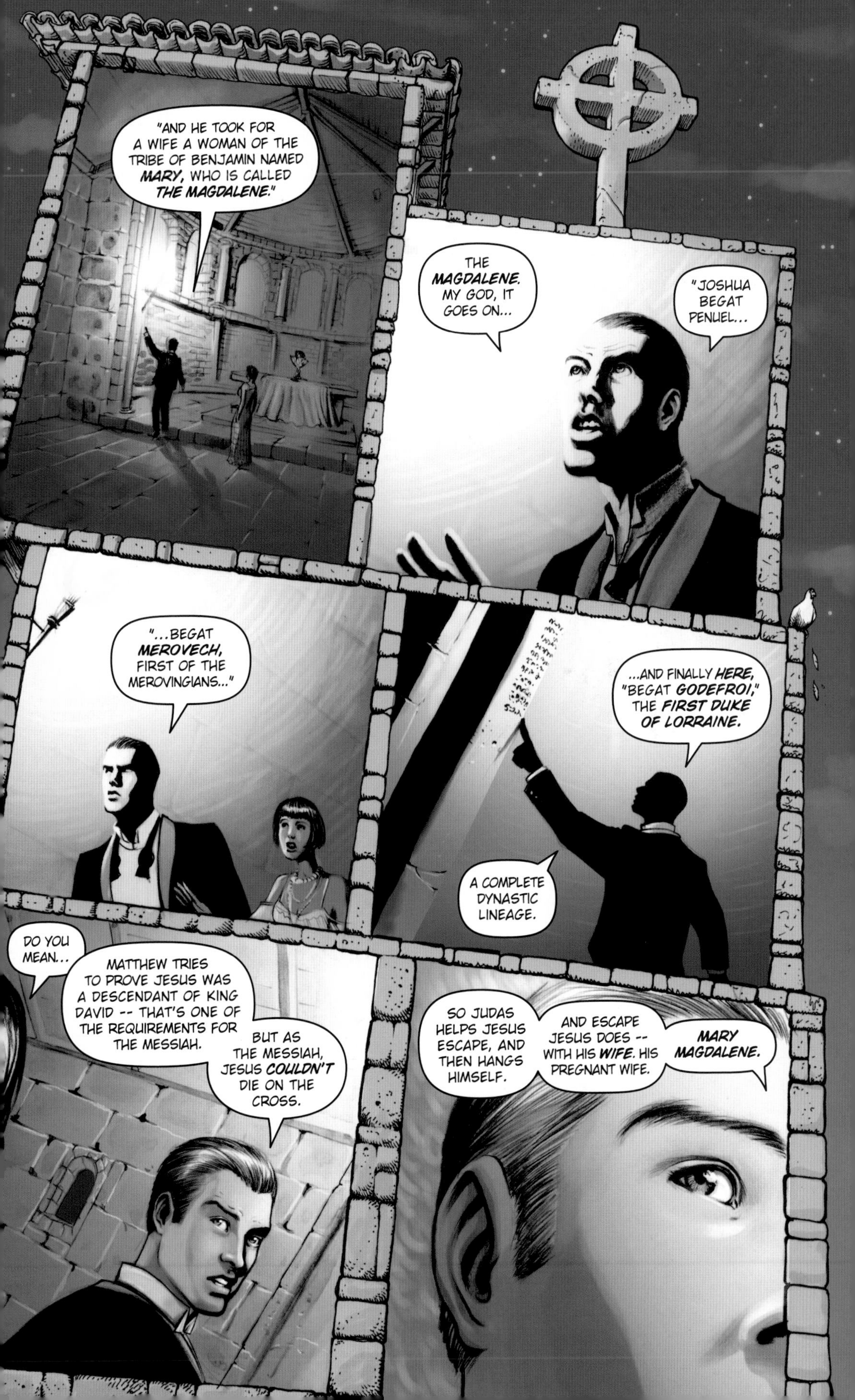
"AND HE TOOK FOR A WIFE A WOMAN OF THE TRIBE OF BENJAMIN NAMED MARY, WHO IS CALLED THE MAGDALENE."
THE MAGDALENE. MY GOD, IT GOES ON...
"JOSHUA BEGAT PENUEL...
"...BEGAT MEROVECH, FIRST OF THE MEROVINGIANS..."
...AND FINALLY HERE, "BEGAT GODEFROI," THE FIRST DUKE OF LORRAINE.
A COMPLETE DYNASTIC LINEAGE.
DO YOU MEAN...
MATTHEW TRIES TO PROVE JESUS WAS A DESCENDANT OF KING DAVID -- THAT'S ONE OF THE REQUIREMENTS FOR THE MESSIAH.
BUT AS THE MESSIAH, JESUS COULDN'T DIE ON THE CROSS.
SO JUDAS HELPS JESUS ESCAPE, AND THEN HANGS HIMSELF.
AND ESCAPE JESUS DOES -- WITH HIS WIFE. HIS PREGNANT WIFE.
MARY MAGDALENE.

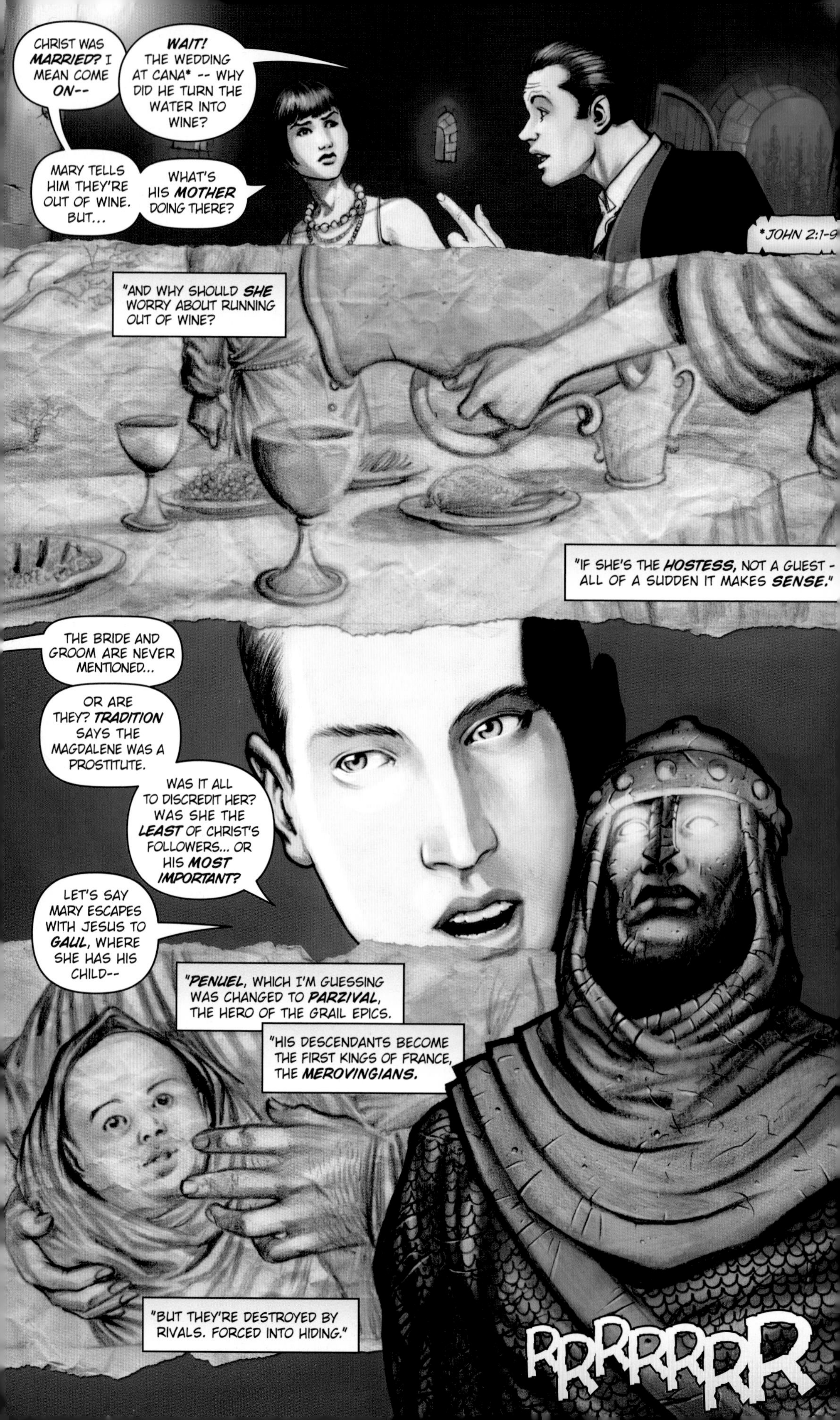
CHRIST WAS MARRIED? I MEAN COME ON--
WAIT! THE WEDDING AT CANA* -- WHY DID HE TURN THE WATER INTO WINE?
MARY TELLS HIM THEY'RE OUT OF WINE. BUT...
WHAT'S HIS MOTHER DOING THERE?
*JOHN 2:1-9
"AND WHY SHOULD SHE WORRY ABOUT RUNNING OUT OF WINE?
"IF SHE'S THE HOSTESS, NOT A GUEST - ALL OF A SUDDEN IT MAKES SENSE."
THE BRIDE AND GROOM ARE NEVER MENTIONED...
OR ARE THEY? TRADITION SAYS THE MAGDALENE WAS A PROSTITUTE.
WAS IT ALL TO DISCREDIT HER? WAS SHE THE LEAST OF CHRIST'S FOLLOWERS... OR HIS MOST IMPORTANT?
LET'S SAY MARY ESCAPES WITH JESUS TO GAUL, WHERE SHE HAS HIS CHILD--
"PENUEL, WHICH I'M GUESSING WAS CHANGED TO PARZIVAL, THE HERO OF THE GRAIL EPICS.
"HIS DESCENDANTS BECOME THE FIRST KINGS OF FRANCE, THE MEROVINGIANS.
"BUT THEY'RE DESTROYED BY RIVALS. FORCED INTO HIDING."
RRRRRRRR

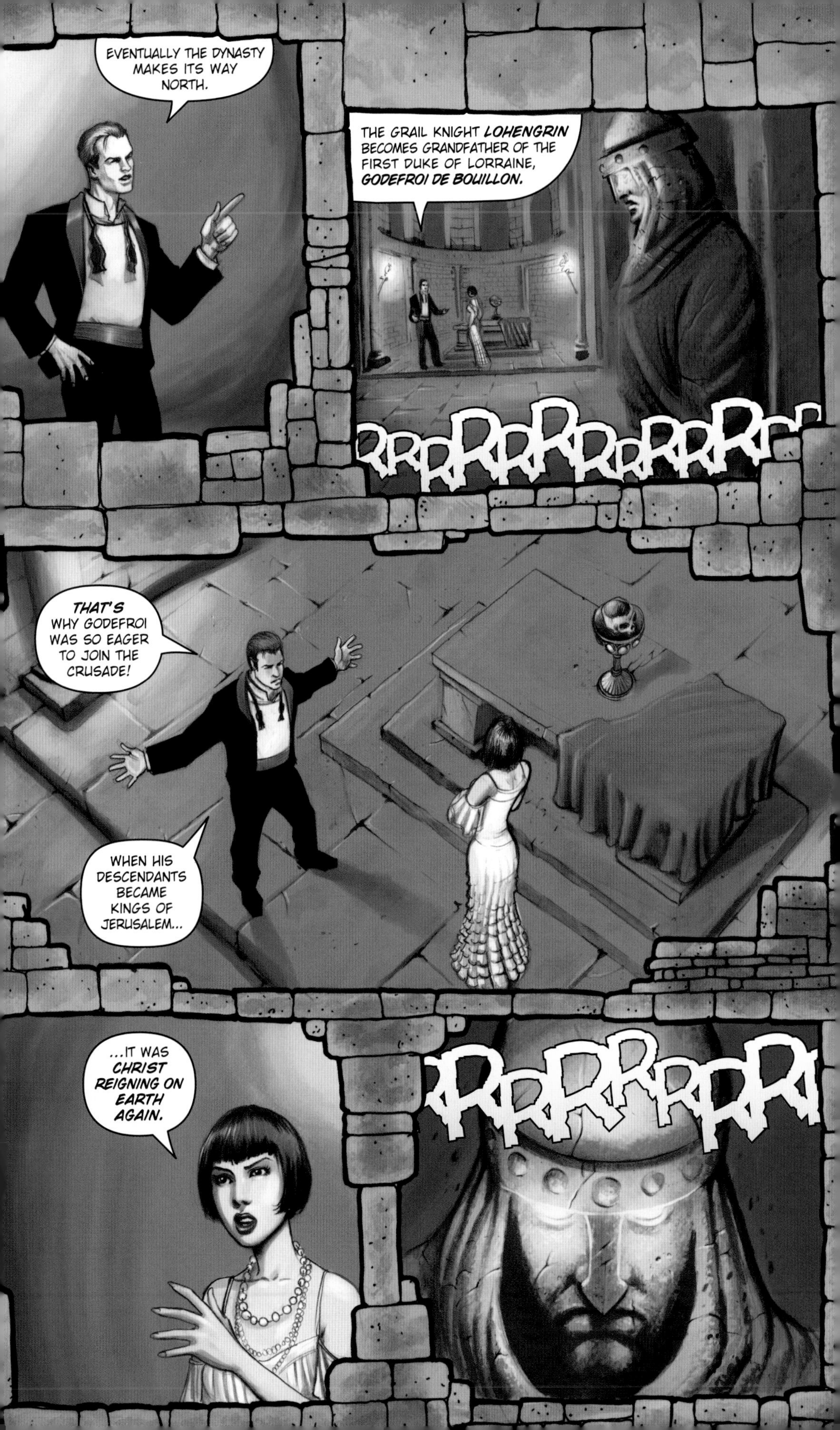
EVENTUALLY THE DYNASTY MAKES ITS WAY NORTH.
THE GRAIL KNIGHT LOHENGRIN BECOMES GRANDFATHER OF THE FIRST DUKE OF LORRAINE, GODEFROI DE BOUILLON.
RRRRRRRRRRRRRR
THAT'S WHY GODEFROI WAS SO EAGER TO JOIN THE CRUSADE!
WHEN HIS DESCENDANTS BECAME KINGS OF JERUSALEM...
...IT WAS CHRIST REIGNING ON EARTH AGAIN.
RRRRRRRR

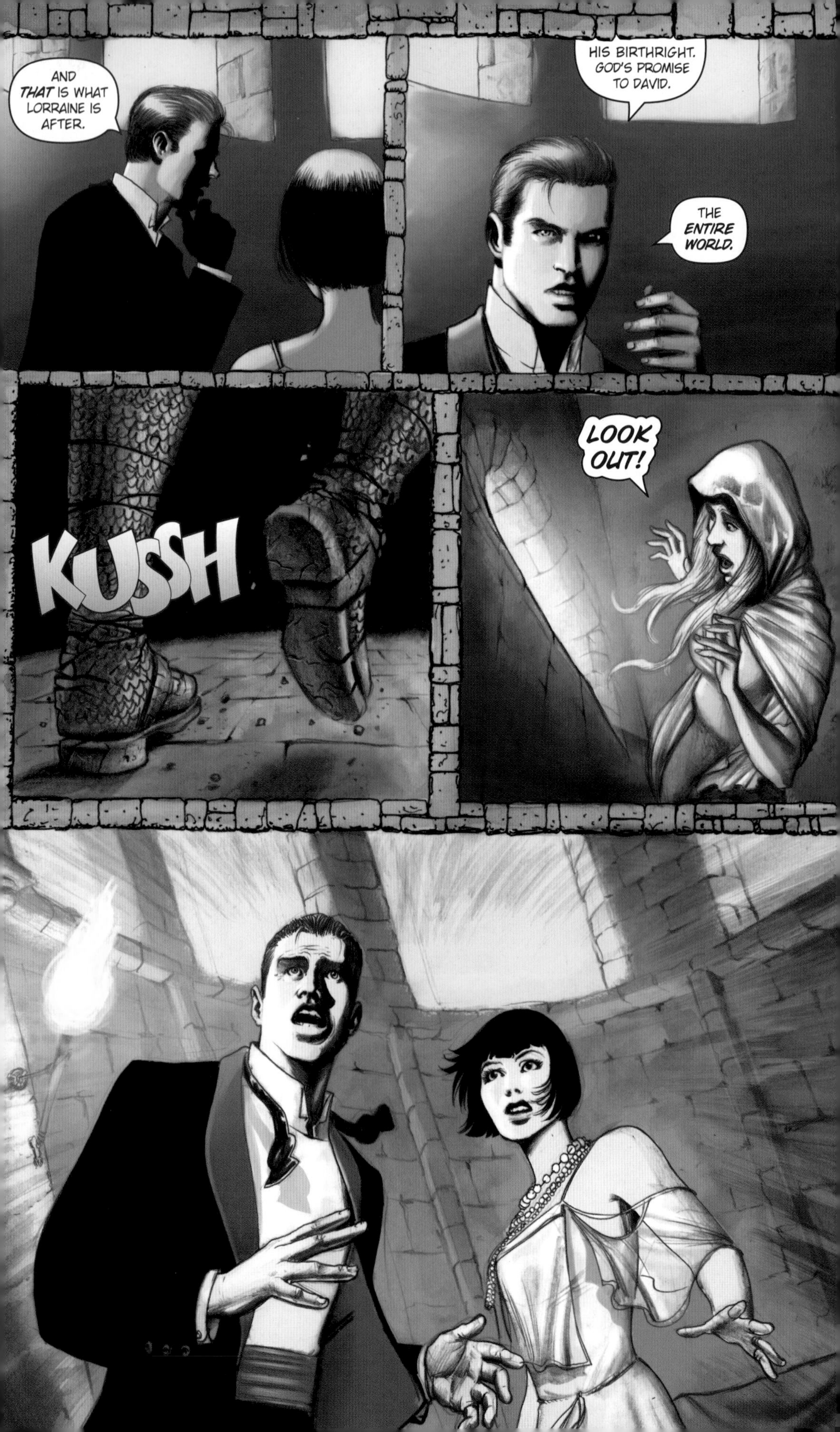
AND *THAT* IS WHAT LORRAINE IS AFTER.
HIS BIRTHRIGHT. GOD'S PROMISE TO DAVID.
THE *ENTIRE WORLD.*
KUSH
LOOK OUT!

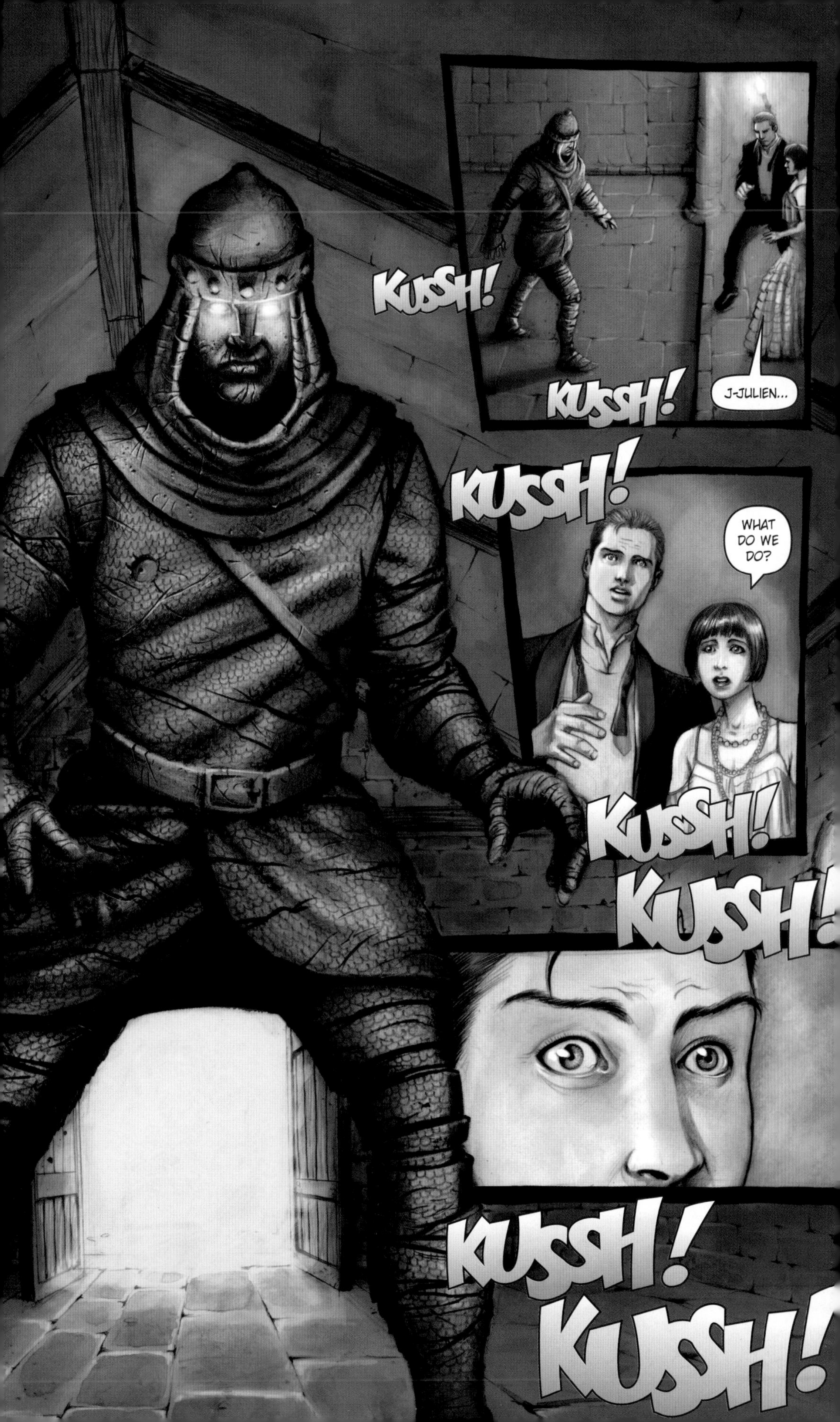
KUSSH!
KUSSH!
J-JULIEN...
KUSSH!
WHAT DO WE DO?
KUSSH!
KUSSH!
KUSSH!
KUSSH!

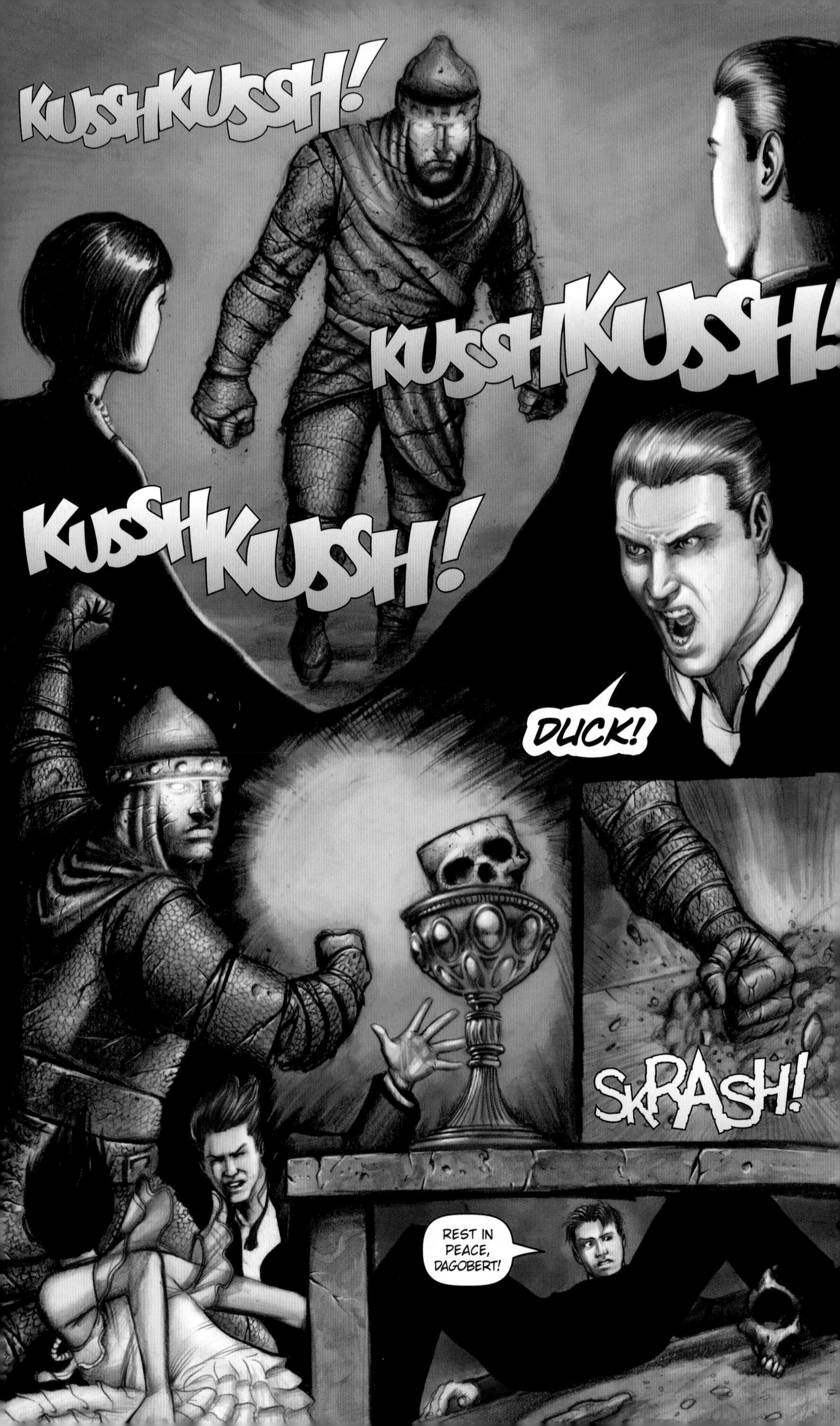
KUSSHKUSSH!
KUSSHKUSSH!
KUSSHKUSSH!
DUCK!
SKRASH!
REST IN PEACE, DAGOBERT!

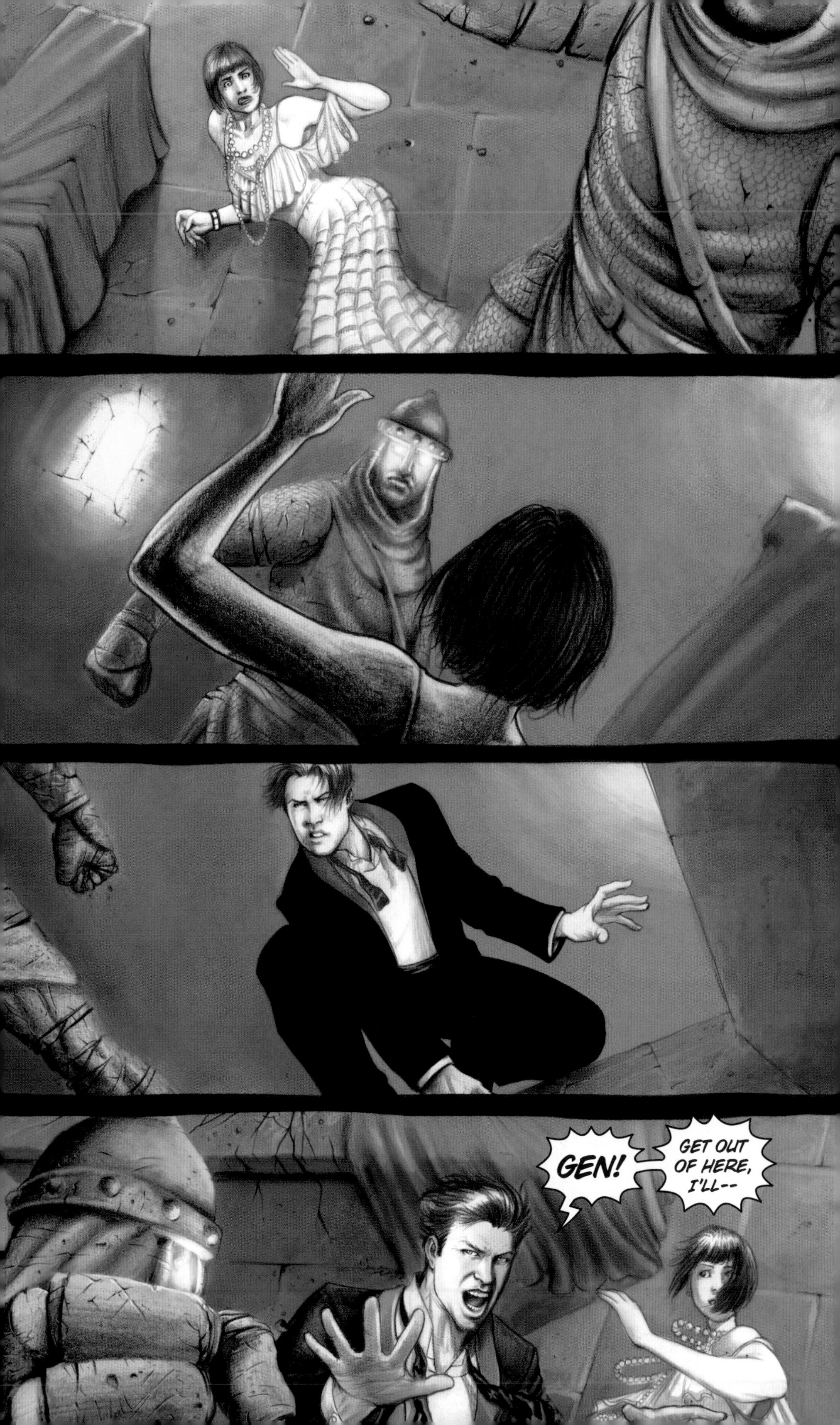
GEN!
GET OUT OF HERE, I'LL--

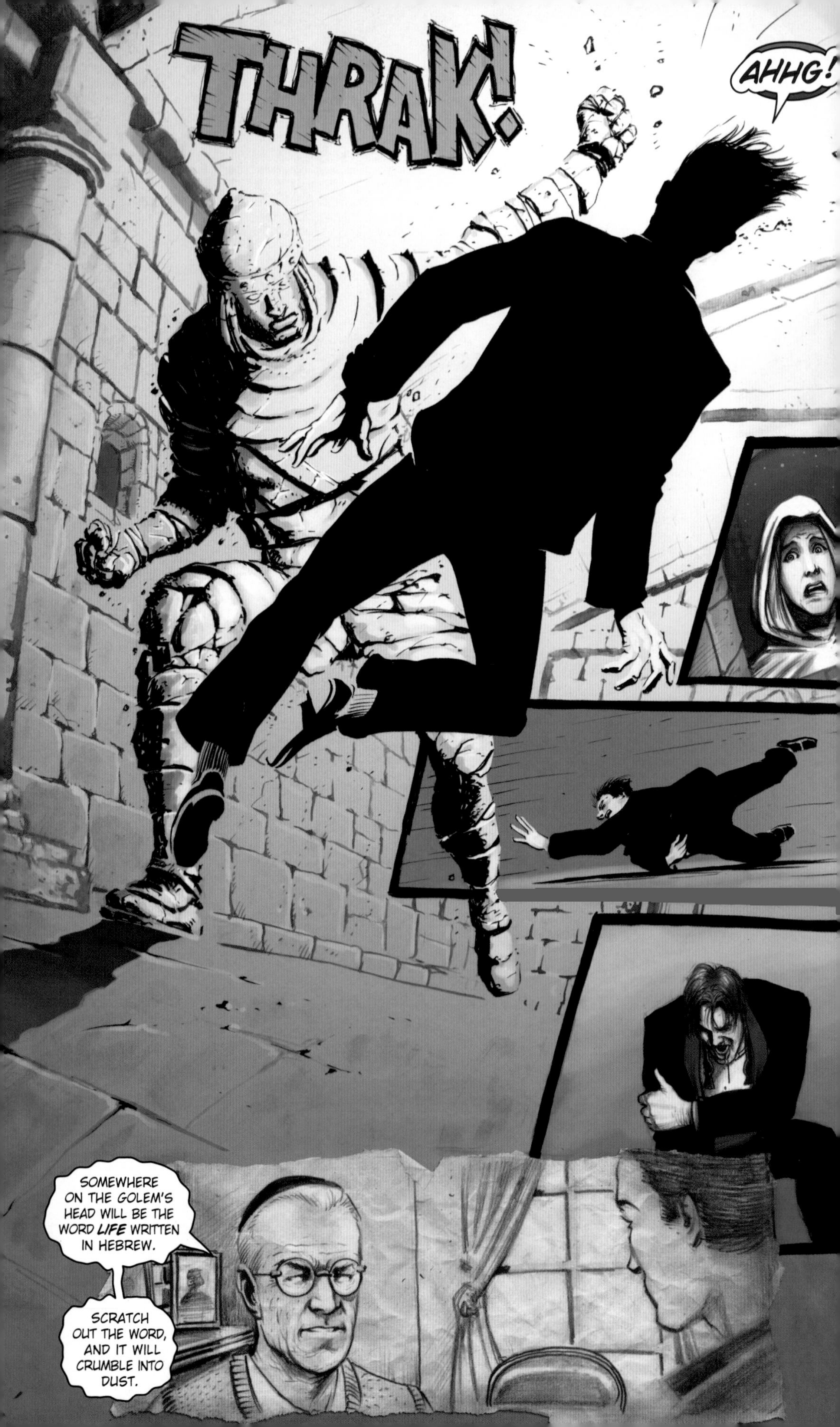
THRAK!
AHHG!
SOMEWHERE ON THE GOLEM'S HEAD WILL BE THE WORD *LIFE* WRITTEN IN HEBREW.
SCRATCH OUT THE WORD, AND IT WILL CRUMBLE INTO DUST.

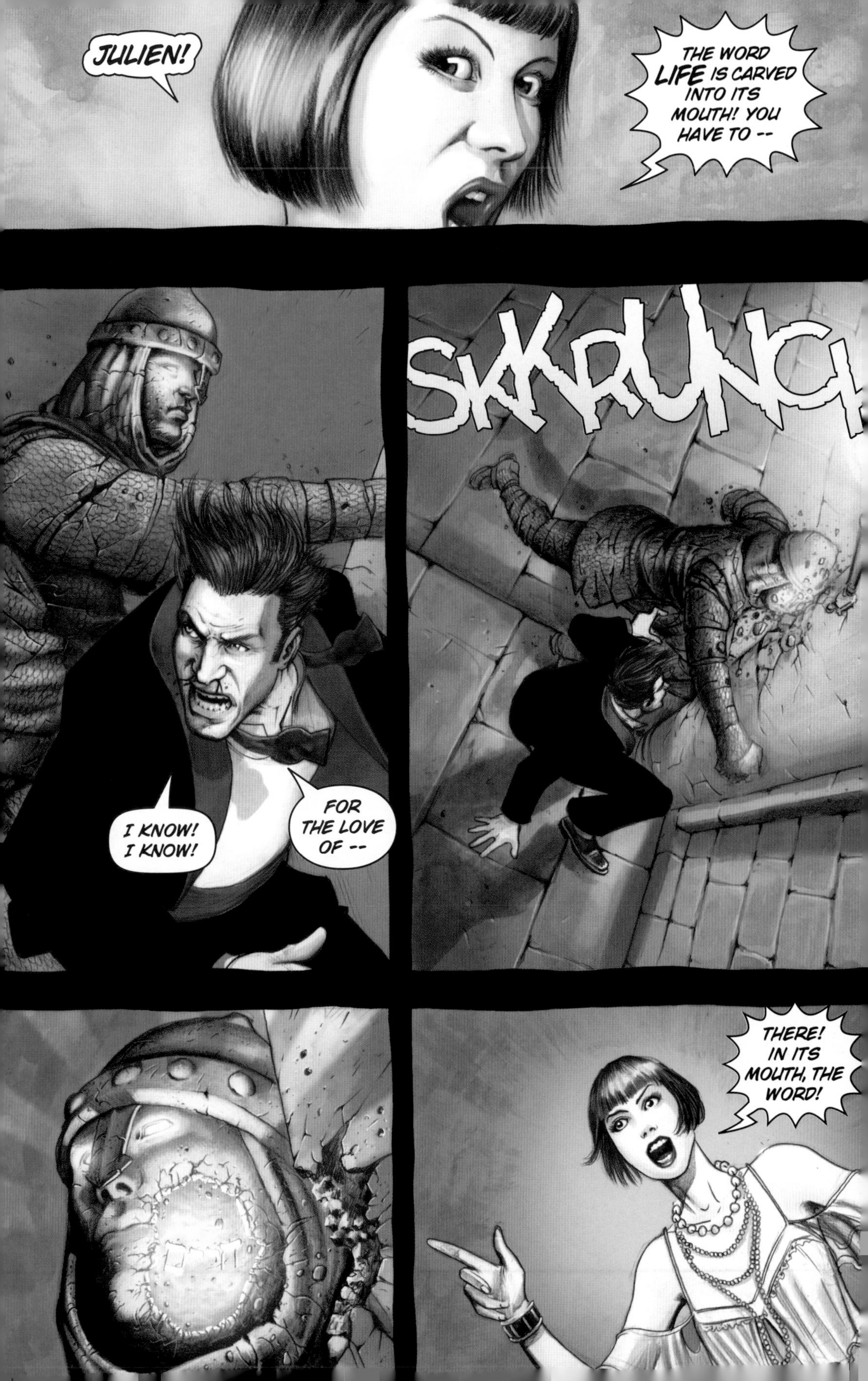
JULIEN!
THE WORD LIFE IS CARVED INTO ITS MOUTH! YOU HAVE TO --
I KNOW! I KNOW!
FOR THE LOVE OF --
SKKRUNG
THERE! IN ITS MOUTH, THE WORD!

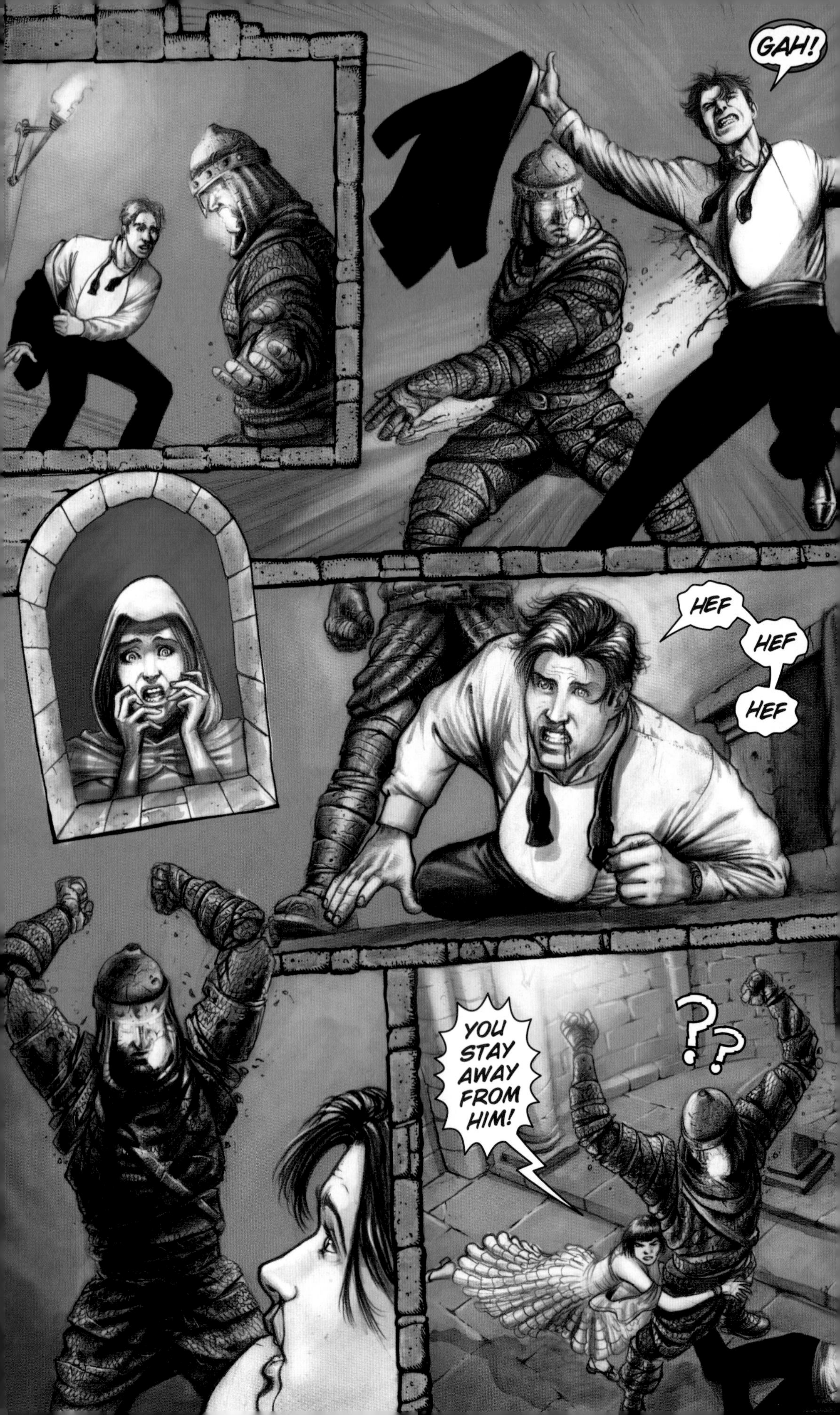
GAH!
HEF
HEF
HEF
YOU STAY AWAY FROM HIM!
??

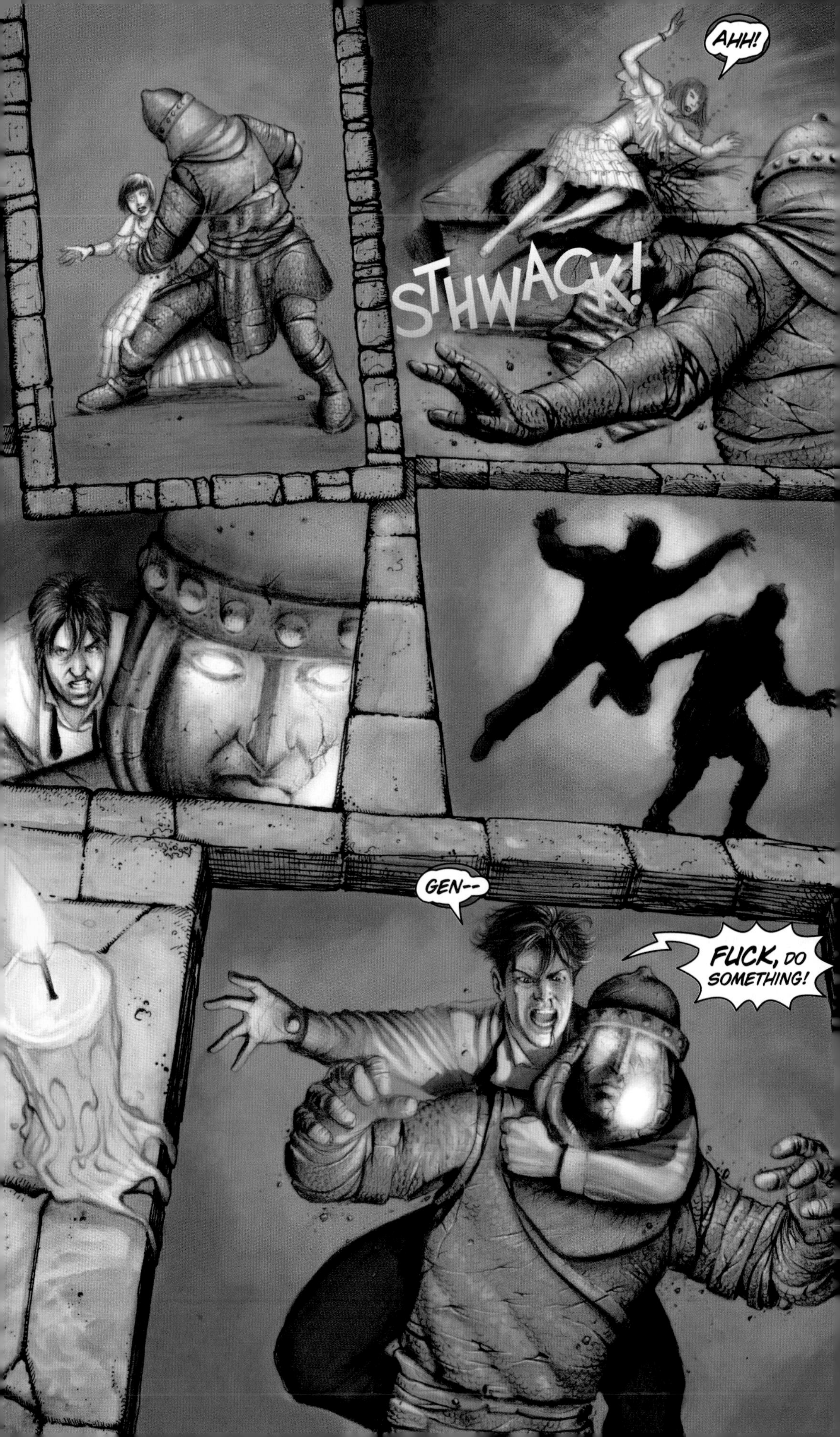
AHH!
STHWACK!
GEN--
FUCK, DO SOMETHING!

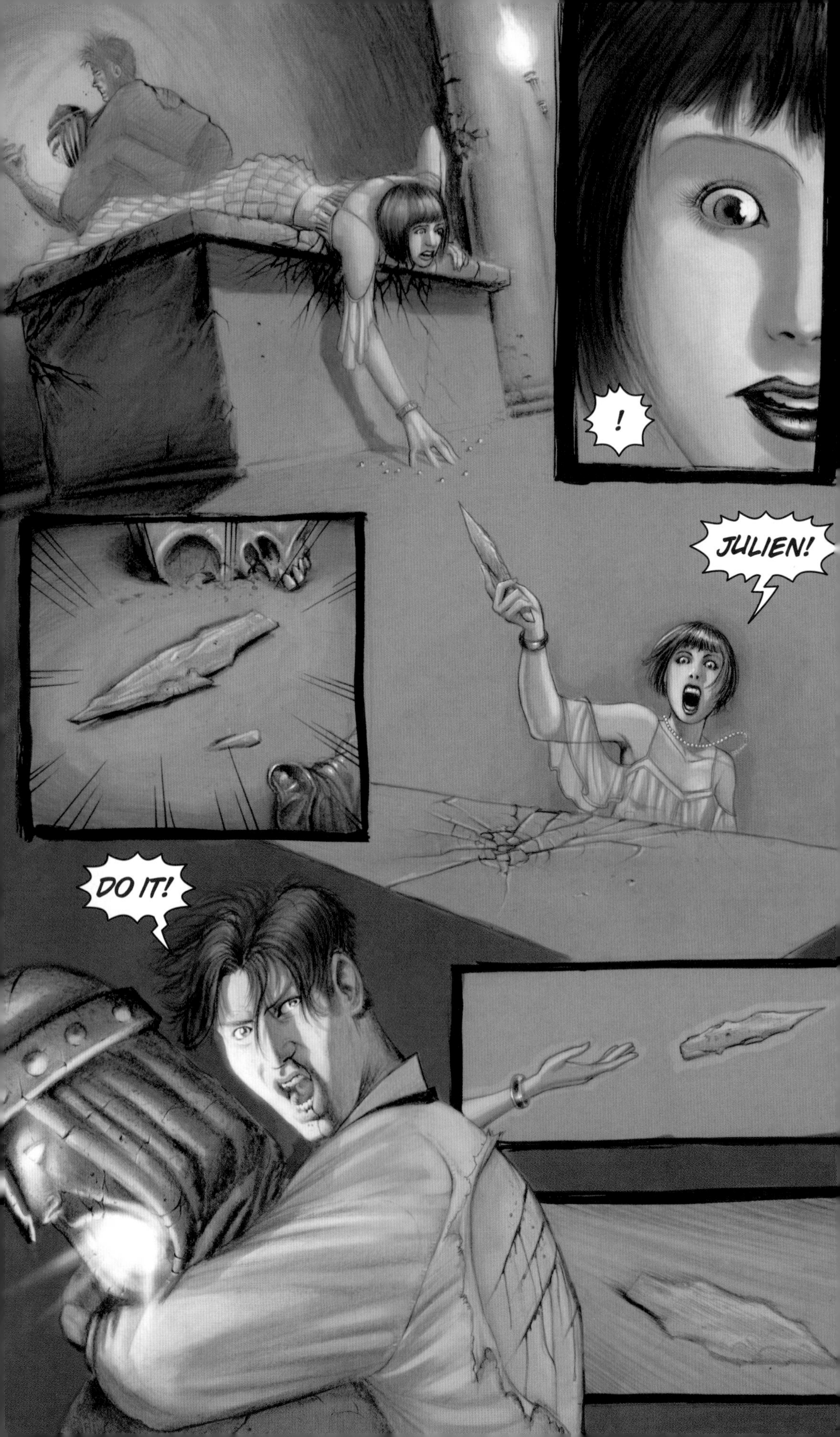
!
JULIEN!
DO IT!

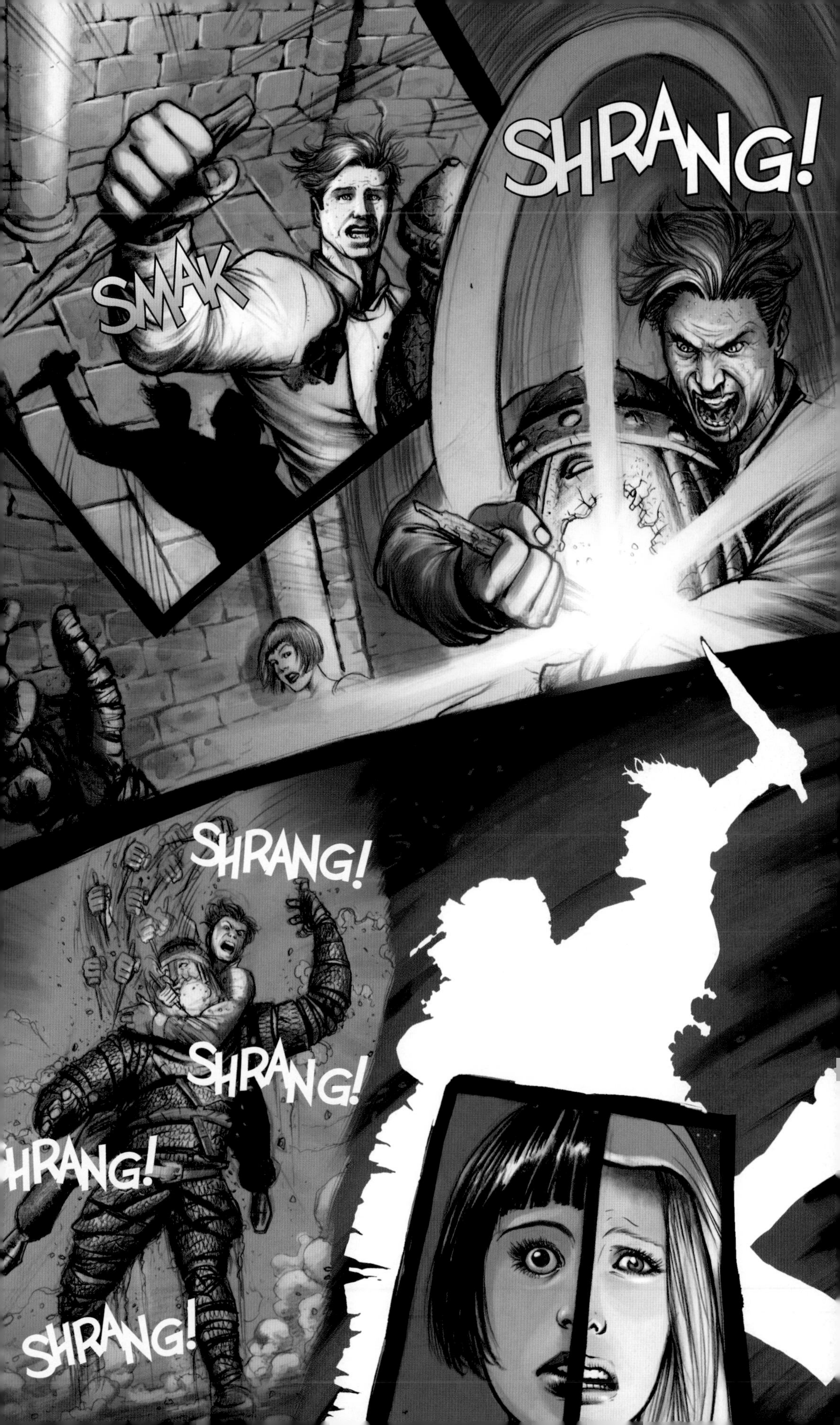
SHRANG!
SMAK
SHRANG!
SHRANG!
HRANG!
SHRANG!

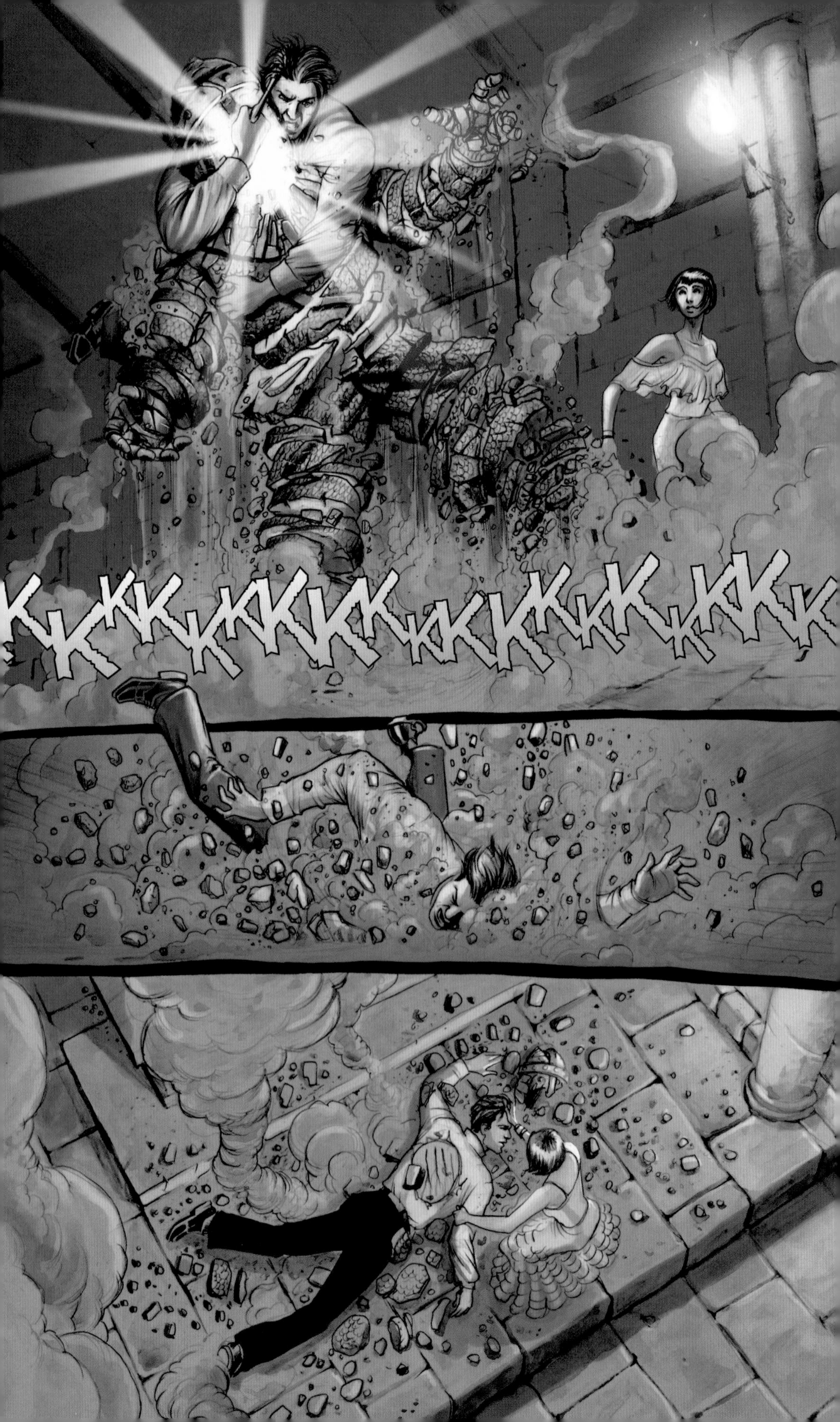
KKKKKKKKKKKKKKKKKK

Le Journal de la Liberté

Paris' leading anglophone newspaper • vol. 205, no. 102 • Nov. 5, MCMXXXIII

Editors in Chief: M. Tait Bergstrom, M. Matthew Pasteris. **Story Editor:** M. Arvid Nelson. **Art Editor:** M. James Di Bartolo. **Photography Editor:** M. Alexander Waldman. **Layout Supervisor:** M. William Kartalopoulos. **Editors Emeritus:** M. Clark A. Smith, M. Howard P. Lovecraft, M. Robert E. Howard. Redacted by the Holy Inquisition under the direction of His Excellency Archbishop Emile-Jean Ireneaux. Le Journal de la Liberté is printed under the benign auspices of his most puissant majesty KING LOUIS XXII of FRANCE. GOD SAVE THE KING.

Papal seal of Approval

FRANCE AT WAR

ASSASSINATION LEADS TO CONFLICT OVER KING LOUIS' OBJECTIONS • PRUSSIA, AUSTRIA WITHDRAW AMBASSADORS
ENGLAND DECLARES HER SUPPORT FOR FRANCE • WORLDWIDE CONFLICT DEEMED "LIKELY"

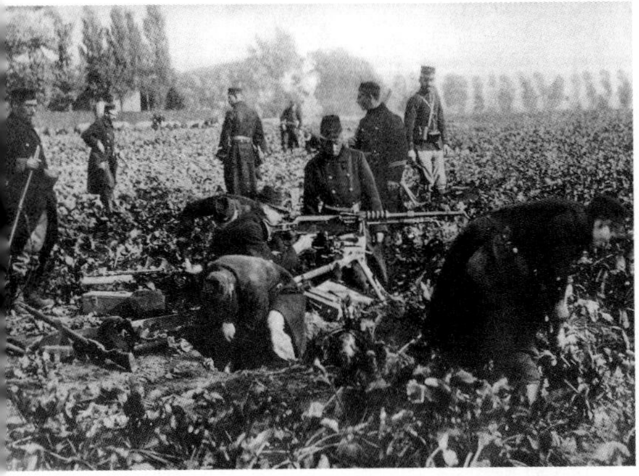

gionnaires in the Duchy of Lorraine brace for the inevitable German sault across Flanders. "Let the Huns come," The Duke of Lorraine said.

atalonia, France – The war imatum proposed by the Duke Lorraine following the Marquis Aragon's assassination expired e other night. Lorraine's sup-rters in the Hall of the Robe bsequently declared war on the nirate of Cordova.

Riots broke out in Paris as ews of the war spread. Royal endarmes and Inquisition of-cials have so far been unable to store order. Conflicting reports the extent of the unrest are nerging from residents fleeting e chaos.

King Louis XXII condemned e declaration of war, but since oth houses of parliament ad-pted Lorraine's ultimatum, his osition was overruled.

Already, members of the Hall the Sword are making com-ents that only a year ago might ave been grounds for charges sedition.

"The King has demonstrated is irrelevance in these past ew days. France needs a strong ader, someone whom our rmed forces can rally behind," e Count of Razes said.

The Hall of the Sword nominated the Duke of Lorraine to lead France's armed forces. Lorraine accepted.

A veteran commander who oversaw the suppression of rebellions in Indochina and Algeria, Lorraine is well liked by the French legions.

"Lorraine, he took the time to learn the names of all of his men. Down to the lowliest corporal. He was one of us, a soldier's soldier." Major Jean-Louis Dupontel said. Maj. Dupontel served as a captain under Lorraine in Indochina.

Lorraine made himself available in a press conference early this morning although he is "deep into preparations" for the offensive against Cordova.

"We're going to hit the Mohammedans with all the furor of our crusading ancestors. This is a conflict to drive Mohammed from Europe, make no mistake," he said.

He dismissed concerns about a joint Prussian/Austrian thrust from the east. "Let the Huns come," he said. "We're ready."

Lorraine's military staff is composed of his most trusted advisors and subordinates from his colonial campaigns.

His senior officers have been overseeing a build-up of troops along the Cordovan border for days. At the time this edition went to press, no order to begin the invasion had been given, and an eerie calm permeated the assembled troops.

"It doesn't feel real yet, but I'm sure it will once the dirt starts flying," Corporal Emmanuel Drouot, stationed on the Cordovan front, said.

King Louis has not made a public appearance since the declaration. Some are expecting him to make a bid to re-establish his authority in the coming days.

Indeed, not all members of parliament are pleased with the war declaration. The resolution for the ultimatum passed by a mere three votes in the Hall of the Robe, the king's traditional support base.

The Robe remains closely divided.

"This is all an aberration. The King's rightful influence over the Robe will be restored in coming days, mark my words," Viscount Aristide Lescot-Noël, a supporter of King Louis in the Hall of the Robe, said. Others are not so certain.

"I fully and unreservedly support the decision to go to war," Baronet Aristide deMandeville, Speaker for the Hall of the Robe, declared in a written statement.

Even members of King Louis' court admit the war is likely to spread beyond France and Cordova.

"All the great nations – England, France, Germany, Russia – they've been plotting and maneuvering for a long time. The only surprise is that it hasn't happened sooner," a member of King Louis' court said.

The German Kaiser and Austrian Emperor have recalled their ambassadors from France. A joint declaration of war by Prussia and the Holy Roman Empire is expected sometime early tomorrow.

"The Kaiser and the Emperor are of a like mind," Prussian Chancellor Karl von Haugwitz said. "Lorraine's belligerence leaves us no choice."

England and Russia are in turn expected to declare war on Prussia and the Holy Roman Empire; England because of political and economic ties to France, and Russia because of rivalry with the Prussians and Austrians for dominance over Eastern Europe.

continued on next page

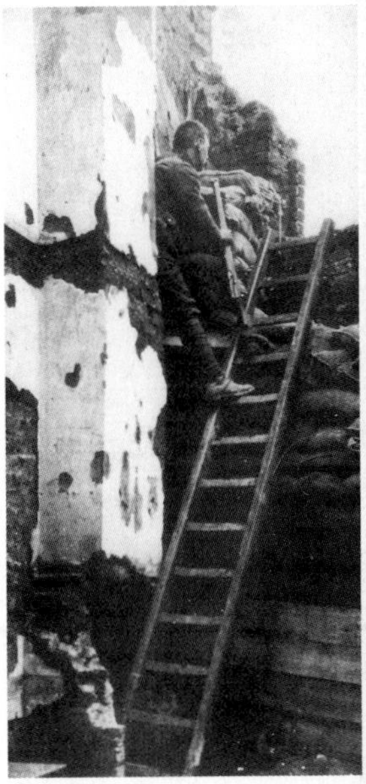

A sentry presides over an uneasy calm on the Cordovan border.

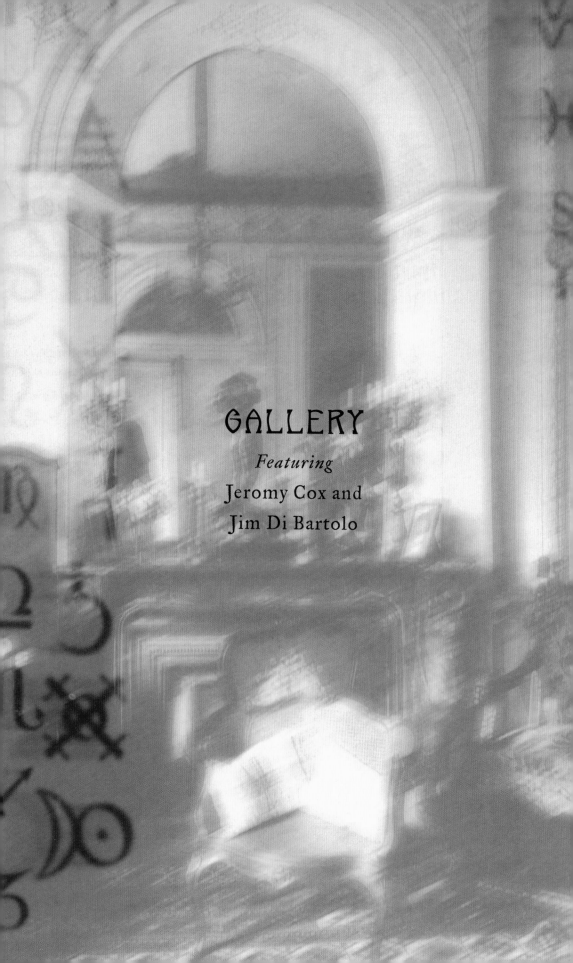

GALLERY

Featuring

Jeromy Cox and

Jim Di Bartolo

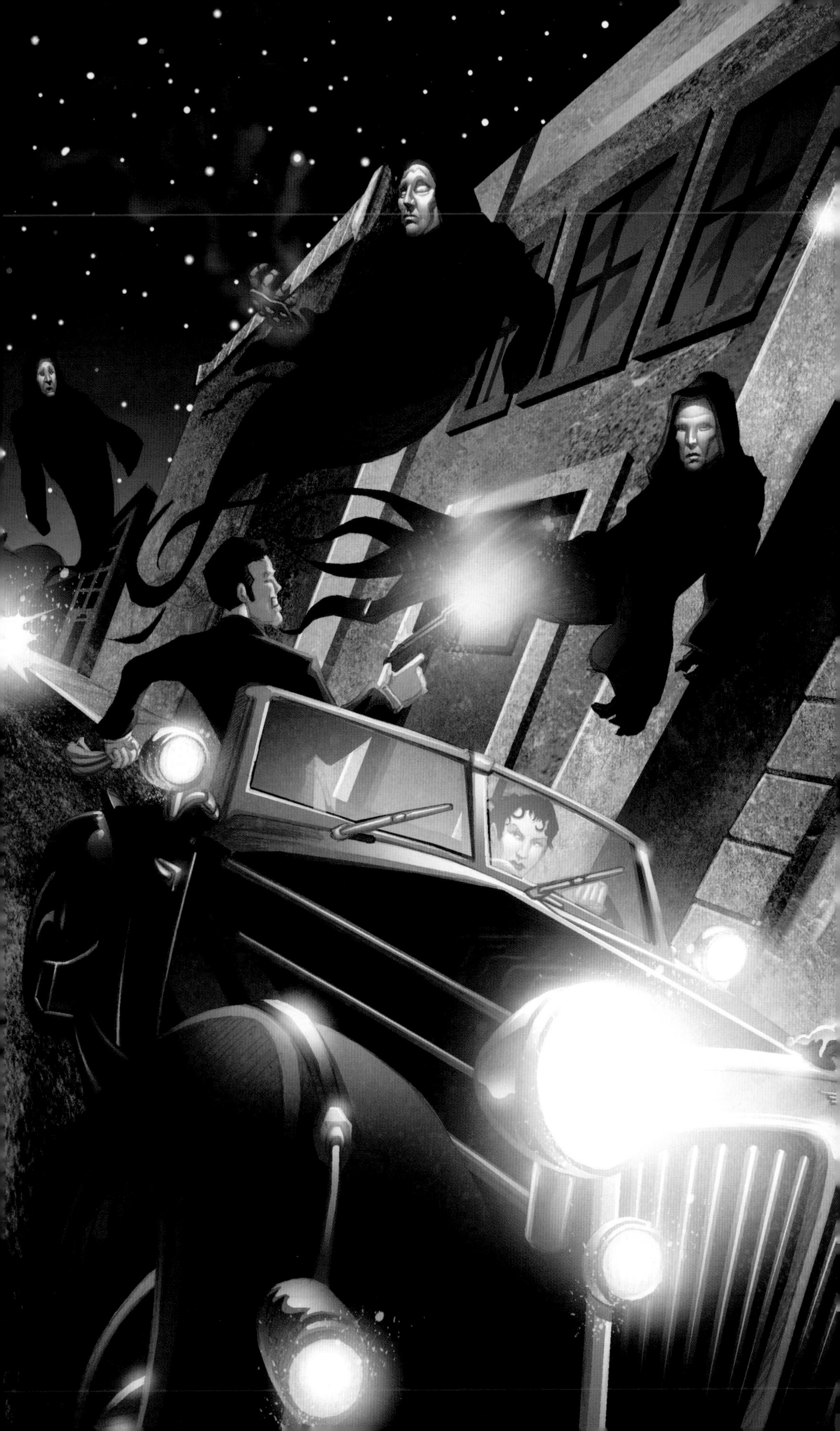

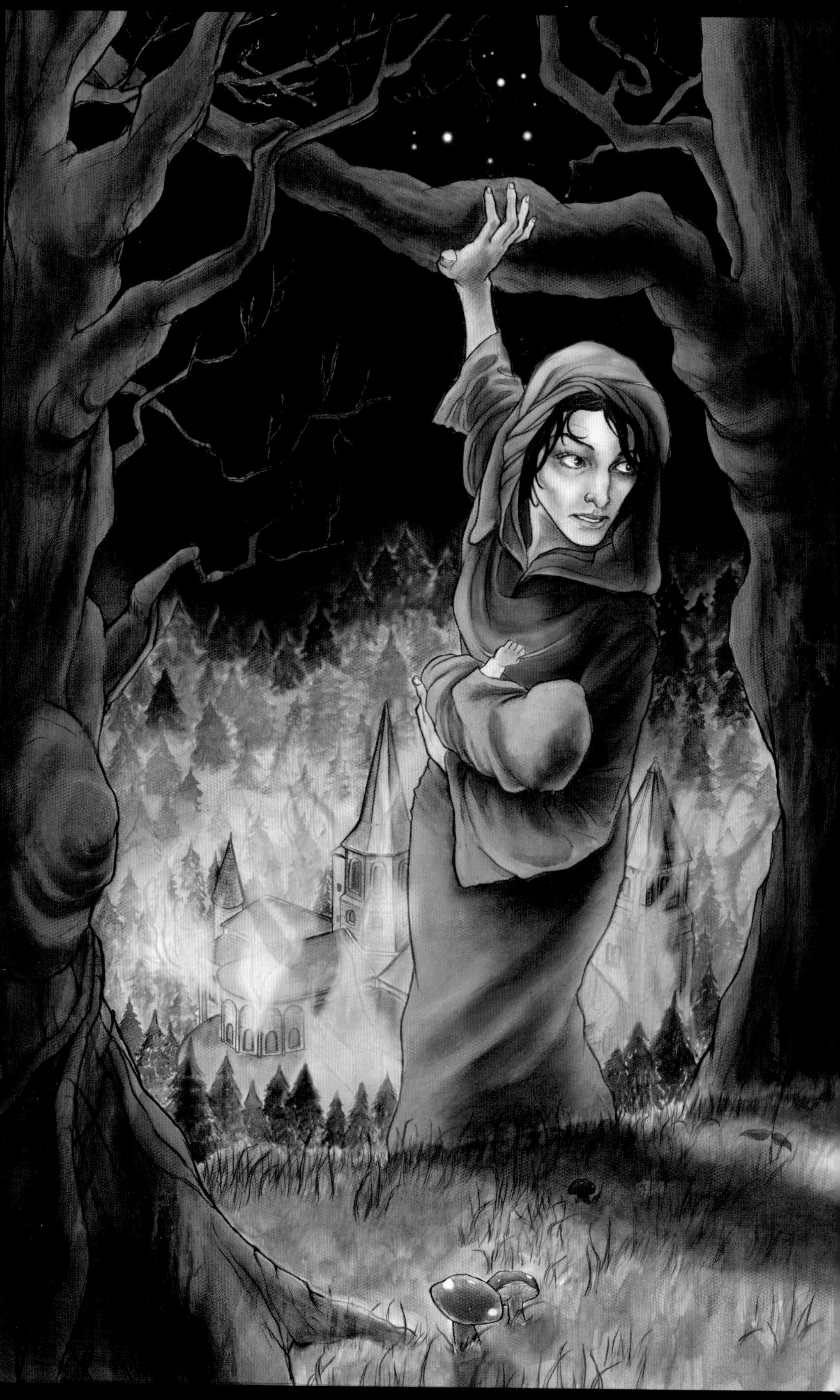

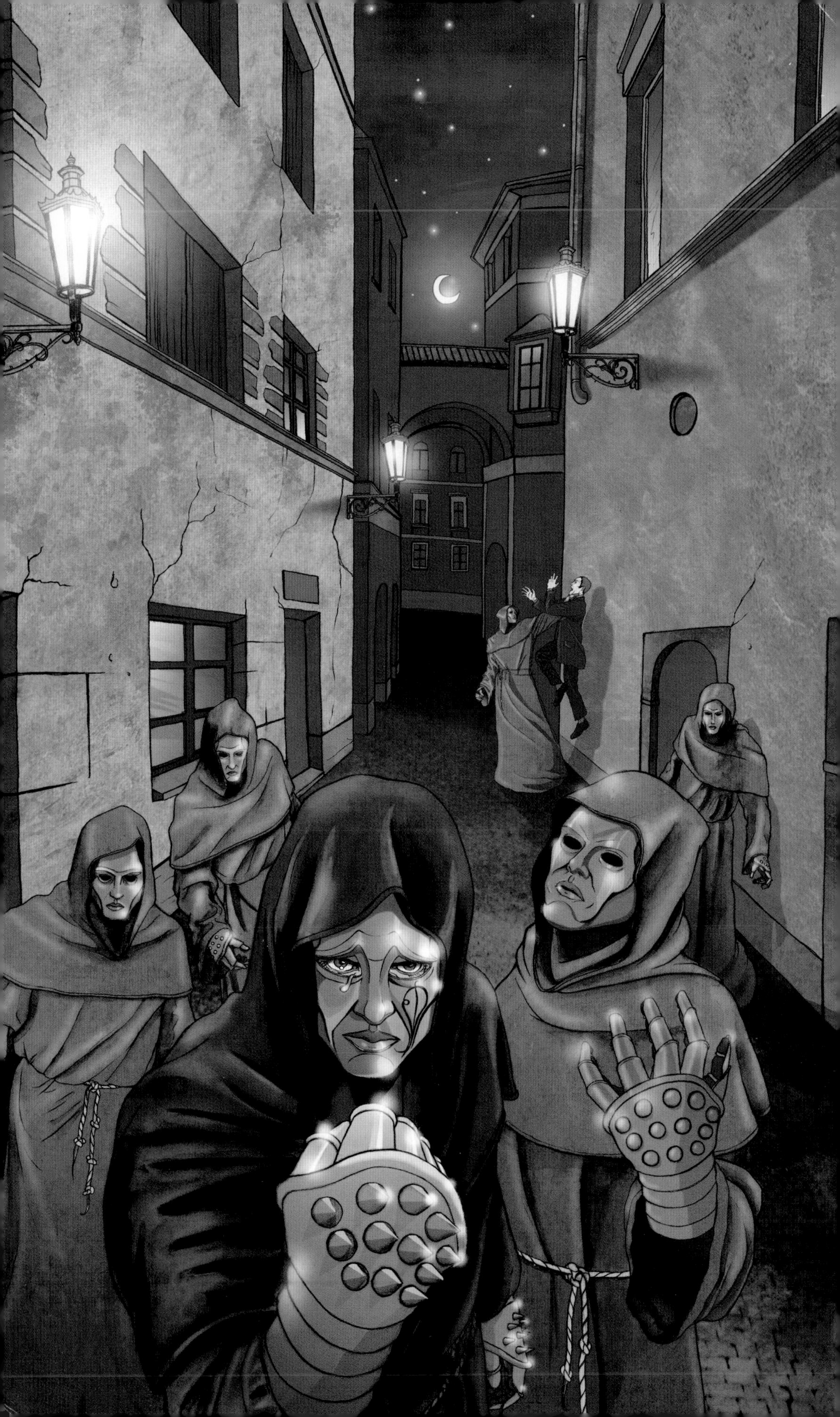

Mike Mignola Jill Thompson Evan Dorkin
Kurt Busiek Keith Giffen Gary Gianni and others
The Dark Horse Book of
MONSTERS

ARK HORSE BOOK OF MONSTERS

Gary Gianni, Evan Dorkin, Jill Thompson, Kurt Busiek, iffen, Arvid Nelson, Juan Ferreyra, and more.

Cover by Gary Gianni

kes Hellboy on a monster-crunching mission and Gary illustrations for a classic tale of South Seas horror by odgson, and there are many more terrifying yarns by st talented folks in comics, in this fourth addition to sner-nominated books of *Hauntings*, *Witchcraft* and

$14.95, ISBN: 1-59307-656-8

MIKE MIGNOLA'S
HELLBOY
WEIRD TALES
Volume Two

HELLBOY: WEIRD TALES VOLUME 2

J. H. Williams III, John Cassaday, P. Craig Russell, Gene Colan, Kia Asamiya, Craig Thompson and many more. Cover by Mike Mignola

Considered the "artist's artist" of contemporary comics, Mike Mignola has accumulated quite a few professional fans over the years. Now, some of the best known writers and artists in comics show their love for Hellboy, telling amazing stories of satanic theatres, a vacation in Hell, and romance in the back of a Cadillac.

$17.95, ISBN: 1-56971-953-5

Revelations
PAUL JENKINS HUMBERTO RAMOS

REVELATIONS

Paul Jenkins & Humberto Ramos

nal next in line to succeed the ailing Pope turns up Yard's finest detective, Charlie Northern, finds him- o Rome with little more than a full pack of cigarettes. a priest, a coroner and one beautiful lawyer, Northern e facts in a place legendary for keeping its secrets.

$17.95, ISBN: 1-59307-239-2

THE GOON
MY MURDEROUS CHILDHOOD
(And Other Grievous Yarns)
by Eric Powell

THE GOON VOLUME 2: MY MURDEROUS CHILDHOOD (AND OTHER GRIEVOUS YARNS)

Eric Powell

Welcome to the Hobo Jungle, where the destitute have given up train hopping for a feral life of cannibalism in the wild. Will the Goon and his best pal Franky end up in a Hobo stew before they can stop a grave-robbing family from replenishing the Zombie Priest's ranks of living dead?

$13.95, ISBN: 1-59307-109-4

AVAILABLE AT YOUR LOCAL COMICS SHOP OR BOOKSTORE

To find a comics shop in your area, call 1-888-266-4226

ore information or to order direct visit darkhorse.com or call 1-800-862-0052 • Mon.-Fri. 9 A.M. to 5 P.M. Pacific Time.

***Prices and availability subject to change without notice**

RK HORSE COMICS® *drawing on your nightmares*

se.com

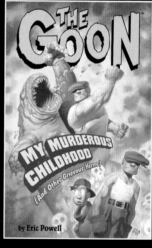